THE ULTIMATE BUSI

How to

AND Unlea

MARTY FOX, CBCP

UltimateBusinessContinuity.com
New York

I

Printed in the United States of America

First Printing, 2017

The Ultimate Business Continuity Success Guide may be purchased in bulk at special discounts for corporate gifts, promotions and educational purposes. For more information please email your request to: Sales@UltimateBusinessContinuity.com

www.UltimateBusinessContinuity.com

Contents

vi

viii

DEDICATION

This book is dedicated to Debbie, David and all my family and friends who put up with the hundreds of weekend and evening hours I devoted to creating this book.

This book is also dedicated to you – the resilience, continuity, emergency management, safety, security, technology and operations professional. You are on the front lines every day empowering organizations, large and small, to become safe, resilient, and prosper in a dangerous world.

ACKNOWLEDGEMENTS

This book would not have been possible without the professional and tireless editing of Debbie Fox. Her daily input, ideas and improvements enabled us to create a product we are proud to share with the world.

I have been very fortunate for the hundreds of friendships I have been privileged to make during a very rewarding career. The many challenges and successes we experienced together created memories that will stay with me through my life. So many wonderful people have had a positive influence on my business continuity and technology careers. It would have taken a book just to name everyone. You know who you are. Thank you for your friendship and professionalism!

A special thank you to two close friends that left us too soon but will always be remembered: Arun Gupta (DataEase) and Greg Urvalek (MetLife).

DISCLAIMER

This book is presented solely for educational and entertainment purposes. The author and publisher are not offering it as legal, accounting, or any other professional services advice. While best efforts have been used in preparing this book, the author and publisher make no representations or warranties of any kind and assume no liabilities of any kind with respect to the accuracy or completeness of the contents and specifically disclaim any implied warranties of merchantability or fitness of use for a particular purpose.

Neither the author nor the publisher shall be held liable or responsible to any person or entity with respect to any loss or incidental or consequential damages caused, or alleged to have been caused, directly or indirectly, by the information or programs contained herein. No warranty may be created or extended by sales representatives or written sales materials. Every company is different and the advice and strategies contained herein may not be suitable for your situation. You should seek the services of a competent professional before beginning any improvement program. The ideas in this book worked for me. You should be mindful of what works for you and what does not work in your program or life. Any likeness to actual persons, either living or dead, is strictly coincidental.

Neither the author or anyone associated with this book warrants the accuracy, reliability or timeliness of any information published in the book, nor endorses any products or services linked from the book, and shall not be held liable for any losses caused by reliance on the accuracy, reliability or timeliness of such information. Portions of the information may be incorrect or not current. Any person or entity that relies on any information obtained from this book does so at his or her own risk.

All product and company names are trademarks™ or registered® trademarks of their respective holders. Use of them does not imply any affiliation with or endorsement by them.

The views and opinions expressed in the book are those of the author and do not reflect the official policy or position of any company or agency of the U.S. government.

PREFACE - WELCOME!

Writing the *'The Ultimate Business Continuity Success Guide'* was a labor of love. I know it sounds like a cliché, but I wrote this book from my heart. It is my small way of giving back to the profession that has meant so much to me. I enjoyed every moment of the process. I truly hope you enjoy it and get value from my effort.

The idea for this book had been brewing in my mind for years. Finally, it became an obsession. I knew the time had come to 'pay-it-forward'.

Initially, I envisioned sharing a short list of my favorite tips and techniques. When you scan the table of contents you will realize I 'failed' in the 'short list' concept. What happened was my passion for business resilience and continuity took over. I wrote and researched most nights and every weekend over the next year and a half. A healthy portion of this book was also written during my daily two hour round-trip commutes on New York's Long Island Railroad.

Simply, the goal of this book is to help you improve business resilience and continuity in your organization, regardless of size. I have accomplished this in the past for Fortune 100 companies, mid-tier companies as well as two person companies. I will share my insights, tips, techniques, technologies, ideas and stories. This book goes beyond the usual here is 'what to do'. This book explains 'how to do it' in the real world.

Who can benefit from The Ultimate Business Continuity Success Guide:

- Business Resilience / Business Continuity (BRBC) Professionals
- Emergency Management Professionals
- Cyber Security Professionals
- Founders and Owners
- Safety & Physical Security Professionals
- Managers and Process Owners
- Employees
- Enterprise companies
- Mid-tier companies
- Small companies
- Global companies

- Local companies

What The Ultimate Business Continuity Success Guide is:
Real World Continuity:

This book is written from my vantage point as a seasoned BC professional who enjoys being on the front lines mixing it up with office employees, factory and warehouse employees, techies, truck drivers, C level execs, facilities, sales-people and anyone else I run into in the hall.

I do not believe you can do this job properly from an executive suite. If you want to do the job right, you must be 'all-in'. You and I are going to be on the front line throughout the book. We will be trapped in an elevator with a C level executive, in meetings with department managers, hosting table-tops and work area recovery exercises, responding to a 2:00 am crisis call, selecting business continuity tools and tackling 'beyond BC projects' that can make or break us.

I did my best to pack this book with 1001+ of my favorite practical 'boots on the ground' ideas, tips, techniques, technologies and resources. These are the nuggets that enabled me to succeed and I believe they will help you.

I will share all my experiences, both good and bad. It is about honesty. Some of my ideas may be a little 'outside the box' and ultra-innovative. But those 'moonshots', as the guys at Google (R) would say, have often had huge payoffs for me. My hope is that they will give you ideas and plant seeds of what is possible.

We will also discuss some things that have blown up in my face, such as activating a mass notification call list exercise as a 'blast' rather than a 'cascade' – more on getting 'dinged' for that one later in the book. There is also the story of an former BC executive who took a 'lickin' and a 'kickin' when he hosted a webinar and unwittingly mixed in some embarrassing instant messages on his shared screen. It can happen to you, so skip that story at your own risk!

Business Resilience:

This book goes way beyond prepare, respond and recover. Throughout the book, we talk about building a resilient program and company. We discuss the importance of building a flexible 'bend but do not break' culture so you can respond to any disruptive event and come back stronger than your prior state.

We also spend a lot of time on how you can position you and your team as a profit center NOT an expense. I discuss many initiatives that have worked for me and can be very important to your company and your career. Believe me, it does not take a whole lot of these 'extra credit – beyond BC' successes to go from being thought of as a cost-of-doing-business to a uniquely indispensable contributor.

This book is also very high on using technology to supercharge your business resilience program. My special niche in life is finding and leveraging technology to improve business continuity / resilience programs. When people ask me where I live I often respond, 'where business resilience intersects with technology'. Sometimes it leads to stares outside a business setting, but hey it is where I live.

On many occasions, it has been my extensive technology experience has led to revenue generating and cost saving opportunities. This is what I love to do. I will share ideas how you can apply technology to building resilience, how to protect against cyber security threats and what your ultimate tech toolbox might look like – now and in the future.

What the Ultimate Business Continuity Success Guide is not:
This book is not intended to replace the fundamental guidance we derive from fine organizations such as DRI and BCI. This book builds on that core information with real-world experiences, tips, techniques, ideas, answers and technology tools that have worked for me. This book is definitely NOT limited to BC 101. You can find lots of basic fundamental information all over the Internet. I tried not to regurgitate what has been published a thousand times. I could not improve on that.

How to use The Ultimate Business Continuity Success Guide:
The Ultimate Business Continuity Success Guide is flexible in how you can use it. You can read it cover to cover or go directly to content specific chapters. Most chapters stand on their own. Some refer to other chapters for additional information. The choice is yours. Use it in the manner that best suits your needs.

Tip – If you are launching a new resilience program you will benefit the most by reading the book sequentially, cover to cover. We discuss all phases of business resilience and continuity.

I am here for you:

Hopefully, The Ultimate Business Continuity Success Guide is not boring. I think some stories might even border on 'entertaining', unless you are that former BC executive I mentioned above. I think you will laugh at some of the stories. In my opinion, that is good. There is no rule against having fun. I believe having fun helps us step up to our challenging job. This is a 'people business' and people like being around others that are upbeat, positive and have a good sense of humor. I love my job and I smile most days going to work. Often, I wish the day were longer. Seriously – I say *'clock, please slow down.'* If you love what you do you will build a great innovative program.

You might not agree with everything I say in the book. Pick and choose what best fits your organizational culture. If you make use of just a few of my ideas, tips or techniques it will be well worth your time. Diversity of ideas is critical to planning and responding. Unfortunately, when everyone blindly agrees that it is okay to situate power generators and vital records in basements of nuclear plants, hospitals and businesses we wind up with Fukushima and Katrina type impacts. More on that later. I encourage you to use what makes sense to you and throw out the rest.

I would love to hear from you. Your feedback and ideas are as critical as a 'less than 1 hour process RTO'. If you have some cool tips, techniques or ideas that have worked for you and you would like to share them (with credit to you) please let me know. Maybe I can include them in a future edition of this book or in an upcoming edition of my newsletter.

In addition, be sure to leverage the Special Bonus – Business Resilience Online Roadmap and subscribe to my free Ultimate Business Continuity Tips, Techniques, Tools and Technologies Newsletter so I can continue to share late breaking information with you.

Finally, most authors usually add their contact information at the back of their book. I decided to put my email at the beginning of the book, in case you have a question or just want to bounce around some ideas.

Marty Fox Email: Marty@UltimateBusinessContinuity.com

I have been in your shoes. I know every inch of the way. I have the successes, lessons learned and 'bruises' to prove it. I have built world class resilience programs for some of the largest companies in the world as well as advised mid-tier and smaller companies. I happily poured one-and-a-half years into creating this book. It is the book
I would have wanted along the way. Everything I discuss in the book I have done or I would not suggest it.

The tone of the book is not a lecture. It is the two of us sitting in your office or the corner pub 'talking shop'. Our focus is on how you can build a successful world class innovative value-laden resilience program with the least amount of B.S. along the way.

The Business Continuity / Resilience profession has a great future! Like any young profession, it must grow and mature, which it is doing. We have only scratched the surface of the extraordinary and sometimes surprising value we can provide organizations. I believe this book will help us develop a mindset that will take us to the next level and beyond. I look forward to the time we will be spending together as we journey through the upcoming pages.

At a high level, there are three over-riding threads that flow through the book:
1.   Real world ways you can implement the fundamental building blocks – Program Initiation, Business Impact Analysis, Risk Reduction and Risk Assessment, Recovery Strategies, Plan Development, Plan Maintenance and Assessment, Testing and Awareness. **Rather than just listing what you should do we discuss how you can do it most effectively!** You must put these in place to have a great foundation for your program. We will also discuss the speed-bumps that could slow you down or derail you. We will talk about it at the street level, the way it gets done in the real world.
2.   How you can leverage technology to its fullest (I do mean fullest and beyond) to build a world-class resilience program for your organization. Where 'business meets technology' is my special place in the world. In fact, after reading this book, you may just 'out IT the IT guys' understanding and implementing great resilience technology.
3.   How you can identify unique opportunities to provide exciting new value to your organization instead of possibly being thought

of as an expense center. Management's mouths will water when they get a taste of what you can do! I scored a few bonuses completing the projects described in this book. I hope you enjoy them. I will provide ideas and help you think broadly about the opportunities in front of you.

The book is comprised of:

Parts I – XI: I share 1001+ resilience / BC related tips, techniques, tools, technologies (4T's) and ideas. Everything is presented in a series of bite size chapters with a few longer ones where required (cyber threats that can destroy your organization and suggestions to prevent/mitigate them are a couple of longer ones that comes to mind). Most of the material I share is not taught in 'business continuity school':

- Tips, techniques, tools and technologies that can help you build and improve each phase of your program. Most of the information we discuss is not the usual material. Many ideas are unique and innovative, especially the ideas that use technology – creating the mini BC plan, automated real-time program metrics, mashing-up value laden exercises, implementing virtual meeting rooms, converting BC plans into highly readable eBooks and a lot more. The book includes strategies that have worked very well for me and I am eager to share them with you

- Technology tool suggestions that can save you time and reduce pain. My passion and specialty is building BC programs powered by world-class technology and I share my thoughts on leveraging technology whenever possible. I am the BC guy that keeps vendors and internal IT 'honest'. I have been known to hijack BC tech calls with system vendors to 'call them out'. We are all understaffed, right? So, let's leverage tools and technology as much as possible. The right tools will help get us to 'world-class', the wrong tools can destroy us.

- Tech skills corner – I will help you become the most tech savvy BC pro at your company. Much more on that later

- Cyber security guidance to help prevent and mitigate ransomware, malware, viruses, worms, data-theft…the nightmare scenarios that can make front page news, for all the wrong reasons. Cyber impacts resilience professions so we had better be comfortable with the concepts. I will help get you get there.

- Techniques to get people excited about upcoming exercises – seriously – excited! Imagine, for a moment, people standing by the water cooler gossiping how they can't wait for the next tabletop or off-site recovery exercise! I know you are smiling right now, but perhaps not quite believing me – yet!

- Golden opportunities to prove your value beyond core business continuity. I discuss projects I have completed and how I did them. I have always been a corporate exec with an entrepreneurial attitude. It worked for me and it will for you.
- Career corner – The book includes my ideas on what makes a great BC professional as well as transitioning into BC/CM/DR from IT. I have been a Business Resilience Director for enterprise companies and I was formerly a Senior Technology Officer for a top 10 financial institution. I guess I did something right along the way and it was not playing politics
- Stories, anecdotes and lessons learned. The book includes believe-it-or-not BC experiences. Some are serious and some hysterically funny

Part XII

Special Bonus 1: The Online Roadmap:
As I was creating the book I knew deep down in my heart that Parts I-XI (above) would really be helpful to people. I had shared bits and pieces of the content with early reviewers and I received a lot of 'thank you Marty comments'. At some point during developing the book something started brewing in the back of my mind – which is sort of the norm for me. So, I said to myself, "Self, you are only going to create this book once so let's go all out and 'take it to the next level'". That is how the Online Roadmap idea was hatched.

I feel the Online Roadmap has value on many levels. I hope you will feel the same way. It is the icing on cherry on the cupcake. I see it as sort of the Resilience Yellow Brick Road to success. A step-by-step roadmap that will guide you toward the reward of resilience. As usual, I include some out-of-the-box ideas – it's what I love to do.

The Roadmap begins on day 1 arriving at the office and moves through a series of steps and ideas that have been very successful for me. I suggest you use the roadmap as a guide as you move through the classical phases when building your program. Many of the steps in the roadmap link to chapters in this book.

My hope is that the Online Roadmap becomes a collaborative effort. I will continue to add to it plus I want to open it up to you to help nurture and grow it. If you have ideas, tips, innovations and techniques that have helped you build your program, I would love to hear about them. Simply email them to me and maybe we can include your ideas in the Online Roadmap.

Special Bonus 2: Free Subscription to the Ultimate Business Continuity Tips, Techniques and Tools Newsletter:
Happily, when you complete the book, it is only the beginning. If you enjoy the book I would like to continue building our relationship by offering you a free subscription to the Ultimate Business Continuity Tips, Techniques and Tools Newsletter. Every issue is packed with my latest resilience tips, techniques, tools and technologies to help you improve your program. To begin your free subscription please visit -> UltimateBusinesContinuity.com/newsletter

Note: There are select links to products, services and conferences I find valuable, use personally, recommend or have tested. In some cases, the organizations offer special discounts to my readers.
Enjoy the Ultimate Business Continuity Book, Online Roadmap and Newsletter! Marty

PART 1 - PREPARE TO SUCCEED

In this part of the book we will set the tone for your success.

I will share what has worked for me and some 'lessons learned'.

We will discuss creating goals, building relationships, partnering with management, understanding your company culture, demonstrating the incredible value business continuity will provide, building teams and a great deal more to position you for success.

We will discuss what resilience means and the wonderful opportunities it can provide us with if we have the right mindset and we position ourselves advantageously.

We will also re-live and enjoy some of my 'based on true stories'.

CHAPTER 1

THE NEW MINDSET - UNLEASHING OUR REAL VALUE!

This is where our mindset begins to change and our journey to organizational greatness truly begins, right here and right now...

If you asked me '*What business are we in?*' My short answer would be:

'We are in the business of Building Real Resilience AND Unleashing Beyond BC Value $treams!'

1. *We instill a confident and knowledgeable culture to insure our organization can proactively understand and respond to any disruptive event we encounter. We might bend but we will NEVER break AND we will spring-back STRONGER than our previous state!*
2. *As we are building resilience we are uniquely positioning ourselves to identify valuable new opportunities. These opportunities can be revenue generating and cost reducing.*
3. *Our value is no longer solely limited to prepare, respond and recover!*

My longer answer would include:
During developing resilience, we can present management with opportunities and risks at a deep level of detail. Currently you are probably deep-diving processes as part of your BIA, doing risk assessments and building plans. We can go much further in providing unique value and we will, possibly breaking new ground in many organizations. Information is power and we are the postman/postwoman. We will deliver!

At a slightly more detailed level – the heart of our value includes but is not limited to:

- The ability to respond to any type of disruptive event in an adaptive and flexible manner. We promote a culture that enables us to solve whatever is thrown at us.
- The ability to gain strength from any disruptive event we encounter **and spring-back stronger** than our previous state. Not the same as before – **stronger and more resilient than before. We learn and get better!**
- The ability to be resilient, which is as much a state of mind and culture as it is having written plans. No plan will be perfect and you must have the attitude, teamwork and skills to work your way through a crisis. We provide all of that!

- The ability to clearly understand management's pain and relieve their pain.
- The ability to implement a high degree of situational awareness through tools and processes. This is critical to being proactive in risk identification, prevention and mitigation. It includes the ability to predict the probability of certain disruptive events becoming a reality.
- The ability to understand our organization from end-to-end, from the tip of multiple supply chain tiers to the customer and every step in between. This includes processes AND data flow. This will enable us to identify new opportunities for revenue creation and cost reduction.
- The ability to deliver quantitative AND qualitative insights to management. This can lead to many surprising opportunities.
- The ability to understand inter-relationships between ALL of our company's assets. This can expose many previously well-hidden opportunities.
- The ability to maintain a 24x7x365 systems infrastructure where required. This is an expectation in many industries in a globally connected world. This can be a differentiator / money-maker in many critical time sensitive industries.
- The ability to clearly understand threats, risks, vulnerabilities and opportunities in real-time and have the capacity to act on them.

Are you excited? I know I am!

How we got from there to here...

In the beginning, there was Core Business Continuity:
When I came into the profession, business continuity was at a relatively early stage. My responsibilities focused on enabling my companies to continue to provide our services at a predefined acceptable level during and after a disruptive event. This was extremely important and ground-breaking at the time and for several years hence. Much of the work entailed understanding our business, our goals, risks, developing recovery strategies, documenting plans, testing and creating awareness. It was very important work.

Unfortunately, it was not easy to quantify the value. Believe it or not, in some circles I was considered an expense! A cost of doing business! Expendable! Fortunately, the story does not end there. Happily, I am now far from being an expense. *Please read on…*

3

Providing extraordinary value through 'Business Resilience' and a curious mindset:

Before we continue, I want to address the issue that some people may be sensitive to which is Business Continuity being referred to as Business Resilience. Keep in mind it is a term and a mindset. You do not have to use the term, although I think it has value. Actions speak louder than words. If you add the extra value, people will be grateful whatever you refer to yourself as.

Over the next few years the world got a lot faster and more complex. Customers and internal users had little tolerance for delays or non-receipt of products or services. The Internet exploded in popularity and became critical to many businesses. Global supply chains became much more complex. Just-in-time inventory created increased profits, as well as additional risks.

The business continuity profession quickly matured, out of necessity. Response and recovery time expectations shrunk and in many cases, went from recovery expectations measured in hours to 24x7x365 'always on' expectations. Tools and technologies were developed that made meeting these more aggressive business expectations a reality.

As I gained experience, my thinking steadily shifted from how I could help develop strategies to keep the business going to how I could help in more quantifiable ways.

I view our profession in a much broader and strategic sense. By employing lateral thinking, I can uncover opportunities beyond core business continuity expectations. I am now an in-house entrepreneur who uses creativity and innovation to identify and communicate to management new opportunities. I have often been rewarded for producing value beyond expectations. It worked for me and it can work for you.

Do not get me wrong, our core business continuity responsibilities are still critically important. Building a strong business continuity foundation is as important today as it ever was. In fact, it is even more important now. We must get that right. What I learned through experience is that it is where our value only begins. It only scratches the surface of what we offer the fortunate organization that employs us. This is where true resilience and creativity kick in!

Throughout the book, I am going to demonstrate through examples and stories how we make companies more resilient in the traditional

4

business continuity sense. I will also share how we can identify possible revenue and cost reduction opportunities, safety and security improvements, disruptors entering our business space (think Netflix-Blockbuster and Amazon-every brick and mortar retailer).

We will also discuss cyber threat mitigation, technology tools, hardware, software and Internet of Things. Each of these can provide great value and new ways to do business throughout an organization. I will keep the discussion simple and to the point.

This new value comes naturally. Due to the nature of our work, you and I are uniquely positioned to deep-dive and bring them to the surface. Incredibly, we can achieve much of it with little extra effort beyond the techniques we use in our profession. Where some projects may entail putting in greater effort they are so interesting, rewarding and trail-blazing that they are fun and time flies by. I know you can do it as I have done it many times.

You do not have to 'sell them' on our value. Simply provide value in every way you can, and they will want to buy what you can offer. People will realize the extraordinary value you provide and will want to be part of your Business Resilience / Continuity Success Story.

Here is a brief taste of how we bring value:

Tip – Communicate the profit / cost saving value possibilities to management, sales, marketing and all other processes. You do not have to commit to anything at this point. Make it part of your elevator speech, which we will discuss in an upcoming chapter. Have a short presentation. Load the presentation up with some of the tips below plus your own.

Tip – Let sales know that when they are competing for a new client, the prospect may require that your company has a business continuity program in place. The answer is yes, you have one! Sales can lead with that without being asked. All things equal, that may be the differentiation in making a sale. If so, the salesperson owes you lunch – and more!

Tip – Provide sales with powerful stories and stats recounting how your company was prepared and had zero business interruption during the last natural or man-made crisis. Competitor X went out of business and competitor Y sustained long customer delays and non-delivery of services. That really angered people. Leverage these stories and if you have pictures, so much the better.

Tip – Your resilience program can lead to process improvement.

Tip – Your resilience program can eliminate redundancy.

Tip –Your resilience program can identify cost savings and revenue opportunities -a few examples in the book include 'Spinning data into Gold' and the 'Golden Opportunities to Generate Beyond BC Value Streams'. There are many other chapters that identify opportunities you may find fruitful.

Tip – Your resilience program can reduce risks across the board – regulatory, revenue, loss of customers, branding. Reduced risk will be appreciated by insurers and may even entitle you to lower premiums.

Tip – Your resilience program can improve data quality. This is an adjunct to what we do when implementing data-driven systems across the organization. Data can be a company's second most valuable asset – behind people, of course. Great data can be spun into dollars – more details on that later. Bad data will be very expensive. We talk a lot about data in the book.

Tip – Your resilience program should have end-to-end mapping of your internal and external supply chain that may identify additional revenue generating / cost reduction opportunities that can provide exciting new ways to do business.

Tip – Your resilience program may identify possible competitive business destroying disruptors entering your niche.

Tip – Your resilience program may identify possible disruptive business strategies your company can leverage to generate revenue and own your business niche.

Tip – Your resilience program can identify cyber risks that can keep your upper management off the front page – read 'Cyber breaches = C's that lost their jobs' in the Risk Management part of this book. We also discuss a lot of technology risks that may scare you a bit but it is better to know about them now then to lose your network and your business.

Special Note: All the above is true and will excite the right people. However, as Ron Popeil used to say when selling on TV, 'but wait, there is more!'… there is no need for you to be satisfied with 'static' results. If you are so inclined you can build a dynamic resilience program to automatically identify new threats, risks and opportunities in real-time! Your system can even automatically serve management a gorgeous daily intelligence briefing, while you are sipping your coffee! Let's talk about that a bit later when we discuss program assessments, tools and technology. That is my special passion!

The story below is based on an entrepreneur's experience in the food industry but it is relevant to you and me. It demonstrates how a slight shift in thinking can present vast, formerly unrealized, opportunities.

Many years ago, I had the same sort of shift in thinking while building resilience programs and it has paid extraordinary dividends. I now apply this 'slant methodology' to many areas of business and life. I discuss my experiences throughout the book. I am confident you are positioned in your organization to derive unforeseen value by way of your daily work. The Founder, a movie starring Michael Keaton, is about Ray Kroc and his significant influence on making McDonald's (R) a leading fast-food chain. I enjoyed the movie. It is an interesting business case-study on how a small innovative hamburger stand in California became a world-wide enterprise.

Ray Kroc was a hard-driving salesperson. The movie opens with him selling multimixers with 'mixed success'. Somehow, he gets an unusually large order from a small fast food restaurant located in San Bernardino, California run by Dick and Mac McDonald. He phones them to let them know they somehow mistakenly ordered several multimixers – only it was not a mistake.
Ray is intrigued. He packs his car and drives from Nevada to personally deliver the multimixers to the brothers. When he arrives, he is mesmerized with their 'lean' fast food business model. To make a long story short, he suggests and they agree to sell franchises.

Ray is passionate about the business and becomes adept at selling McDonald's franchises to people in all walks of life. Unfortunately, his contract with the brothers earns him a meager few cents on each hamburger sold and not much more. It seems somehow the more he sells the less he earns. At a point of desperation, he meets a finance maven named Harry J. Sonneborn. Ray and Harry hit it off and Harry winds up reviewing McDonald's cash flow and balance sheets.

In my favorite part of the movie during Ray's lowest point, Harry asks Ray the seemingly silly question, *'Do you know what business you are in?'* Ray is dumbfounded and replies, *'The Hamburger Business, of course.'*
Harry pauses and delivers the gold, **"*No Ray, you do not seem to realize what business you are in. You're not in the burger business; you are in the real estate business*."** This 'out of left field' insight and a brief explanation of how to turn his business into a goldmine instantly turned the light on for Ray (this scene is on YouTube).
Location is everything. Franchisees needed great real estate locations. It is in limited supply. Ray started leasing real estate and sub-leasing it to franchisees at a healthy markup. Later he started buying real estate and leased it to franchisees at an even healthier markup. Whether a

franchisee made money or not this new revenue stream flowed to Ray. It was brilliant and it applies to us.

Developing resilience puts us in a unique position to understand our organizations and develop value way beyond our core responsibilities. We must keep our eyes and ears attuned. We must think like internal entrepreneurs. We must be bold. We must think beyond mediocrity and create greatness. Make a better future for your organization and yourself!

Going forward we will dive into a series of chapters that will help you start building a solid foundation. Many of the techniques can also be applied to projects beyond resilience. Perhaps, they can benefit some of your colleagues in other business parts of your organization. We will discuss getting off on the right foot, building relationships and selling yourself. We will discuss embracing and overcoming any challenges you encounter. There will be challenges but nothing will stop you from moving forward and attaining true business resilience!

I am thrilled you are joining me on this ground-breaking journey!

CHAPTER 2

POSITIONING YOUR PROGRAM FOR SUCCESS

Congratulations! Whether you are building a new business resilience program or enhancing an existing one, what lies ahead is an opportunity for you to build great value for your company and reap the rewards that come with it for you and your family.

But before you jump in, perhaps take a deep breath, sit back with a hot cup of coffee, tea, cocoa and decide where you want to take this exciting opportunity.

What are your goals? What do you want to achieve short term and long term? What will make your management happy? What will make you happy going to work every day? As Steve Jobs used to ask, *"what makes your heart sing?"*

Tip – Write down your goals. Writing them down makes them real. You will be able to refer to them as you progress. You do not have to go into precise details at this point, as you have not even gathered requirements from your management and process owners. Just start thinking about those high-level goals and write them down.

In my case my overriding passion is leveraging technology to create exceptional value. You will hear a lot more about how I have taken companies to a 10x level later in the book. The reason I mention it now is when I start a new program I promise myself and my teammates that I will help build a 'state of the art' resilience technology infrastructure for our company. It is always my goals and I am proud to say I always achieve it.

By relentlessly focusing on my high-level goals I have been able to make them a reality every time. So, if you can list 5-6 high level goals you will have an end-game to work towards. You will have targets. I learned early on when I was a software developer to start at the end. Understand management's goals and your goals and then work backwards to make them realities. That will allow you to build the more detailed steps and delivery dates to reach each goal in the required time-frame. This process has worked for me every time and it will for you as well.

Tip – Approach the challenge of building a world-class business resilience program in a relaxed and confident manner. Don't stress! Life is too short. Being tense and uptight won't help. I used to worry about everything that could possibly happen. It never did me any good. Later

9

in the book in the handling stress chapter I talk about how a few small adjusts on how I looked at life made all the difference to my success both personally and professionally.

Tip – Make your teammates better. For me it has been easy to do that as I have been blessed with great business continuity and Information Technology teammates throughout my career. The thing about business resilience and continuity is that you are most likely understaffed for all that you would like to accomplish. Leveraging the varied skills and passions of your entire team is critical. We all have our strengths. I have learned so much from my teammates and hopefully I have been able to pass some knowledge on to them.

Tip – Make management and employees better. It is all about them. If you help them succeed and alleviate their pain, you will succeed. If you solve the answers to the question you ask them, *'What keeps you up at night?* ', you will definitely succeed.

Tip – Be persistent. It is so important. If you are persistent and do not give up, you will find a way to get it done. Most people encounter resistance and quit on the two-yard line (American football analogy). It is sad but true. Do not let that be you.

Tip – Build great relationships! The relationships you build will be so valuable to you while building your program and at time of crisis. If you can bring the right people into the conversation you will be successful. If you try to do it as a silo effort you will fail. You must be building relationships and fostering communication on a regular basis. This one tip helped me get through many disruptive events with flying colors!

So, relax, have fun and go out there and build a world-class program! You can do it!

CHAPTER 3

ALWAYS BE READY, WILLING AND ABLE!

There is a saying that I have lived by in my professional and personal life; '*Preparation is 90% of success.*'
Being thoroughly prepared has proven to be a success factor for me in school, sports and in my professional career. If you are prepared you will be confident, organized and productive. Preparation will enable you do a great job 100% of the time.

There is never a good time to have a disaster but they seem to have a way of occurring at the most inconvenient times. Usually during your most critical business timeframes or at 2:00 a.m. during a great dream or Sunday evening when you are at a concert – you get the idea. It goes with the job that you are on-call 24x7x365. I **ALWAYS** keep my work and personal mobile devices next to my bed and yes, I have on occasion received calls between 2 am and 5 am.

I once had to call one of my AT&T telecom buddies during the Great Northeast Blackout to utilize our toll-free routing tables to reroute calls to an alternate recovery location. He did it while he was on vacation on the 15th fairway playing golf! I was afraid to ask what he shot on that hole. Great guy!

You can use your commitment to being available 24x7x365 and your expectation of 2:07 am calls as selling points if you interview for a future business resilience job. Stress to the interviewer that you understand and 'live for' the 24x7x365 expectations. Encourage the interviewer to test you if he or she wants to! Yeah, tell them to call you at 2 a.m. It will clearly demonstrate your passion. In my experience, it impresses them and only one took me up on the offer.

As part of your responsibilities you will be in a key position of supporting the Incident Commander during a disruptive event. You will be a focal point, sort of the glue holding everything together:
Tip – have all the critical supplies, communications and plans you will need at the command center
Tip – have everything you need at home – do a little scenario walkthrough to make sure
Tip – have everything you need on the network
Tip – have everything you need in your plans

Tip – have easy-to-use checklists and cheat sheets so you won't forget anything at crunch time. Checklists saved me a bunch of times (more on checklists later in the book)

Tip – have current lists of critical contacts at hand – always! Sorry, systems are down so you can't get to your intranet

Tip – think about what is missing

Later in the crisis management portion of the book I will provide a lot more tips and experiences relevant to managing a disaster and what to expect.

Tip – As you know, responding at 2 a.m. might very well be in your future so be ready! Now is the time to do your own little tabletop scenarios focusing on how you will help manage a crisis. I regularly play through various scenarios to insure I have everything I need when I need it. It has proven valuable in the past and makes me more confident. Sometimes I do it while exercising or in my sleep. I may be a bit over-the-top in my planning but in our business, it works. You and I should leave nothing to chance.

Tip – Even with diligent preparations, no two disruptive events are the same. Cascades from primary events can cause unforeseen impacts. Be resilient, cool, and collected. You and your team will be successful.

Lesson learned – I did have one occasion in my career where I had my cell phone ringer on mute one evening and I missed a important call from management. It was during the initial phase of building my program. I was new in the organization and trying to prove myself. Fortunately, there was no business impact but it was far from the ideal way to start. I eventually overcame the mishap by taking pride in always being available at any hour. I wanted to share that experience early in the book so there is no chance of you getting burned as I did.

I am not trying to jinx you but just in case something happens today, 'Always be prepared and ready!'

CHAPTER 4

FAST START ACTION TIPS...READY, SET, GO...

These tips are universal in value but may be especially helpful if you are new to the organization or initiating the business resilience program. I remember how those first few days can be long and stressful.

Remember, your goal is to implement great continuity plus added value through a holistic resilience program. Everything you hear and do day-by-day should be positive steps in that direction.

Perhaps some of these ideas will help you as much as they have helped me:

Tip – Settle in and learn about the organization. Learn about the culture. It is critical that you adapt and 'fit in'.

Tip – Request an organizational (org) chart. Get your arms around the scope of your business continuity program and what lies ahead.

Tip – Order your business cards and when you get them hand them out liberally. Perhaps add a helpful tip or two to the back your cards. I have done that and people appreciate it.

Tip – Make lots of friends. You are in a people business so get out there and meet people on all levels. Hand out your business cards and encourage people to reach out to you anytime – 24×7.

Tip – Use your 'it's about you' elevator pitch – more about that later in the book.

Tip – If you support multiple sites, cities, states or countries obtain lists of managers and all other key contacts at each location. Those contacts will be critical as you build your program.

Tip – If you are responsible for multiple locations buy a wall map and 'pin' the various locations. Identify geographic patterns and distances. This will be critical when you begin designing resilient, cost-effective recovery strategies. Management loves in-house solutions and you will too.

Tip – Obtain a webinar account. When you can't be there, webinars are the next best thing AND often they are better than being there when you consider the time and hassle of traveling and the personal cost of being away from your family and friends. I have probably hosted more webinars than there are grains of sand on the beach.

Tip – Obtain a smartphone. Did I really say that in our mobile world?

Tip – Obtain a satellite phone.

Tip – Obtain a laptop and a backup laptop.

Tip – Obtain a tablet – if budget permits. Idea: if they give you a hard time about getting a tablet and you are responsible for supporting mass notification activation's, that may help you justify the expense.

Tip – Make detailed notes and stay organized. Your notes will be so valuable as you build your program.

Tip – Build a tracking spreadsheet. It will be used to track successes (for reports and yearly reviews) and challenges/issues that must be escalated to management. In the book, I list the type of data that should be captured.

Be organized and track everything important. It is too easy to forget things and let them 'fall through the cracks'. Those are the ones that come back to bite you.

5

UPPER MANAGEMENT - A KEY TO YOUR $UCCESS!

One of your first action items should be to meet with upper management (leadership) as early as possible.

- Understand their goals
- Set the tone
- Begin communicating the extraordinary value you will provide the organization
- Get them excited

Begin with a high-level discussion to level-set the scope and goals of the business resilience / continuity program. Make sure to clearly identify your value. On a business continuity level make sure they understand that you will keep the business going during any type of disruptive event. Products will continue to be shipped, security trades will be completed, customer calls will be taken. Work the phrases, 'we *will build redundancy* 'and '*we will eliminate single points of failure that could seriously impact our ability to continue business*' into your value statements. Be sure to read the chapter later in this part of the book on crafting your elevator pitch and why you should stay away from the acronyms.

Keep it simple and to the point. If upper management actively endorses your efforts, you will get cooperation from process owners and their direct reports. You will be gold!
Let management know that as you build the program you will gain a unique understanding of how the company works from end-to-end. This can lead to new opportunities to generate revenue and/or reduce expenses. Your willingness to go 'above and beyond' demonstrates you have initiative and want to help in any way you can. Management usually welcomes that type of team-oriented progressive thinking.

On the other hand, if upper management does not understand the true value you and business continuity bring to the organization they will not actively support you or they might think of you as an expense of doing business. Over time that can become a real problem. There will be negative cascades. Unfortunately, if upper management does not 'get it' you will most likely be burnt toast. You may have to eventually dust off your resume.

If upper management does not 'get it' then it is your duty to make it crystal clear to them that everyone's job, especially theirs, will be in jeopardy when, not if, a disruptive event impacts your organization and you do not have a resilient and well tested business continuity program in place.

Learn upper management's goals and expectations for the business continuity portion of the program. Notice their body language and inflections. Read between the lines. One of my favorite questions is, *what keeps you up at night?* That question has proven to be worth its weight in gold to me. Try it and let me know how it works for you.

Some of the things that keep them up at night will include:
- Active shooter
- Cyber related issues
- Enterprise systems not being available
- Critical hardware that is a single point of failure and cannot be easily replaced
- Weather related threats
- Union strikes
- Disruptive technology trends. For example, Uber disrupted the taxi industry, Netflix disrupted Blockbuster and Amazon disrupted the brick-and-mortar retail world
- Pandemic

Actively listen, listen and listen some more. Write down as many of their pain-points as possible while maintaining eye-contact. As soon as possible add the pain points to a checklist, database or spreadsheet. Stay organized. Soon you will have an ocean of information flowing through your desk. Staying organized will serve you well as you build your program. Do not let tasks slip through the cracks or you will get bitten in the end.

Tip – Schedule steering committee meetings with management regularly over the life of your program. If all the meetings are not required, it is ok to cancel. Management is busy so meet when it is important but cancel when you or they have nothing on the agenda. They will respect that.

Tip – During this type of interview meeting, whether it is with upper management, process owners or line workers, if you are speaking more than they are then you have a problem. Dial it back. You will be happy you did. You never learn anything while you are speaking. The old saying 'we have two ears and one mouth for a reason', is so true.

6

STRATEGIES FOR BUILDING CRITICAL RELATIONSHIPS

In addition to upper management, getting middle management's support is extremely important to your success. Without it you will have a difficult time implementing and maintaining a world-class program. With it you will have a much easier path to success.

Process owners, directors and department heads will be your critical partners on the front lines. I have been fortunate in my career to have had committed partners and it worked to everyone's benefit. Some of the stories in this book reinforce that.

Tip – It is all about them. Emphasize you want everyone to keep their jobs during and after a disruptive event. Mention some of those industry horror stories that have impacted other companies in your industry. People have bills to pay so they will 'get it'. You are here to make sure that your company can respond to any type of event.

If you package it right, managers will dedicate time and energy to building and testing their plans as often as necessary. Early in my career I had a positive experience with a Director of Securities Trading. He was an important person with a busy schedule but he 'got it'. Together we spent time carving out innovative ways to recover the trading processes before most companies were doing it. It proved valuable when disaster struck. I tell the story in more detail later in the book.

Tip – In my experience a great way to get full support from all levels of management is if upper management hosts a lunch for you your first week on the job introducing you to the middle-managers and other key partners. It will clearly demonstrate upper management's support and buy-in for you and the resilience program. To kick off the meal they will speak to the attendees about the importance of having tested plans in place. Trust me, it means a lot coming from leadership. Even more than coming from you or me. You will also have the opportunity to meet many people that will be critical to the success of the program. Meetings and time commitments from middle-managers and line workers will fall into place when they realize upper management is committed to building a culture of resilience.

In one company I worked for, upper management hosted a lunch for me during my first week on the job while one of my counterparts in

17

another region of the country met with the middle managers 'cold' (no upper management hosted support lunch prior to the meetings). Coming into the meetings 'warm' made my job easier and very effective. People knew I was on-board to help them. My counterpart, on the other hand, was seen as an efficiency expert. Perception is everything. It is hard to change first impressions. People unfortunately thought he was brought on-board to reduce expenses by cutting jobs. Unfortunately, my teammate left the company within a year.

So, get managements backing and spread the word. A power lunch or dinner will move things along very nicely. Good luck.

7

PROVIDE MANAGEMENT THE GREAT METRICS THEY NEED, LOVE AND DESERVE!

Management loves and needs great metrics. Really, they love them. Sometimes it makes me teary-eyed when I feed them some dynamic dashboards full of real-time program pulse numbers and real-time graphs from my real-time tools (we'll get to that later) and they start getting ga-ga eyes and begin caressing and crunching those important metrics. I once had to step out of the room.

I completely understand how important metrics are to the success of an organization. They are critical for management to gauge program progress and identify risks and opportunities as they arise. Give them great metrics and management will be your best friend. Keep them in the dark and you... well you were forewarned not to withhold. With managements help you WILL fast-track your resilience program. It is important that you proactively and regularly provide management with whatever they need.

A key to providing the right metrics is to clearly understand what management requires. Some managers like informal written summary reports and others prefer weekly or monthly face-to-face meetings and detailed reports. You should package your metrics to match their preferences. The best way to understand their needs is to ask and actively listen. They will tell you through their words and body language what they require.

Depending on the level of management, different types of metrics will be required. For example, middle management might want quantitative metrics including the number of plans built and the number of recovery exercises completed during a time-frame. Upper management might prefer a higher level real-time critical risk dashboard describing the health of the overall enterprise.

Basketball superstar LeBron James is very good at understanding where his teammates want the ball – outside, inside... that is why he makes players better and they win championships as a team. Superstars that look inward and make it all about themselves rarely win championships. Get management the ball, I mean the metrics, they need to succeed and you will succeed.

Tip – Don't worry, your metrics report probably does not have to be fancy. A simple progress report on a bi-weekly or monthly basis may be what they want and need BUT – if you want to supercharge your metrics program read on…

Ideally, the metrics you deliver are real-time! This is where the right software and hardware in your toolbox become critical to your ability to deliver big. I use powerful tools to deliver real-time metrics to management AND to understand risks and opportunities. It has made all the difference between good and world-class. Later in the book we will discuss technology tools that can empower you to deliver the right metrics at the right time.

If you are not fortunate enough to have a powerful business continuity management system you can build a dashboard using a spreadsheet such as Excel or Google Sheets. The dashboard should include completion percentages and deliverable dates of the major phases of your program – Initiation, BIA, Risk, Strategy development, Plan development, Testing, Awareness and Maintenance. A spreadsheet solution will do the job to a certain degree but I am more into delivering metrics on a real-time basis. You will need to go beyond a spreadsheet to do that.

In conclusion, be like LeBron! Provide your management with the metrics they need and communicate regularly with them. Never hide anything. Be transparent. Supercharge your program. Deliver beyond expectations. Doing so will pay off big! 1

8

HOW TO ALWAYS BE ALIGNED WITH YOUR STEERING COMMITTEE

Your steering committee typically consists of upper management decision makers. They are crucial to the success of your program. They have the final decision as to program expectations and budgetary decisions.

Meet with your steering committee early and often. Certainly, before you begin the Process Owner BIA meetings. Schedule steering committee meetings on a regular basis. I typically begin with bi-weekly or monthly meetings. Get the meetings on upper managements schedules well in advance. Be real, some months they may have to skip a meeting – these are typically very busy people.

I am always respectful of steering committee members time, as I am of all employee's time. Hey, I promise you business continuity is not the top thing on their minds. Of course, you and I know how critical it is. Have the meetings when there are important items to discuss. On the other hand, if there is nothing to discuss, either cancel the meeting or make it a short and sweet touch-point meeting. They will appreciate the brevity. They will know when you do have a meeting, important stuff will be discussed.

You must clearly understand the steering committee member's goals and expectations. Do they expect business-as-usual (BAU) recovery time-frames or do they prefer that you develop cost effective recovery strategies aligning to the critical business processes recovery needs, although perhaps not BAU?

For example, if the steering committee expects all employees to be working day one instead of only a smaller percentage (the critical recovery employees) you must design recovery strategies with redundant locations and equipment to meet these expectations. Possibly hot sites with shadow staff. This will likely come at a high cost in comparison to 'keeping the business going' but not business as usual. Agreeing on expectations will insure there are no surprises later on. You will be able to partner with the process owners to develop recovery strategies that will align with the goals of your organization.

21

Tip – I have found process owner's recovery expectations stated during the BIA interviews line up fairly accurately with management's expectations. Some very time-sensitive processes do truly require real-time recovery, such as:

- Investment security traders – must have very aggressive RTO and 100% staff
- Customer service – must have very aggressive RTO and high percentage staff
- Security – aggressive RTO and 100% staff
- Safety – aggressive RTO and 100% staff
- Facilities – aggressive RTO and 100% staff (plow snow, melt ice, building assessments)

Tip – For most processes your marching orders may be – 'we do not require business as usual, rather we want to maintain continuity of our operations.'

Whatever you hear get it in writing. It may come in handy later. Make sure you communicate upper management's expectations accurately to the process owners. Do not give process owners false expectations that 100% of their employees will be part of the recovery team on day 1, unless they will.

9

HOW TO ACE THE IMPORTANT BUSINESS PROCESS / DEPARTMENT OWNER MEETINGS

One-on-one business process owner (department manager) meetings are directly related to the success of your resilience program. Lots of learning and relationship building can take place in these meetings. I encourage you to prepare properly to achieve the maximum value.

The cool thing is if you do them right you will make lots of friends you can call on at any time. I am proud that I have an 'open door' to speak with my process owners practically any time I want. And it is a two-way street; if they need to speak or meet with me I will re-arrange my schedule to accommodate them.

Prior to scheduling the one-on-one meetings learn your organizations norms and culture. Ideally upper-management will have already hosted the meet-and-greet power lunch we talked about earlier to properly introduce you to the team in a relaxed setting. The lunch is a great setting to 'break-the-ice' and to start getting a feel for how people interact and what their personalities are like. Try to pick up as many queues as possible. **Watch, listen and learn.**

Soon after the upper management hosted lunch your next action item is to schedule the one-on-one meetings with each process owner. I like to make these low-key relaxed meetings, friendly and not too long. That has worked well for me. It also fits my personality so I think I conduct them well. Your style may be different but just as effective. You must be yourself. As my cool friends say, *'you have to be real Marty!'*

Tip – Be prepared, set goals, have a game plan and have an agenda for the meetings. Know what you want to accomplish.

Tip – I like to think of this meeting as a kick-off meeting. You will provide a brief 'about them' knowledge share of the value you can bring them. They may remember some things from the management hosted lunch but here you can go a bit deeper here and maybe show a few (less than 10) info slides and pictures. I have found showing one or two 'horror story pictures' of a hurricane ravaged warehouse or a critical office environment in ashes or under water from a flood really hits home! After that brief but powerful intro, you will ask questions but they must be doing most of the talking.

Tip – This first round of meetings can be a great opportunity to begin learning what response and recovery capabilities are currently in place.

During the meeting ask the process owner how they would currently recover their process. Answers can range from 'I never thought about that' to a well thought out plan. Possibly they will describe a disruption when they had to recover at a sister-site or work from home. If that is the case drill down with follow-up questions such as – how did that go? How could it have been better? …

If the opportunity presents itself in the natural flow of the conversation, ask a few other simple Yes/No capability assessment type questions. The purpose is not to turn the conversation into a full dependency analysis. That will take place during the BIA interview/survey. At this stage, it is to level-set a bit. I find it advantageous to squeeze in the following questions to get a sort of informal baseline of where we are starting from:

- Do you maintain an updated contact list for your team? Is it available when you are home or travelling?
- Do your managers have company issued laptops?
- Can managers work from home, if necessary?
- Can your team work from multiple sites or is it necessary for everyone to be physically in one room?
- Do you have critical customer facing toll free numbers? Can you currently re-route the calls if necessary? Have you tested re-routing them recently?

You might be pleasantly surprised. Some organizations have a resilient culture. They are practicing emergency response and business continuity principles even if they do not have a formal program and written plans. If so, it is a great start! That will make your job easier.

Whatever the process owner tells you will be valuable. You will understand the baseline level of maturity and how far you must go in building your world-class program. You will also instill confidence in them when you let them know the great news that you are there to partner with them to insure they will be able to continue to work regardless of whatever disruptive event we encounter.

Tip – Prepare for process owner meetings and be ready to collect both qualitative and quantitative data. Both types will be very valuable to you as you move forward. (I also mention this tip in the BIA part of the book).

- **Qualitative data:** is data that is non-numerical. It is a messier type of data than quantitative data. It is more subjective and cannot be precisely measured but can provide important information. For example, you may ask, 'are you confident employees are aware of what to do and not do when the fire alarms sound?' The response may be 'I am not too confident at all.

I am very concerned about safety'. It can also be observations you make during a conversation. For example, if you ask the process owner about employee morale and he/she rolls his/her eyes and shakes his/her head in a negative manner it is an important indicator there is a need for improvement.

- **Quantitative data:** is more precise numerical data. For example, 'how many sub-processes do you have'; 'how much is a fine for late payment'; 'how many regular employees do you have in your process?' This is data that is easy to build reports and dashboard metrics around.

Tip – Prior to each business process owner meeting learn something about the process owner. Be a sleuth. No, I am not suggesting you troll them on the Internet but just do some light research that will make the meeting more enjoyable. Finding commonality between you and the process owner will help you bond.

Tip – Start the meeting off low-key and maybe bring up something not business related. Smile and be friendly. People do business with people they like. Open with something they enjoy speaking about to break the ice. You will immediately notice their enthusiasm and the positive direction the meeting will begin to flow in. If you meet in their office there will be all sorts of queues. Perhaps they coach little league. Perhaps they run. Perhaps they have a Dallas Cowboys picture on the wall...

Tip – Be careful, I have seen 'green' business continuity professionals come on too strong and blow things up from the start. For example, setting up three hour meetings centered around presentations or lectures consisting of 120 PowerPoint slides using an 8-point font! Ouch! That is certain to cause process owners to squirm in their seats, 'glaze over', start looking at their watches and desperately try to find creative excuses to somehow get the heck out of there. Maybe there is an app for that. Put yourself in their shoes; imagine an auditor inviting you to a three-hour meeting – yikes – no thanks!

Tip – Leave your PowerPoint in your office. They will love you for 'forgetting it'. Just talk to them as you would a friend with passion in your voice. It is much more effective. Hey, if you ever auditioned for a Ted Talk you know they frown on PowerPoint slides (I am aware of this as I was recently invited as a finalist to give a TedX talk at a major University).

Tip – I have also witnessed 'whet behind the ears' over-eager business continuity professionals barge into process owner's offices without proper introduction and behave like efficiency experts looking to reduce expenses by cutting jobs. Whoa, slooooow down bucko. Please, do not be that person. Complaints to upper management the first week from middle management are not the ideal way to launch your program.

Tip – During these meetings you should diminish their fears. Keep it all about them. Remind them of some industry related crisis horror stories where people lost their jobs and how the impacted company went out of business because they did not have a tested business resilience program. In my experience this sort of story is highly effective. It will get people nodding their heads. They will relate. It really hits home or more to the point; it rightfully scares the sh*! out of them. Hey, they have bills to pay. There are lots of statistics validating the high percentage of companies that go out of business when they encounter a disruptive event and do not have a tested plan. I mention several of them throughout the book.

Tip – During meetings it is important to let the process owners talk. If you are doing most of the talking then there is a problem. Throttle it back. You should actively listen and ask probing **open ended** rather than Yes/No questions. Build on what they are communicating to you. Ask questions and listen intently. You should be listening more than speaking. Let them talk and with the right open-ended questions they will describe their pain, process criticalities (time sensitivity) and single points of failure.

Tip – If you do these intro meetings in a light, relaxed manner the info will begin flowing naturally, sometimes like an ocean. You will hear some amazing things such as, '*I can't remember the last time we had a fire-drill*' or '*I do not even know what a rally-point is*!' Jot everything down while trying to maintain eye-contact throughout. This is important information you are collecting and you will want to refer to it later.

Tip – Make eye contact! Looking people in the eye and connecting shows sincerity. It opens people up. In recent years, we have gotten so used to looking down at our devices that we often forget the importance of making eye contact. Make eye contact works – it works.

Tip – Do not interrupt them or finish their sentences. The more they talk, the more you get to know their pain points. You do not learn anything when you are talking.

Tip – Begin understanding their business process and 'what keeps them up at night'. Learn which business processes they depend on (upstream) and which processes depend on them (downstream). This information will be critical when you map the upstream and downstream dependencies as part of your BIA. Keep great notes.

Tip – One of my favorite questions is 'what keeps you up at night' often people will say 'going to the bathroom', which is cool as it indicates they are loosening up and you are beginning to build a relationship. Make sure you laugh. Ok, give it a try. Please practice how you will laugh at their joke now so it does not sound phony during the real meeting. I will wait…. good but relax …one more time… please laugh………. excellent!

26

Tip – Keep the meeting to the allotted time. I usually schedule the first meeting for 47 or 49 minutes – not 60. If you really think you need 60, please make it 55. Give them back that 5 minutes to prep or get to their next meeting. Trust me, psychologically it works. Remember, most process owners are really busy so please be respectful of their time. It will pay off with less people blowing off your meetings.

Tip – Reflection works. I have become very good at reflecting the person I am speaking with. It enables them to be more comfortable and open with me. Reflection is about getting on the same wavelength as the person you are speaking with. Psychologically, people enjoy speaking with people like them. Here are some tips on reflection that have become natural to me:

- Learn to pace your words. If you are speaking with someone that speaks verrrry slowly you should slow down your words. If they speak fast you speak fast

- Watch their body movements. Reflect some of the gestures they use. Just remember you do not want to blatantly imitate them. So, if they pick their ear or another body part, don't automatically do that. No, the trick is to subtly get on the same wavelength as the person you are having a discussion with

- Use words and phrases, they will clearly understand. I was having a meeting with a process owner a couple of years ago, and I kept referring to their 'process'. They nodded and nodded as there was someone with us at the time. After the meeting the process owner took me aside and asked me what a 'process' was They were ashamed to ask the question in front of the other person. So, my bad. In this company they referred to a process as a department. Saying 'department' would have been much better in that meeting. Take nothing for granted

Tip – Buy them lunch. Sharing a meal fosters openness and makes everything easier. They will quickly open up to you. Try it. Plan what you will order before-hand. Unless you are a neater eater than I am you might want to refrain from a big bowl of spaghetti and sauce. It is my favorite food but I had  it one time with a process owner at lunch and more sauce wound up on my shirt, face and on him than in my mouth. The young man in the picture eating spaghetti is neater than me. For me, maybe a salad might have been more appropriate for this meal.

Tip – Quote a true stat during the meeting such as '73% of businesses without a tested plan that encounter a crisis go out of business within three years.'

Tip – Most people have no idea what business resilience or business continuity is. If you start talking about BIA's, RA's, sub-processes, blah, blah, blah you will often see people glaze over. These terms are second nature to us but Pig Latin to most business people. You are there to help them keep working. You are there to keep the company in business. You are there to insure the company become stronger. That it bends but does not break. For a true story of the importance of clearly communicating the criticality of business continuity read the chapter, 'How and Why You Need a Powerful Continuity Elevator Pitch Today', in this part of the book.

Tip – Don't worry if the first couple of meetings are not perfect. In fact, set the first couple with processes you have an inkling will be less critical (time sensitive). Possibly begin with marketing and merchandising to get the marbles out of your mouth. Ok, if you are in marketing or merchandising please do not be offended – I always include you as vital to recovery but your process may not be as time-sensitive as others although in the long run no company can survive without marketing and merchandising.

Tip – Over the course of many meetings you will hone your pitch. In sales people buy from people they like. In our profession, it helps if they like us and it makes your job more pleasant. We certainly do not want them to run when they see us – 'uh oh, here comes the BC guy or gal',

Tip – Finally, PLEASE, I REPEAT PLEASE, DO NOT assign them 'homework' at this point. Always hand them a couple of your business cards and let them know they can call you anytime – including weekends and nights – and mean it! You are there to serve them. The rewards will come back to you.

10

TERMS AND ABBREVIATIONS

In the business continuity / resilience profession we use quite a few terms and acronyms. Some can overlap and others can be down-right confusing. Too often we take things for granted, when we should not. Some terms are specific to a company. Hopefully, as our industry continues to mature we will develop a clear and consistent standardization of terms. I realized the value of standards during my technology career.

Below are terms and acronyms I use in the book:
New Acronym – Business Resilience / Business Continuity (BRBC) – As 'The Ultimate Business Continuity Success Guide' went to print our profession was in a phase in which business continuity was rapidly maturing and broadening to business resilience. As I mentioned before if you do not like the term Business Resilience just do not use it.

- I use the new acronym **BRBC** when I refer to the encompassing of the business resilience / business continuity profession. I have referred to myself as a BRBC Professional the past few years. I realize BRBC is a new acronym, which I believe I invented and it may take a few chapters to get used to it. However, in the long run the 4-letter acronym will save you reading time and I believe it conveys the overall value of the profession

- I use business continuity (**BC**) when we discuss traditionally core phases such as 'prepare, respond and recover' and the associated deliverable's

- I use business resilience (**BR**) when we discuss concepts and opportunities such as 'bending but not breaking', 'becoming stronger after facing adversity' and the next phase of adding 'beyond BC' value streams

Company Specific Terms
- Process = Department. I have been the cause of confusion when using the term 'process' in companies that typically use 'department'
- Process owner = Department manager
- Incident Commander = Site Leader
- Emergency Operations Center = Command Center
- Rally Point = Muster Point = Assembly Point = Evacuation Assembly Area

General acronyms

I tried not to use too many acronyms in the book. You are probably familiar with most of the abbreviations that follow but to eliminate any confusion later, here is a list of business resilience / business continuity / emergency management related abbreviations.

Tip – Before you use these on unsuspecting management or employees please read the chapter coming up soon, '*How and Why You Need a Powerful Continuity Elevator Pitch Today* '. It might be important

Tip – When speaking with people outside of the business continuity profession never use more than one of these acronyms in any sentence. Keep it simple and convey the value you bring to them. Be outward, not inward.

BCP – Business Continuity Plan

BIA – Business Impact Analysis

CBCP – Certified Business Continuity Professional

CMP – Crisis Management Plan

CMT – Crisis Management Team

DRP – Disaster Recovery Plan

EAP – Emergency Action Plan

EMP – Emergency Management Plan

EOC – Emergency Operations Center

ERP – Emergency Response Plan

ERT – Emergency Response Team

ICS – Incident Command Systems

IMP – Incident Management Plan

MAD – Maximum Acceptable Downtime

PITA – Pain In The Ass

RA – Risk Analysis or Risk Assessment

RPC – Recovery Point Capability

RPO – Recovery Point Objective

RTC – Recovery Time Capability

RTO – Recover Time Objective

SETAPL – Squirrel Eating Through A Power Line

SLA – Service Level Agreement

SPOF – Single Point Of Failure

UPS – Uninterruptible Power Supply

WAR – Work Area Recovery

WTF – What The F*!k

11

YOU MUST ACHIEVE YOUR DELIVERABLE DATES OR IT MAY CO$T YOU!

Let's take a couple of minutes to dig into a really important subject that can impact your program and career in a positive or negative way – deliverable dates.

Deliverable dates are very important. Business resilience is a project driven business. Without deliverable dates and deadlines projects can go on forever. That is bad. I have seen many 'forever projects' in my career. As a former large scale project manager, I cannot stress enough that **every project and the tasks that make up a project must have start and end dates.**

- Achieving your deliverable dates is great. It means you have delivered value on or before expectations. This can result in positive feedback from management and users. Hopefully it can also result in more money in your pocket around bonus and raise time
- Missing deliverable dates, on the other hand, is very bad for you and your company
- Unfortunately, it is all too common in my experience, for projects to get kicked down the road as priorities change. Often failed projects begin with missed deliverable dates

In a minute, I will provide a few tips on attaining your deliverable dates but first, to set the tone, a true story that unfortunately happened to me years ago but still irks me to this day:

At the time, I was:

- 'Carrying' a Fortune 100 business continuity program (my VP's words not mine)
- Implementing a global intelligent mass notification system (domestically and to 32 countries)
- Scheduling 2,000+ yearly exercises (yes 2,000+)
- Personally, hosting twenty-five tabletops manually
- Supporting large work area relocation exercises throughout the United States with up to 150 participants in each exercise
- Supporting national and global day-to-day business continuity BIA, risk assessment, plan development, assessment and maintenance in 32 countries (14 hour workdays were a reality)
- AND automating our resilience program to a high level.

31

My boss actually told a fellow employee that I was a 'work-horse' which I consider a complement. Right?

I met all my deliverables except one – and it was a minor one with zero impact on our business. I missed it by one day! Two days before Christmas! Because a critical business subject matter expert was on vacation.

I believe that one missed deliverable cost me my yearly bonus, at a time in my life when I needed it the most. My son was in college and I had bills galore. That was the only time I missed a bonus in my long career. Sad but true. I suppose it was a 'lesson learned'. I do not blame anyone but myself. My advice to you – never miss deliverable dates unless you have a very good reason and you communicate the reason.

Here are some tips that may help you estimate realistic deliverable dates and deadlines. These originate from first-hand experience. I promise you not meeting them really hurts:

Tip – Do not over-estimate what you/we can get done – It's mid-November or maybe December. Everyone is in a great mood as it is Holiday time and possibly bonus time. It is my favorite time of the year. It is time to have an off-site meeting to plan for next year and have some fun.

On the agenda is the list of projects we will complete the following year – all 31 new systems (true story when I was in IT). Well, we have 5 people in the department and we are going to build 31 new enterprise systems? Even the VP who is presenting this at our fancy-resort off-site meeting was apologizing for these upper management, 'you got to be kidding me' marching orders.

Or maybe you are the new business resilience / continuity director, manager or analyst. You want to impress management so you nod your head when they tell you they want to go from no BC Program to the highest level of maturity in three months – or maybe three weeks.

My advice is don't get caught up in the moment. Do not overestimate. It is better to be honest and to set realistic expectations. Maybe even set the bar a 'teensy-weensy' bit low and then work you butt off to over-deliver in a big way!

Tip – Do thorough research and planning. Perhaps you have a project such as implementing a major new BCM tool, maybe a situational alert system or an intelligent mass notification tool. Big systems all of them. You read an advisory report by Gartner or other service. It say's so-and-so product is in the upper right quadrant. Cool. You set a production delivery date of 3 months out. You put it in writing to management that you will get it done. Hey, 3 months seems like a long time, right? A quarter of a year – wow – that is a long way off – it won't come so soon – 90 days – a couple thousand hours – what could go wrong? Well everything can go wrong! Time flies!

Tip – We are in the 'planning for what can go wrong business' so we should know better. Even so, I have seen inadequate research and planning in both IT and in BC. Maybe, I have even been over-enthusiastic myself at times. Most IT system implementations in large companies fail due to poor planning and lack of communication. It is true. I come from IT and I have seen it first-hand. We in business continuity often rely heavily on IT for DR testing and help with system implementation so be careful.

Tip – Make sure IT has the resources to support your projects. You will need them. Make sure they are doing what they are supposed to be doing, when they are supposed to be doing it. Otherwise, it quickly can turn into finger pointing between internal IT and the vendor, with you in the middle. You DO NOT want to be there, I promise you. For those of you that have been there you are nodding your head right about now. If you are still in that situation you are not smiling. Am I right?

Tip – I have implemented many BC related system tools. It is my specialty. Establishing accurate deliverable dates means really doing your homework. Research as much as possible on what it will take to implement that process or end-to-end system solution. Identify any of the challenges that can delay the implementation.

Tip – Define the scope of the project early and have the deliverables signed off on. If the scope is a moving target once the development starts you will likely run into dreaded 'scope creep'. I have seen scope creep first-hand from both sides of the table, when I was in IT and as a user. Scope creep is bad. Scope creep can turn into 'forever projects'. I do not care if the development is being done in agile, waterfall or any other development process. Scope creep can occur regardless of the process so do not be fooled.

My suggestion is once the deliverables are set and signed-off on the new features become version 2, after version 1 is delivered.

Tip – When you understand the high level-components of implementing a solution, break it down into more detailed steps. For example, when implementing an intelligent mass notification tool, a major deliverable is getting accurate HR employee contact data into the system and building a process to insure it is kept up-to-date and accurate. That one step alone might entail multiple meetings with HR, Legal and IT. Then there is the long process of updating the employee information. Dealing with the integrity of employee data is critical to the success of the project. Unfortunately, employee contact data quality may never have been addressed prior to your project. It can take months just

33

to get that right (more on HR data and data quality improvement ideas later in the book). The point is, you must factor in all facets of the project in your deliverable timeline.

Tip – Build a project plan. You can use a spreadsheet or a project tool such as Basecamp, Trello or Microsoft Project. Make sure you estimate dates, determine resources and tasks. If you have never done a project before you may want to do some Googling or get a book at the library or online that focuses on project planning 101. It does not have to be complicated.

The bottom line is before you commit to deliverable dates put thought and research into it. Once it is in writing you will be held accountable.

12

YOU NEED A POWERFUL CONTINUITY ELEVATOR PITCH TODAY

It's BC Story time!!!

Grab some coffee and cookies and get comfy while I take you on a wild-and-crazy 'based on a true story' ride straight up – or down depending on how you look at it!

It is important to have a clear concise value-laden business resilience / continuity elevator pitch. If you do not have one, I encourage you to develop a short version (30 seconds or less) and a longer version (31 seconds to 1 minute maximum).

If you do not think you need an elevator pitch I suggest you pour that coffee, digest some cookies and enjoy the following story. It just might strike a nerve.

Value of your elevator pitch:
1. An elevator pitch will help you make a **great first impression**.
2. It will eliminate the possibility of a **career breaking bad first impression**.
3. You only get one chance at a first impressions – so don't blow the opportunity.
4. You never get a second chance at a first impression.

Your elevator pitch must concisely convey the enormous value you and business resilience bring to your organization. Until you have your elevator pitch ready be very careful who you share an elevator ride with. The last thing you want is for Big Shot Vice President (BSVP) to bump into you in the elevator and the following, based on true events, nightmare unfolds. I promise you, one bad experience will keep you up at night replaying *shoulda, woulda, coulda…* If you do not know that person standing next to you, make believe you just got a call and take the next elevator until you are ready to pitch.

The Elevator Ride to Nowhere – '*based on a true story*'

Starring: Billy B. Boring…as himself

Co Starring: Big Shot Vice President (BSVP)…as herself

Scene 1 setup:

Time: 11 am – Billy B. Boring's first morning at Always Available Investments and Trading …

Please read the next sentence in your best Rod Serling Twilight Zone Voice. He was the creator, host and writer of many Twilight Zone episodes in the 1950's and 1960's. They still hold up well today. Reruns can be seen on SciFi TV and during Twilight Zone marathons every year around Holiday time in December.

'I submit for your approval Billy B. Boring, a freshly minted Business Continuity Analyst. It is his first day on the job and unbeknownst to him… he is about to enter the Business Resilience Twilight Zone; in **'The Elevator Ride to Nowhere'.**

Action!

Billy B. Boring just completed his mandatory two hour booooooring HR indoctrination at Always Available Investments and Trading.

'Wow', he sighs, *'it feels like it is 5 pm.'* Billy checks his watch. *'Yikes! It is only 11 am! Did my watch stop?'*

Sorry Billy, HR meetings can move in slooooow motion. It really is only 11 am – in the Business Resilience Twilight Zone. The good news is it is time to go straight up to the 72nd floor to meet with your new business continuity teammates.

The creeky elevator door opens. This bandbox has seen better days. Definitely a never-restored 1930's relic. Billy rushes in and presses the well-worn copper button for the 72nd floor. Haltingly, the door grinds shut. Immediately, sweat begins seeping from Billy's pores as his mind races back to 1993 and the time he got stuck in an antiquated elevator with a broken door exposing bare concrete between floors 53 and 54 for an endless 45 minutes in the Marcos owned but neglected 40 Wall Street building. He worked for the Manufacturers Hanover Trust Company at the time. That event freaked him out and he has never been the same. As every good business resilience professional knows, every crisis has learning opportunities and Billy definitely learned he is claustrophobic (much like me – hmmm).

Immediately Billy feels a presence over his right shoulder. Well, look who is standing shoulder-to-shoulder with him? Yup, it's Big Shot Vice President (BSVP). Billy briefly shook hands with her a couple of weeks ago, during his final job interview. Of course, at that time his hands were dripping with sweat from interview anxiety. Today it is claustrophobic anxiety – sort of a sweeter, stronger, more pungent smell. Wow, today is his lucky day.

BSVP's office is in the penthouse on the 75th floor. The button is faintly lit. Billy was never great at math but he rattles off some quick calculations and approximates the travel time in this tin can of an elevator – 1 Mississippi, 2 Mississippi, 3 Mississippi – 2nd floor – carry the 1… his calculations indicate it will take almost two minutes to get to his sky-high destination. Why-oh-why couldn't his office have been on the 6th floor?

By the 7th floor Billy is a wreck, the elevator is belching, wheezing and straining… and it is only going to get worse the higher it goes kiddo. BSVP glances over at him and matter-of-factly says, *'hey, do I know you? What do you do around here?'*

Oh s!*t we're off to the races. Unfortunately, unlike you and I, Billy never took the time to develop his elevator pitch. He was too busy drinking and partying. Sorry Billy, you can't go home and get under the covers – you have officially entered the Business Resilience Twilight Zone.

Billy, panics and just says the first things that pop into his mind. 'Well hello I'm Billy B. Boring, I am the new BC guy. I do BIA's, DA's, RA's, BCP's and WAR exercises. Oh yeah, I have a CBCP.'

BSVP: with bewilderment says, *'huh, what did you say?'*

Fear not, Billy has a few more juicy acronyms that BSVP won't give a crap about, but Billy is going to have to hurl them at her anyway. He starts slinging…

'I also analyze RTO's, RPO's, build RACI charts and when I have all of that finished two years from now I will document it in a BCP!'

Billy Boring, **WTF did you just do?**

BSVP is so glazed over by now she is the one with the anxiety sweats. She instantly taps the button for the 12th floor – yeah you're not even at 12 yet Billy. She didn't get to her lofty position without thinking on her feet. It is life or death in her mind, a few more acronyms and she might be screaming for help by the 18th floor. Billy is slinging like an out of control pitching machine at a dusty old arcade.

She literally spits out (so keep your distance): *'Billy, it sounds like that acronym mumbo-jumbo might mean something to somebody but I just realized I have to get off at 12 to speak with HR about someone. It sort of just came up. I hope you enjoy your day here.'*

Uh-oh. Billy is rightfully concerned – *'hmmm what did she mean by it just came up and you enjoy your day here?'*

End of Scene 1

Ok, so maybe we can learn from this career crisis event. Some sage tips from someone who has been there, done that and learned from his ways:

Tip – When trying to make an impression don't sling an endless stream of fancy acronyms only you, me and our fellow ACBP, CBCP or MBCP's can decipher (yikes, now I'm doing it!).

Tip – Do make the pitch all about them. Focus the value as it applies to the person you are speaking with.

Tip – Do make your pitch simple and clear. Sort of like you are designing the business continuity pitch version of the iPhone.

Tip – Do let them know what you really do is 'empower your business to successfully respond to any type of disruptive event through preparation and practice.' You can even guaranty it, because if the business does go under – you are gone anyway.

Tip – Do remind them of the big storm when poor competitor 'YouPickIt Company' got crushed by that hurricane and had no tested business continuity plans in place. Shareholder lawsuits galore, all jobs lost…eventually they went out of business. Remind them of that. It is very effective. That will never happen here! You keep people in jobs so they can lead happy lives, send their kids to school and pay their bills. Always use a value first approach.

Tip – Do let them know how, as part of building a resilient business continuity program you will become uniquely familiar with all the processes and how they interact. This will enable you to point out ways to improve processes, increase efficiency, save them money and possibly make them a great deal more money! They will love it!

More good news for you. Take these tips seriously and you probably will get an invite to the next upper management luncheon. **Hey, with your cool new elevator pitch – I want to hire you!**

The best part is, everything in your value-laden elevator pitch is true or should be true – if you are doing your job to the best of your ability.

THE BOTTOM LINE IS – SELL YOURSELF! Make it 30 seconds they will never forget! Write it, tweak it, memorize it and practice it in front of a mirror until it just rolls off your tongue. Role play it with friends. Do an exercise – practice it in an empty elevator – yeah I do that. Whoever is monitoring the security video footage must think I am a bit crazy talking to myself and gesturing with my hands. But who cares. An untested elevator pitch is a worthless elevator pitch!

Make them gravitate to you when they see you in the hall, instead of running the other way.

When they get off that elevator ride make them wish it was going to the 150th floor!

HOW TO REALLY UNDERSTAND BUSINESS PROCESSES
AND MAXIMIZE VALUE

After meeting with the process owners, the real fun begins! Now is the time to begin spending time with the people that do the hands-on work. The people that 'make it happen'. The people that make the processes and sub processes *GO!*

Keep your eyes and ears wide open. You will learn a lot!

Tip – Spend half or full days meeting with the people that do the hands-on work: accountants, human resource professionals, customer service representatives, delivery drivers, salespeople, factory and warehouse workers, marketing professionals, security traders... Even if you have to work evening and early morning shifts – do it. It is worth the effort.

Tip – If you do it right they will show you the ropes and they will reveal detailed information that will be critical to you as you build a strong resilience program. You must love upper management and the process owners but some of them may have been removed from the hands-on work for a while. The worker bees will show you the real-deal intricacies of the job.

Tip – Building relationships and good-will (social capital) are keys to your success. DO NOT come on like a cost cutting efficiency expert. Stress that you are there to make sure they still have a job if your company encounters any type of disruption. Make it all about them, as you did when you met with upper management and the process owners.

Tip – You will uncover a great deal of low-hanging BC and non-BC fruit working with the people in the trenches. Take legible, detailed notes. Your notes will be golden nuggets as you build out your program and suggest valuable improvements.

Tip – Value the precious time employees spend with you. Most of these folks are very busy. Some are rated on metrics indicating how many calls they answered or how many route deliveries they made. Keep it to the point. Thank them before and after. Give them a couple of your business cards and let them know sincerely that they can call you any time about anything. Send a quick note to their manager giving 'props' to the employee.

GOLDEN OPPORTUNITIES TO GENERATE BEYOND BC VALUE STREAMS

Opportunity is Plentiful.
Be Creative * See Opportunity Everywhere * Question
Everything * Think Outside the Box
Reduce Risk and Expenses * Empower $ales Team to Increa$e
Revenue

I am very excited to share the information in this chapter with you. I consider projects including those listed below key to my success formula. Focusing on providing 'beyond the expected' value has enabled me to: build highly resilient continuity programs, discover surprising value streams, write books, create videos, develop B2B enterprise software and succeed at the national level in athletic endeavors. You can do it too! Much of it is mindset!

I have successfully completed all the resilience related projects in this chapter and many more. Each project has helped my organizations become more resilient and often they have produced significant expense reduction and revenue opportunities beyond my core responsibilities. The projects are universal and can be initiated for any type of organization.

I suggest you do not limit your value to these projects. The seeds for many of my projects are a result of the unique holistic view you and I have of organizations when building our programs. We have the privilege of understanding our assets, vulnerabilities, capabilities and risks. Often, we understand assets better than anyone in the organization. As you read about the projects in this chapter and throughout the book, think about projects that are specific to your industry and organization. My intention in this chapter is to provide examples that you may be able to leverage, but also to inspire your thinking beyond core prepare-respond-recover. If you maintain a positive, creative, innovative, think big, open minded attitude – you will provide extraordinary value to your organization in many ways!

Throughout this chapter a common thread is that data is a top asset for many organizations. Due to our positioning in the organization and as a by-product of our core responsibilities, we can monetize this for our organization and ourselves. Your contribution can be incredibly valuable low-hanging fruit. The results can impact every department in your organization and the payoff can come through many revenue and cost reduction opportunities.

Your Sales Department can use the resilience you build to generate revenue: After you have successfully responding to and recovered from a disruptive event your sales team can use your success to help close sales. Imagine speaking with a prospect that had a nightmare experience with your competitor when important products could not be ordered. Imagine the frustration on their part with the revenue and customer confidence they lost. Imagine how their brand was impacted. This cascade goes many levels downstream. A savvy B2B salesperson could 'mine the news' for these unfortunate businesses stories and hopefully have them become customers of your highly resilient company.

Get Ready to Prospect!
I suggest every day you ask yourself:
- How can the data I am collecting provide new benefits to my customers or internal departments?
- Can I increase value if I dig a little deeper into the data?
- What golden nuggets are hidden below the surface?
- How can I create new value if I 'mash up' the data I collect with other internal or external data streams available throughout my organization? Sometimes the sum is greater than the parts!
  o Can mashing data streams provide new value that can be used as a competitive advantage?
  o Can mashing data streams be used to perhaps create a new product or service? I know of commercial products that are built on creatively using public data for spectacular results!

Before we review specific projects, here are some general project tips, techniques and tricks that have helped me succeed on many occasions both in my career and my personal life. Additional examples are abundant throughout the book.

Tip – Do not get overwhelmed. I know at a first glance some of these projects may seem imposing and may take time and effort. For example, the book you are reading has been one of the most challenging projects of my career. There was a lot of information I wanted to share with you and I had limited time beyond my day job to create it. I systematically completed my ambitious book project using the advice I suggest in this chapter and throughout the book. You will find a way and in the end, you will complete all the projects you attempt.

Tip – Understand what you want to accomplish. It helps to think of the outcome (deliverable's) and to work backwards. I learned to work backwards when I was a software developer and it has served me well in all walks of life.

Tip – Develop a written project plan. It does not have to be fancy. You can use a spreadsheet or project planning software. There are excellent commercial and free systems available.

Tip – Be organized, focused and respectful of start and end dates. Understand your resources. Set a realistic completion of goals and reward yourself along the way.

Tip – BREAK THE PROJECT INTO SMALL STEPS (TASKS). Every big project is a series of small steps. Listing the small steps is a key to your success.

Tip – BE CONSISTENT. If you complete a few tasks every day it really adds up over a month or year. That is how I wrote 10 books, developed resilience programs and succeeded in every other large project I have attempted.

Tip – Each project is a journey, enjoy it.

Tip – If you hit a wall find a way around it, over it or under it – never let it stop you!

Tip – Be creative and think outside the box

Tip – Never give up AND Never say 'I can't'! I live every day of my life by those credos.

Finding low hanging fruit: Perhaps, you have already gathered some or all the data for the projects described in this chapter during your BIA or when building your plans. Perhaps, the data exists in full or part in a 'gold copy' database somewhere in your organization. Sometimes data is gathered and just sits there collecting dust. You may be able to leverage that data in it's current format or by looking at it from a slightly different slant. Often that uncovers surprising new value.

I believe information is best served being stored and accessed from a centralized 'gold copy'. You need that one source of 'truth' as opposed to 10 conflicting databases or 50 siloed spreadsheets. If the data is modified in one place it should be reflected throughout your organization. Imagine how many data errors and how much manual effort that would eliminate! That will translate into cost reduction and revenue. I have experienced it.

Building high hanging fruit is worth the effort: If the data that makes up the projects does not exist you must compile it from the ground up. There are many ways to do this such as through interviews and surveys. Depending on the size of your organization it can be simple or complex to create. In some cases, it is cost effective to bring in an admin or an intern to assist you in collecting and inputting large data sets.

If you love to explore, research and solve puzzles, you will really enjoy these projects. It is time to start prospecting for golden nuggets…

$ – Toll free phone number identification project: I discuss this project in detail in the next chapter in the book, 'Spinning Data into Gold'. Identifying and building resilience for customer facing critical toll free phone numbers is essential. Customers are your lifeblood. You must be available to them. During a disruptive event, you still must communicate with them.

But wait there is more! While you are doing your data prospecting you just may happen upon tens or hundreds or even thousands of toll free phone numbers your company is still paying for that are no longer being used. I promise you it happens. There is an industry built on auditing telephone bills and tracking organizational phone numbers. I have savings in the six and seven figure range by cleaning up mistakes. You can do this analysis in-house. Please read the 'Spinning Data into Gold' chapter for details on my strategy.

$ – Laptop / Tablet recovery project: I discuss this project in detail in the chapter entitled, 'Reduce Expenses and Improve Resilience with The Laptop Re-use Project' This project has produced increased resilience and significant savings for my clients. The potential savings for a large company of mid 6 figures to low 7 figures is possible. In some cases, I could initiate the project with a few phone calls and some coordination with IT. Management loves this project. I can't blame them. It is a win-win project- increased resilience and cost reduction.

$ – Generator project: loss of power is one of those 'fairly common' types of disruptive events. A generator can keep the lights on until power is restored. Commercial generators can be used for office locations or personal generators can be used to keep the lights on for critical employee's homes.

During the aftermath of a blizzard we drove a personal generator to one of our IT executives who lived off-the-beaten path. We installed it and he worked through the rest of the blizzard. Mission accomplished. Had we not planned we would not have been able to purchase a personal generator, as they were all sold out during and after the storm. He was thrilled and we earned brownie points.

43

The effort to gather the data needed for this project can be a standalone project or as part of a comprehensive location capability data gathering effort.

Gather a list of all your locations and the facilities managers. You can get this information from the facilities or real estate department. You then send an email to the facilities people asking if they have a generator, what section(s) of the facility it covers, how long the generator can run and the last time it was tested. If you will store the data in a centralized database, provide them with a link.

They can then open a simple form and populate the database. When they complete the form it can trigger an alert or run a report on the current results so you can follow-up where more information is required.

The results can then be mapped to your BIA impact results to understand risk. You can then present your findings to management and discuss remediation. Perhaps you will purchase the first generator for a location that has none or add additional generators to cover an entire building rather than only part of it.

Tip – The generator assessment can be part of an overall automated process that sends update reminders to the facility managers. Include a link in the message so the managers can review the current location data in your system and make modifications. After they click the 'reviewed button' trigger an algorithm that analyzes the new data against the requirements for the location. This is truly understanding risk and capabilities in real-time.

$ – Supply Chain Project: Many companies rely on just-in-time inventory and complex supply chains. If the supply chain breaks and suppliers are not available, it can have a devastating impact on a company's ability to do business. LuLu Lemon and Toyota are just two of hundreds of companies that have experienced the pain and embarrassment of a broken supply chain.

Hopefully your purchasing department has this information but if not it is a great exercise. I suggest you map the supply chain end-to-end. Identify critical suppliers. Identify single points of failure. Identify Tier 1, 2 and 3 suppliers. Does each node in the chain have a tested business continuity plan? Has your company reviewed their plan?

If you are using a great BCM system mapping the supply chain can become a much easier effort than trying to do it manually. Also, gaps can be identified in real-time as data changes (see the automating assessments chapter for an example of the real-time process). In addition, my favorite BCM systems can visually display the supply chain.

Tip – You have the most leverage on insuring a supplier creates a business continuity plan and implements redundancy when contracting with a new supplier or when renewing their contract depends on them having a tested plan.

$ – Vendor project: your company may have a great deal of vendors you work with to procure supplies and equipment. Perhaps vendors can be mapped to locations or regions. Some may be national vendors that service your entire company. Whether the vendor provides snow removal, copy machines, pallets, boxes, commercial vehicles… if they are not available it can severely impact your business.

Hopefully vendor information was collected during your BIA or possibly your purchasing or accounting department maintains an up-to-date master database of all your vendors. Otherwise, it can be a valuable exercise to initiate a thorough analysis of all your vendors. Identify critical vendors. Identify single points of failure. Identify alternate vendors. Do each of your primary and alternate vendors have tested business continuity plans?

You may discover that you are using different vendors for the same product or service in many different locations. Perhaps that can be consolidated to contracting with one vendor for all your locations. This can result in significant volume savings and simplification. If you do consolidate to one vendor do be sure to have backup contingencies in case that vendor does not deliver.

Tip – You have the most leverage on a vendor that they create a business continuity plan and implement redundancy when contracting with the vendor or when renewing their contract.

$ – Systems gap analysis project: In mid or large organizations, this can be a complex project that is talked about but sometimes just never gets completed. Although the analysis may be time consuming, it is critical that your organization understands your upstream and downstream system vulnerabilities and capabilities.

During this exercise map all your internal and cloud systems end-to-end. Understand all dependencies. Is there a Tier 2 system sitting between two highly critical Tier 1 systems? Is there an ftp data file needed to drive those Tier 1 systems? Are you getting that ftp file from an outside vendor? Do the vendors have a good backup plan? Can they meet their systems level agreement (SLA)? Have they experienced 'down time' that could impact your ability to service your customers?

This project can also identify redundant systems that may present opportunities for consolidation, simplification and cost savings. It will also identify systems that do not meet the required business RTO and

RPO. I have even seen this project result in tremendous savings where dedicated servers were migrated to virtual servers, running multiple systems on the same server. Consolidation of servers can reduce costs for hardware, software, electricity and data center space requirements. I have seen saving in the 6 and 7 figures. Another feather in your cap!

Warning Tip – Just because a system is in the cloud, does not mean it is resilient. There are many horror stories of cloud systems being unavailable and businesses stopping. I have read about companies where people 'go to lunch' when a critical cloud system is unavailable. This could cause loss of clients and revenue. Audit your cloud provider to be certain they have a robust plan in place should they be hacked or hit with a Distributed Denial of Service attack. I have witnessed cloud providers being down for an unacceptably long period of time. That becomes a huge business continuity issue. If you insure cloud providers a resilient you are providing way above and beyond value to your organization.

$ – Employee skills and certifications project: There can be significant value in doing a comprehensive analysis of employee skills and certifications throughout your organization. HR might have some of the skills and certification information but there may be room for improvement. Speaking with them to learn what information they have collected would be a good starting point.

The value of understanding the skills and certifications of employees can be critical during disruptive events. For instance, if employees in a certain region are not available, you may have the required skill-set to keep the business going in a different region of your organization. This project also has incredible value from a safety aspect. You will understand who is trained in CPR, as an RN… Clients I have advised have found surprising value in many parts of their organization. You never know what skills people have until you ask.

Work with HR and approach this project with care. Sometimes this exercise is performed prior to an upcoming merger or acquisition. People can rightfully become concerned. So, communicate honestly the reasons for building a skill and certification repository.

$ – Shipping project – I have completed this project on two occasions and it reduced expenses significantly in both instances. Once I completed this project for a catalog company and the other time for a manufacturing company. In both cases the subject of shipping costs arose while doing the BIA dependency analysis for the shipping process.

The process owners were complaining about the high cost of shipping by UPS and FedEx to customers. They provided me with some data which listed shipping costs by weight, distance and size of the packages. Each company was being billed more than $20,000 per month. I have a friend that owns a company that built complex algorithms and a highly-automated process to analyze shipping expenses and significantly reduce expenses.

The shipping process owners I was working with submitted a very short form consisting of one month's billing to me and I ran it through my friend's website. In each case the cost savings were well over six figures on an annualized basis. The best part is there was no expense to my clients for the service. My friend's company works on a fee from the percentage of savings.

$ – Always Always Always seek opportunities to improve data quality, streamline the flow of data vertically and horizontally through your organization and break down those awful department silo's:
You will have the unique privilege of seeing how data moves vertically (within departments) and horizontally (across departments, suppliers and customers) from end-to-end. Amazingly you may be the only person in that position. Often IT departments are too busy working on new systems and maintaining current systems to examine the end-to-end flow of data. Unfortunately, data inefficiencies and errors can be very expensive to your organization. Suggesting improvements can be a goldmine to you and your career.

As you work with department managers and their employees watch how data is input into systems. You will learn a great deal. Map where the data comes from (upstream) and goes to (downstream). Ask managers about issues they are having with data they receive. It is an important question, as what often happens is a data error is made a step or a few steps upstream and the cost to the organization is not felt until it is used downstream. For example, imagine your company receives a supply of widgets and the person doing data entry makes an error in the number of widgets received. Perhaps inputting 1,000 instead of 100. If a mistake is not caught immediately it might incorrectly seem you have enough supplies when in truth you will fall short, which could be costly in many ways including brand image, loss of customers and wasted time and money fixing the errors.

Do not laugh, I encountered this type of data input error years ago, when a colleague ordered 1,000 custom portfolios for our team to give

47

out at BC Offsite Meetings instead of ordering 100. Let's just say we never had to re-order portfolios.

Tip – Many data errors can be corrected on the front end – when data is being collected and input into systems. If systems are not designed with proper data validation controls at all upstream data entry points, then downstream processes and ultimately revenue will suffer. You will have a continuous data cleanup black hole.

Tip – Business managers must take ownership of data quality.

Tip – When selecting tools or developing your own database systems use field validation on input fields whenever possible. A few examples that are simple, highly effective yet are often overlooked include:

- Required fields such as employee ID must be entered or the record cannot be saved
- Formatted (masked fields) such as telephone numbers should only accept numbers and can only be a certain length
- Date fields should have a consistent and defined structure
- End dates cannot be earlier than start dates
- Pick-lists and lookup fields should be used whenever possible, otherwise information will not be normalized and the system can quickly become an expensive to cleanup mess.

As you watch the data entry process being performed and ask questions you will find many possible low hanging fruit improvements.

Also, please read the Chapter 'Database or Spreadsheet' for much more information on database design best practices.

If you have any questions on these projects, please contact me.

I am reporting on additional revenue generating and expense reduction business continuity related opportunities in upcoming issues of the Free Ultimate Business Continuity Tips, Techniques and Tools Newsletter.

15

SPINNING DATA INTO GOLD

This story describes a perfect example of how your business resilience team can go beyond core business continuity responsibility and add revenue generation or expense reduction value to your company in non-BC areas. Management loves these extra credit efforts!

Always look for these types of golden hidden opportunities to shine. Be curious. Your normal resilience and BC functions will provide you with a unique view of your organization which will open these goldmine opportunities up to you for the taking. You can ultimately be seen as a profit center!

You never know when an opportunity will present itself, so '**always be ready** '. I draw a parallel to when very smart athletes make it to the professional level. Even if they are third or fourth on the depth chart, for the first time in their lives, the smart athletes 'practice with a purpose' every day just as if they are in the starting lineup. When the opportunity presents itself, and it will, they will be ready! **That must be your mindset as well.**

Here is an example how with a little out-of-the-box thinking an opportunity presented itself to me. I found that by going the extra yard and digging a little deeper I was able help my company save hundreds of thousands of dollars. This one 'stretch project' rewarded me in many ways. By the way, I LOVE 'stretch projects'. You should consider challenging yourself with stretch projects in your professional and personal life.

It all started when I was implementing a recovery strategy for customer service toll free numbers for a Fortune 500 Company. Building a resilient customer facing toll free number recovery strategy is critical and fortunately it is one of my specialties. It intersects technology and aggressive business process needs which is a challenge I really enjoy. I get to express my tech, resilience, BC skills and have a ton of fun doing it! Don't tell my employer but I would do this stuff for free!

The customer service process I was focused on would need to recover approximately 60 customer facing toll free lines during a disruptive event. Many of the lines had numerous sub-prompts which enabled the callers to reach employees with the exact skill-sets needed to answer their specific questions. I had implemented this type of call re-routing recovery strategy many times in the past so it was smooth sailing.

- I went through the process of meeting with the customer service process owner to review the customer facing numbers and the time sensitivity of each line. They had some documented in their business continuity plans but it is important to double check to make sure you have all the customer facing numbers in scope and all are accounted for in the telecom provider's routing tables.

- Next, I worked with our in-house telecom expert and the process owners to build the routing tables. I set up and hosted the meetings. Getting these conversations going with the right people is invaluable. Know your resources and plug them in where required.

- Next, I partnered with our third-party recovery vendor to square away routing the calls to the alternate recovery site and to the proper skill set recovery personnel wherever they happened to be sitting in the work area recovery room. The beauty of the routing tables is that once the number is set up, it can be sent to any location – vendor location, mobile trailer, your in-house sister-site or work-from-home.

- I was also able to implement features at the vendor work area recovery site such as call forwarding, conferencing, call recording and many other cool features the business required. It entailed working with their telecom team and our telecom team.

- We then did a great deal of testing. We started with simple tests and later got quite complex while thoroughly testing each feature. We 'embraced' each issue we encountered in testing, fixed them and re-tested.

Tip – The first few times you go through this type of project it can be tricky but you will do a great job and you will learn a lot. Subsequent implementations will be much easier.

Tip – Make sure you create a detailed project plan or a checklist so you do not miss any steps in the process. Make certain you have listed the people accountable for completing each task. It is important to document realistic deliverable dates for each task.

Tip – Don't worry, you do not have to be a telecom expert, just pull the right partners together and you will be fine. There is no way I could have successfully completed this type of project without knowledgeable partners.

The value of the resilient toll free re-routing strategy was critical during the Great Northeast Blackout of 2003 (next chapter in the book) when

50,000,000 people on the east coast of the United States were without power. New York City was severely impacted and our company had to 'declare' and enact our business continuity plans. Everything worked well for us. Now let's get back to the focus of this chapter, which is finding golden opportunities in your business continuity travels.

Discovering the gold in the data:
While reviewing the toll-free numbers in scope for the customer service toll free numbers I started thinking – if this department had upwards of 60 toll free numbers and within other department business continuity plans including other customer service departments we had an additional 300-350 toll free numbers documented, might there be additional toll free numbers throughout our 85,000-employee organization that we had not accounted for and have strategies built to recovery? Might some of them be time-sensitive? I became really curious and soon it became an obsession to uncover ALL the toll-free numbers in our huge organization.

So, I had to figure out a way to dig deeper into locating toll free numbers on an enterprise level instead of just the ones directly involved in this project or the ones we had accounted for in the business continuity plans. Fortunately, I am a 'data rat'. Working with big data is another passion of mine. I know it sounds funny but I love data and I feel very comfortable being immersed in even terabytes of data. My hope is someday to have the opportunity to analyze a zettabyte of data!

During my career, I have discovered that where there is a lot of data – there is often opportunity to make money, save money and improve an organization in many ways. Big data is changing our world. A very creative use of big data is how Jawbone(R) and Fitbit(R) are using data from their wearable personal health devices. One example is the analysis Jawbone did on sleepers during an early morning Napa, California earthquake. Surely directional analysis could be layered on top of the metrics and perhaps someday this could help us with early warnings provided personal information were not used. Just an idea of mine.

Sometimes big data ideas come to me in the strangest places – when I am sleeping, in the shower or on a long run. I suggest you keep a note pad with you at all times to jot ideas down or they will 'flitter' as described in the 'Ideas Flittering Away' chapter in the book. You can also voice record notes in your smart phone if you prefer.

If you have ever worked for an enormous global organization with 85,000 employees, you can appreciate the scope of this project and the sleuthing necessary to get to the gold – the big toll free list(s) – if such a list or lists even existed.

The key to my detective work was the many great relationships I had built over the years. Building corporate and industry relationships is valuable social capital. Sometimes half the battle in a big corporation is knowing the 'players' and having an open door to contact them. It can take years to build this social capital. If you build these types of relationships, they will benefit you immensely. Network, network, network!

I systematically contacted people in my corporation I thought might be able to get me closer to the golden list(s). One connection led to another and to another until finally after digging ten people deep I finally discovered the 'keeper of the toll-free list'. I was so excited!
She was very helpful and sent me a list with 5,387 toll free numbers. Seriously! 5,376 toll free numbers! I still get excited just thinking about it. I pulled the list into a simple spreadsheet and methodically began analyzing it. Next, I started randomly calling and testing some of the numbers. Interestingly, many of the numbers 'busied-out' or were dead. Yikes!

I dug a bit deeper. Many of these numbers were assigned to sales-people that had long ago left the organization. Hmmm. On a hunch, I contacted accounts payable. I learned we were still paying for many of these useless numbers that had been changed or abandoned over the years. Often, they simply fell through the cracks and were still on our books! Believe it or not there is a whole industry built around telecom auditing.

I calculated the lost revenue and turned the results over to upper management. The potential cost saving on these numbers was in the six figures. Ka-ching! In addition to current savings, a process was implemented so we could automatically identify future toll frees that were not actively in use. Future savings would also be significant. Ka-ching! Management was thrilled and they showed their appreciation.

Being a resilience / continuity professional provides you with a unique opportunity to see the organization holistically. You will see the big picture. Bring value and it will make you unique and indispensable. Dig into the data and the process, think outside the box, be creative, go that extra mile and provide value beyond core business continuity expectations. I share additional revenue generation and cost reduction opportunities throughout the book.

16

REGIONAL POWER OUTAGE: A DETAILED CASE STUDY OF RESPONSE AND RECOVERY TO AN HISTORIC EVENT

During the early afternoon of August 14, 2003 I hosted a tabletop exercise at my company's New York City headquarters. The scenario we played through during the tabletop was a power outage. The tabletop was fun, went well and a lot of valuable info was shared by the participants.

Does August 14, 2003 sound familiar to you? For me, it is a day and event I will never forget. Late in the afternoon I was travelling home to Long Island from Manhattan. Uh oh, maybe you guessed it, the lights went out across the Northeast portion of the United States impacting approximately 50 million people in the Great Northeast Blackout of 2003. I like to think of the timing of the power outage tabletop and the same day real event as fortuitous.

Unfortunately, the folks in our NYC office referred to me as 'Marty the Jinx' for years hence. But they were so well prepared! So yeah, I will gladly 'take one for the team' and happily live with the nickname.

Creatively Recovering Our Time Sensitive Processes

The Great Blackout of 2003 is one of my most memorable preparedness, response and recovery stories. Our very time sensitive (critical) trading (<1 hr RTO) and customer service (<1 hr RTO) processes were in Manhattan, NY. The many risks of being in Manhattan after the horrendous 9/11 World Trade Center attack heightened the need for robust emergency response and business recovery solutions. We spent a lot of time and effort developing and testing our strategies with the safety of our employees foremost in mind.

Our primary business recovery strategy if something should happen in Manhattan was to recover at one of our sister sites across the Hudson River in New Jersey. If we could not recovery in-house for any reason, the secondary strategy was to recover at our third-party vendor work-area recovery location. It is important to always have multiple recovery options ready and thoroughly tested.

I had the responsibility of designing and building out the recovery capability but I give credit to my boss, who during one of our first continuity discussions described how he had implemented a strategy at a former employer where he leveraged a lunchroom as a recovery space and had PC's and phones on carts ready to roll into place at a moment's notice – and he did this in the 1990's! Always a guy ahead of his time and a great person to work for.

Tip – It is important to have a mentor to learn from. I hope I am now considered a mentor to some people.

I took inspiration from his insight and designed a similar strategy for our critical customer facing processes enabling us to recover in a conference room in New Jersey. Fortunately, we built and diligently tested our recovery strategies often. We ran through tabletops AND physically tested recovery by rolling out the carts and working from recovery desktops in the recovery conference room! Much more on interchangeable work area recovery exercises (IWARE) later in the book.

As you can imagine all hell broke loose on my way home that evening in 2003. 50,000,000 people were literally in the dark, including me. At first, many of us thought this might be a large-scale cyber-attack on the electrical grid by a terrorist group. It was an understandable thought as we were in NY and the recent events of 9/11 were ingrained in our thoughts every day, as they always will be. We learned this event was not terrorist related, although I firmly believe we will face an attack on our infrastructure at some point from a terrorist group or nation-state. The Northeast blackout was caused by human error and a series of cascading infrastructure events escalated the impact to historic proportions. Cascades accompany many types of natural and manmade events.

Tip – Always consider cascading events when planning. Unfortunately, in some high-profile recovery mishaps organizations never considered cascading impacts.

Tip – Human error triggering disruptive events is not unusual. Back in my IT days I learned to be very careful when making changes to programs or the network, especially late in the day when I was tired or in a rush. Software developers are smart not to commit changes to production late in the afternoon on a Friday. That had a way of wrecking a weekend.

The evening of the 2003 power outage I got home at 5 pm. I had scheduled the tabletop early in the day so I could get home early for some much-needed R&R. Well, as you are well aware in our profession we are on call 24x7x365 and duty called that night and for the following week. But that is what we BC Professionals live for! I always say, 'if I do not step up and get our company though a crisis – FIRE ME! ' It is where the 'rubber meets the road.' **Tip** – use my FIRE ME line in interviews (with passion) and you will have a good chance of getting the job – but you must be prepared to live up to it.

Ready – Set – Go!

On the first night of the Great Blackout I opened our crisis team conference line. Every member of our experienced crisis response team stepped up. We kept that line open for 72 straight hours. It was probably the only time since my college days or my big-time coding years in the 1990's that I worked 72 hours straight, with only 3 quick naps. **Tip – Keep lots of coffee brewing!**

Throughout the event the importance of communication was driven home. We had active participation from the Incident Command Team (ICT), Emergency Operations Team (EOT) and critical IT and telecommunications partners throughout our enterprise. So many fruitful discussions focused on various scenarios we expected to play out. Situational awareness information was so important and it flowed to the people that needed it as the situation escalated.

Everyone stepped up. If you have ever been in the middle of a crisis situation you know it can be a bit surreal and you might agree that time seems to either fly by or go in slow motion. Information had to be digested and big decisions had to be made in an intelligent manner.

By 2 am the Mayor of New York (NY) was 'hopeful' of getting train service going by the morning rush hour. By 3:30 am it was far from a sure bet. Our team weighed our options. Wisely, our Incident Commander made the decision to have our facilities in New Jersey (NJ) begin readying the business recovery rooms in the event mass transit was not running and we had to recover there.

Facilities and technical employees in NJ reported to the recovery site and rolled-out the PC's that were on the carts. They fired them up to insure they connected to the network, checked that the latest image and patches were in place (we updated the images often so there were no issues). They wired up and tested the phones (wireless could not be used for sensitive trading calls). We were ready to work!

Simultaneously our ICT and ECT teams assimilated all the information available to us and we reached out to public agencies we had relationships with to get news as it happened. We were fully prepared to recover in NJ or work from NY if the situation changed for the better at the last minute. We were on partial generator in NY but transportation was a factor to consider. At 5 am we made the final decision to enact our plans and recover our critical NY processes at our now ready NJ campus. As I mentioned, we had practiced for this type of scenario many, many times which enabled us to close many potential gaps prior to this event. Practice, practice, practice and a great team gave us confidence we would make this work.

We contacted teams at the recovery site and let them know that recovery personnel would be arriving by 8 am.

Process owners had communicated with employees throughout the evening and early morning hours. They utilized their up-to-date well tested call trees they kept at home. We knew everyone that lived near our locations in NJ from detailed mapping information in our plans. At the time, everyone had land lines which had power from the phone company. Today we would have used additional multi-modal means to communicate – more on that in the mass communication chapters in the book.

Impressively 100% of the trading and customer service recovery employees in New Jersey were contacted and made it to work by opening bell that morning.

Telecommunications re-routed all customer facing toll free numbers (documented in our internal phone routing tables). So, all calls that were destined for NY were now ready to be taken in NJ! We had tested this often.

I kept the conference line open throughout the event. It was our focal point to smooth out any speed bumps we encountered during the day. For example, the need to gather a few more headsets, replace a couple of dead batteries, get additional trading forms – all things we had available at the recovery site as part of our plan. Low-hanging fruit because we kept extra supplies on hand.

During a crisis, not everything works perfectly so you have to be resilient and be able to adapt. You should build and promote a culture of resilience. I promise, it will serve you well!

At the end of each day we did a recap/hotwash meeting (we used to call it a post-mortem – but eventually we shied away from that term as it sounded sort of negative) to see what went right and what could be improved for the next day and the next inevitable event. We documented all issues and opportunities for improvement in an issues log, tracked and closed them one-by-one. You really do learn from every event. The key is to act on what you learn. Unfortunately, industry research shows we do not always act on those 'lessons learned' opportunities. That should not happen. Acting on them and fixing them for the next time really pays off.

On day two of the Great Blackout we again worked from NJ and finally on day three we could begin returning to our primary production site in Manhattan. We did this in a couple of waves of employees rather than all-at-once just in case the Manhattan power infrastructure was not stable. You probably can relate that power has a way of going up and down – if you have ever been through one of these events.

I am so proud that our company responded so professionally and effectively to such a difficult challenge. I attribute it to a culture of resilience, the dedication of management, professionalism of employees, communication, teamwork and testing. Everyone knew their role and performed it well. No egos – no glory mongers. It was a stressful week but also the best feeling as we were 'zoned in' as a team throughout the event.

17

HOW TO CREATE A HIGHLY SCALABLE RESILIENCE PROGRAM

Have you ever seen a business continuity department that was overstaffed? I haven't. Most likely you are working 'lean-and-mean'. If you are a large organization, you must implement an elastic and resilient organizational hierarchy. Technology tools can also help empower you to successfully scale your program. We will discuss those throughout the book.

I have managed global enterprises spanning the U.S as well every continent – except Antarctica. To successfully build and maintain strong and resilient business continuity programs I like to build hierarchical hub-and-spoke frameworks.

Tip – If you are a global enterprise a good scalable strategy is to appoint an English-speaking BC liaison to work directly with the process owners and employees in their country or region. Your Enterprise BC / resilience team should guide the program but to scale I suggest you give responsibility to each country management to do the hands-on implementation, testing, awareness and maintain compliance. The results of their efforts should be reported to you in a timely manner.

If there are questions from employees in the countries have them bubble up from process owners to country BC coordinators to regional liaisons. Your enterprise team should be available to the regional liaisons whenever they need assistance answering questions as well as partnering on table-tops and off-site recovery exercises. Assist with awareness communications, posters and newsletters that the regional liaisons localized to each country. It is really cool seeing posters and newsletter in different languages such as Japanese,

The same sort of hub-and-spoke hierarchy can work well for states, divisions and regions throughout the domestic part of an organization. Again, your enterprise team should be responsible for oversight but each region should be responsible for their own program which must be in compliance with your corporate guidelines.

Tip – The key to making this work is for management to completely buy into this type of hub-and-spoke hierarchical structure. They must support it for it to have any teeth. They must actively enforce it when 'push comes to shove'. I have seen it both ways. When management supports the initiative, it works well. Without management support, it will likely fail. If it fails (flattens out so you do all the work) you may not have the resources to provide the value your organization deserves.

I have had extraordinary success building hub-and-spoke domestic and international programs. Every crisis my companies have encountered including the tsunami in Japan, earthquakes in Chili, pandemic in Mexico and terrorism in England have been handled as a successful partnership between the local team with support from the core our enterprise teams. I found it to be highly scalable and efficient. It can work exceedingly well if built and supported correctly. Good luck!

18

BE READY FOR THE UPCOMING 2:00 A.M. CRISIS CALL!

Hurray! It is that time again – BC Story Time!

It is 2:00 a.m. and you are about to dunk over LeBron James (wait that's my dream) or whatever else you dream about.

Ring – Ring – Ring… you wearily open your peepers and EEKS you realize from the caller ID it is Big Shot Vice President (BSVP). Hmmm, the time is 2:07 am so chances are this is not a pleasure call. More likely, *'It is now, show time!'*

You immediately hear the trembling in BSVP's voice because his/her job is very much on the line, as is yours. You can just anticipate BSVP's next quivering words;

BSVP: 'hey <<your name goes here>> I just got a call from facilities that a water pipe burst in headquarters! To make matters worse it burst directly over the fu&%!''ing call center and trading room. Water everywhere! It's bad, real bad. I just texted you a picture that facilities sent me.'

BSVP continues: 'Without our call center and trading room up-and-running at 9 am we are up s*?t's creek. What the heck (although likely a more colorful adjective) is the plan?'

If you are like me, you will not be worried. It is your time to shine. We live for this. It is the moment of truth for you. In an instant, you will either reply with a piss-poor response such as:

You: 'Uh oh! We did not plan for a flood. Whaddaya think we should do?'

Well, if that is your response; pull the phone away from your ear as quickly as possible. Please just do it. It is going to get real loud – real fast. You officially have one foot out the door. You will hear a stream of rather negative words and soon you will be known as the 'former business continuity director/analyst/consultant' at your former company.

On the other hand, if your response is similar to mine:

You: 'BSVP, no problem! We have documented and well tested emergency response, communications and business continuity plans in place that will allow us to account for our employees and recover our critical business processes in the recovery time-frame we agreed on during our planning discussions. So, customer service and trading will be up-and-running by the opening bell. We will make it happen. You have no worries.'

Nice! If that was your response congratulations – you are gold! The next sounds you hear over the phone will be a long sigh of relief from BSVP followed by sobs of joy and an invite to lunch after all this is over.

I have lived these types of situations (in fact, one almost identical to the one I just described) and each time it worked out well for me and my employer. Yes, you will encounter a lot of stress, especially the first few times you go through the early morning wakeup call process, but if you have done your job, are confident and stay 'in-the-moment' everything will work out well.

19

PRODUCTIVITY - HOW TO IMPROVE YOUR MEETINGS -
A SUPER DUPER IDEA THAT SAVED MY PROGRAM

This meeting productivity technique has been worth its weight in gold to me. It has worked every time I have used it. It initially helped me improve the quality of an international (non-domestic) business resilience program. I later applied the same technique to domestic programs in numerous companies I have advised and it worked every time!
So, what was the problem?

Through the years, I have built International Business Resilience Programs from the ground up. This has included many countries in Asia Pacific (APAC), Latin America (LATAM) and Europe (EU). I think Antarctica is the only continent I have not touched – so that is on my bucket-list (if you know of a company doing business in Antarctica that needs guidance please let me know).
To manage one International program early in my career
I would hold monthly touch point meetings with each region. All the countries within a region had to be represented on the group call. The regional liaisons partnered with me in hosting the meetings. BC coordinators from each country in the regions attended the meetings. The meetings were conference calls that would have attendees from 8-12 countries. Representatives from each country reported on progress, challenges, issues and concerns they or their employees had in building their portion of the overall enterprise business continuity program.

To cover all the countries and to hopefully learn from each other we allotted 10-15 minutes for each country in the region to report. Frustratingly, the great majority of the responses from each country were short or non-existent I knew they were working hard and took business continuity very seriously but often they provided one word answers, even to open ended questions!
Something was wrong. I knew people had questions and concerns. Often, they were communicated offline. But during the large regional conference calls these issues were never communicated. Our global program was falling behind. It was getting sad and soon management would become irate.

The simple solution – that would never have occurred to me without a co-worker's advice...

One of my colleagues was an international auditor and she would attend these calls as a business continuity partner. She had a great deal of international experience, far more than I had at the time. One day she pulled me aside and explained that she had encountered similar issues years before and one small change to her meeting process made all the difference in improving her program by leaps-and-bounds. She suggested I schedule shorter calls with each country individually for 10 minutes instead of holding the large regional 90-minute call.

Even though it was more of a hassle to schedule 30+ individual calls each month, I took her advice. Well, immediately information, issues and questions started flowing from each country during these more private calls. It turns out, even though I positioned the regional calls as learning experiences, etc., people were not comfortable asking questions in front of their peers from the other countries. Sure, I had made them comfortable and told them no one has all the answers... but they just did not want to look like they did not know as much as the leaders in other countries. In hindsight, I saw the error of my ways. Their reluctance to share was totally understandable. Lesson learned.

Separating the calls into mini meetings made it more personal and much less stressful. We accomplished so much from that point on and it made all the difference to successfully building out all the regional and country programs. Together we faced many disruptive events over the years from tsunamis to earthquakes to civil unrest and so many others and to each one we prevailed. We may have bent a bit but we never broke and we came back stronger every time.

Going forward I continued having the regional touch points with multiple countries attending on a less frequent quarterly basis. I still believe the larger group dynamic has many benefits in sharing information. In those meetings, it was more of voluntarily tips, successes, ideas and having fun – sometimes at my expense – but I loved it. Over time those meetings worked well. Many of us met in person, became close friends and remain friends to this day.

20

PRODUCTIVITY - HOW TO PREVENT YOUR GREAT IDEAS FROM 'FLITTERING' AWAY

This tip hits close to home. I am good at coming up with resilience and technology ideas and even better forgetting them in an instant. I had to prevent this from happening and I did...

My mind is always working at hyper speed – granted some of my ideas are a bit 'out there' (perhaps you will agree when you get to the robots, drones and virtual reality training part of the book) but these have often resulted in my biggest successes (hey a grandmother running a senior focused web site – crazy but it went viral – NY Times, CBS News, Fox News and helped thousands of people globally).

We all dream about our programs – right? Well, occasionally I wake up at 3 am with great business resilience / continuity ideas.

Unfortunately, if I do not write my ideas down immediately they often flitter away (hmmm – I wonder if the domain name flitter is available – I better write that down and check when I finish this chapter).

My simple 5 step process for forgetting world-changing ideas:
1. I come up with a great idea!!!
2. My wife asks me what time it is
3. I say 7:45
4. ...and next thing I know I am asking myself, 'Marty, *what was I thinking about?*'
5. Idea Gone!!!

My simple solution and suggestion:
Tip – Keep a pad nearby and write that idea down or record it on your mobile device. Next, consolidate all your ideas in a simple idea list spreadsheet.
I know, it sounds so simple but the trick is to condition yourself to do it. In my case I over estimate myself. I say, 'well I will remember this one...' and some other priorities instantly come up and I forget the idea. You can then organize, prioritize and when the time comes act on them.

So, if you come up with an idea before hosting that tabletop – write it down. If you are going for a run and you come up with an idea write the idea down or record it on your smartphone.

Tip – categorize your ideas as short, medium and long term. You can also categorize them into different phases of your business resilience / continuity program – for example a new resilience related game to increase awareness, a dynamic email sig program to append rotating resilience quotes to your emails for awareness and branding...

So, write all your ideas down, I know you will be glad you did.

21

PRODUCTIVITY - HOW CHECKLISTS CAN CHANGE YOUR LIFE AND SUPERCHARGE YOUR PROGRAM

We have so many tasks to attend to as we build our programs. If you are like me, you are almost always working on multiple projects simultaneously. Multi-tasking is a way of life, even though it has been proven that it is not the most productive way to work.

I live by checklists:
For many years, I have jotted down a simple checklist each-and-every morning listing everything I want to accomplish that day. In fact, I cannot remember a day that I have not made a checklist. I learned, through experience, to include even the simplest tasks so absolutely nothing falls through the cracks.

I use solid bullets for work related tasks and hollow bullets for non-work tasks. I circle the tasks that are most time sensitive. Those are the ones I want to insure I complete early in the day. Crossing each task out as I complete it gives me a sense of accomplishment. This disciplined methodology leaves nothing to chance.

For example, I may put on a list:
- Schedule Accounting BIA review meeting
- Schedule HR BIA meeting
- Analyze that RTO gap analysis
- Begin the Supply Chain mapping strategy
- Do the Sales plan walk-through
- Steering committee meeting at 3:00 pm
- Write two chapters for the book
- Buy train tickets
- Pick up dinner

These simple checklists have made me super productive. They have enabled me to complete even my most complex and challenging work and side projects. Checklists have enabled me to create commercial software, author books, create videos, prepare for speaking engagements AND build real-time resilience programs.

When planning large projects, I create elaborate checklists so I do not miss any steps in planning and execution. Sometimes the checklists morph into full-fledged project plans. Whether it is planning an exercise or implementing a new automated system – checklists work for me every time!

Tip – When implementing business continuity tools such as a BCM system or mass notification tools I will develop a more robust project plan. A project plan is really a supercharged checklist listing the steps and the resources required to complete a project. The 200+ step business continuity roadmap included with this book can be thought of as a big checklist.

Tip – I use checklists in every phase of building my resilience programs. They are especially valuable during a crisis so nothing important slips through the cracks. I create scenario specific checklists to prepare for different types of potentially disruptive events. For example, during a blizzard I use checklists to make sure we have attended to snow removal, securing or removing outdoor items, updated the employee emergency hotline... I do a checklist run-down with all departments. They appreciate it and I do not have to worry that we missed something important.

Tip – Leading up to a tabletop or recovery area exercise I maintain a checklist for every step from day one of preparation through the post exercise meeting. It has never failed me. I have never missed an important step.

Tip – It is important to be brief but to include enough detail so you clearly understand each task on the list.

Tip – For quick and dirty daily tasks I typically use a paper checklist I keep in my shirt pocket. It is 'old school' but I can easily update and refer to it many times during the day as I add new tasks. It is very mobile. There are also lot of good checklist apps.

Tip – A good book about checklists is, *'The Checklist Manifesto'* by Atul Gawande. He implemented checklists in many hospitals which significantly helped reduce mistakes that were made during surgeries. This resulted in reducing post-op infections. His checklists were simple bullet items and very effective.

In order to come up with his health-related checklists he studied how the aviation industry has been using checklists as pre-takeoff check-downs as well as responding to in-air irregularities. Airlines also keep a large detailed manual on each plane but it is the checklists that prevents a lot of potential mistakes from happening in the first place. The checklists make it much simpler, easier and faster to respond to disruptive events. They obviously work, as the aviation industry has been using checklists since the 1930's.

Checklists make me feel free, calm and organized.
I encourage you to create your own checklists and use them daily.
Make them a part of your routine.

22

BEWARE DANGEROUS FACTORY, WAREHOUSE OR OTHER NON-OFFICE ENVIRONMENTS. YOU MUST READ THIS...

Factory and Warehouse Lessons Learned
*IMPORTANT – Speak with your Safety Team and learn ALL of the safety policies and precautions before walking through your factory or warehouse. They are the experts. *
Ok, so you worked your entire career in an office setting for a financial company and you just got the job as a Business Resilience Director for a distribution company with a warehouse or factory. Well actually something similar happened to me a few years ago, I am not the safety guy but...the number one safety tip I can give you from personal experience is – be careful and always be aware of your surroundings! If you have never worked in a warehouse or factory you will quickly learn it can be a very dangerous place if you are not concentrating.

So below are a few 'Marty lessons learned'. Some are a bit embarrassing, but what the heck – if they help one person it's worth my dignity:
Stay focused – I have the nasty habit of walking and texting. While on vacation in Baltimore a few years ago, I was walking and texting and came within 5 feet of walking off the dock into the Baltimore Harbor. I think I would have survived as the fall was approximately 15 feet and I only had a 50/50 chance of being impaled on one of the wooden stakes below.

On a few other occasions, I have tripped on an uneven patch of sidewalk while multi-tasking. During one particularly bad fall while I was racewalking on my way home from work I was lucky to only have ripped my palm and fortunately did not hit my head. I almost hit my face on the concrete (maybe it would have been an improvement). I came back stronger and I was racewalking the next day, my wife called me **'resilient!'** I thought that was so cool.

I quickly learned that a warehouse or factory has a whole different level of safety concerns compared to an office environment. I have numerous stories – all my fault and all from when I was a 'beyond the office' newbie a few years ago. Here is my most frightening experience:

I was walking on the third floor of a inventory module and rapidly approaching an opening that was clearly marked, unfortunately my head was down. I glanced upward and, I kid you not, I was within 3 feet of tumbling off and plummeting 20 feet to bare concrete. I stopped myself in the nick of time. One more stride and I would have fallen. I was surreal.

I made my way down the stairs and just looked up to the spot I would have fallen from. I got chills and still do every time I pass that spot, even though the incident occurred years ago, had anything happened it would have been all my fault!

In addition, people are driving forklifts which you do not want to walk into. There could also be broken glass or sharp metal that can cause injury. Situational awareness in these environments is so important. Know your surroundings always! Focus on every step you take!

Please – please – never text and walk in a factory or warehouse – or near a harbor for that matter. Really concentrate and know your surroundings every step of the way.

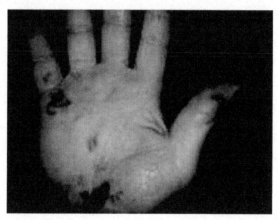

In a factory or warehouse:
- Always wear a luminous vest
- Always wear the correct shoes
- Always wear a hard-hat if your company requires it
- Always do everything else your company advises for safety

I say 'Always' as it is that one time you skip a step that can be disastrous. So be careful – ALWAYS!

You, your family, your company and this author need you to be around a long time. I need you out there recommending this book! (kidding)

*IMPORTANT – Speak with your Safety Team and learn **ALL** the safety policies and precautions before walking your factory or warehouse. They are the experts. *
Please be safe!!!

23

THE BC COMEDY VIDEO - FUNNY AND A GREAT!

We have covered a lot of ground in the Prepare for Success Part 1 of the book. Before we jump into Part 2 - The Crisis Management part of the book sit back and have a little fun! You deserve it.

Believe it or not, there is a funny business continuity on-line video AND it conveys a message. It might even be a cool addition to your next tabletop exercise to loosen everyone up. I have used it and it was well received. Ok, it's not Kevin Hart or Jim Gaffigan funny but I think you may appreciate it.

Tabletop attendees are often tense and think they must know all the answers during an exercise, which is not true. Often people cram and 'stress-out' when, in reality, the goal of the tabletop is to flesh out the gaps and close them prior to a real crisis event. Our best tabletops are the interactive ones, right?

Your relaxing opening statements to start a tabletop and perhaps using this video will put attendees at ease and everyone will have a fun learning experience.

Here's the video, enjoy – https://www.fema.gov/media-

library/assets/videos/80069

PART 2 - CRISIS MANAGEMENT TIPS AND TECHNIQUES

The Crisis Management part of the book includes suggestions, tips and techniques that can help you successfully manage a crisis.

A resilient organization might bend but NEVER breaks! A culture of resiliency and preparation enable us to survive any disruption! We always spring back STRONGER than our previous state!

You must have a tested crisis management plan in place. Planning is essential. Your plan is your roadmap to success. Crisis management plans are created in many different formats. There is no one size fits all. Huge overly complex plans numbering in the hundreds of pages often do not work well. A more streamlined approach of checklist format tasks, contact lists, team responsibilities, emergency response best practices are preferred by some organizations. I lean toward a streamlined approach but you must decide what is best for your organization.

You must have the right leadership and culture of resilience in place that meets the needs of your organization and employees. Every crisis is different and you must have a team that can adapt. Having the right people on the team is crucial.

Our number one priority is Employee Safety. There must be awareness throughout your organization of safety, security and continuity best practices. Emergency procedures must be documented for different scenarios.

Evacuation procedures must be thoroughly tested and clearly understood. Communications must be well thought out – it is critical to your employees and the continuity of operations. Ready.gov and Homeland Security have good information that can help you with content for your emergency response plan - https://www.ready.gov/business/implementation/emergency. I have consolidated some of their guidance in this part of the book.

High level phases of managing a crisis that must be included in your planning and testing include:

- Prevention – understanding threats and vulnerabilities and implementing the necessary controls
- Response – managing the crisis from start-to-finish
- Resumption – resuming your time sensitive processes in the required timeframe to keep your business going
- Recovery and Restoration – how you will recover and resume normal operations

Communicating during a crisis is critical.

Crisis management tools such as situational alerts and mass notification as well as data quality are discussed here and in the technology part of the book

I hope you find the upcoming chapters useful additions to your current planning strategy.

24

BUILD RESILIENCE FAST AND STRONG - BY GOING WIDE AND DEEP

I will bet Peyton Manning looked into the eyes of his wide receivers in the huddle thousands of times over his successful career and said, '*Go wide go deep* '. When I played wide receiver, I loved when the QB told me to go wide go deep! Aggressively going wide and deep, can be keys to your building a strong resilience program.

I see it way too often. An organization decides to implement a new Business Continuity Program or improve their existing program. They are gung-ho but move sloooowly. Management interest and support begins to wane. There is not that sense of urgency that crisis management and continuity of operations requires. This is bad.

The nightmare scenario is you spend a year or two focusing on a few locations. Unfortunately, a disruptive event does not know you are not ready and severely impacts a location. It could be a life threatening natural / man made event or a continuity of operations disruption such as a squirrel (more on squirrels later) eats thru a single point of failure (SPOF) power line or a backhoe cuts power and the impact is all your systems are down. Possibly a hurricane makes a direct hit on one of your locations. If you do not have plans in place and are caught sitting on your hands you know who will be in the hot seat – YOU.

You will forever be referred to in the former tense (if the company is still in business), 'remember Wilbur the BC guy, very nice guy. But he should have worked with a sense of urgency and had something in place to respond…'

Hence my strong advice is to be proactive! Drive your program forward today. Touch all points of the organization.
Yes, we must be detailed. Yes, we may have hundreds or thousands of locations and employees. Yes, some processes are more time-sensitive than others. I completely understand all of that. The point is to get at least the basics out there for crisis management, emergency response and continuity of operations.

Show progress. Win management and employees over with your aggressive – value laden approach. If you wait too many weeks, months or years – trouble will surely find you at some point. You can only dodge

this bullet so long. If something happens and you are not prepared –
you might not get a second chance.

Tip – Do not fall into the trap of paralysis by analysis. Don't overthink
it.

Tip – A quick win would be to call or email the senior officer at each
location to introduce yourself. Begin building relationships.
Communicate crisis management and emergency response best
practices- critical phone numbers, evacuation, accounting for
employees… Start building those critical relationships and
disseminating information early.

Tip – You must have contact information for the key people and
backups at every location in your organization.

Tip – Get crisis management, emergency response and basic business
continuity plans into the field. Don't drag your feet on this. You can
then improve your resilience maturity level on top of the basics you
have already put in play. You will sleep better knowing this information
has been distributed. Your employees depend on it.

Tip – add a short (or long) online quiz:
To analyze the level of crisis management understanding and to insure
the streamlined plan you sent was read by the recipients you can add an
online quiz. Incident Commanders can take the quiz after reading the
streamlined plan. When they 'submit' the answers your back-end system
can score it and save the results. No human intervention required!
It is a win-win process. Even if the person taking the quiz answers
incorrectly the system can automatically send a reply with the correct
answer and some supporting information. This process creates a
positive feedback loop. It is beautiful, non-threatening and an
opportunity to create awareness.

Here are three ways you can add an automated quiz to your Go Wide
Go Deep Emergency Response / Business Continuity Plan Initiative:
1.   Use your Business Continuity Management (BCM) system to
     create, send and score the survey. You can use assessment criteria,
     triggers and workflows to implement an end-to-end solution if you
     have a powerful BCM tool. We will discuss BCM system selection
     criteria later in the book. I do not name BCM products in the
     book, as they change and new ones come on the market. Please
     contact me - marty@ultimatebusinesscontinuity.com if you would
     like suggestions based on your requirements.

2. Use a survey specific tool such as Survey Monkey. It has full featured surveys and it is priced fairly. The down-side is if your goal is to tightly integrate the data with your in-house BCM tool it may be difficult. You can try to do it with the Survey Monkey API. I will be testing the API and I would be happy to provide you with an update if you contact me.
3. You can build the quiz process in-house using your email system and a data repository for the results. I have done this on occasion and it worked, but unless you have the luxury of extra time and enjoy coding on the weekends and nights (which I love to do), you would be better served using either your BCM system or a tool such as Survey Monkey.

Do not procrastinate:
Perhaps, the initial iteration of your plans will not be perfect but it is far better than waiting a year or two or three to get plans in place throughout your organization. Remember, what we always preach to users, "73% of companies that incur a disaster and do not have tested plans in place go out of business within three years." Unfortunately, disasters do not wait until you are ready for them.

Once your initial set of crisis management, emergency response and business continuity plans are in place, aggressively test, update and improve them. You can even call the initial versions 'interim plans' to level-set that they are 'living documents' and will improve over time.

The important point is to begin today. Do not wait to start building your foundation and distributing critical information.

Go wide go deep – you will score that winning career touchdown!

25

SAFETY OF PEOPLE IS OUR #1 PRIORITY!

I HAVE ALWAYS STRESSED EMPLOYEE SAFETY AS A COMPANY'S NUMBER #1 PRIORITY SINCE THE FIRST DAY I STARTED BUILDING BUSINESS RESILIENCE PROGRAMS AND IT WILL ALWAYS BE THE TOP PRIORITY FOR ME.
LIVES CANNOT BE REPLACED. EQUIPMENT, LAPTOPS, PHONES, SUPPLIES CAN BE REPLACED.
WHEN YOUR EMPLOYEES ARE SAFE AND SECURE YOU WILL BE ABLE TO SUCCESSFULLY RECOVER YOUR BUSINESS.

**This chapter and the entire book includes emergency response information but it is not intended to be a thorough training manual. That is beyond the scope of this book. You should work closely with your safety and security experts.

Tip – Always keep your eyes open and report everything that can be of danger to management, your safety department and any other people that should know about the threats. Do it verbally and in writing.

Tip – Partner with Safety and Security to assist them in any way you can. The safety of employees is their direct responsibility. We must coordinate and support their efforts. In my opinion, if you have dedicated Safety and Security teams at a site then evacuation procedures and evacuation drills should be their responsibility. I realize it differs at many organizations.

Tip – Create a RACI chart that clearly indicates what Safety and Security are responsible for and what you are responsible for. There should be no confusion over responsibilities.

Tip – Perform regular evacuation drills. Everyone must participate in all the drills no matter how high on the org chart they sit and however big they think they are. They should be reported to management if they do not participate. During 9/11 there were accounts of senior executives staying on the phone and not evacuating in a timely manner. Time the drills. Start with announced drills and then do surprise drills!

Tip – When performing tabletops and during one-on-one discussions with process owners try to gauge their level of evacuation and rally point awareness. Are they confident in the process? You should ask how they would account for their employees. Sending a fireman into a building needlessly if an employee is on vacation or left the building for any other reason is very dangerous and unnecessary.

Tip – If you do not have emergency response resources or experience bring in an outside company that specializes in employee safety to help build or audit your program.

Tip – Begin your tabletops emphasizing employee safety best practices.

Tip – Bring in representatives from the fire department, police department and Red Cross to speak with employees.

Tip – Encourage active shooter response training. It is critical!

Tip – Review FEMA scenario guidance and response training. Some good links in the 'Hazards Central' chapter in this part of the book.

Tip – Implement an employee hotline – it can be employee's lifeline during a crisis.

Tip – Implement a thorough crisis communications plan.

Tip – If you are a mid-size or large organization you are beyond manual calls trees, in my opinion. In my experience, manual call trees will break down and you will waste precious seconds/minutes/hours attempting to contact employees when seconds can mean the difference between life and death. Do your employees and company a favor and consider implementing an automated mass notification solution. This is one of my specialties and I discuss it in detail throughout the book.

Tip – Let people know the importance of being accountable for their own safety. Public first responders are great but they cannot be counted on being on-site at 'minute zero' of a crisis. Employees must know what to do. Awareness and practice will greatly improve the odds of surviving a crisis.

Tip – Your plans should account for people that may require assistance during an evacuation. Partner with process owners, HR and safety on this often delicate but critical subject.

Tip – Perform a thorough risk assessment. Identify threats and vulnerabilities that can impact your people and your business. Implement controls to prevent, mitigate or transfer risk where possible. I discuss this in more detail in the risk assessment chapter.

Tip – Monitor risk in real-time – I discuss tools and techniques that may benefit you in the technology chapter.

You Need an Emergency Action Plan – The purpose of an Emergency Action Plan (EAP) is to facilitate and organize employer and employee actions during workplace emergencies. The elements of the plan should include, but are not limited to:

- Evacuation procedures and emergency escape route assignments
- Procedures to be followed by employees who remain to operate critical operations before they evacuate
- Procedures to account for all employees after an emergency evacuation has been completed
- Rescue and medical duties for those employees who are to perform them
- Means of reporting fires and other emergencies
- Names or job titles of persons who can be contacted for further information or explanation of duties under the plan

A great resource for emergency action planning is the planning guide created by the California Department of Labor and the United States Department of Labor – http://www.bepreparedcalifornia.ca.gov/BEPREPARED/BUSINES SES/Pages/EmergencyandEvacuationPlanningGuideforEmployers.as px

I suggest you read it. You must carefully write your plans and include your organization's specific details including teams and risks. You must then review your plan with management, safety and security for input and updates. You must also test the finished plan to insure it meets your needs.

ACTIVE SHOOTER - THE TIME TO PLAN IS NOW!

If you have an Active Shooter response program in place, that is great. If you have robust controls in place I applaud you for considering your employees!

Your employees must know best practices when confronted with an active shooter scenario. Provide them with that guidance.

Professional in-person training seminars and classes can be potentially life-saving. One of the active shooter response classes I took was at my local library given by a top professional. It was well worth the time!!!

A valuable booklet is the Homeland Security Active Shooter – How to Respond booklet -
https://www.dhs.gov/xlibrary/assets/active_shooter_booklet.pdf

Your employees will appreciate your concern for their safety and security!

IT TAKES A VILLAGE - TEAMS AND PARTNERSHIPS

To achieve real-world resilience, you must build strong and well-coordinated teams. Teams must meet and test often to be ready. A culture of resilience is critical to be truly prepared for disruptive events.

The Crisis Management Team is critical as it is tasked with managing a crisis from start to finish. It includes the Incident Command Team, Emergency Operations Team, Crisis Strike Teams and specialized sub-teams. Crisis Management capabilities and training should be part of your program as early as possible at every location. Both employee safety and continuity of operations depends on it.

The crisis management team structure and process I favor in the business world, is based on The National Incident Management System (NIMS) and Incident Command System (ICS) but it has been optimized to align with business processes and structure.

If you are interested in learning more about NIMS in detail here is a link to the National Incident Management System (NIMS) Incident Command System (ICS) Forms Booklet. The NIMS booklet contains many templates you can leverage for your program - http://nationalincidentmanagementsystem(nims)incidentcommandsyst em(ics)formsbooklet/

Incident Command Team (ICT):
This team consists of key people that will provide information to the Incident Commander. There is no hard and fast rule as to who must be included on the ICT, but they should provide value during minute zero and beyond. As I mentioned, you need an ICT in place at **every location** as soon as possible. Employee safety, location assessment, systems availability are all in scope for the ICT.

Drill the ICT on a regular basis. These professionals must be practiced, confident and ready to react 'on a dime'. They must be a well-oiled machine. Everything starts with the ICT collecting valuable data and turning it into insight. This team makes important decisions.

Below are suggestions for ICT members (add or delete to customize for your company and locations):
- Security
- Safety

- Facilities
- IT
- HR
- Operations
- Trading
- Customer Service
- BC
- Warehouse
- Finance
- Logistics

Emergency Operations Team (EOT):
This team consists of process owners (department managers) and alternates. This team will provide information to and get information from the Incident Commander (Site Leader in some organizations) and will communicate information back to their process staff. This is a key team in the decision-making process. These people know the business and must be part of the discussion.

For example, if a disaster is declared and people must recover to an alternate recovery site, members of this team will coordinate with the staff to make it happen.

Tip – Make sure you can communicate and reach every member of the EOT. It is important to regularly review contact lists and encourage team members to provide multiple contact devices they can be reached on. This will increase the probability of reaching them when they are needed. Contact lists change often. Team members leave and new ones join the organizations. You should have a process in place to keep the information current.

Below are suggestions for EOT members (add or delete to customize for your company):
- Management
- Legal
- Human Resources
- Communications
- Public Relations
- Insurance and Risk Management
- Safety
- Finance
- Labor Relations

- Operations
- Trading
- Facilities or Property Management
- Engineering
- Security
- Medical
- Information Technology
- Purchasing, Supply Chain and Distribution
- Quality Control
- Warehouse
- Delivery

Public external team partnerships:
Leveraging external resources is critical as you build out your real-world resilience program. Unfortunately, building these relationships is often overlooked. It is wise to establish them as soon as possible.

Preparing for a disruptive event, responding to an emergency, executing business recovery strategies and other activities often require support that comes from outside your organization. For example, if there was a fire in your building, you would call the fire department. Contractors and vendors may be needed to help repair and restore a building, salvage moldy vital records, remove snow, fix equipment....

An understanding of the availability and capabilities of external resources is needed to make decisions. How long would it take the fire department to arrive? How do you reach a contractor late at night and how long will it take them to arrive? Determining the response time and capabilities of external resources will help you identify gaps between what you need and what is available. Strategies must be developed to close these gaps.

Tip – During your tabletops try to schedule representation from local fire and law enforcement for at least a preset few minutes. I respect how busy they are and it is not fair to ask them to stay for 3 hours, but unless their resources are not available they always make time to attend my exercises. Even thirty minutes of their time can really make a difference. They can communicate important information on best practices such as what to do during a fire or active-shooter incident. They are the experts. I have learned so much from them over the decades. Your employees will benefit greatly.

83

Tip – During minute zero of a crisis you will be dependent on your internal resources. It happened during Katrina, 9/11 and Hurricane Sandy. Public agencies will not be on the scene immediately. I suggest you read, *'Five Days at Memorial – Life and Death in a Storm Ravaged Hospital'* *by Sheri Fink* for a riveting account of the first few days at this major hospital during Katrina. Also, I suggest you read, *'The Unthinkable – Who Survives When Disaster Strikes' by Amanda Ripley* for a sobering account of response during 9/11 from a survivor. The book also includes the heroic story of Rick Rescorla. You will identify with his bold take-charge actions. Both books are listed in the Recommended Reading chapter toward the end of the book.

The following suggested external resources should be identified within your plans. Include their contact information and any additional instructions required to quickly reach them.

Public Emergency Services

(Note: one agency or department may provide multiple services)

- Fire
- Law enforcement (local, county, state police)
- Emergency medical services
- Hospital or emergency health care provider
- Hazardous materials
- Public health
- Public works

Contractors and Vendors

- Emergency services (hazardous materials cleanup, facility repair and restoration)
- Systems and equipment (procurement, inspection, testing and maintenance)
- Information technology (equipment procurement, data backup, recovery solutions)
- Business continuity (generators, temporary equipment, leased space, office trailers)

Partnerships

(Reciprocal or mutual aid agreements. Get in writing, if possible)

- Business partners (suppliers, contractors, vendors and professional services firms that could lend assistance with services, temporary work-space and other resources)
- Businesses or civic organizations in the community

84

28

A STRONG INCIDENT COMMANDER IS CRITICAL FOR SUCCESS

I have partnered with all types of Incident Commanders (called Site Leaders in some organizations) during my career. Some were great and some not so great. I can confidently say that a strong, intelligent, confident, calming, take-charge, decisive leader is critical to successfully leading an organization through a crisis. My advice to you, if you have input, is to appoint an:

1. Intelligent, decisive Incident Commander. Employee safety and continuity of operations can be dependent on this person's decisions
2. Intelligent, decisive Alternate Incident Commander (backup). You NEED that backup person to be ready to step in if the Incident Commander is not available

Perhaps he or she is head of operations, security or safety. In fact, one of the best leaders I had the good fortune of working with was Director of Security for a global company. He had 30 years' experience dealing with life and death situations throughout his career. No matter what crisis he faced he answered the call and led the team through the event in a calm, confident manner. Tornadoes, Hurricanes Katrina and Sandy, major power outages, winter storms, anthrax scares… it did not matter. He did a great job!

It is critical that the Incident Commander (IC) be provided with up-to-date situational awareness information. It will enable the IC to understand events as they are unfolding and the impacts of these events on your assets including people, locations and systems. The IC can then assimilate the information into knowledge and insight.

The resulting insight leads to actionable steps which will get your company through the crisis – if you have prepared properly. In the technology part of the book we deep dive free and commercial situational alert tools that I have found valuable.

The technology is improving so rapidly that by the time you read this, there will be additional tools available to benefit your organization. I will keep you up to date on new tools through the Ultimate Business Continuity Tools and Technologies Newsletter.

A great leader does not get rattled. At the core of resilience is the ability to adapt to a rapidly changing environment. A while ago I was on a series of early morning calls (1 am – 4 am) because a system that managed a complex series of factory logistical devises was not operational, Had the system not been fixed by 5 am, it could have resulted in a serious business impact.

He was faced with obstacle after obstacle. It was a toughie. I know, as I am still a techie at heart. 1 am, 2 am, 3 am… He just calmly and firmly moved forward to isolate the needle-in-the-haystack. He logically eliminated all possible causes for the breakdown. A few times he had to repeat himself to people on the scene in the factory, as the technicians were on cell phones and it was very noisy. But he never lost it. Not even once. You just knew he would get the problem solved and he did. Very impressive.

Remember, appoint the right people in the Incident Commander and Alternate Incident Commander roles and your resilience and confidence will skyrocket!

29

EVACUATION – ACCOUNTING FOR EMPLOYEES

Your organization MUST be able to account for employees during an evacuation.

IF YOU THINK AN EMPLOYEE IS STILL IN THE BUILDING BUT IN ACTUALITY HE IS NOT, A FIREMAN MAY HAVE TO GO IN NEEDLESSLY TO LOOK FOR HIM – AND THE FIREMAN COULD POSSIBLY LOSE HIS/HER LIFE!

If your process to account for employees during an evacuation, as documented in your emergency response plan, needs to be improved begin working on it immediately. Upper management must actively support your effort. Remind them that they can be held responsible if a tragedy occurs and they did not put forth an effort to fix a broken process they were aware of.

You must have a bullet-proof process to account for employees during an evacuation. Partner with Safety and Security on building the process.

A few tips:
Tip – Make sure rally points / evacuation assembly areas are known to ALL employees and visitors. The first few evacuation drills I suggest safety and your team walks people to the rally point so they understand exactly where they should go.

Tip – Regularly check that the rally point signs are highly visible. Paint the pole and make sure growing shrubbery is not obstructing the signs.

Tip – Supervisors should be aware who is in the office and who is not.

Tip – A log book at the front desk can record visitors in the building. Someone must have the responsibility to bring it to the rally point.

Tip – I have found employees are wary when they must record the time the leave the building and return in the log book. You might want to consider them simply putting a check-mark in the log book rather than the actual time.

Tip – Employees MUST understand the criticality of reporting directly to a rally point / evacuation assembly area. They should not be jumping in their cars or chatting with friends.

Tip – Attendance MUST be taken at the rally point and provided to the Incident Commander.

Tip – Complications can arise when there are multiple rally points and an employee depending on his whereabouts when the evacuation occurs, may report to one of multiple rally points. Implement a good process to communicate between rally points, the Incident Commander and the fire department officials. Teams should use walkie-talkie radios plus all other communication methods available to them. I use a push to talk (PTT) app in conjunction with radios. I find the PTT app provides value. In fact, my family caught on to it quickly and we use it constantly. The bottom line is – do not have a single point of communications failure.

Tip – There should be a process for employees that hear about the crisis and are not on site to report they are safe.

Tip – If you are in a high-rise or shared building, coordinate rally points with the other tenants. You do not want to encounter mass confusion with a sea of people at the rally point. Every second wasted can be the difference between life and death.

Tip – Automated check-in solutions can be helpful but are not a 100% solution.

30

EVACUATION - DRILL TIPS AND TECHNIQUES

Make sure you team with your Safety and HR management before publishing any of these. They may not be in line with your corporate policies and procedures. You hopefully already have your own awareness tips in place.

To the person that thinks he or she is too important... No, you are not too important to participate in evacuation drills!'

Everyone must participate in evacuation drills on a regular basis. To repeat — Everyone must participate in evacuation drills on a regular basis. Employees must be made aware they will be held accountable for participating.

In my experience, having done many evacuation drills and training, almost everyone follows instructions and participates as they should. I say 'almost everyone' as I sometimes encounter the one or two individuals that just think they are too important or too busy to participate in evacuation drills. They think, *'why practice, nothing will ever happen* ', until it does!

In my experience, it is rarely a clerical or janitorial person that does not want to participate. Often, it is an executive that has a hard time getting his/her head through the doorway. They are just above it all.

A peer of mine described a scenario where the fire alarms and sirens went off and a high-ranking executive just continued with his phone conversation. He thought he was above the rules. Believe it or not, he yelled a bunch of f'in this and f'in that, then he ripped off his brown suede shoes and fired a couple of perfect strikes with plenty of velocity squarely hitting the fire alarm!
In a different setting, if there were a baseball scout nearby, it would be 'sign him up'. Direct hits. I even had to wonder if he practiced this. Well, he knocked out a siren, smiled and just continued his conversation!

Unfortunately for him but fortunately for the company the Fire Marshall wrote him up. The Senior VP had a straight-forward talk with him immediately following the drill. Guess what? It never happened again with that person He cooperated from then on.

Tip – Everyone Must Participate! That means everyone! Including C level employees and guests!

Tip – Management participation is critical. Management sets a positive example by participating and they set a negative example when they do not think it is important enough to participate.

Tip – Know beforehand who may need assistance during an evacuation and have a buddy system in place. Develop contingencies where necessary.

Tip – Never waste time going back for belongings – even your laptop and keys – leave them behind.

Tip – Proceed to the nearest exit.

Tip – Don't run, walk fast.

Tip – Use the staircase, never use the elevator.

Tip – Walk along the LEFT side of the staircase. Yes, the left side. Leave the right side for the fire department and rescue teams.

Tip – Don't talk, text or email while you walk.

Tip – Give first preference to the physically challenged, expectant mothers and the elderly.

Tip – Proceed to the pre-determined rally points.

Tip – Do not re-enter the building until the all-clear signal is communicated

Tip – Evacuate in an orderly manner.

Tip – In high rise buildings special evacuation rules apply. Learn the rules in your building.

Tip – If you are in a high rise building you must make full evacuations part of your testing. You should not just meet at the elevator for a brief discussion and go back to work. Prior to 9/11 there were no full building evacuation drills in the World Trade Center. 90% of the people never tested evacuating the buildings to the street. Many people did not know how many exits there were. Tragically, some people went up the stairs to the locked roof instead of evacuating down the stairs. Read *The Unthinkable: Who Survives When Disaster Strikes'* by Amanda Ripley for a riveting account.

Tip – Don't panic.

Tip – Do not purposely schedule evacuation drills when top management is offsite so they will not hassle you about participating. If anything, they should be onsite and reported if they do not participate in all drills.

Also, do some of your drills when the building is full. Maybe a sales meeting is occurring or a regional operations meeting. I know it is scary and you will ruffle some feathers but it is far worse if a fire occurs when the building is full and there is mass confusion, as people are not conditioned to respond immediately to the alarms and to go directly to the rally points. Every second counts!

Tip – Proper testing and awareness could be the difference between life and death!

Tip – Make sure your rally points are a safe distance from your building. Explosions and building collapse must be considered. Public officials must have access and cannot be blocked.

Tip – Clearly identify your rally points. Paint them a bright color, have large signs. Make them very visible.

Tip – Employees must not jump in their car or 'coffee-klotch' with their buddies. Not reporting to the rally point(s) can cost lives!

Tip – No Smoking!

Tip – If your company is in a building with other tenants, coordinate with them regularly to insure there are not multiple companies vying for the same rally point locations. This can cause mass confusion at time of evacuation. It can impede accounting for employees and endanger lives.

Tip – if your parking lot is backed by a railroad, plane runway or other threats make sure you have multiple rally points and people know what to do. In fact, you should always have alternate rally points, just in case.

Tip – Team with Safety and Security to consider all possibilities.

Bottom line – Everyone must be made accountable for their actions – even executives and would be pitchers. Everyone must participate and take drills seriously. It very well could be the difference between life and death.

Make sure your employees are well prepared!

EVACUATION - EVERY SECOND COUNTS!

This true story taught me to never take anything for granted. Every second counts during an evacuation and you should never waste time. You should never needlessly put yourself in peril. Employee Safety is the Ultimate Concern.

I was hosting a tabletop for a company in the mid-west and playing out a simulated fire scenario.
1. Smell of smoke
2. Alarms go off
3. Orderly evacuation… you know the scenario.

So far so good. I patted myself on the back that we did a good job of awareness and training. These folks really 'get it!' Then an employee raises his hand and adamantly states, '*well I must go back for my laptop as my recovery strategy is work-from-home and I must have my laptop or I will be in trouble with my management.* ' OUCH! Whoa bucko! Say whatttt!!!

I explained in a very straightforward no-nonsense manner that even if it only takes a few seconds to go back – **NEVER endanger yourself or others to retrieve a piece of equipment, car keys, pocketbook…** We will get you a laptop to work on or you can recover to an alternate recovery site and use a desktop. Equipment can be replaced – lives cannot be replaced.

If you waste time during an evacuation you might not see the light of day again.

Square this away with employees asap. I learned to never take anything for granted.

32

EVACUATION - WARDENS AND SEARCHERS

I suggest you team up with Safety and Security to insure you have a strong network of wardens and searchers. These people are critical to the safety of your employees and the overall evacuation process. Also, network with the fire department to insure you have everything covered.

Here a few tips that may help:
Tip – Assign searchers to quadrants of your office to insure the entire office will be searched.
Tip – Assign backups to the primary wardens and searchers.
Tip – Assign female and male searchers for the bathrooms.
Tip – Provide two-way communication radios (walkie-talkies). I suggest you also consider supplementing the walkie-talkies with push to talk (PTT) apps which I discuss later in the book and in more detail in the Ultimate Business Continuity Tips, Techniques and Tools Newsletter. Test the ability to communicate on all devices on a regular basis. It is critical.
Tip – Provide all equipment including but not limited to vests, whistles and chalk so rooms that were searched can be marked with a big X.
Tip – Replace searchers as necessary!
Tip – Practice, practice and practice some more!

A friend told me the story of a searcher her organization appointed years ago, who immediately ran out of the building when the kitchen popcorn-maker over-heated.
One whiff of burnt popcorn and he could have easily won the Olympic 100-meter dash – he covered the distance from the lunchroom to his car 100 meters away in 9.29 seconds – a new world record! Thankfully, he was replaced the same day.
Unfortunately, it sometimes takes an incident to determine the best people for the job. What people say and what they actually do under pressure can be two very different things.

93

EVACUATION - WHO IS RESPONSIBLE FOR DRILLS?

I have found in the real-world there is often confusion as to who is responsible for evacuation planning and drills. If you encounter confusion, it is important to clarify the roles and responsibilities of each person as soon as possible.

If you have Safety, Security and Business Continuity teams, I believe Safety or Security should assume lead responsibility. BC should actively partner with them and assist in every way we can.

To clear the confusion before a disaster, have active discussions with Safety, Security and Management. When you come to an agreement create a RACI (Responsible, Accountable, Consulted, Informed) chart so everything is documented.

If your company has never done an evacuation drill or it has been a couple or many years since the last one, fix that as soon as possible. Perhaps do an announced drill as a first step and then build to unannounced drills. I stress the importance of working on this immediately.

The Fire department will gladly come to your company to do a brief presentation on best practices during a fire, such as testing doors with your forearm instead of grabbing the handle, getting close to the floor and they can offer much more critical advice that can make the difference between life and death.

EMERGENCY OPERATIONS CENTER - IMPORTANT TIPS AND CONSIDERATIONS

An Emergency Operations Center (EOC) or Command Center is a central command and control facility responsible for carrying out the principles of emergency preparedness and emergency management at a strategic level during an emergency, and ensuring the continuity of operations for your organization.

Having a well thought out Emergency Operations Center is critical to successfully managing your response and recovery.

Here are a few tips:

Tip – You should implement multiple options for your physical EOC /Alternate EOC in case one or more is not available at the time of crisis. Options include your production site, a sister site if geographically feasible, hotel or vendor location.

Tip – Your EOC /Alternate EOC can be dedicated space or a meeting/conference room that will be commandeered during a crisis.

Tip – Your physical EOC /Alternate EOC must include equipment and a battle box with all supplies and documentation you will need to make decisions and communicate both internally and externally. Visit the Emergency Operations Center on a regular basis, especially if you will be using a conference room in a sister site. Make sure your supplies are locked up and have not disappeared. Please inspect batteries, headphones, supplies, water and laptops. You do not need any surprises at time of disaster. It is frustrating to have headsets available but the batteries are dead or missing. Use a checklist to review all important supplies, equipment and plans to insure you are ready and do not miss anything.

Tip – You will need subject matter experts to help with making decisions. Make sure your conference number is full-featured. Muting and operator assistance are essential, as you could have a lot of people on the call and invariably in the real-world someone will put you on hold and there will be background music. Did that ever happen to you with 50 people on the call? It sucks if you cannot stop the music!

Tip – You must also have a virtual Emergency Operations Center. A conference line is essential, as there will be times you must meet at a moment's notice during non-working hours. In my experience, many incidents occur during the evening, weekends and very early morning. Welcome to our world!

Tip – Make sure the conference line can accommodate more people than you expect to call. Getting a 'conference full' during a crisis is real nasty. I have seen that on occasions and it is BAD! If you think you might top out at 50 people on a call – get a line that supports 150 or more!!

Tip – Here is a little trick you might find useful: if you are inviting people to the conference call by email or text and you know they are using an iPhone you can format use 'phone number', 'password#'. An example would be 5555555555,1234#. When the recipient clicks on the link, the iPhone will automatically dial the phone number, automatically input the participant code and automatically drop the caller in the conference. If you are using Android, it will dial the phone number and you can then manually input the participant code. You may even come up with improvements by the time you read this. Any manual input you can eliminate to make it easier for people – do it. Every second counts.

Tip – Insure there is a high level of awareness of the EOC /Alternate EOC options.

Tip – Insure the EOC /Alternate EOC is in a centrally located site allowing rapid response

Tip –Insure the EOC /Alternate EOC is in an area that avoids congestion (i.e., transportation choke-points such as inadequate thoroughfares, bridges, etc.).

Tip –Insure the EOC /Alternate EOC is in a facility that has structural integrity.

Tip – Insure the EOC /Alternate EOC is in an area that can be quickly secured.

Tip – Insure the EOC /Alternate EOC is not located in a known high-risk area; e.g., floods, earthquakes, nuclear power plant, Hazardous Material (HAZMAT) sites, etc.

Tip – Insure the EOC /Alternate EOC is located near an adequate road network for ease of access.

Tip – Insure the EOC /Alternate EOC space, whether it is dedicated (set aside and configured for EOC use only) or for multi-use not dedicated (such as an office, administrative, or conference area that is used for day-to-day functions), will be made available to support emergency response and management operations. Typically, the day-to-day staff are displaced to another location. Get the agreement in writing so there is no confusion at time of disaster. Trust me, the can move the sales meeting or retirement party. As you know – when you need the command space – you need the space command space!

Tip – Consider using one large room rather than several rooms that collectively comprise the EOC /Alternate EOC. You will have better communication.

Tip – Insure the EOC /Alternate EOC has adequate space to support the emergency response staff.

Tip – Consider if the EOC /Alternate EOC can survive the effects of relevant risks; e.g., natural and man-made hazards.

Tip – Consider implementing special structural capabilities to improve the EOC /Alternate EOC survivability.

Tip – Consider the EOC /Alternate EOC having a collective protection system for Chemical, Biological, Radiological, or Nuclear (CBRN) agents.

Tip -Consider the EOC /Alternate EOC having protection from blast effects.

Tip – Consider the impact of where the EOC /Alternate EOC is located, whether it be above the ground floor, on the ground floor, or below grade. This will depend on your risk factors.

Tip – Is the EOC /Alternate EOC and any multi-use space connected to a local dial central office? These telephones are just like those found in a home or office. The advantage is that if the EOC /Alternate EOC loses power to the PBX, telephones connected directly to the dial central office will continue to function.

Tip – If you require it, insure EOC /Alternate EOC telephones have – 1) Recording capability 2) Caller ID capability 3) Voice conferencing capability.

Tip – Consider the need for the EOC /Alternate EOC telecommunications capability be configured to support the scale of emergency response and management activities.

Tip – Consider the need for the EOC /Alternate EOC and any multi-use space to have the capability to display video feeds for situational awareness information.

Tip – Consider the need for the EOC /Alternate EOC and any multi-use space to have video teleconferencing capability.

Tip – Insure you have the proper number of printers available in the EOC/Alternate EOC and any multi-use space adequate to support emergency response operations.

Tip – Perform ample scenario based testing from the EOC / Alternate EOC. Play through crisis events from start to finish. You will learn a lot of valuable information you can apply to your real-world readiness program.

IDEAS FOR YOUR DISASTER SUPPLIES KIT - BASIC, BEYOND AND WAY BEYOND

Employees should keep a kit at home and you may want to consider purchasing kits and go-bags to be kept at work. Leverage FEMA and the Red Cross for additional ideas. This is a starter list, not a definitive list of items. You must add, delete and modify to fit your policies and procedures. Partner with Safety and Security on this project.

BASIC DISASTER SUPPLIES KIT SUGGESTIONS

A **basic emergency supply kit** could include the some or all the following items:

- Water – One gallon of water per person per day for at least three days, for drinking and sanitation
- Food – At least a three-day supply of non-perishable food
- Battery-powered or hand crank radio and a NOAA Weather Radio with tone alert and extra batteries for both
- Flashlight and extra batteries
- First aid kit
- Whistle to signal for help
- Dust mask to help filter contaminated air and plastic sheeting and duct tape to shelter-in-place
- Moist towelettes, garbage bags and plastic ties for personal sanitation
- Wrench or pliers to turn off utilities
- Manual can opener for food
- Local maps
- Cell phone with chargers, inverter or solar charger
- Prescription medications and glasses
- Infant formula and diapers
- Pet food and extra water for your pet
- Cash or traveler's checks and change
- Important family documents such as copies of insurance policies, identification and bank account records in a waterproof, portable container.
- Sleeping bag or warm blanket for each person. Consider additional bedding if you live in a cold-weather climate.

- Complete change of clothing including a long-sleeved shirt, long pants and sturdy shoes. Consider additional clothing if you live in a cold-weather climate.
- Fire extinguisher
- Matches in a waterproof container
- Feminine supplies and personal hygiene items
- Mess kits, paper cups, plates, paper towels and plastic utensils
- Paper and pencil
- Books, games, puzzles or other activities for children

FIRST AID KIT SUGGESTIONS

In any emergency, you or a family member may suffer an injury. If you have these basic first aid supplies, you are better prepared to help your loved ones when they are hurt. In addition to this list you should review the Red Cross suggestions.

Knowing how to treat minor injuries can make a difference in an emergency. You may consider taking a first aid class and CPR training, but simply having the following things can help you stop bleeding, prevent infection and assist in decontamination.

- Two pairs of Latex or other sterile gloves if you are allergic to Latex
- Sterile dressings to stop bleeding
- Cleansing agent/soap and antibiotic towelettes
- Antibiotic ointment
- Burn ointment
- Adhesive bandages in a variety of sizes
- Eye wash solution to flush the eyes or as general decontamination
- Thermometer
- Prescription medications you take every day such as insulin, heart medicine and asthma inhalers. You should periodically rotate medicines to account for expiration dates.
- Prescribed medical supplies, such as glucose and blood pressure monitoring equipment

Non-prescription drugs:
- Aspirin or non-aspirin pain reliever
- Anti-diarrhea medication
- Antacid
- Laxative

Other first aid supplies:

- Scissors
- Tweezers
- Tube of petroleum jelly or other lubricant

SUPPLIES FOR UNIQUE NEEDS

Remember the unique needs of your family members, including growing children, when making your emergency supply kit and family emergency plan.

For Baby:
- Formula
- Diapers
- Bottles
- Powdered milk
- Medications
- Moist towelettes
- Diaper rash ointment

For Adults:
- Denture needs
- Contact lenses and supplies
- Extra eye glasses

Ask your doctor about storing prescription medications such as heart and high blood pressure medication, insulin and other prescription drugs.

If you live in a cold climate, you must think about warmth. It is possible that you will not have heat. Think about your clothing and bedding supplies. Be sure to include one complete change of clothing and shoes per person, including:
- Jacket or coat
- Long pants
- Long sleeve shirt

Documents – placed in a waterproof container:
- Driver's license or government ID card
- Social security card
- Marriage license
- Credit cards
- Phone numbers of family and friends
- Bank account numbers

AVOID CONFUSION - STREAMLINE REPORTING CRITICAL EVENTS

Team with Your Safety and Security Professionals on the following tips.

Tip – Place local fire, police and ambulance contact numbers plus the 911 emergency number on all desk handsets.

Tip – Create wall signs and display them to re-enforce awareness for these potentially lifesaving critical numbers.

Tip – Ask employees to also add these emergency resources as contacts in their mobile phone.

Tip – Using the local fire department phone number to report a fire may shave seconds or even minutes rather than using 911 in some areas. Speak with your safety and security professionals and the local fire departments to determine if this is true in your locale.

SHELTER IN PLACE - DANGEROUS ISSUES TO CONSIDER

During certain events, **external to your location** such as chlorine gas in the air, a chemical spill or a fast approaching tornado it often makes sense to **shelter in place (internally)**.

Develop a plan so that your organization can provide for your employees for 72 or more hours sheltering in place. Consider storing ample water, non-perishable food and sleeping cots. Medication can also be a concern. You may want to have the American Red Cross visit your company to help you design your shelter in place strategy and plan. I have called on them in the past and they have always provided wonderful value.

Even with a shelter in place plan there may be times when an employee simply does not listen to your advice and insists on leaving. Your company must have a policy on how to handle these types of situations. Employees may be putting their life in danger if they venture into the path of a tornado or into an area that has noxious fumes.

Your policy may be to do everything possible to explain the hazards of leaving to the employee but to not keep people in the building against their will. This is something HR, legal and upper management must decide before it is rolled out to the enterprise.

A friend told me about an experience a few years ago, in which an air conditioning unit failed in the middle of a hot July day. It took a few days to get parts to repair the unit. They kept large fans in-house as part of their plan to address such an event but it was still sort of warm in the building.

Management made it known that anyone who felt uncomfortable could leave. Some employees could work from home and others from a nearby sister location until the HVAC was fixed. HR stepped-up and decided to pay all employees, even the people that could not work from home or the sister location.

'IN CASE OF EMERGENCY' (ICE) SAVES LIVES! SPREAD THE WORD!

Emergency Safety Tip

You can get a lot of mileage out of this In Case of Emergency (ICE) tip. I learned this tip while hosting a tabletop exercise years ago, one of the participants mentioned it and I have paid it forward during hundreds of tabletops, blog postings, newsletter alerts, dinner conversations with friends and now in my book!

ICE is a global initiative that enables first responders, such as paramedics, firefighters, and police officers, as well as hospital personnel, to reach emergency contacts identified in your mobile phone to obtain important medical or support information. The phone entry should supplement, not replace, written information or indicators, such as a wallet card.

ICE info can be lifesaving and you never know when you will need it. I was playing full court basketball in July 2015 in a playground on cement and tripped over a players' foot. Brilliantly I broke the fall with my head instead of my hand. It was the worst fall I ever took. Fortunately, I have a hard head but had my skull cracked the ICE info might have helped save my life.

ICE Tips:
Tip - Add a name or relationship to the contact entry such as 'ICE – Marty' or 'ICE – Husband'.

Tip – Add multiple emergency contacts such as 'ICE1', 'ICE – Husband', etc.

Tip – Add an ICE app to a password protected phone. Search for "ICE" or "ICE lock screen" in your appropriate app store to find one that works on your phone. Apple has also added an emergency widget to the home-screen of iPhone's. Even if the phone is locked the widget can be clicked to pull up an emergency contact. Please test this for yourself.

Tip – Add an ICE sticker to your phone. You can clearly hand write it and tape it to the back of your phone. I have it on all my phones.

Tip – You can optionally include important health information on your ICE card. Children can carry the card in their back-pack.

Tip – Obtain a blank ICE card and keep it in your wallet. Many Doctors offices have them. The AAA website has a template online that you can print.

Tip – Create awareness for ICE. Ideas include a blog post, newsletter article or email alert.

39

PLAN FOR PET(S) - THEY ARE FAMILY

Our pets depend on their human 'mommy and daddy'. How we plan for our pets prior to encountering a disaster can mean the difference between life and death!

Pets are part of our family. I know my rescue dog Flakes (aptly named as he is a bit flaky and very 'yappie') could not survive a disaster without pre-planning.

I suggest you make pet awareness a part of your business continuity blog and newsletter. Also, invite the ASPCA to participate in your next lunch and learn. Devoting even 10 minutes during an upcoming tabletop would be valuable. Believe me, the attendees will appreciate the 'beyond business' concern for their pets' welfare.

The tips and resources below can help keep pets safe when disaster strikes:

Tip – Find shelter for your pet – family pets left behind during an evacuation rarely survive on their own. Make sure there is a predetermined place they can go because not all shelters allow pets. There are some very sad stories of pets that were left behind. Do not let it happen to your beloved pet. Perhaps you, your family and friends can create a reciprocal plan to care for each other's pets during a crisis. If you plan early enough, some pet shelters will make reservations. Other options include hotels, boarding facilities or veterinarians.

Tip – Develop a plan for 'regular emergencies' – your pet may suffer if you encounter a 'regular emergency' such as getting stuck on the highway or forgetting to turn on the A/C. Plan with neighbors, friends or relatives to make sure that someone is available to help. I set up a plan with my neighbors and I now travel with less worry in case I am delayed.

Tip – Create a pet emergency kit. Some items to include are:
- A pet first-aid kit with all pet medications
- Enough food to last up to a week, stored in an airtight, waterproof container
- At least three days of water specifically for pets

- Toys to occupy pets. To our chagrin, Flakes considers our TV remote control a toy and enjoys when I chase him around the house to get it back. I bought a safe remote control toy that I now keep in the kit to make him happy.
- A collar with ID tag, harness or leash
- Important documents such as copies of registration information, adoption papers, vaccination documents and medical records in a clean see-through plastic bag or waterproof container
- A crate or other pet carrier
- Sanitation supplies, which may include litter and litter box, newspapers, paper towels, plastic trash bags and household cleaner
- A physical and digital online picture of you and your pet together in case of a possible separation during an emergency – you may need help in identifying your pet

I also recommend you review this PetSmart article for some great tips on caring for your pet in extreme weather http://www.ultimatebusinesscontinuity.com/petsmart

Tech can help:
- The ASPCA recommends micro-chipping pets so they can be identified and returned to you even without tags. Another option is to invest in a GPS tracker so you can find your pet without a third party
- This ASPCA app (http://www.aspca.org/mobileapp) will also help you keep track of animal records required to board pets at an emergency shelter and has other helpful tips for a variety of situations
- New home automation devices allow you to watch your pet from your smartphone. You can also control the temperature and lights in your home from anywhere. I hooked up a simple camera at home that allows me to rotate the view 360% from a mobile app. It even can notify me if there is motion detected. You can implement it for under $100.

40

HAZARDS CENTRAL - RESOURCES, CHECKLISTS, PLAYBOOKS AND TABLETOPS

Hazard information at your fingertips! There is more natural and man-made hazard related business and personal information below than you or I could ever hope to assemble. Fortunately, we do not have to!

Disclaimer: Because every emergency is different, it is important for your safety that you follow the directives of your state and local emergency management authorities and local utilities. The information provided through these linked sites and in this book, is intended for general informational purposes only and is not an endorsement of any particular material or service.

The Ultimate Business Continuity $uccess Guide eBook has clickable links to each resource listed in this chapter. For my print book readers, I placed this chapter with all the links below at: www.UltimateBusinessContinuity.com/chapter40

Emergency Management Offices:
Here is a link to a great list of emergency management offices for every state and some additional countries which offers incredible information at your fingertips. Each office has location specific information. Many provide alert services. For example, in New York I rely daily on Notify NYC for many types of disruption alerts. Often, I get these alerts before the news services report on them.

Alert services I rely on that offer free online versions:
- Department of Homeland Security – they have a terrific newsletter
- FEMA.gov – they offer a great deal of worthwhile info and templates
- USGS – Earthquake Notification Service – they have a somewhat hidden real-time feed
- American Red Cross – great institution with important information
- NOAA- National Weather Service – is the feeder for most TV and radio reporters
- Wunderground.com – Weather Underground. I value their predictions. During a recent blizzard in New York their scientific discussions provided me with unique insight that the event would

not impact some of my assets as severely as 99% of other services predicted they would be impacted. Weather Underground was correct!

- Windmapper.com – this is my favorite wind specific site. Detailed maps, speed, direction, etc. Search by zip or city. It has served me well in numerous storms. Review all the tabs, as there is a lot of information on their site
- OpenWeatherMap.org – this service fascinates me. Great info is searchable by city AND for a programmer like me, it has a really cool API. I am making time to test the API as soon as I complete the book you are now reading. I will report the results in the free Ultimate Business Continuity Email Newsletter

Hazard Information:
The two FEMA links below are favorites of mine. They have information and checklists on many hazards in convenient pdf format. Use them as is or customize them for your crisis management program.

- https://www.fema.gov/media-library-data/20130726-1549-20490-4629/natural_hazards_1.pdf
- https://www.fema.gov/media-library-data/20130726-1549-20490-2128/natural_hazards_2.pdf

Special Triple Mashup Resource:
Three additional resources I use on a regular basis are Ready.gov Prepare for Emergency Page, the DisasterAssistance.gov site and FEMA's 'Know Your Hazards' site. They contain hazard related guidance, checklists, videos and FEMA scenario specific playbooks for organizations, **including tabletops**. I encourage you to visit all three sites.

BONUS – For your convenience I created a special triple mashup consolidation of the three sites. The list below contains most, but not all, of the hazards described on the sites. The first resource for each hazard is from Ready.gov, then the FEMA playbook (where available), followed by additional resources:
Biological Threats – Learn what biological agents are and how they can be spread. You can also learn what to do to prepare in anticipation of an attack and what to do if you're exposed.

- Biological Threats (Ready.gov)
- Bioterrorism – Learn what bioterrorism is and the categories of biological agents. You can also learn about specific agents and get fact sheets. There is also information for healthcare professionals and first responders. (Centers for Disease Control and Prevention)

108

- Biodefense and Bioterrorism – Learn about agents such as anthrax and smallpox as well as research, treatment, and tests. There is also an option for you to sign up for email updates. (U.S. National Library of Medicine)
- Bioterrorism and Drug Preparedness – Learn about drug therapy and vaccines and receive advice on medication for certain biological agents. (U.S. Food and Drug Administration)

Bomb Threat and Explosion Information
- Bomb Threat and Explosion Information (Ready.gov)
- Please read the next chapter in the book – 'Homeland Security Bomb Threat Checklist, Guidance and Video' for detailed information

Chemical Threats – Learn what chemical agents are and how they can be released. You can also learn the possible signs of a chemical attack and what you should do if you've been exposed.
- Chemical Threats (Ready.gov)
- Household Chemical Emergencies – Learn the guidelines for safely buying and storing chemicals in your home, and what to do in an emergency. (Ready.gov)
- Chemical Emergency Preparedness – Learn how you can prevent chemical accidents as well as prepare for an emergency. You can also learn how you may be exposed to a chemical and how to respond. (American Red Cross)
- Chemical Emergencies Overview – Learn what chemical emergencies are and the different chemical types. You can also learn about sheltering in place, evacuation, and decontamination. And there's information for healthcare professionals and first responders. (Centers for Disease Control and Prevention)

Drought – Nearly every part of our country experiences periods of reduced rainfall. If we plan for drought, then we can enjoy the benefits of normal or rainy years and not get caught unprepared in dry years.
- Drought (Ready.gov)
- U.S. Drought Portal – View maps, local news, and fact sheets to help you monitor droughts in your area. (National Oceanic and Atmospheric Administration)
- National Drought Mitigation Center – Get current news and monitoring tools, and learn how to plan for a drought. There is even a section just for kids! (University of Nebraska–Lincoln)
- Drought Preparedness and Water Conservation – Learn about the four types of drought and what they affect. You can also learn

109

how to conserve water indoors and outdoors. (American Red Cross)

- Water Conservation Tips – Learn how you can save water in the bathroom, kitchen, laundry, and outside your home. (Washington Suburban Sanitary Commission)

Earthquakes – Sudden rolling or shaking events caused by movement under the earth's surface. Earthquakes occur along cracks in the earth's surface, called fault lines, and can be felt over large areas, although they usually last less than one minute. Earthquakes cannot be predicted — although scientists are working on it! All 50 states and 5 U.S. territories are at some risk for earthquakes. Earthquakes can happen at any time of the year.

- Earthquakes (Ready.gov)
- Prepare Your Organization for an Earthquake Playbook (FEMA)
- USGS – Earthquake Notification Service
- Earthquake Preparedness – Learn about risks and get an Earthquake Safety Checklist. You can learn how to prepare for and what to do during an earthquake, both inside and outside. Also become informed on how to let your family know you are safe after an earthquake. (American Red Cross)
- Surviving an Earthquake – Find out how to prepare ahead and deal with home hazards. Learn about what to do in specific situations during an earthquake, such as if you are in a crowded public place or have impaired mobility. You can also learn what you need to know about food, water, and other safety issues after an earthquake. (Centers for Disease Control and Prevention)
- Earthquakes can trigger fires, floods, landslides and tsunamis, so it's good to learn how to stay safe from these hazards, too.

Fires – Fires can start by accident, acts of nature, or even by arson. They are common across all locales. You can help keep your family and co-workers safe during a fire by making sure smoke alarms work and by practicing a fire escape plan. The resources below can help you learn what to do to prevent or recover from a fire.

- Fires (Ready.gov)
- After the Fire: Returning to Normal (PDF, 406 KB) – Learn what to expect and how to handle the damage after a fire. There's also a checklist to help you record vital details to keep on file. (FEMA)
- Also, please read the sample tabletop chapter in the Testing part of this book. I incorporate a sample fire scenario.

Floods – Learn some flood terms, facts and safety tips to help you before, during, and after a flood. You can also read about flood insurance.

- Floods – (Ready.gov)
- Prepare Your Organization for a Flood Playbook – includes a tabletop (FEMA)
- Key Facts About Flood Readiness – Learn basic steps to prepare for a storm and pending evacuation. You can find out what to do if you're under a flood watch or warning, and what emergency supplies you need. The site also has information about clean-up and food and water safety after a flood. (Centers for Disease Control and Prevention)
- Flood Safety Checklist (PDF, 80 KB) – Get a checklist that answers three questions to help you prepare for a flood: What should I do? What supplies do I need? What do I do after a flood? You can also learn about the "Safe and Well" website. It allows you to register to let your family know you are safe. (American Red Cross)
- What Consumers Need to Know About Food and Water Safety – This page offers food and water safety facts to help you prepare for and respond to a hurricane, power outage, or flood. For floods, you can learn specific steps to help keep water and food safe during and after a flood. There is also a link to a PDF file if you want to save a copy of the information. (Food and Drug Administration)
- Flooding – Get tips on how to recover after a flood. Tips such as how to use a generator safely, how to handle private wells and septic systems and how to deal with disaster debris, mold, clean-up and renovation are provided. You can also find information on water and food safety. (Environmental Protection Agency)

Hurricanes – Learn terms, facts, and safety tips to help you before, during, and after a hurricane. You can also read about the Saffir-Simpson Hurricane Wind Scale and the five hurricane categories.

- Hurricanes – (Ready.gov)
- Prepare Your Organization for a Hurricane Playbook – includes a tabletop (FEMA)
- NOAA- National Weather Service
- Hurricane Safety Checklist (PDF, 80 KB) – Get a one-page checklist to help you prepare and respond to a hurricane. Learn what supplies you'll need and what to do after. (American Red Cross)

- Hurricane Toolkit
- Hurricanes – Information for Protecting Health and the Environment – Learn how to prepare before a hurricane. Learn how to plan for things like drinking water, food and disaster debris. Also learn how to handle other health and safety hazards like flooding and mold. (Environmental Protection Agency)
- Medical Devices and Hurricane Disasters – Get safety tips for using medical devices during and after a hurricane. Learn how you should deal with power outages, water, heat and humidity, and keeping things sterile. There is also a special section about blood glucose meters. (Food and Drug Administration)

Landslides

- https://landslides.usgs.gov/ – USGS Landslide Hazards Program
- http://www.redcross.org/get-help/how-to-prepare-for-emergencies/types-of-emergencies/landslide#Before – Red Cross Safety
- http://www.conservation.ca.gov/cgs/geologic_hazards/landslides – California Geological Survey (CGS)
- http://geology.com/usgs/landslides/

Power Outages – Basic safety tips and what to do before, during and after a power outage.

- Power Outages (Ready.gov)
- Generator Safety (Energy.gov)
- Many chapters in this book refer to power outage preparation, response and recovery

Radiation and Nuclear

- Nuclear Power Plant Emergency – Learn the potential radiation exposure danger from a nuclear power plant emergency. Learn how to prepare a supply kit and how to make a family emergency plan. You can also find out what you should do during and after the emergency. (Ready.gov)
- Nuclear Blast – Learn what a nuclear blast is and the hazards of nuclear devices. Learn how to prepare your home and family before a nuclear event, and what you should do during and after. (Ready.gov)
- Hazardous Materials Incident – Find out what different hazardous materials are and where they can be found. Learn how to build an emergency supply kit, how to protect yourself during a hazardous materials incident and what you should do after. (Ready.gov)

- Contamination vs. Exposure – Learn the difference between contamination and exposure and how you can limit contamination. (Centers for Disease Control and Prevention)
- Acute Radiation Syndrome (ARS) – Find out what you need to know about radiation sickness. Learn how you can get it, what the symptoms are and how it is treated. (Centers for Disease Control and Prevention)
- Potassium Iodide (KI) – Read frequently asked questions about the use of KI in radiation emergencies. (U.S. Food and Drug Administration)

Thunderstorms & Lightning – All thunderstorms are dangerous. Every thunderstorm produces lightning. While lightning fatalities have decreased over the past 30 years, lightning continues to be one of the top three storm-related killers in the United States. On average in the U.S., lightning kills 51 people and injures hundreds more each year. Although most lightning victims survive, people struck by lightning often report a variety of long-term, debilitating symptoms.

- Thunderstorms & Lightning – (Ready.gov)

Protecting your property from high winds can involve a variety of actions, from inspecting and maintaining your building to installing protective devices. Most of these actions, especially those that affect the exterior shell of your building, should be carried out by qualified maintenance staff or professional contractors licensed to work in your state, county, or city. For buildings with Exterior Insulation Finishing System (EIFS) walls, a type of wall often used for commercial buildings, one example of wind protection is inspecting and maintaining the walls.

Tornado – Get tornado facts and learn the conditions to stay alert for. Find out how to shelter in different structures or even if you are outside. Learn how to stay safe, inspect the damage, and clean up after a tornado. There's also information on how to prepare a safe room.

- Tornado – (Ready.gov)
- Tornado Playbook (FEMA)
- Tornado Safety – Learn the difference between a "tornado watch" and "tornado warning," and the danger signs to watch for. Read about warning systems, and how to prepare your family and your home ahead of the storm. Learn what to do to stay safe during a tornado and how to recover after. (American Red Cross)

- Tornadoes – Get information on how to prepare before a tornado, and how to stay safe during and after. Learn what to do when you re-enter your home and how to safely handle flooding or debris. (Centers for Disease Control and Prevention)

Tsunamis – Find out how to protect yourself and your family before a tsunami. Learn how to make a family communication plan and what the warning signs are. Learn what to do during a tsunami and how to stay safe after.
- Tsunamis – (Ready.gov)
- Warnings and Forecasts – Learn how the Tsunami Warning System works and how to respond. You can also find links to other tsunami information like "The Tsunami Story," event databases, and news articles. (NOAA)
- Emergency Preparedness and Response – Tsunamis – Find information on the health concerns and effects of tsunamis. You can also get tips on food and water safety. (Centers for Disease Control and Prevention)
- Tsunami Preparedness – Learn the warning signs of a tsunami and the best sources for information. Get tips on how to prepare and be aware of the area around you. You can also learn how to respond during a tsunami, what to do after and how to let your family know you are safe. (American Red Cross)
- Tsunami Hazard Mitigation – Get facts about tsunamis and learn what to do if you are on land or in a boat when a tsunami arrives. (University of Washington)

Volcano - Learn the many hazards of a volcanic eruption. Learn what you need to be aware of during an eruption.
- Volcano – (Ready.gov)
- Volcano Preparedness – Do you live in a known active or dormant volcano area? If so, you need to know about your local warning systems and emergency plans. Learn the other hazards that can be caused by an eruption and how to prepare before an event. Find out what to do during an eruption, whether indoors or outdoors, and how to protect yourself during ash fall. You can also get tips on how to stay safe after. (American Red Cross)
- Volcanoes – Get information about how to prepare for a volcanic eruption. You can also learn how the EPA responds and you also learn about the health and environmental impacts after. (Environmental Protection Agency)
- Volcanoes – What You Should Know – Get advice on how to protect yourself and your family after an eruption. There are also

links to help you learn about other hazards that can occur with an eruption. (Centers for Disease Control and Prevention)

- Volcanic Ash – Learn what ash is, what it can do, and how to prevent damage. Get tips on what actions to take for clean-up and disposal. You can also view brochures about volcanic ash from the International Volcanic Health Hazard Network (IVHHN). (U.S. Geological Survey)

Winter Storm – Learn the terms for winter weather conditions and how you can plan for a storm. Learn what you should do during a winter storm or in extreme cold, such as if you are stranded in a car. You can also learn how to find a shelter if you lose power or heat and don't have any way to stay warm in your home overnight.

- Winter Storm – (Ready.gov)
- Prepare Your Organization for a Winter Storm Playbook (FEMA)
- Winter Weather – Learn how to deal with extreme cold and its health hazards. Get winter weather checklists and learn how to prepare your home and car for winter emergencies. You can also learn what to do during and after a winter storm. (Centers for Disease Control and Prevention)
- Winter Weather Safety – Find out about the coming winter weather outlook, get forecasts and warnings, and winter storm preparedness tips. There is also a link to help you find weather awareness safety events in your state. (National Weather Service)
- Winter Tips – Get tips on how to stay safe, save energy, and reduce waste in the winter season. (Environmental Protection Agency)
- Winter Storm Preparedness – Learn how to prepare before a winter storm. One way would be to make a supply kit. You can also get tips on how to stay safe during a storm and learn about carbon monoxide, frostbite, and hypothermia hazards. (American Red Cross)

A GOLDEN DOZEN VALUABLE GOVERNMENT RESOURCES

These are some of my favorite government resources. I use and recommend them on a regular basis. They have provided me with exceptional value. Most of them have newsletters and real-time feeds. Subscribe!

A few are duplicated from the Hazards Central chapter but I thought it would be handy if you had them as part of this overall Golden Dozen.

The Ultimate Business Continuity $uccess Guide eBook has clickable links to each resource listed in this chapter. For my print book readers, I placed this chapter with all the links below at: www.UltimateBusinessContinuity.com/chapter41

I will be adding to the online page so please check it out.

Homeland Security: www.dhs.gov

FEMA: www.fema.gov

National Weather Service: www.nws.noaa.gov

U.S. Cyber Security: www.dhs.gov/topic/cybersecurity

Emergency Alert Ready.gov Info: www.ready.gov/alerts

U.S. Centers for Disease Control and Prevention: www.cdc.gov

U.S. Citizen Corps: www.ready.gov/citizen-corps

U.S. Department of Energy: www.energy.gov

U.S. Department of Homeland Security: www.ready.gov

U.S. Environmental Protection Agency: www.epa.gov

U.S. Fire Administration: www.usfa.fema.gov

U.S. Nuclear Regulatory Administration: www.nrc.gov

HOMELAND SECURITY - BOMB THREAT CHECKLIST, GUIDANCE AND VIDEO

It is critical to prepare for a bomb threat. The Homeland Security Checklist, Guidance Brochure and Video information and links below are excellent! You can use it as-is or customize for your company. I leverage them for my programs and I wanted to share this important information with you.

Similar to the previous two chapters, this chapter includes several important links. The Ultimate Business Continuity $uccess Guide eBook has clickable links to each resource listed in this chapter. For my print book readers, I placed this chapter with all the links below at: www.UltimateBusinessContinuity.com/chapter42

DHS-FEMA Bomb Threat Call Procedures

DHS Bomb Threat Checklist

DHS-DOJ Bomb Threat Guidance Brochure

DHS-DOJ Bomb Threat video – expand the video section to watch the video

For your convenience, I have included a portion of the Homeland Security Bomb Threat Page:

What to Do – Bomb Threat
Bomb threats or suspicious items are rare, but should always be taken seriously. How quickly and safely you react to a bomb threat could save lives, including your own. What should you do?
The guidance and resources listed below outline in-depth procedures for either bomb threats or suspicious items and will help you prepare and react appropriately during these events.

If You Receive a Bomb Threat
Bomb threats are most commonly received via phone, but are also made in person, via email, by a written note, or other means. Every bomb threat is unique and should be handled in the context of the facility or environment in which it occurs. Facility supervisors and law enforcement will be in the best position to determine the credibility of the threat. Follow these procedures:

- Remain calm.
- Notify authorities immediately:
- Notify your facility supervisor, such as a manager, operator, or administrator, or follow your facility's standard operating procedure. (See below for assistance with developing a plan for your facility or location.)
- Call 9-1-1 or your local law enforcement if no facility supervisor is available.
- **Refer to the DHS Bomb Threat Checklist for guidance, if available.**
- For threats made via phone:
- Keep the caller on the line as long as possible. Be polite and show interest to keep them talking.
- **DO NOT HANG UP**, even if the caller does.
- If possible, signal or pass a note to other staff to listen and help notify authorities.
- Write down as much information as possible—caller ID number, exact wording of threat, type of voice or behavior, etc.—that will aid investigators.
- Record the call, if possible.
- For threats made in person, via email, or via written note, refer to the DHS Bomb Threat Checklist and Guidance for more information: (https://www.dhs.gov/publication/dhs-bomb-threat-checklist) and DHS-DOJ Bomb Threat Guidance (https://www.dhs.gov/publication/dhs-doj-bomb-threat-guidance-brochure)
- Be available for interviews with facility supervisors and/or law enforcement.
- Follow instructions given by authorities. Facility supervisors and/or law enforcement will assess the situation and provide guidance regarding facility lock-down, search, and/or evacuation.

If You Find a Suspicious Item

Together we can help keep our communities safe—if you see something that is suspicious, out of place, or doesn't look right, say something. A **suspicious item** is any item (e.g., bag, package, vehicle, etc.) that is reasonably believed to contain explosives, an improvised explosive device (IED), or other hazardous material that requires a bomb technician and/or specialized equipment to further evaluate it. Examples that could indicate a bomb include unexplainable wires or electronics, other visible bomb-like components, and unusual sounds, vapors, mists, or odors. Generally speaking, anything that is hidden, obviously suspicious, and not Typical (**HOT**) should be deemed

118

suspicious. In addition, potential indicators for a bomb are threats, placement, and proximity of the item to people and valuable assets.

NOTE: Not all items are suspicious. An **unattended item** is an item (e.g., bag, package, vehicle, etc.) of unknown origin and content where there are no obvious signs of being suspicious (see above). Facility search, lock-down, or evacuation is not necessary unless the item is determined to be suspicious.

You may encounter a suspicious item unexpectedly or while conducting a search as part of your facility's or employer's Bomb Threat Response Plan. If it appears to be a suspicious item, follow these procedures:

- Remain calm.
- Do **NOT** touch, tamper with, or move the package, bag, or item.
- Notify authorities immediately:
- Notify your facility supervisor, such as a manager, operator, or administrator, or follow your facility's standard operating procedure. (See below for assistance with developing a plan for your facility or location.)
- Call 9-1-1 or your local law enforcement if no facility supervisor is available.
- Explain why it appears suspicious.
- Follow instructions. Facility supervisors and/or law enforcement will assess the situation and provide guidance regarding shelter-in-place or evacuation.
- If no guidance is provided and you feel you are in immediate danger, calmly evacuate the area. Distance and protective cover are the best ways to reduce injury from a bomb.
- Be aware. There could be other threats or suspicious items.
- Every situation is unique and should be handled in the context of the facility or environment in which it occurs. Facility supervisors and law enforcement will be in the best position to determine if a real risk is posed and how to respond. Refer to the DHS-DOJ Bomb Threat Guidance for more information.

Have a Plan – Guidance for Facility Owners, Operators, and Managers

Having a plan makes the response to bomb threats, unattended items, or suspicious items as orderly and controlled as possible, reducing risk and the impact of false alarms on regular activities. Facility supervisors—such as school, office, or building managers responsible for the facility—should:

- Review the DHS-DOJ Bomb Threat Guidance.

- Develop a Bomb Threat Response Plan for their organization or facility. Contact the Office for Bombing Prevention at OBP@hq.dhs.gov for more information on planning workshops.
- Train employees, tenants, and/or visitors to take appropriate actions in the event of a bomb threat and/or identification of an unattended or suspicious item.

Developed in partnership with the Federal Bureau of Investigation, the Department of Homeland Security (DHS)-Department of Justice (DOJ) Bomb Threat Guidance is a quick reference guide that provides facility supervisors with details on pre-threat preparation, threat assessment, staff response guidelines, and evacuation and shelter-in-place considerations. Download the DHS-DOJ Bomb Threat Guidance for more information.

School-specific bomb threat guidance can also be found at ThreatPlan.org and the Readiness and Emergency Management for Schools (REMS) Tech Assistant Center.

Bomb Threat Training Video

It's important to know what steps every day citizens can and should take in the event of a bomb threat. This video, developed by the University of Central Florida, in conjunction with the International Association of Chiefs of Police (IACP) and the Office for Bombing Prevention within the National Protection and Programs Directorate's Office of Infrastructure Protection, teaches viewers how to respond in the event they receive a bomb threat. It actually uses the checklist discussed above. **Click here and expand the bomb video section to watch the video (https://www.dhs.gov/what-to-do-bomb-threat#)**

43

SALVAGING VITAL RECORDS - ACT FAST AND ALL MAY NOT BE LOST!

You should strive to have copies of all vital records backed-up in digital format and physically stored safely off-site.

If vital records are damaged it is important to have a process in place and a trusted vendor that can jump in and help save them. A good professional mitigation partner is your best bet.

Here are some tips and resources on salvaging moldy and contaminated vital documents:

Tip – DO NOT store vital records in the basement. You might be surprised how often they wind up in the basement.

Tip – Always ask process owners where the originals are stored. You might be surprised and perhaps dismayed.

Moldy Documents:

Tip – If documents are soaking wet for a long period – days, weeks, they will likely mold. If it is humid that will compress the time-frame for mold to begin forming.

Tip – Air drying wet documents is effective for small amounts of documents prior to mold forming.

Tip – Freezing wet documents can stop mold growth.

Tip – After freezing wet document they should then be vacuum freeze dried. Doing this will remove the frozen water so it cannot go through the liquid phase. It is the a very effective way to dry frozen documents.

Tip – It is important to understand that freezing does not kill mold. It suspends mold growth if the documents are frozen. So, moldy documents still must be treated after freezing and vacuum freeze drying is finished. Any leftover mold should be cleaned off in a separate step by a vendor wearing protective gear.

Tip – Drying methods not recommended for documents include: thermal, desiccant, vacuum thermal drying or de-humidification. Using these will harm the documents.

Contaminated Documents:

Tip – Documents can be contaminated by the contents of the water that impacted them.

Tip – Documents soaked in muddy water still must be dried to remove residue on them, possibly in addition to the mold, after freeze and vacuum drying are complete.

Tip – If the water that impacted the documents has, or might have, biological contaminants then you must sterilize the documents. **Do not do this yourself**. For safety, your vendor should do this, not your team.
Tip – Two sterilization methods your vendor might consider using are: fumigation with ethylene oxide, and gamma irradiation. Again, let you vendor advise you on sterilization.

Vendors:

I highly recommend you speak with vendors BEFORE a disruptive event. Understand their capabilities. Speak with some of their current clients. Perform your due diligence, and as always (I know I am preaching to the choir, please forgive me) have redundant vendors just in case the primary vendor is not available.

I discuss other aspects of discovering and documenting vital records in more detail in the risk, BIA and plan development parts of the book.

44

EMERGENCY GUIDEBOOKS (DESK GUIDES, FLIP BOOKS). GOOD THINGS COME IN SMALL PACKAGES

I suggest you consider making your guidebook simple, mobile, attractive and compact so people can easily carry it and have it on hand always. If it is too large and cumbersome it defeats the purpose, people will not use it. I have seen some huge monstrosities in my day. If the intention is to leave it in the office or command center that is fine but do not expect people to lug a large document to the beach or on a 5k run! These voluminous plans might be handy to do forearm curls if you do not have your weights handy but in a crisis, they would not be so valuable.

You should additionally (not to replace the physical guidebook) consider an Incident Management app with all the above in it. It should not be used as a replacement for the physical guidebook. You can brand the app with your logo. I discuss app creation in the technology part of this book.

Tip – Create a compact colorful emergency guidebook that includes emergency response and business continuity best practices. Partner with your Safety, Security, HR and graphic design experts on this project. They will have valuable information to contribute.

Tip – Briefly detail response procedures. Detail responses to probable threats such as fire, hurricanes, earthquakes, active shooter and terrorism. Customize it by location to align with their most probable risks.

Tip – Diagram your rally points. Perhaps, use custom insert pages so you can easily change them without reprinting the guidebook. If rally point locations change or you add additional ones you can simply replace the necessary pages.

Tip – List critical police, fire and medical phone numbers on the cover or inside cover.

Tip – Leave space on the inside cover for the user to list personal contact info and prescribed medications, etc. – discuss this with your HR and Legal departments.

I include my favorite custom guidebook publishers and specific Incident Management app recommendations in the free Ultimate Business Continuity Tools and Technologies Newsletter.

123

PART 3 - CRISIS COMMUNICATIONS

The ability to effectively communicate prior to, during and following a crisis is of the utmost important. This sub-section of Crisis Management includes information on:

- Your crisis communications plan
- Audiences you will need to keep informed
- Quality contact data
- Incoming notification tool
- Outgoing notification tool

45

YOUR CRISIS COMMUNICATION PLAN AND DATA QUALITY IS CRITICAL FOR SUCCESS

I consider crisis communications one of the most important things we do as business resilience / continuity professionals. You will undoubtedly be judged by management on how well communications are triggered and maintained throughout a crisis. Communications can make or break you, so I implore you to give it a lot of thought. You must get it right the first time and every time!

A robust and practiced crisis communications plan will empower you and your company to respond quickly, accurately and confidently throughout any disruptive event.

When a disruptive event occurs, such as a tornado, earthquake, active shooter, etc. the need to communicate can be immediate. These are fast breaking events where every second counts. Employee safety is your number one concern – ALWAYS.

Other events have a longer lead time – hurricane, winter storm, union strike… You have more time to prepare and release communications. Employees and their families must have clear, accurate and consistent information. Neighbors living near your site may need information—especially if they are threatened by the incident. Keeping all this balanced will be much easier if you spend time preparing and practicing your plan. Templates are also valuable to save time and prepare you so you do not forget anything during early frantic moments of a crisis. Have these prepared, signed-off-on by management and tested before a disruptive event.

Beyond employee safety the continuity of operations is critical. If business operations are disrupted, customers will want to know how they will be impacted. Depending on your industry, regulators and local government officials may have to be updated on your status. I lived this in the finance sector for many years at some of the largest global companies. So be ready to communicate. Do not go into a shell at 'crunch time'.

Throughout the book, I discuss communications as it is at the core of what we do as business resilience / continuity and emergency management professionals. This chapter provides guidance and suggestions on the different audiences you may want to maintain communications with.

If you have a sizable company and are still using manual call trees, you may want to rethink that. Tools such as intelligent mass notification systems and a scalable – cost effective national employee emergency hotline will be incredibly valuable provided you select the right tools and implement them correctly. I specialize in implementing communication tools that empower organizations. My door is always open to you beyond this book. You have my attention if you need it. Just email or call me for advice.

I am sure you will want to modify the information in this chapter to fit your business but it will provide a solid foundation to build on. Understanding potential audiences is key, as each wants to understand: "How does it affect me?" So here we go:

Audiences you must include in your crisis communications planning:

Contact Information:
Accurate contact information for each audience must be readily accessible to you. Existing information such as customer, supplier, vendor and of course employee contact information probably are available within your organization. Leverage what you can. Try to maintain a gold copy of contact information. Otherwise it will become impossible to maintain the data quality (integrity) of these critical lists. We talk about data quality below, in the Golden Opportunities chapter and in the technology part of the book. Data is one of my passions. Great data is power while bad data is...really, really bad, counterproductive and can become very expensive to an organization.

Include as much information for each contact record as possible (contact name, business telephone number, business cell number, business email address, personal cell, home phone, personal email address...). A big caveat though – if you are using a cloud / SAS vendor for your mass notifications, upload only the data necessary to contact employees. For example, there may be no valid reason to upload the home street addresses but city, state, zip code can be beneficial for geo-location to target messages for employees in location of concern. This was very useful to me during the Boston Marathon bombing when I had to do notifications to particular towns and zip codes as the event progressed and shelter in place was advisable by authorities. In addition to this chapter there is more information on improving contact data in the technology part of the book.

126

Contact lists must be updated regularly, secured to protect confidential information and available to authorized users at the emergency operations center or an alternate location for use by members of the crisis communications team.

Pay close attention to contact data integrity. Partner with Human Resources (HR) to improve the quality of the contact data. In my opinion, HR should own the contact data portion and possibly have Sales own the customer portion of the data. You cannot and should not try to do it all.

I also suggest you implement an automated process to keep data fresh and accurate. DO NOT underestimate the effort it will take to keep your contact data pristine. It might take a large effort from multiple departments to do this but it is well worth the effort. You will get extraordinary value from clean accurate data.

After you have clean data in-house you must get it into your notification system. Stay clear of manually uploading spreadsheets. I favor a simple automated process to add/update/delete data to a mass notification tool:

YOUR COMPANY IN-HOUSE GOLD COPY -> sftp upload OR real-time synch-> MASS NOTIFICATION TOOL

This type of automated process takes the human element out of the data uploads. The automated upload can be triggered as often as you like. Daily is often sufficient but I have also implemented real-time data synchronizations so when a change is made locally either in an HR system (SAP, Taleo…) or BCM system, a trigger is activated and the mass notification system is updated in a few seconds with the revised contact information. Even if you have 100,000+ employees the updates can occur almost instantaneously with the right tools and processes in place. In the database world, my world, 100,000 records are 'teensie tiny' (Marty technical term). Never let a vendor tell you that is a lot of records. I have created real-time database updates for databases with millions of records. My son has me beat – he has designed graph database solutions with over 12 billion nodes and no latency

Notifying Employees:

OK, allow me to be repetitious, **employees are our number one priority. They are our life-blood. They are our most valuable asset.** They must always be kept up-to-date with consistent accurate information. In my opinion Human Resources (HR) should own and assume responsibility for the day-to-day communications with employees regarding employment issues and benefits administration. HR management should assume a similar role on the Incident Command Team and the Crisis Communications Team. HR and Corporate Communication should coordinate communications with management, supervisors, employees and families.

They should also coordinate communications with those involved with the care of employees and the provision of benefits to employees and their families. Close coordination between management, company or division spokesperson and HR is needed when managing the sensitive nature of communications related to any incidents involving death or injury.

If you have a mass notification tool HR should be trained to be able to do notifications with your support if they need assistance. Don't fall into the trap I did years ago, of doing all the notifications by yourself. This can cause issues for your company and your health. It was a learning experience and partially my fault for letting it happen. I later trained representatives throughout organization to be able to do their own notifications. It became so much better for everyone, including me!

Tip – Develop pre-defined and approved templates for various scenarios. It makes it easier to modify them at time of launch rather than writing them from scratch and getting them approved. We will discuss a lot more on mass notification tool best practices elsewhere in the book.

To recap – HR should own the quality of employee data that is used for crisis management purposes. You should not own it. The data should originate from a gold source such as SAP. Make sure they understand that. Document it in your RACI chart or elsewhere. It could come in handy if finger pointing starts.

Notifying Management:

Oh boy!!! Protocols for when to notify management should be clearly understood and documented. Trust me, you had better keep management informed. IF MANAGEMENT GETS BLINDSIDED you are toast! You want to be the person that notifies management. If they hear it from their management or from some cowboy that should not be reporting-up but sees it as an opportunity to score brownie points that spells BIG trouble for you.

For you, management notification is the MONEY SHOT! Get it right and you are set – get it wrong and it ain't pretty. After the crisis is over you want them to call you with praise for making them look good. The last thing you need is to receive the dreaded call from the Big Kahuna asking why you 'dropped the ball'.

128

Providing consistent updates to management by phone, email and **secure** text messaging is especially critical during and after a crisis! If I had to choose between under communicating and over communicating I would skew toward over communicating every time.

It should be clear to staff the scenarios that require immediate management notification and the proper process to notify them. If it is important then you must notify management at 4 am. Don't worry about waking them up. Similar protocols and procedures should be established for notification of directors, investors and other important stakeholders. Trust me, management does not want to learn about a problem from the news media Wake them up!

Tip – Sometimes local teams are hesitant to give management bad news. My advice is to be honest and open at all times. If you hide things it will come back to bite you in the worst way and may even rightfully cost you your job.

When communicating status using email:

- Use a clean-consistent structured email template
- Include pictures if they add value to help management make decisions
- Always mention the next scheduled status update date and time
- Test the message beforehand on all types of devices you will send to such as mobile phones and tablets – especially if you are using rich text formatting to delineate fields in the message

Be sure to include update information such as:

- Date of Incident
- Type of Incident
- Time of Incident
- Location of Incident
- Current Status
- Business Impact Rating – Low/Medium/High
- Business Impact Description
- Overall Description
- Management Response
- Current Update
- Next Steps
- Photos Attached
- Additional Info Links – Internal and/or External Sources
- Next Scheduled Update
- History of Prior Update(s) – Optional

129

Tip – Be consistent. Using a structured format will enable you to deliver important information that will allow management to make decisions. There will be no surprises. Each update brands your name to management, which is an extra benefit for you. Just make certain you get it right. When review and bonus time comes around they will remember how proactive you were keeping them informed.

I would strongly suggest you also consider using a mobile Incident Management tool. I provide more info on the value of such tools in the technology part of the book.

Notifying Customers:

Customers are critical to staying in business and prospering. Providing customers with accurate and timely information is a top priority. Customers may become aware of a problem as soon as their phone calls are not answered by customer service, sales or their orders are not processed. Your business continuity plan should include action to redirect incoming telephone calls on customer facing lines (possibly toll free's) to an alternate call center (if available) or to recovery employees crossed-trained to take calls until you are able to get the primary staff to their recovery locations.

A voice message indicating that the business is experiencing a temporary problem can be used but I dislike using voicemail. I strive to do better than that! I only use VM as a last resort in the most extreme circumstances when all else fails and only for as long as absolutely necessary. Perhaps a few minutes until calls can be redirected to recovery personnel.

Your customer service business continuity plan should also include procedures to ensure that customers are properly informed about the status of orders in process at the time of the incident. Customer service can make outgoing calls to your most important customers. Make sure you have an accurate list of customer contact information.

You can also consider adding your customers to your mass notification system. This will greatly compress the time it takes to notify customers and to keep them regularly informed of progress throughout a disruptive event. They will appreciate it and they will remember how proactive you were! It could result in keeping them as customers in the future when the competition tries to snatch them away. You should speak with your mass notification vendor regarding any licensing concerns when using the system beyond employee contacts.

Notifying Suppliers and Vendors:

Your crisis communication and business continuity plans should include documented procedures for communicating with suppliers. Typically, I include this in plans for purchasing, facilities and all other processes that deal directly with suppliers. Also, this information should roll-it up to your division and regional plan as backup. Procedures should identify when and how suppliers should be notified. Also, remember to implement redundancy for critical suppliers and vendors along with contact details. Test the ability to contact representatives just as you would employees. You do not want to find out at crisis time that you cannot reach a critical vendor or supplier.

Notifying Government Officials & Regulators:

Communications with government officials depends upon the nature and severity of the incident and regulatory requirements. I spent a good portion of my career in the securities industry which is highly regulated. I was on a lot of calls with SIFMA, the SEC and the Federal Reserve during Hurricane Sandy. The calls were really interesting and valuable. It was cool being part of decisions that impacted the entire financial system. Make sure you can reach the proper regulators in a timely manner.

Notifying Your Community:

If there are hazards at a facility that could impact the surrounding community, then the community becomes an important audience. If so, the procedure detailing how you will achieve community outreach should be part of your crisis communications plan. This is often overlooked. Your plan should include coordination with public safety officials to develop protocols and procedures for advising the public of any hazards and the most appropriate protective action that should be taken if warned. You should have these numbers available to you for all your facilities.

Beyond Continuity Value – This can also be an opportunity to help your community. It is the right thing to do. You may have excess resources – space, food, fuel that can benefit the community and possibly help your company in the future. Remember, the community includes customers and perhaps future customers. Be a good neighbor.

Communicating with the News Media:

If the incident is serious, then the news media will probably seek you out in person, by phone or email to obtain details. There may be numerous requests for information from local, regional or national media. The challenge of managing large numbers of requests for

131

information, interviews and public statements must be planned. In our information age, requests can come from the established media or from bloggers – some of whom can be very influential. Prioritization of requests for information and development of press releases and talking points can assist with the need to communicate quickly and effectively.

Develop a company policy that only authorized spokespersons are permitted to speak to the news media. Communicate the policy to all employees explaining that it is best to speak with one informed voice. Determine in advance who will speak to the news media and prepare that spokesperson with talking points, so they can speak clearly and effectively in terms that can be easily understood. You have probably seen carefully worded responses to major cyber-attacks that frequently make front page news. I suggest you make the process for communicating to the news media part of your tabletops scenarios.

News Media TIP – 'No Comment' is not a good comment:
It is very important to make employees aware of the proper procedures if they are approached by a member of the media for comments during a disaster. Incorrect comments regarding the safety of an employee or the impact to your organization because of a fire or other crisis can be devastating. It could affect a family or customers. You definitely do not want them reading sensitive information in the news or hearing it on TV rather than receiving correct information directly from your organization.

In many organizations, the procedure is never to say 'no comment', rather it is to direct the media person to an official organization spokesperson that can make a well informed accurate statement. Employees must have awareness PRIOR to an event on the procedures and who to contact. When you develop the official process make it part of your training and awareness program. I include it in all my tabletops. I have it in my example tabletop later in the book.

Your best course of action is to meet with HR and Corporate Communications to develop a holistic strategy, the proper language and process when communicating with the media.

46

THE IMPORTANCE OF INCOMING AND OUTGOING COMMUNICATION TOOLS

Emergency Hotline and Mass Notification Tools

This chapter will serve to frame the value of two types of communication tools that can be of great benefit to you and your organization – incoming and outgoing communication tools. These are two of my passions and specialties.

In the technology part of the book we will discuss in detail how to select and implement these tools.

Tip – To provide your employees with the most value, provide them with both a way to call in for crisis information and a way for them to receive information on their personal and work devices. To accomplish this I recommend implementing BOTH an emergency hotline (incoming) and a mass notification system (outgoing).

Tip – To eliminate the possibility of providing employees with mixed/contradictory messages during a crisis, you MUST develop a process so your emergency hotline message is aligned with your outgoing mass notification system message.

How an Emergency Hotline (incoming) complements a Mass Notification System (outgoing):

Emergency Hotline:

An emergency hotline can be a phone or bulletin board system. The hotline can use voice recordings or textual messages on web pages (bulletin board feature). It can optionally allow employees to speak with operators or post responses, pictures, video... during a disruptive event. The emergency hotline must be able to support a large volume of simultaneous callers, so do not use a line that will only support 10-15 employees if you have 3,000 people in your company. Always allow room for growth. If you think you will need to accommodate 50 simultaneous callers – then implement capacity for 100+.

Mass Notification System:

A mass notification system enables you to send large numbers of people a consistent interactive message using multiple modes of communication in seconds or minutes. For example, during hurricane Sandy I sent out 38,000 voice calls, emails, text messages and push notifications all in less than five minutes. Try that with a manual call tree! Mass notification systems empower you to send consistent messages and get important responses from recipients.

Tip – Some mass notification systems I recommend have the capability to also act as your emergency hotline.

Why my recommended solution consists of both an Emergency Hotline + Mass Notification System:

I believe you need both types of systems. During an ice storm, you may use your outgoing mass notification system to blast a message to two groups of employees, alerting one group that there will be a one hour delayed opening for location 'abc' and the other group that location 'def' will be closed for the day. As part of the messages you would request the recipients to, '*continue to check the emergency hotline – 800-XXX-XXXX for important updates before leaving for the office* '. This provides both push and pull benefits for the people that require critical information.

The benefit of employees calling into the emergency hotline becomes important if they are not able to be reached in a remote area with your outgoing mass notification system (Tip – a sat phone would eliminate that vulnerability). The ability to pull information from the emergency hotline allows employees to call in from any phone and receive critical information. For example, if an employee's mobile device is out of power or they are in a location with poor cellular reception or they simply do not have their phone handy (I know not having your mobile phone in your pocket nowadays sounds ludicrous, but it could theoretically happen). In those instances, they will still have the option to access a message on the emergency hotline from any landline or a friend's mobile device.

Tip – Many organizations brand outgoing messages with the emergency hotline number as the caller ID. In my experience, including an important number that employees are familiar with will **significantly increase** the number of people that will answer the call. When people receive a call from a strange number they are not familiar with they often think it is an annoying telemarketing sales call and they will ignore the call.

I have used emergency hotlines and mass notification tools to keep employees well informed during disruptive events including:

Weather events:
- Hurricanes
- Ice and Snow Storms

- Blizzards
- Earthquakes
- Floods
- Tornadoes

Man-made events:
- Power outages
- Terrorism

The following are some tips I have learned through the years. Also, later in this part of the book I have a extensive list of 'according to Marty' mass notification best practices. In addition, in the technology part of the book there is a chapter dedicated to mass notification selection criteria and suggested vendor questions.

Tip – A top-down formalized emergency response protocol should be used to create consistent messages. This will eliminate the possibility of unauthorized, inappropriate and possibly conflicting messages being placed on the incoming emergency hotline or being blasted out to employees with the outgoing mass notification system. I have heard of this happening. It gets messy, so be careful. Customize templates where possible to reduce errors.

The Incident Command Team, including the Incident Commander and management representing HR, Legal, Safety, Security, Communications, Operations, Business Resilience / Continuity, Sales and additional processes in your organization, could be the authoritative team that develops the appropriate messages to be delivered to employees. I have enjoyed success when HR and Corporate Communications take the lead on the proper wording.

After the message is developed, it is recorded and posted to the emergency hotline and launched with the outgoing mass notification system by an employee trained in the administration of the systems. Often, this person is an HR or Corporate Communications manager to insure a consistent message is communicated through all channels.

Tip – If you contract with an emergency hotline vendor consider front-ending their number with one. Callers will call your number and it will redirect (pass through) to the vendor end-point number. That way if you ever need to change vendors you simply point your toll-free hotline phone number to a different end-point.

Tip – Multiple emergency hotlines can create confusion:
If you have many locations multiple emergency hotlines can create confusion. For example, imagine if you work in New York and travel to your location in Nebraska or Hawaii (hopefully). What if there was a crisis event and you needed crisis updates in the state you are visiting. Would you know their emergency hotline phone number? What if there was an ice storm and the local management team decided to delay the opening due to extremely dangerous road conditions? Wouldn't you want to know that rather than driving to the office in dangerous conditions, assuming unnecessary risk and discovering the location is not even open? Yikes! I know I would be pissed off.

To exasperate the situation, as organizations grow and expand to new locales emergency hotlines have a way of multiplying like bunny rabbits which leads to significant confusion, complexity and cost. What an unnecessary mess.

Tip – The above issue is for emergency hotline contact. Good mass notification systems (outgoing) have interesting options for automatically detecting through geo-fencing where you are currently located and can dynamically include you on outgoing notifications for the site you are visiting. More on that when we deep-dive mass notification system selection criteria in the technology part of the book.

Tip – Consider this solution – One National Emergency Hotline
In my experience, a single national emergency hotline may be a better solution than multiple local emergency hotlines.

I have experienced both scenarios; organizations that used multiple emergency hotlines with inconsistent results and Fortune 100 companies with 75,000+ employees that very successfully used one national emergency hotline during local and regional events.

Advantages of one national emergency hotline include:
- Simplicity – only one number for employees to remember wherever they are will greatly increase their ability to access the system – especially if the number is an easy to remember acronym such as 800-CRI-SIS1.
- Using one vendor simplifies billing and reduces costs. Most of the time the emergency hotline will not be in use and paying multiple vendors is a waste of money which is compounded as you add new local numbers.
- Updating one national emergency hotline by a central 24x7x365 team is much simpler, less stressful and error prone than having to maintain and remember how to update multiple local emergency hotlines by administrators who rarely use the system.

Sample Emergency Hotline and Mass Notification Message Tips:
When posting a message to the emergency hotline or launching a notification it is very important to indicate the precise location that is impacted. The message should inform employees of the current status and any call to action. For example:
'Due to the ice storm the 123 Main Street, New York, New York location is scheduled to open at 10 am EST on Monday January 8, 2018. Please continue to check the emergency hotline for updates before travelling.'

Tip – If there are many locations simultaneously impacted and opening at the same time you could use:
'Due to the north-east ice storm the following locations will open at 10 am Monday January 8, 2018: 12 Main Street, New York, New York, 456 South Avenue, Clifton, New Jersey and 789 Beacon Road, Hartford, Connecticut. Please continue to check the emergency hotline for updates before travelling.'

Tip – If there are many offices simultaneously impacted and opening at various times you could use:
'Due to the northeast ice storm the following locations will have a delayed opening on Monday January 8, 2018. The 12 Main Street, New York, New York location will open at 10 am. The 456 South Avenue, Clifton, New Jersey location will open at 11 am. Please continue to check the emergency hotline for updates before travelling.'

Tip – On days when there are no crisis messages the emergency hotline should have a message to the effect:
'There are no emergency messages for Thursday February 1, 2018.'

Tip – Emergency Hotline Awareness:
Here are a few tips to help improve emergency hotline awareness. Customize for your organization:

- Each employee should have the emergency hotline phone number on the back of their employee ID badge. Labels can be affixed to the back of employee ID badges rather than printing new badges.
- Emergency hotline labels should be placed on desk phones.
- Wall posters should remind employees of the importance of the emergency hotline.
- Emergency contact wallet cards should be made available to employees. Critical contact numbers including the emergency hotline will then be readily accessible to them wherever they are.

This is especially important if you do not have an emergency hotline with an easy to remember acronym.

- Employees should be encouraged to add the emergency hotline as a contact on their mobile phones.
- The emergency hotline should be publicized in national and local corporate newsletters.
- The employee section of the corporate website should include the emergency hotline phone number(s) and reminders that it is our 'life-line' during a crisis event.

NEXT: The next few chapters discuss some of my favorite Mass Notification System tips and techniques

PREPARE ULTRA TIME SENSITIVE NOTIFICATION PROCEDURES TODAY!

I wanted to break-out this brief discussion so you can get a head start on this important issue. I have seen this go wrong and I do not want it to happen to you. I have documented many additional mass notification best practices in the upcoming chapter, 'Marty's Favorite Mass Notification System Tips, Best Practices and Lessons Learned'.

Now is the time to plan! During extremely time-sensitive disruptive events, wasting precious seconds can mean the difference between life and death! I strongly suggest you meet with management and the Incident Command Team as soon as possible. Develop procedures detailing how you will respond to extremely time-sensitive disruptions that require you to quickly alert employees and other groups. Make sure HR, Communications, Safety and Security are part of the meeting.

Imagine you received a time sensitive alert regarding a tornado, earthquake, tsunami or active shooter either from your situational awareness tool or from a phone call, email or text from an employee:

- What are your immediate next steps?
- Do you clearly know what to do and who to notify?
- Do you have a tested process in place? It is essential.
- Communication decisions must be made very quickly, but you must get it right.
- Are you authorized to send the notification or does management must review it? What if they are not available? To repeat, what if they are not available?
- Remember, every second counts. It can make the difference between life and death.

Other scenarios such as a hurricane, winter storm or union strike have longer time frames to respond, but you must have a communications strategy prepared for those as well. After your team decides the proper procedures for each type of impact, you must document them so there is no confusion at time of crisis.

MARTY'S MASS NOTIFICATION SYSTEM BEST PRACTICES

In this chapter I list some of my favorite mass notification system tips, tricks and techniques. Many of these have served me well. Some I learned the hard way and I have the bruises to prove it!

Message Creation:

Tip – Use a consistent message intro such as – 'This is an important message from ABC Company'... Consistency avoids confusion and conditions people to realize the importance of the message. This will increase the number of people that read/listen to the entire message and the number of responses. Another way to say it is – it will reduce the hang-ups.

Tip – Specify the site location in detail including the exact address, city and state.

Tip – Mention the effected work day/night shifts, if your company has multiple work shifts.

Tip – Specify info such as date, day, time and time zone – so there is no confusion.

Tip – Specify the reason for the message – test exercise, weather, power outage... Be very clear and concise.

Tip – Clearly specify the action(s) to be taken.

Tip – Specify how the recipient can/will get more information. For example, 'Continue to check the ABC Company Emergency Hotline – 555-555- 5555 for further updates' OR – 'The next status update will be sent at Date / Time

Tip – Begin all **test activation messages** with **THIS IS A TEST.** I have seen some really bad mistakes with this – including two by mass notification vendors trying to sell me their systems.

Tip – Eliminate superfluous words! Keep messages short and to the point. This improves delivery speed, comprehension and response rate.

Tip – Avoid acronyms. Speak clearly regarding the action that should be taken by the recipient. Do not assume they understand acronyms.

Tip – When recording a message be ready to hit the # button (or other button) to end the recording. Otherwise, if you delay before ending the recording, when the recipient receives the message he will hear 'dead air' and could hang up before a subsequent polling question is asked.

Tip – If time allows, write your message out before recording it.

Tip – End the message with an appropriate closing such as: Thank you, please use precautions when travelling, Stay safe, etc.

Tip – Speak slowly when recording phone numbers or addresses.

Tip – Listen to your message before saving it. Re-record it if necessary.

Tip – Repeat important information twice in voice messages. If your message is short, try to repeat the entire message.

Tip – Use a polling question, if possible. This enables you to capture valuable data, such as whether the employee or student is safe, will he /she be able to come to work and it also provides acknowledgement that the message was listened to by the recipient. You can then generate response driven metric reports to provide management a real-time pulse of the human impact of the crisis. Finally, asking a question provides consistency which will condition people and improve response rates. They will be happy you are concerned for their wellbeing.

Tip – When using text-to-speech listen to the message. Use phonetics if necessary to clarify words the system has trouble speaking. Text-to-speech is surprisingly good in some systems but on occasion will mangle some words.

Tip – Specify in messages that employees should 'continue to check the Employee Hotline Phone number for updates. Say the number in the message in case they do not know it'.

Tip – Record messages in your voice, if possible, rather than text to speech. It will validate the message.

Tip – Keep text messages short and to the point so they do not have to be split into separate messages due to length.

Tip – Schedule call-list exercise notifications for approximately 7:30 pm local time. Do not schedule after 9 pm. People will get upset if they are called with a test message too late in the evening, especially if they have small children that may be sleeping. Been there, done that with a too late notification approximately 8 years ago. Hey, I can't blame them, lesson learned!

Tip – Practice doing notifications with your team. Stay sharp! Every second counts during a real crisis. The more you use the system, the more comfortable and confident you will be activating it during a real crisis. In my experience, most people do not practice enough. Even if you train people to do notifications, which you must, there will be times that you and your team will be called on to do the complicated ones, when they just do not remember how to use the system or the pressure gets to them during a real crisis. Activating to 38,000 people the first few times can be terrifying. So, my suggestion is you should be very comfortable with your mass notification system.

Tip – Before hitting the 'send' notification button review your message and make certain it is correct. Also make certain you are using the proper recipient list. You do not want to send the wrong message or contact

141

the wrong recipients. I have seen this happen. Listen, if it does happen to you it is not the end of the world. Simply send a 'sorry please disregard' message to the wrong list you used and send the message to the correct list. Don't stress too much. Just another 'lesson learned'. You must stay focused, never get rattled and move forward.

Tip – Understand device-retry rules. Knowing how device-retry rules work will enable you to answer questions concerning non-receipt of a message. I promise you, if the list you send to has 100+ recipients you will get 'why didn't I get a call, email, text, etc.?'

Check the call log. Check the call retry' s. Ask the recipient to check their spam filter. Ask if they opted in. Ask if someone else in their household might have answered the call and forgot to mention it? The bottom line is, in my experience, the system may have hiccupped and not sent a call, but that is few and far between for the good systems. Usually it is incorrect contact data, which we discuss elsewhere in the book, or they received it and did not realize it until you ask them to research a bit. I have actually won a few lunches betting that they received the message.

Tip – Use a consistent naming convention when creating call lists. You may eventually have hundreds of lists so it is important to be organized.
Tip – Use a consistent naming convention when creating scenario templates. You may eventually have hundreds of templates so it is important to be organized.
Tip – Advise employees what to expect in a call list exercise so they are not surprised or confused. I send a very detailed pre-exercise email to the recipients prior to the first call list exercise. The first couple of call list tests should be announced leading up to the exercise rather than using a surprise exercise. I send an email a couple weeks before the date of the exercise and then a couple of reminders the week of the exercise. You can use the system to send the reminder messages. It is good practice for you.
Tip – Use a meaningful caller ID number for voice calls. I favor branding messages with the Employee Hotline Number (see the previous chapter for employee hotline info). If people recognize the phone number, it will significantly increase the likelihood that they will pick up the call. Otherwise, they may think it is a telephone solicitor and will disregard the call.
Tip – Use care when sending a recipient required PIN number to listen to the message. Most systems allow you to add a PIN that the recipient must enter to listen to a secure message. For mass crisis alerts I suggest you do not use a PIN. Imagine there is a tornado warning and someone must scavenge around for their PIN.

Tip – Send a survey from the mass notification system after every call list exercise. Recipients will provide valuable feedback you can use to gauge their satisfaction and improve future notifications. Plus, you will be able to provide management with some nice testimonials.

Tip – When sending text messages use a short code that identifies your company to the recipient. Generally, mass notification vendors can supply you with a short code.

Tip – During a real event, if time permits (not for a time-sensitive event like a tornado), try to get the wording for notification requests emailed to you from the requestor. If the message is time sensitive and the authority cannot email it, have them dictate it and you read the message back to the requester and get their acknowledgement that it is correct. The last thing you need is to hit the send button and they say 'hey I didn't say that'. Yikes, we do not need finger pointing at crunch time.

Tip – Generate pre-designed metrics reports on the results of all test notifications. It is a good way to measure your current ability to reach employees and keep management abreast of progress. Also, generate reports during and after real crisis notifications.

I hope you enjoyed these tips. I provide a regular stream of tips in the Free Ultimate Business Continuity Tips, Techniques and Tools Newsletter.

Great news! There is more mass notification system information in the technology part of this book.

49

MASS NOTIFICATION SYSTEM - BLAST OR ESCALATION?

You just never know when the poop will hit the fan. Seriously! Oh yeah, I once '*got slapped upside the head*' for ringing and pinging too many devices simultaneously. But I would do it again! Read on...

All modern full-featured mass notification systems allow you to send messages by blasting to all contact devices as quickly as possible or using an escalation. Escalations allow you to determine which devices are contacted and spread the messages over a pre-determined time period.

The devices are contacted sequentially rather than simultaneously (blast). For example, you could specify a 20 second buffer between each device attempt for a particular recipient. If a device is answered by a live person (as opposed to an answering machine) the escalation for that recipient stops. The system will not call his/her other devices, as it succeeded in reaching the person.

A blast notification, on the other hand, sends the message to all devices for all recipients as quickly as it can fire them off. In the real world, each recipient will receive the text and email first followed by calls to their voice device(s). The system must queue-up the voice calls and it may take seconds or a couple of minutes to being blasting out to them, depending on the size of the list. All the messages can arrive simultaneously to a user's devices.

For a time-sensitive notification such an approaching tornado, I ALWAYS use a blast, as every second counts. There is greater probability of reaching a person if you contact all their devices. That is one of my selling points when asking users to register multiple devices. On the other hand, for a notification sent the evening prior for an anticipated next-day-storm, I lean toward using an escalation, as the event is not as time sensitive, as measured in seconds or minutes.

I used to prefer sending blasts during call list exercises to test as many devices as possible and familiarize recipients with the way the system works in an extreme emergency. Often, I could identify disconnected devices the employees no longer owned. They just forgot to update their HR record to indicate a new contact number. This data allowed us to

144

loop back to the employees and HR to improve data quality for future notifications.

Be very careful though, as you might find management is 'uncomfortable' with simultaneously receiving calls on multiple devices. Been there, done that. It was not pleasant. One Senior Vice President just could not handle more than one device ringing at the same time. He went ballistic and let the whole world know that his night was ruined because a couple of his phones rang simultaneously and he also received an email and a text message. He just melted down from the confusion. Oh boy! Imagine that! Definitely not the type of person you would want as an Incident Commander.

He immediately had me 'called on the carpet' to explain why I wanted to test all devices. I explained to him the importance of testing as many devices as possible prior to an actual event, but he did not buy it. I had to take one for the team. However, if it helps you guys, it was well worth it.

My advice is even though you send awareness emails 4 weeks, 2 weeks, 1 week and 48 hours prior to a call list exercise, to make people comfortable with the system and the calls they will receive, you should clear whatever process you will use with management or it might cause you a lot of post exercise grief.

50

CRISIS COMMUNICATION CHANNELS - BASIC, BEYOND AND WAY BEYOND

A handy-dandy list of my favorite communication channels. You might want to consider using some or all of these to reach people.

Some are basic and others may be considered innovative such as a favorite of mine – PTT (push to talk). The more methods you have to reach people the better your odds are to be able to connect and communicate important information.

Use these and add your own.

Voice:
- Work desk
- Work mobile
- Home phone
- Personal Mobile
- Google Voice, Skype or other IP phones
- Satellite phone (Sat phone)
- Zello, Mororola, walkie talkie type push to talk (PTT) apps (many can also connect to two-way radios). As an aside my family is hooked on Zello. We use it every day for non-crisis communications. It is fun and efficient.

Email:
- Work email
- Personal email

SMS – text messaging
- Work mobile device
- Personal mobile device

Push Notifications
- Some mass notification systems include apps that allow for push notifications with geo-fencing capabilities so you can dynamically send messages to people within a certain geographic area. More details on this benefit are in the technology part of this book.
- Cable TV – crawl on bottom line. I currently use this as a communication channel for my employees.

Radio Broadcast – many people depend on radio during disruptive events.

Public address system

Alarm system

Other communication tools to consider:

- Desktop alerts – a small widget that allows you to send alerts to thousands of user's desktops in seconds. A must-have in a crisis, such as an active shooter. My favorite mass notification tools include this feature/benefit.
- Slack – I use it for instant messaging and much more. I like using it for disruptive events and business as usual communication and collaboration. It is getting very popular
- Yammer – organizations are now catching on to this collaborative communications tool
- Skype for Business – instant messenger, voice, video conference, auto-attendant
- Twitter – Twitter – Twitter – it can offer great value if used in an intelligent manner
- Facebook organization private page. Zuck is focusing on additional ways to help people report their status during a crisis
- XML, JSON and Really Simple Syndication (RSS) feeds – these are great methods to send and receive news. They have free readers for IOS and Android. An incredible number of sites allow you to access their RSS feeds
- Face-time voice, videoconferencing. Fun fact – I had a part in bringing to market one of the earliest desktop video-conferencing systems in the 1990's named VIDEOVU
- Virtual presence meeting places – Second Life, SoCoCo
- Digital signage boards – They are valuable when employees are moving around your locations. Messages can be dynamically pushed to the boards through an application programming interface (API) from various software systems including my favorite mass notification systems.
- Pagers – I will bet you $1 there are still a bunch out there. I know some hospitals that still use them. Why not, they are reliable.
- Smoke signals and drums. Oh, I am just kidding, OR am I? I can think of at least one influential use-case where it is being used to signal an important appointment of a person.

New methods of communication are being developed all the time. Keep your eyes open to interesting new channels, apps and

Internet of Thing (IoT) devices that you can use for crisis communication. Amazingly, computers can be controlled with brainwaves and eye movement which is wonderful for people that cannot move their hands. At some point in the not too distant future direct mind-to-mind control will become a reality.

51

VOICE OVER INTERNET PROTOCOL (VOIP) CAN BE YOUR COMMUNICATIONS LIFELINE

I have received a great deal of positive feedback from employees regarding the tip discussed in this chapter. If you agree it has value please pay it forward to your employees during a tabletop, in your newsletter or any other way you see fit.

Most of us love our mobile devices, well at least most of the time. They do so much. They are little computers – in size – but have far more computing power than that massive mainframes that put astronauts on the moon, back-in-the-day. Gordon Moore, co-founder of Intel (R) Corporation, stated in 1965 that the number of transistors per square inch on integrated circuits had doubled every year since their invention. Through the ensuing decades his observation, famously known as Moore's law, proved an accurate prediction of the future of computing.

A growing percentage of us, including my son, only own mobile devices – no landlines. Unfortunately, in a crisis mobile cell service can fail us. Cell towers often become overloaded, just when you need to make or receive a critical voice call. Callers may get a busy signal or no signal at all. Yes, sometimes text messages can still be received, as they ride a different transport protocol, but there are times it is important and comforting to hear someone's voice. Plus, believe it or not, some people do not text!

Google Voice and other Voice Over Internet Protocol (IP) based phone services may be beneficial in those situations. Generally, they are free or low cost. I have experience with a number of such services. I happen to enjoy Google Voice. I even use it during non-crisis situations. In fact, I rarely use the desk phone in my office anymore. The only drawback is there is a 3-hour limit per call. Believe it or not, I have actually hit the limit during some conference calls that lasted too long. One way around that is to call into the conference call from another device when you are nearing 3 hours and then calling back on Google Voice and you get another 3 hours. If you somehow max out the next 3 hours you have a bigger problem of insanely long conference calls!

Google Voice is feature rich and just keeps getting better and better. You can make clear voice calls over the Internet to any phone. It does not have to be to another Google Voice number. You even get your own Google Voice phone number. That is handy when you do not want to give out your home or personal mobile numbers. You can set the Google Voice number to forward to any landline or cell device. It works great! Google Voice essentially acts as a call-forward to any device you choose. It has so many other cool options.

If the internet is available, even if cell towers are down, you may be able to reach employees or a family member.
I enjoy Google Voice and you may too. Here is a link to the Google Voice site - https://voice.google.com/.
Please let me know what you think.

P.S. I actually learned about Google Voice while hosting a tabletop quite a few years ago. I have hosted hundreds of tabletops over the years and I thoroughly enjoyed each of them. From feedback I received I believe the attendees felt the same way. I learned from them as they did from me. Then I 'pay what I learn forward' in future exercises. I will have much more to say about conducting tabletops a little later in the testing part of the book.

PART 4 - BIA AND RISK ASSESSMENT

In this part of the book we will cover performing a thorough Business Impact Analysis (BIA) and Risk Assessment (RA) which are the building blocks to making you more resilient and providing incredible value to your employees and organization beyond core business continuity.

To build a solid foundation, we must...

- Understand our assets at a detailed level
- Understand threats that can impact our company, the probability of a threat becoming a reality and the level of impact if the threat becomes a reality. We need to address our vulnerabilities and ultimately our risks
- Understand how we can reduce bad risk
- Understand how we can think laterally to identify and take advantage of 'good risk' opportunities. The result can be an increase in revenue and/or a decrease in expenses.
- Understand how we can use situational awareness tools to our advantage

The BIA and RA will help you identify and evaluate potential impacts (including: financial, life/safety, regulatory, legal/contractual, reputational) of natural and man-made events on your assets. Understanding impacts and probable risks enables you to develop controls to prevent, mitigate, transfer or accept the risks.

The BIA combined with the RA also affords you a tremendous opportunity to add value to your company beyond traditional business continuity! Working through these two foundation cornerstones will enable you to connect the dots and analyze your organization from end-to-end at a level of detail that has probably never been attempted. You and management will gain clarity in ways to reduce bad risk and possibly increase revenue and reduce expenses.

Some of the insight you will derive from the BIA includes:
- Understanding which are your most time sensitive processes.
- Understanding how processes map to each other upstream and downstream – from supply chain to customer and every step in between
- Uncovering redundancies

- Identifying single points of failure
- Discovering process improvement opportunities
- Unleashing surprising internal and external revenue generating and cost reduction opportunities!

All this actionable information can be a goldmine to your organization.

You can then leverage all the information you collected in the BIA and the RA to begin understanding threats, vulnerabilities impacts and risks to your organization. You can intelligently present your findings and suggestions to management. Usually you do it through an executive report and meetings. Appropriate actions to deal with each risk can be decided upon and implemented.

After we discuss BIA tips and techniques I will share my tips and techniques on the RA and risk in general:

- Discover why the sometimes controversial, risk assessment is important to your program
- Learn how to approach risk from a business continuity standpoint
- See what a risk assessment is all about.
- Learn how to do a risk assessment
- Discover the importance of understanding situational awareness
- Predicting events
- Mitigation ideas
- Top threats list
- Learn why risk is a moving target and how we can monitor it leveraging technology

Bonus Cyber Security Threat and Remediation Chapters – Learn about Mobile and Desktop Cyber Security and Internet of Things (IOT) risks, insights and tips.

I have major concerns about desktop, mobile, Internet of Things and Cyber Security threats and risks. Cyber risk is the number one concern for many CEO's. There are people that will cause major harm to our networks and systems if we leave the door open. If your company is like most, then it is critical your networks and systems are up-and-running. Even one serious compromise of a network can seriously impact and even put a company out of business. The kicker is that a lot of breaches and errors originate from employees and contractors – intentionally and unintentionally.

Unfortunately, many critical processes rely on complex systems to operate. There is no going back to doing it manually, as you would in the old days. Remember, a single network compromise, whether it is a

152

virus, worm, malware… can quickly become a major business continuity event – sometimes without a good solution. That will directly impact you.

I suggest after reading this book you begin taking immediate action. Speak with IT, speak with management. At least get your concerns voiced and in writing. You do not want what happened to SONY, The Democratic National Convention, AWS, GitLab and many other companies and public organizations to become a nightmare for you. Take this seriously and prepare before you turn on your computer one morning and there is a ransomware demand – that you very well might be forced to pay. I hope it does not come to that, but we do not operate on hope.

To give you additional leverage when bringing up these important risks to management I included a chapter entitled, *'Cyber breaches = C's on the hot seat!'* Sadly, the list of ousted C's is growing at an alarming rate. Use the list when communicating the seriousness of cyber threats. I am sure it will get management's attention.

P.S. If you are not interested in the cyber security technical information in this section of the book simply skip those chapters at your own risk. I feel strongly that by reading the information and understanding cyber security threats, vulnerabilities and controls in this section it will help you. Even if you just become familiar with terms like botnet, phishing, malware, ransomware and understand the fundamental differences of each, it will make you more comfortable in meetings with IT, Cyber Security and management. You might even offer some insights that will surprise the right people.

The next few chapters will focus on BIA and RA tips and techniques that have worked for me.

Onward and Upward!

52

RECIPE FOR A SUCCESSFUL BIA

The Business Impact Analysis (BIA) will empower you to clearly understand which processes are time-sensitive (critical) to your organization's ongoing success based on several factors. You will be able to accurately gauge when each process needs to be up-and-running and the **impact** to your organization if it is not available when the business requires it.

The BIA also provides information that can provide value beyond core business continuity. It can help generate revenue and identify cost reduction opportunities. I discuss many of those throughout the book. In this chapter I describe the BIA process and interject my techniques, ideas and tips that I have cultivated over the years. You do not have to use them all. Pick, choose, customize and improve the ones you find valuable and interesting.

Tip – I do my initial BIA before doing the Risk Assessment (RA). Some people do the RA and then the BIA. Some very experienced professionals believe it is only about impact and they choose not to do a Risk Assessment at all. I discuss each of these options and my preferences in the Risk Assessment chapter, which follows this one.

The BIA data will provide valuable insight, some of which might well be new to your organization:
- Financial, operational, regulatory and legal impacts on the organization if a process is not available due to a disruptive event
- Which processes are most time-sensitive (critical)?
- What is the most logical order of process recovery?
- Upstream and downstream dependencies

Tip – Prepare for process owner BIA meetings and be ready to collect both qualitative and quantitative data. Both types will be very valuable to you as you move forward. In part one of the book we discussed in detail tips and techniques to get the most out of process owner meetings.

Qualitative data is non-numerical. It is a messier type of data than quantitative. It is more subjective and cannot be precisely measured but can provide important information. For example, you may ask a process owner, '*are you confident your employees are aware of what to do and not do when* *the fire alarms sound?* ' The response may be *'not too confident. There is room for improvement '*.

It can also be observations you make during a conversation. For example, if you ask the process owner about employee morale and he/she roll their eyes and shake their head in a negative manner, it is an important indicator there is a need for improvement.

Quantitative data is more precise numerical data. For example, 'how many sub-processes do you have? how much is a fine for late payment, how many regular employees do you have in your process?' Each of these questions can be answered with a number.

Tip – Process based inter-dependencies upstream and downstream are important. Be sure to include all processes and the end-to-end supply chain as part of the analysis. There could be single points of failure lurking a few levels upstream that could cause peril to your organization if not identified and considered during recovery.

Many companies run lean-and-mean operations. They use just-in-time inventory which makes any breakdown in the supply chain especially disastrous. For instance, the impact from the Fukushima tsunami and power plant meltdown caused Toyota to tumble from the number 1 automaker to number 4, in part because of impacts on their supply chain (parts and paint became issues). Toyota is a model of efficiency so this surprised me. They did eventually regain the number 1 position by analyzing and acting on 'lessons learned' from Fukushima and increasing redundancies.

It is smart to map the supply chain and all upstream and downstream dependencies visually, in addition to textually. My favorite Business Continuity Management (BCM) systems automatically create visual mapping and RTO/RPO gaps for upstream and downstream processes including your supply chain. Also, when analyzing the supply chain be sure to include Tier 1, Tier 2 and Tier 3 suppliers in your analysis. Tier 2 and Tier 3 are often left out of an analysis and that can lead to trouble.

BIA Data Collection and Analysis:
I include the following data elements when collecting process information and dependencies for each process and their associated sub-processes. The fields I list here should be considered a starting point. You know your business better than I do, so add and delete as many fields as you need to build the perfect list for your organization. If the data is important, ask for it!

155

If you are using a robust automated BCM tool ALL this information should AUTOMATICALLY feed your Business Continuity Plans from the BIA collection process. You DO NOT want to go through the error prone and time consuming effort of manually inputting this data again.

Be very detailed in your data collection effort. I suggest analyzing down to the sub-process (sub-department level). Break the recovery dependencies down to timeline buckets, such as: <1 hour, 4 hours, 24 hours...). This will be critical information for you to understand and build appropriate recovery strategies. It will also be important in the event you have to declare a disaster and enact your business continuity during a real crisis. Facilities and IT will need this information to bring processes up in the correct order.

With the right tool, you can automatically do ALL of the above in real-time!

Data collection list – starting point:
- Process (Department) Owner
- Alternate Process (Department) Owner
- Employee dependencies at various time-frames (<1 hr, 4hr, 24 hr, 72 hr, 1 week). Both regular employees and recovery employees
- Employee skill-set matrix. It is important you know the required skills. Additionally, if you map employee skills throughout the organization you may be able to leverage employee resources you might not have initially considered. You can unearth interesting 'hidden' resources. It has happened to me.
- Normal process start-time and end-time (include time zones)
- Work shifts – Great to reduce workstation area recovery seat requirements – especially valuable when you are paying by the seat. I was able to enjoy significant savings using the same seats spread over multiple shifts. More on that later. It can be a nice win for you.
- Critical processing times of the year
- Supplier dependencies at various timeframes (<1 hr, 4hr, 24 hr, 72 hr, 1 week)
- Vendor dependencies at various timeframes (<1 hr, 4hr, 24 hr, 72 hr, 1 week)
- System dependencies at various timeframes (<1 hr, 4hr, 24 hr, 72 hr, 1 week)

156

- System recovery time objectives (RTO) and recovery point objectives (RPO)
- Vital Records – what kind and where they are stored. Hopefully, not in the basement
- Hardware dependencies at various timeframes (<1 hr, 4hr, 24 hr, 72 hr, 1 week) – include the required amount of each item. I included a tip on probing for 'special' equipment below. In my experience, recovery sites have printers, copy machines, etc. It is the special equipment that can be a bigger issue.
- Equipment dependencies at various timeframes (<1 hr, 4hr, 24 hr, 72 hr, 1 week) – include the required amount of each item
- Supplies- include the required amount of each item and when needed

Do you recall the following questions from the process owner high level meeting chapter in part 1 of the book? If you have already asked them, great. If you did not ask them earlier, then now is the time to gather this information. This will be valuable later as you build your recovery strategies. Here they are again:
- Do you keep an updated contact list for your team with you at all times?
- Do your managers have company issued laptops?
- Can managers work from home, if necessary?
- Can your team work from multiple sites or is it necessary for everyone to be physically in one room?
- Do you have critical customer facing toll free numbers? Can you currently re-route the calls if necessary? Have you tested re-routing them?

Tip – In my experience process owners are generally accurate in their assessment of the time-sensitivity of their processes. It is important to communicate to them when they are suggesting a very aggressive RTO – for example <4 hours for marketing, that there will be additional costs involved in building such an aggressive recovery time-frame. Be sure to advise them, if this is the case in your organization, that the goal is to keep the business going and not to attain business as usual. Often the process owners will say, '*hmmm*' and modify their expectations when they realize there is an associated cost with a compressed time-frame and management will ultimately have to sign off on it. **It is your job to level-set this information with the process owners before their responses get to the BIA – RA Management Report.**

Tip – For each process, compare the number of business-as-usual employees in the process to the number of recovery employees required by the process owner. If you are scarce on in-house recovery seats or you are using a third-party recovery vendor and are paying by the seat you should be especially sensitive to the number of seats the process owners need for recovery.

For example, if the sales department has 200 employees and they indicate the require 200 recovery seats you should definitely question that. Remind them the expectation is not 'business as usual'. For example, salespeople often have great flexibility where they can work from. Work from home can be a good option. I only use sales as an example, you should assess the requirements for every process. Consider building this in as one of your automated assessment metrics (discussed in the Automated Assessment chapter later in the book). For each process, establish a baseline of BAU vs recovery employees. When process owners change these data elements you will identify any potential gaps in seat availability and can act on it.

Tip – Multiple shifts can be another way to save on seats. This can be very useful whether you are contracting for seats or building your own recovery site. You may be able to size it smaller if you can utilize shifts. So, probe if there are any constraints on processes splitting staff into 1st, 2nd and 3rd shifts. Customer Service might be difficult unless you are servicing customers in different time zones or globally. Remember, if you are building your own recovery site, do factor in growth. I have built recovery sites both domestically and internationally and shift work was an important factor in each instance. I discuss this in more detail in the Recovery Strategies part of the book.

Tip – Map the process owners' view of the world to IT's view of the world. You may identify important gaps:
Collecting the business view of RTO (process recovery time objective) and RPO (system recovery point objective) against information supplied by IT during an AIA (application impact assessment) provides great value. This will allow you to do a gap analysis that may uncover gaps in what the business needs and what IT is capable of actually delivering. You can do this manually, but a good BCM tool should be able to do calculations and uncover gaps automatically. The benefit is real-time 'even while you sleep' metrics. More on that in the automating assessments chapter.

Tip – Process owners will have no idea what RTO and RPO mean. Explain the purpose and value of each in very simple terms so they can give you accurate answers.

RTO and RPO data will be valuable to:
- Insure the proper backup and recovery strategies are in place to meet the business needs. For example, if you need a system back in 1 hour and you are backing up to tape, there is a big gap between expectations and capabilities. On the other hand, you may be able to save money by doing the analysis and identifying systems that have an overly aggressive recovery solution and the associated expense. You may be able to reduce the expense with a more appropriate recovery solution. For example, you may be running a system active-active for real-time data mirroring – which can be expensive when it is not necessary based on the business requirements to have the system back in 72 hours.
- In addition, you will be able to do system upstream – downstream analysis that can uncover well-hidden gaps in system dependencies that can jeopardize recovery. For example, a critical Tier 1 System may have dependencies on data from a supposedly non-critical Tier 3 system. Perhaps, when restoring systems, your network team will need to bring up that Tier 3 system or the Tier 1 system will not function properly.

System inter-dependencies and business requirements are dynamic, not static. If you build your automated real-time system correctly to monitor all of this information you will uncover gaps in real-time. Otherwise, if done manually, it will be like finding a needle in 10,000 haystacks.

Tip – Over the years I have migrated from using the term 'critical' to using 'time sensitive' when referring to the recovery time-frame for processes. For me, that simple adjustment has worked well. Process owners understandably feel their process is critical and they are right! If the process was not critical, why would the company pay people to do it? If someone hears their process is not 'critical', they might understandably think 'the writing is on the wall' and the company is seeking to dissolve or scale down the process and employees – uh oh! It is easier for process owners to digest that certain processes are more 'time sensitive' than others and it makes sense to give them priority during recovery. We discuss this and other interpersonal tips in the process owner meeting chapter.

Tip – Be open minded when performing your BIA. Experience has taught me that it is advantageous to examine all processes during the BIA analysis, rather than a subset of pre-determined critical processes. I am still not sure how criticality can be accurately determined prior to actually performing a BIA. There could be financial impacts and critical dependency issues that only become apparent when interviewing the process owner and mapping processes and systems upstream and downstream.

An example that hits close to home is when I recently conducted a BIA interview with a seemingly non-critical process. Unfortunately, in many BIA's this process might not have even been included. During the BIA, after some prompting, the process owner said, '*Oh, by the way Marty, there is this one regulatory issue that could come up…* ', Digging a bit deeper, we identified a possible $1,000,000 regulatory risk that could have severely impacted our organization with regulatory, revenue and customer confidence issues. Seems like a time sensitive process to me.

During the same meeting, I discovered the process owner that I was interviewing was the most qualified person to be my onsite business continuity backup if I were not available during a crisis. He was quite knowledgeable about crisis management and business continuity. He described how he helped build plans for a local school as a volunteer. That made my day!

If I had approached the BIA meetings with the notion that this process was out of scope for the BIA analysis, when the inevitable disaster occurred my butt would have been on the line for having not identified the potential regulatory impact. Plus, I can now take an occasional vacation (which I rarely do) knowing I have a qualified backup!
My advice is to go into the BIA with an open mind and let your thorough analysis of each business process define what is time sensitive and what is not.

Tip – Probe for Specialized Equipment and Supplies
When you are doing your BIA follow-up interviews with process owners, ask them about any specialized equipment and custom supplies they will require during a disruption. Make them really think. Present a scenario where they do not have access to their office and must work from home or an alternate recovery site. When you probe them, they may come up with equipment they did not capture on the first draft of the template. (In the Recovery Strategy part of the book I included a chapter on storing specialized equipment off-site).

160

Examples of equipment and supplies I have uncovered during probes:

- MICR printers (check printing)
- checks
- custom forms
- high-speed scanners
- rubber stamps
- headphones
- mice
- extra batteries…

Tip Reality Check: Getting the BIA back on time – some will and some won't:

Some people will be more receptive than others to devoting time to completing their BIA. If you think you will send out twenty emails to process owners asking them to complete their BIA and you will receive them back on time fully completed and then everyone will show for their scheduled BIA follow-up review meeting, I have a bridge in Brooklyn I would like to sell you… In reality, some will and some won't. Follow-up with the people that did not comply, mention the drop-dead due date and then it goes to management on an exception report. People hate being on exception reports! If, after two follow-ups you do not get the survey from them, tough luck on them – report them to management! I realize this is not their main job but you must keep the program moving forward.

Tip – In the BIA intro email to the process owner it helps if you mention that the person of authority, such as the Senior Vice President, endorses the program and will review the results on 'such and such day'. You will get a far higher percentage of completed BIA's returned on time. You will also get a far higher percentage of not getting blown off for the follow-up meeting request. People never like being on management 'lists'.

Tip – Technology can SUPERCHARGE the value of a BIA and make your life easier:

The BIA is NOT a onetime event – or at least it shouldn't be. It is an ongoing process. At the very least you must 're-BIA' once a year. There are so many moving parts in your organization. Things can change on a daily or weekly basis. Here are just a few critical dependencies that can and will change:

- Staffing dependencies
- Time sensitivity requirements

161

- Upstream and downstream process dependencies
- System dependencies
- Telecom dependencies
- Equipment dependencies
- Vendor dependencies
- Please add additional dependencies important to your organization

In fact, if things are not changing in your organization you may have bigger issues. It could be a sign that your business has become stagnant. In today's world of disruptive technologies, disruptors (Netflix, Amazon, Uber) entering your niche may be a growing risk! Identifying this lack of change can be enlightening to management. I build this into my algorithms when automatically assessing my program

The ideal solution is to make your BIA dynamic rather than static. Leverage technology to monitor all changes to your program in real-time. As visionaries, such as Elon Musk and Jack Dorsey say – 'Take it to the 10x level!'

Automation will allow you to identify changes that impact your organization from end-to-end. You can build simple or complex rules (algorithms) and workflows to trigger events and alert the right people instantaneously. This impact/risk insight can simultaneously be automatically reported on a detailed level to process owners and/or summarized to middle and upper management in a dynamic colorful high level dashboard. Imagine a cool real-time dynamic chart changing colors to alert the right people of risks and opportunities. Most importantly, it provides them with a holistic real-time vision of the organization they have never had before. There is immense value and career payback to you for implementing such a visionary system. The automating assessments chapter provides detailed information on the power of having a real-time pulse on your program.

BIA checklist steps:
(All of these steps, and more, are listed in the BCM Online Roadmap included with this book)
1. Decide on the type of data you want to capture
2. Decide on the type of repository you will use to capture and store the information you collect from process owners. Will it be in a spreadsheet (not recommended for mid to large organizations), in word processing docs (again not recommended for mid to larger organizations) or a business continuity management (BCM) system (recommended for many reasons listed throughout the book)

162

3. Decide on which processes will be in scope for the BIA. I suggest **all processes** are in scope for the analysis. Experience has demonstrated to me that pre-conceived notions can be inaccurate and dangerous. In basketball, players on occasion say to refs on a perceived bad foul call, '*ball don't lie*'(refs do not like to hear that). Well, the BIA equivalent would be,'*data don't lie* '. Go by the data you collect to decide what is really time sensitive and what is not!

4. Decide on the type of data collection process you will use. Two popular options are 1) having the process owners take a first try at filling out the BIA in a meeting or 2) emailing them a survey they will fill out. I have done it both ways. I enjoy meeting with them and helping them the complete the BIA. It is fun and I always pick up interesting info. I have also had good results in cases when it was not practical to meet in person so I send them the survey and they complete it. The next few steps describe if they are taking a first cut at completing the BIA

5. I always try to make the BIA very straight-forward. I include simple step-by-step instructions with a description of each field in the template and why we are collecting the information. The process owners take a first cut at completing the BIA. I encourage them to contact me with questions or concerns. We then do follow-up meetings in-person, if practical, or by webinar to review each piece of data

6. Develop a clear concise introductory email that helps process owners understand the goals of the BIA. They must clearly understand what you expect of them

7. Include your BIA template as an attachment or preferably a link to the online version. If they will be completing the BIA in a BCM tool, so much the better. It will save you time, as the BIA data will naturally flow into the Business Continuity Plans and anywhere else you want to analyze and report on the data. The key to normalizing data in all aspects of your program is to enter data only once (gold source) and get value from it in as many ways as possible. Well-designed database systems separate the presentation and data layers. I discuss good basic design in the 'Database or Spreadsheet' chapter in the Technology part of the book

8. Always set a due date for completion and return of the BIA survey. If you keep the survey clean and simple, seven days is plenty of time. Mention that upper management wants to have the process completed by the due date

9. Also, set up a follow-up meeting for ten to fifteen days after you send them the survey. This puts some urgency for them to have their first draft of the BIA back to you before the meeting, so you can review it with them. The purpose of the follow-up meeting is

to walk through the information the process owner provided. You can answer questions and provide additional guidance if needed. You can then finalize the BIA

10. Compile and summarize results in preparation for the upcoming executive management report (to be discussed in an upcoming chapter in this part of the book)

11. Treat yourself to a nice dinner!

12. 'Re-BIA' manually on a regular basis or preferably automate the process and re-BIA in real-time when any piece of information anywhere in your organization changes!

In the next chapter, we will discuss the BIA's partner; The Risk Assessment.

53

RECIPE FOR A SUCCESSFUL RISK ASSESSMENT

The goal of a risk assessment (RA) is to calculate risk as it relates to threats, probabilities, impacts and vulnerabilities. If you think creatively, the risk assessment can also tip you off to business opportunities and revenue generators! This chapter provides one framework for developing a risk assessment. There are many ways it can be performed. There are entire books written on assessing risk.

As with BIA components assessing threats and understanding risk is an ongoing process. It is not a onetime annual or even monthly event. Using the correct situational awareness, database management tools and algorithms you can build an automated risk monitoring engine! This can provide you and management with an understanding of risks and opportunities on a daily and minute-by-minute basis. In some cases risk alerts will be generated in near real-time. I will dig deeper into ideas for automating your program in the 'Automating Assessments' and technology parts of the book. For now, let's chat about fundamentals. As always, I encourage you to modify the information I provide to meet the needs of your organization.

The components of a risk assessment include:
1. Threats – What can potentially hurt us?
2. Probabilities – How likely is it that those threats will impact our assets? What is the probability of each of the threats becoming a reality?
3. Vulnerabilities – What controls do we have in place to deal with the threats?
4. Impacts – If it does happen, what are the consequences?
5. Risks – take all the above into consideration to identify risks and opportunities
6. After we compile the information we list the risks and often graph them!

The risk assessment plus the BIA help us understand:
1. What assets require protection
2. What level of protection is required
3. How an asset may be compromised
4. What is the impact if protections fail

Tip – As you are developing your risk assessment research historical and geographical impacts to the areas your locations are situated in. For example, have there been annual floods or tornadoes impacting your location or the general region?

Tip – As more and more building is being done in coastal areas or near lakes, additional risks arise. If you are located near the ocean consider global warming, rising sea levels, hurricanes and tsunamis. Make sure you have mitigation plans in place. Katrina is a classic example of what can go wrong. I recommend you consider reading *Fives Days at Memorial* by Sheri Fink. She offers a chilling account of what can go wrong and discusses how emergency planning should not be done.

Tip – In addition to partial loss I suggest you always include worst case scenario impacts in your risk assessment, recovery strategies, plans and testing. For example, consider a direct impact completely destroying your hospital, factory, warehouse, securities trading exchange. I realize this is difficult to plan for, as I have done it, but I envy people faced with this sort of challenge. Embrace it! When you figure out the solution, and I know you will, you should rightfully feel proud.

Tip – Make sure you consider the threat of executive leadership not being available at the time of disruption. Plan for succession of ALL key executives.

But wait, there is a bit of controversy regarding business continuity related risk assessments:
I am confident we all can agree it is critical to perform a BIA, which we discussed in the previous chapter. Although there are not too many hard-and-fast standards yet in business continuity, performing a BIA is as close as you will get to a standard. There are companies that skip the BIA and go right to Business Continuity Plans but that is not advised.

What is more controversial is whether we should perform a thorough Risk Assessment, a Risk List or neither.
Many companies do a simple Risk List and some do nothing. In fact, some very influential people in the business continuity profession have published articles on how the Risk Assessment has outlived its usefulness and is a waste of time and effort. Google it, you will see for yourself. You know what? If it works for them that is fine. But I would disagree with them. I am convinced a thorough Risk Assessment can provide great value and will enable you to build a stronger program.

166

Why we need a Risk Assessment:

I realize there are thousands of threats in the world and it would not make sense to create detailed plans for all of them. For example, a volcano is a threat – but is it a risk to my location in Manhattan? I don't think there is a volcano within 1,000 miles of Manhattan, so if I suggest to management we spend money to mitigate the threat of lava flowing down 42nd Street in Manhattan and develop a volcano specific response strategy, it might seem a bit ridiculous. Also, as Nicholas Taleb discussed in his book, 'The Black Swan', no matter how many threats we consider, there are events we would not even think of planning for – until after they occur – and in hindsight we needlessly beat ourselves up for not considering that Black Swan.

Many companies will conduct basic impact planning and simply break down impacts into 3 or 4 high-level buckets such as impacts to people, locations and/or systems. Before we get too far I will go on record that I agree with impact planning and I bake it into my response strategies and plans BUT I also believe we can create so much more value by digging deeper to understand what specific threats have a high probability of occurring (based on data), what the impact would be if they occurred and what we can do to reduce the risk.

For example, performing a thorough risk assessment might make it apparent that your security traders are located on an earthquake fault line, or the geo-location latitude-longitude places your major distribution center in the middle of a flood-zone. Perhaps some of your sites are in a high-crime area... you get the picture. This type of situational awareness is very important to you.

Mapping the probability of certain disruptive events occurring (earthquake on a fault line) to the impacts identified in your recently completed BIA will help you focus on whether it makes business sense for you to do mitigation, risk transfer or at least discuss the risk with management. If they decide to do nothing, well at least you did your due diligence and you will sleep better. **Also, when that next earthquake, flood or fire does occur you will have 'covered your butt', as we say in the profession.**

After you identify and categorize risks, you can then implement controls. The final decision for the type of controls that are needed lies with management. During the risk assessment, your job is to identify and quantify the risks. Some risks you may try to prevent, mitigate or transfer. Others you may decide to accept, if the impact is low and the cost to mitigate is high.

Tip – During the Risk Assessment you will be researching and gathering data. It is also fruitful to brainstorm what-if scenarios with your teams. Discuss possible scenarios. Gather ideas from different people. Encourage them to speak up! Diversity of views is critical to a resilience program. It was a lack of communicating diverse views and everyone simply agreeing that allowed a generator needed to cool nuclear reactors to be placed in the basement in Fukushima, which ultimately contributed to the melt-downs.

- What-if there was an active shooter in the building?
- What-if there was a pandemic and people could not travel?
- What-if you are a logistics company and a major thoroughfare is closed?
- What-if a dirty bomb went off on your block?
- What-if there was a Pandemic?
- What-if there was a plane crash or a railroad derailment adjacent to your location?

If any of these threats can impact your employees or business you can build them into your analysis, controls, planning and tabletop tests.

Threat examples:
- **Natural** – Flooding, Dam/Levee Failure, Severe Thunderstorms (Wind, Rain, Lightning, Hail), Tornadoes, Wind storms, Hurricanes, Tropical Storms, Winter Storms (Snow/Ice), Earthquakes, Tsunamis, Landslides, Volcanos
- **Biological** – Pandemic Disease, Foodborne Illnesses
- **Human – Accidents** -Workplace Accidents, Transportation Accidents (Motor Vehicle, Rail, Water, Air), Structural Failure/Collapse, Mechanical Breakdown
  - **Human – Intentional Acts** – Active Shooter, Labor Strike, Demonstrations, Civil Disturbance (Riot), Bomb Threat, Lost/Separated Person, Child Abduction, Kidnapping/Extortion, Hostage Incident, Cyber/Information Technology (Malware Attack, Hacking, Fraud, Denial of Service, etc.), War, Geopitical, Workplace Violence, Robbery, Sniper Incident, Terrorism (Chemical, Biological, Radiological, Nuclear, Explosives), Arson
  - **Cyber Security** – Ransomware, Virus, Worm, Malware, data theft, Internet of Things
  - **Information Technology** – Loss of Connectivity, Hardware Failure, Lost/Corrupted Data, Application Failure

168

- **Utility Outage** – Telecommunications, Electrical Power, Water, Gas, Steam, Heating/Ventilation/Air Conditioning, Pollution Control System, Sewage System
- **Fire/Explosion** – Fire (Structure, Wildland), Explosion (Chemical, Gas, or Process failure)
- **Hazardous Materials** -Hazardous Material spill/release, Radiological, Accident, Hazmat Incident off-site, Transportation Accidents, Nuclear Power Plant Incident, Natural Gas Leak Supply
- **Supply Chain Interruption** – Supplier Failure (Ties 1, 2 or 3), Transportation Interruption
- **Environment** – Commercial or Commuter Railroad derailment behind the parking lot, Proximity to Airport crash or equipment dropping from sky (it happens), Dangerous Neighbors (chemicals, fireworks)
- **Black Swans** – scenarios we cannot imagine until they occur and then we sort of connect the dots (after the fact) and think we should have thought of them (Taleb)

It is critical to know your assets:
- People
- Locations
- Systems
- Supply Chain
- Equipment

Probabilities (what is the likelihood of our assets being at risk):
This is where it starts to get really interesting and where we can go above and beyond by doing some analysis and data mining. There are many public and commercial data repositories you can data mine. I mention some of my favorites in the technology part of the book.

Never say never! Even if the probability is low – high impact events can and do occur:
- NY Earthquake – Manhattan has experienced earthquakes. There is a fault line in Manhattan. Manhattan is overdue for a significant earthquake. If it should occur the impact could be high. Structures in Manhattan are often very close together. I have measured inches between some building and 20-30 feet between them is not unusual. New York buildings are not designed to earthquake resistant specifications, as they are in San Francisco.

- 100-year hurricane. In reality, it happens more often than every 100 years. New Orleans levees and a sea wall were built to withstand any hurricane…Until they encountered Katrina.
- Floods in the desert – Las Vegas and many other cities have had their share of severe flooding.
- Japan had sea walls prior to the Fukushima earthquake / tsunami. It gave people a false sense of complacency. That can cause people to build near the ocean.
- Nuclear and Dirty Bomb's – Plan for worst case! Many cities are now doing emergency response exercises for full scale nuclear and dirty bomb events. Either can happen but a dirty bomb is easier than a nuclear weapon for terrorists or rogue nations to acquire or build and activate.
- Elecro Magnetic Pulse (EMP) device – could take out significant portions of the electrical grid. Easier than a nuclear weapon for terrorists or rogue nations to build and activate.

Tip – A GREAT SOURCE for hazard information including in many cases, hazard maps, mitigation strategies, planning, success stories and more is **FEMA's Directory of** Emergency Management Agencies **(https://www.fema.gov/emergency-management-agencies)**. In addition to every state in the United States it lists Guam, Commonwealth of the Northern Mariana Islands, Majuro, Republic of the Marshall Islands, Federated States of Micronesia, American Samoa, Koror, Republic of Palau, Puerto Rico and the Virgin Islands. It has a wealth of value.

Vulnerabilities (what are our weaknesses that can increase the impact more than necessary):
For each threat list your vulnerabilities (weaknesses) that would make an asset more susceptible to damage. Vulnerabilities include deficiencies in building construction, process systems, systems security, protection systems and loss prevention programs. They contribute to the severity of damage when an incident occurs. For example, a building without a fire sprinkler system could burn to the ground while a building with a properly designed, installed and maintained fire sprinkler system would suffer limited fire damage. Also, systems that have no login security or employees that are not required to change their login password or laptops that are not encrypted are vulnerabilities. These can lead to cyber security issues. Fortunately, there are simple controls that can be put in place to reduce the risk. I speak to some of those controls in the cyber security chapters in this part of the book.

Impacts:

Understanding the impact if a threat becomes a reality can be derived from the results of your business impact analysis. Look at all factors when considering impacts including:

- Casualties
- Business Interruption
- Location damage
- Loss of customers
- Financial loss
- Fines and penalties
- Lawsuits

Risk Calculation Formula:

When you have identified the threat level, vulnerabilities and impacts (from the BIA), you can plug those into the following risk formula or you can use your own preferred formula:

Risk=Threat x Vulnerability x Impact

Risk Profile Chart Examples:

After you calculate the threats, impacts and vulnerabilities you can rate and profile your risks based on probabilities vs. impacts. Here are a couple of the many types of charts commonly used to visually display risk impact. A simple search on the Internet will provide many additional examples. Usually the upper right portion displays the highest impact risks and the lower left displays the lowest impact risks.

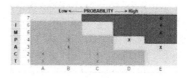

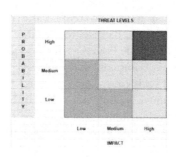

Risk Reduction Strategies:

When you understand your risks and rank them you can then apply the appropriate controls. I provide risk reduction ideas throughout the book including the upcoming cyber chapters.

Prevent or Mitigate the Risk

There are many mitigation strategies you can implement that can reduce damage from threats. Site selection is one such strategy. Natural disasters are not usually caused by nature, often they are caused by humans. Selecting a site that is not subject to flood, storm surge, significant ground shaking from earthquakes or in proximity to hazardous facilities is a first consideration.

Building construction must meet applicable building codes that include requirements for fire protection and life safety. Carefully review high valued assets including data centers, expensive production equipment and hazardous processes to determine the most appropriate protection in accordance with national standards. Computer security should be evaluated on an ongoing basis to determine whether electronic information is secure. New cyber threats arise on a regular basis.

Implement strategies to mitigate electrical power loss include providing uninterruptible power supplies (UPS) and an emergency standby generators for critical equipment. Your business continuity plans with recovery strategies is a key tool for risk mitigation.

You should research applicable fire prevention regulations, national standards and best practices to identify mitigation opportunities and requirements. Confer with your insurance agent, underwriter or broker to determine if they provide consultation services to assist with the development of customized protection specifications for a new or renovated facility. Highly protected facilities may be eligible for reduced insurance premiums. Always work with a respected professional.

Transfer the risk:

Purchasing insurance is a way to reduce the financial impact of a business interruption or loss/damage to a facility or critical equipment. Insurance companies provide coverage for property damage, business interruption, workers' compensation, general liability, automobile liability and many other losses. Losses caused by flood, earthquake, terrorism or pollution may not be covered by standard property insurance policies. Flood insurance coverage for a facility located within a flood zone may possibly be purchased through the National Flood Insurance Program - http://www.floodsmart.gov/.

172

Earthquake, terrorism and pollution coverage may be purchased separately or as an endorsement to an existing policy. Coverage for other hazards such as mold may be provided as part of the basic property insurance, but the amount of loss payable under the policy may be limited.

Business interruption coverage is available to reimburse profits during the business shutdown and certain continuing expenses. Contingent business interruption coverage is available to reimburse losses caused by a supplier failure. Endorsements to standard policies can cover extra expenses, such as the additional costs for expedited delivery of replacement machinery following an insured loss.

Review your insurance policies with your agents, brokers or directly with your insurers to determine whether your insurance policies adequately cover your potential losses. Consider the following recommendations. An **acceptable risk** is a risk that is understood and tolerated. Generally, it is tolerated because the cost or difficulty of implementing an effective countermeasure for the associated vulnerability exceeds the expectation of loss.

Include the supply chain as part of your risk assessment:
A worthwhile exercise is to do an analysis of all of your suppliers and vendors. If a critical supplier failed, would that impact your business? For each entity collect all information that is important to your organization including:

- Their level of criticality
- Are they a single point of failure?
- Do you have alternate suppliers or vendors if the primary one is not available?
- Do they have a tested business continuity plan in place? Can you review results of recent tests?
- Have they been audited by an outside audit company? Can you review the results?
- Can they provide you with a SAS 70 or another certification? I would also recommend an in-person walk through of critical vendor facilities such as data centers

The results of the BIA and the RA will enable you to understand your organization and produce a consolidated report for management. We will discuss the executive report in the next chapter.

54

REPORT YOUR BIA/RA FINDINGS TO MANAGEMENT - AN OPPORTUNITY FOR YOU TO SHINE!

You completed the hard work. Not it is time to wow management with what you have done and what you can do going forward!

After you have completed your Business Impact and Risk Assessment it is time to build an executive report for management's review. I like to do one comprehensive report including both the results of the BIA and RA. The report can also be done separately for each analysis if you prefer. Either way the analysis will provide management with a comprehensive view of criticalities, dependencies, threats and risks.

Go into the meeting confident and proud. You will see, they will love your analysis.
Toward the end of the report include high level recovery strategy recommendations. They do not have to be finely detailed, as strategy development occurs in the next phase of the cycle. Let them know what might make sense and the options that are available. Management will most likely provide valuable input.

Work-up some costs versus impact rationale. During the early years of my career I did not include high level recovery strategies in this report and it was requested by management so I improved the process. These value-added suggestions have always been very well received.

Tip – Great news: having completed a thorough analysis of recovery time-sensitivity, impact and risk your business continuity plans will accurately reflect the reality of your business.

Tip – More great news: if you use an automated BCM system much of the dynamic content in your ensuing business continuity plan will be automatically populated and updated in real-time.

The executive report must be formatted in a professional – visual manner. When I did my first few executive reports years ago I Googled 'executive reports' for ideas on formatting. I admittedly do not have a very 'visual eye'. When I used to develop software systems I would develop the back-ends – databases, logic, algorithms, etc. and I would leave design to the front-end folks. Again, if you are using a BCM tool you may have a nicely formatted and easy to customize Executive Report template that automatically populates – how cool is that!

I structure the sections of my combined BIA, RA Executive Report as follows. Every organization is different so please customize the report for the needs and requirements of your management:

1. Give a short high level overview of the work that was performed
2. List the objectives of the BIA
3. Describe the process you used to gather the information
4. Provide a listing of the processes in scope. I prefer to include all processes in my BIA's
5. Describe the time buckets of time-sensitivity (criticality) to recover the process
6. Provide a list containing each process/sub-process in time sensitivity order from most time sensitive to the least time sensitive.
7. Include the process owner name and a brief description of the major impacts for each process
8. Graph of the process/sub-processes, grouped by time sensitivity buckets, i.e. 1-4 hours…
9. List of process/sub-processes by time sensitivity buckets, i.e. 1-4 hours…
10. Provide regulatory impacts – I list each sub process with a criticality rating, authorities, fines…
11. Provide revenue impacts – you can often get these from sales and/or accounting
12. Provide brand impacts
13. Provide customer loss impacts
14. List IT Systems. Map systems to processes. Include the RTO, RPO
15. List process staffing head-counts – both regular and recovery requirements. I group by time-buckets
16. List employee skills and certifications
17. Provide a summary of general findings during the interviews
18. List threats / hazards to each of your locations
19. Calculate the probability of threats becoming a reality
20. List vulnerabilities
21. List impacts
22. List risks
23. Include the BIA questionnaire you used to collect the results and the responses
24. Include the risk assessment analysis including threats vulnerabilities and impacts

175

25. Include the risk assessment charts (see risk assessment chapter for examples)
26. Summarize all of the findings
27. Describe high level prevention, mitigation and recovery strategies for each process/sub-process

Tip – For discussion purposes with management, include the previously mentioned high level recovery strategies you think are appropriate to meet the business recovery requirements. I show maps with arrows and icons illustrating some possible recovery strategies. I emphasize how I am being cost conscious where it makes sense and I will save them money while still building resilience into the business. I include pictures of workstation area recovery rooms, tech'ed out mobile trailers recovery solutions, etc. Executives are probably not familiar with what is possible to keep their business going. **Wow them with what you can really do!!!**

Executive Report Cycle Steps:
1. Send the comprehensive report to management along with a meeting invite to discuss the report and to answer all of their questions. Give them a few days to read the report prior to the meeting.
2. Meet with them and discuss the report. Some executives will read the report prior to the meeting and some will not. They will have questions and comments. Go through each section with them during the meeting. Keep the acronyms to a minimum. Answer any and all questions.
3. During the meeting, they will probably provide updates and adjustments for you to incorporate in the report. In some cases management might have a different view of the time sensitivity for recovering some of the processes. Occasionally, their view of a process is less time-sensitive than seen through a process owner's lens. I have rarely seen anything drastically misaligned between management and process owners. You will then make the adjustments they request and resubmit the report to management for final sign-off so you can move forward.

Congratulations on getting to this significant milestone. Yes, it is time to celebrate. Enjoy dinner at your favorite restaurant.

A little later in the book we will deep-dive options and ideas for resilient, innovative and cost-effective recovery strategies!

55

MARTY'S TOP THREATS

Welcome to our world!

Every day I get hundreds of threat alerts from situational awareness sources I monitor. They include earthquakes, floods, shootings, fires, power outages, protests... Some sort of threat event occurs every few seconds somewhere in the world.

I analyze the threat data for trends and possible impacts to my organization. Geo-location enables me to manage the avalanche of threats to those most likely to impact my assets. In the situational alerts chapter, in the technology part of the book, we will dig deeper into alerts services you can leverage.

Be forewarned, you might not want to leave your home after you turn on the 'threat faucet' although it is far better to learn about them than to be blindsided. Even worse than you being blindsided is your management getting blindsided. That happened to me once many years ago and I will not let it happen to you if I can prevent it. Fortunately, at this point you and I can lead with the news.

It is important to keep in mind that threats pose different risks to each of your locations. For example, the threat of a major flood in the middle of a desert is minuscule, although they do occur (Las Vegas has had its share of severe floods), while the threat of a flood to your location 100 yards from the Atlantic Ocean in Florida with a data center in the basement is much more of a concern.

Tip – There are many threats we can plan for. There are also ones we cannot plan for. The ones we cannot plan for are described by Nicholas Taleb in his seminal book, *'The Black Swan'* as outliers we cannot see coming. My suggestion is to take a two-prong risk response approach:
1. Plan for high probability specific threats
2. You cannot predict every specific 'Black Swan' threat (meteor, zombie attack...) so also plan your response based on broader
3. 'impacts to critical assets' – people, locations and systems

Tip – When reviewing threats measure your response maturity level. Ask yourself questions such as:
• Have we planned for this?

- How would we respond?
- Have we done training?
- What can we do better?

Examples of high impact threats:
- Active shooter
- Cyber breaches and viruses these can get you on the front page for all the wrong reasons
- Natural disasters – earthquakes, hurricanes, winter storms, floods, avalanches… (location dependent)
- Terrorism
- IOT – Internet of Things security breaches
- Industry disruptors – If you do not see them coming you can be destroyed! For example, Netflix – Blockbuster, Amazon – most brick and mortar retailers.
- Mechanical breakdowns – factory and warehouse equipment… any critical equipment that is a single point of failure (SPOF)
- Supply Chain – Tier 1,2,3 (do not forget tier's 2 and 3)
- Internal mistakes – 'Human Error'
- "Black Swans' – as described by Taleb (mentioned above). These disruptive events are impossible to plan for and can have a huge impact. We cannot see these outliers coming but after the fact we tell ourselves we should have connected-the-dots. This is where impact planning becomes essential!

Below are examples of threats that often-become reality and your headache. Be ready – I can almost guaranty one or more of these are in your future:
- Power outages – local and regional
- Phone systems unavailable – customer service, trading… can't take calls
- Critical software systems unavailable
- Weather that impacts travel
- Squirrels, birds, backhoes… lesser publicized but more frequent

178

56

VITAL RECORDS - CRITICAL LOW-HANGING FRUIT

Vital Records – So critical, yet so often an afterthought...

I can almost bet that there are vital records lurking in cabinets in private and public organizations that would cause an impact if they were not available during a disruptive event. There may even be some important documents 'safely tucked away' in that damp, dusty basement that floods every so often.

Act Now – Before it is too late!
Safely storing and/or imaging vital records is low hanging fruit. It is a quick win with only and upside and no downside. The risk of damaged or lost vital records can easily be mitigated nowadays. The excuse that they are too expensive to scan and image or there is not enough disk storage is 'old school' thinking. You can probably store thousands of your documents on a thumb drive – but please do not do that to prove me right. It is too risky! We will discuss thumb/USB drive risks as well as many other technology related risks in the cyber chapters later in this part of the book.

Carefully and thoroughly gather vital record information during the planning process. I have seen it done during the BIA or plan development stages. Your choice. I prefer to doing it during the BIA dependency analysis. If you happen to join an organization after the BIA and plans were developed and vital records were not included or included as an afterthought, I suggest you make vital records a separate in-depth analysis project. Otherwise, if there were a fire or flood and critical documents were overlooked, guess whose butt will be on the line.

If you can scan paper docs into digital format and store them on your intranet or your secure cloud environment you will save yourself a lot of headaches. Notice I said – secure cloud environment – NOT a personal cloud drive account. Personal cloud storage accounts pose a huge risk for organizations. I discuss that in the risk section of the book. It is one of my top risk factors for organizations.

If your organization has a records information management (RIM) program in place, that will be of great value to you. There may be policies and procedures for properly maintaining critical records. Also, keep in mind it is critical to understand when records should no longer be kept. Speak with the RIM team and your legal staff for more information.

If you do not have a RIM program in place I see a great opportunity for you to bring tremendous value to your organization by leading the vital record protection and compliance projects. Discuss it with management. If they like the idea, which they will, volunteer to participate in the creation of an enterprise RIM program. Partner with HR, legal and any other organizational partners that can help make this happen asap.

In case your vital documents are damaged I also included a chapter in the crisis management section of the book that discusses salvaging damaged vital records.

I suggest you reach out to process owners to understand your vital records vulnerabilities before a flood or fire!

I have used the email below with good results. You can modify it for your own use.

Subject: Vital Records Protection and Compliance

Dear <<process owner name here>>,

Imagine you do not have access to your office, whether it is caused by a fire, flood, gas leak or any other scenario that could impact your office. Take a minute to look around:

- Are there any critical documents you will need to continue your process that are in your office file cabinet and not backed up in digital format?
- Are there any paper or cardboard forms or checks that you would need to continue to do your work?
- Are there any paper documents in the basement? If so, they may be at risk. A flood or fire can destroy them.

If you have any questions, please contact me as soon as possible so we can discuss possibly storing these critical documents off-site and in digital format. You will then have access to them from any recovery site.

Thank you!

<<your name and contact information here>>

57

BEWARE OF THE MORE COMMON 'LITTLE' RISKS - THEY CAN CREATE MAJOR HAVOC

Or – 'How Sandy the Cute Little Squirrel Can Take You Down!'

Many people, including management, often mistakenly believe business continuity and resilience is limited to preparing for major disasters such as hurricanes, earthquakes or terrorism. Although, it is critical to prepare for these large-scale events, in my experience it is more likely that you will be impacted by a lower profile but more probable disruption than one that makes front page news. In fact, it is reasonable to assume you could be impacted by these more probable events a few times a year. Been there, experienced those.

There are occasions these localized disruptions that may only impact your organization can have a larger impact than a more widespread event that impacts everyone. If you are the only organization at a standstill it poses an opportunity for the competition. In a large-scale event, it can be more an even playing field and perhaps, as we discuss in the book, a revenue opportunity for you.

For years, I have incorporated squirrel stories into my tabletop exercises. Whenever I get to the slide showing a cute little squirrel gnawing on a power line everyone laughs. Laughter, during a tabletop, is often a good sign because people arrive at the tabletop tense, mistakenly thinking they must have all the answers or they will get in trouble.

I go on to explain to the attendees that it is not only the less frequent highly publicized events we have to prepare for such as hurricanes or terrorist events, but the more common events such as a backhoe cutting a power line, a car crashing into a telephone pole or a squirrel lunching on a power line. I go on to describe a few stories to them about my experiences with each type of 'I never thought about that' threat and how preparation paid off. The attendees enjoy the stories. Often, they had not thought of these types of threats as a danger to their business.

I tell them a story I lived through during the early years of my business continuity career. I was visiting one of our smaller Connecticut offices to host a tabletop exercise. At 10:15 am we lost power (I know, disruptive events seem to follow me). Luckily, we had a generator that kicked in for part of the building. So, we were able to keep the business going. We tracked the culprit down to a little squirrel that had brunched on a power line. Incredibly, when we found him he was still alive.

There are millions of variations on these types of 'squirelly' power line scenarios. Consider Sully Sullenberger making a perfect landing in the Hudson River off Manhattan after birds got caught in the engines of the airliner he was piloting. That is why from a resilience perspective, my advice is to prepare for specific high impact events such as hurricanes in Florida or tornadoes in Tulsa, but also take a broader approach and prepare for any impact on people, locations and systems regardless of the   cause.

Finally, here are a few case studies of squirrel induced impacts:
Squirrel Causes Electrical Outage in Patchogue: Squirrel eating thru a 700-volt cable. If you are squeamish maybe don't read it: http://patch.com/new-york/patchogue/squirrel-causes-electrical-outage-in-patchogue
Large power outage in Bayshore restored: ATLANTIC HIGHLANDS — Police say a blown transformer triggered a power outage throughout parts of Atlantic Highlands Sunday. A JCP&L spokeswoman said an animal made contact with a piece of equipment, which triggered the outage. About 2,500 homes are affected, she said. http://www.app.com/story/news/local/emergencies/2016/03/27/large-power-outage-bayshore/82329696/
DISNEYLAND, PARTS OF ANAHEIM EXPERIENCE BRIEF POWER   OUTAGE
– http://www.app.com/story/news/local/emergencies/2016/03/27/large-power-outage-bayshore/82329696/
Squirrel sparks Halloween voting outage in Ohio – they had to implement their BC plan! Also I love the squirrel picture in the article
– http://www.cnn.com/2016/11/03/politics/squirrel-voting-outage/
Squirrel causes power outage for 45,000 in East Bay
– http://www.berkeleyside.com/2015/06/08/berkeley-experiences-power-outages-across-town/
This a cool article from the New York Times entitled – 'Squirrel Power!' It has lots of squirrel induced metrics
– http://www.nytimes.com/2013/09/01/opinion/sunday/squirrel-power.html?pagewanted=all

A site called Cyber Squirrel has amazing information on disruptions caused by squirrels, birds, snakes, raccoons, rats and martens. As of 2017 they display 1588+ unclassified animal related disruptions that they have confirmed. 819 of those events were caused by those cute 'lil squirrels I am so fixated on. The events are displayed on an interactive map with pushpins that can be clicked to read more details on each event. Disruptions can also be sorted and read by type of animal. It is such a cool site. The URL is: http://cybersquirrel1.com/

So, think about inserting a cute little squirrel slide in your tabletops. You will get a laugh and more importantly you can drive home the point that we need to prepare for any disruptive event not just the headline makers. If someone asks, '*can a squirrel really impact our organization and take our systems down?*' You can prove to them with confidence that it has happened hundreds of times and it will happen again – but not to your organization!

YOU MUST BE THE DISRUPTOR NEVER THE DISRUPTEE

Disruptive innovation can be a positive and help you generate revenue OR a negative and destroy your business. Either way, it MUST be on your radar. It is a business resilience factor.

I was watching Emily Chang's technology interview show recently on BBC (R) Channel 105 in New York. According to my wife, odds are that you did not see the show. She tells me I am one of the few people that watches tech shows like Studio 1.0, SciTech, Horizons, Click, Hello World and Henry Ford's Innovation nation. Every weekend I watch them all! I love every minute of them. So, what were we talking about again? Oh yeah, disruptive innovation and how it may impact you.

Emily was interviewing Troy Carter the CEO of Atom Factory (R) which is a Mergers and Acquisitions firm. They were talking about his investment in Uber (R), which is about as big a disruptor as you can find. Uber is disrupting the 'people moving' sector. They have already changed the way people move from one place to another and Troy mentioned there is a lot more innovation in the planning stages.

Wikipedia defines **disruptive innovation** as an innovation that creates a new market and value network and eventually disrupts an existing market and value network, displacing established market leading firms, products and alliances. The term was defined and the phenomenon analyzed by Clayton M. Christensen beginning in 1995. In the early 2000s, "significant societal impact" has also been used as an aspect of disruptive innovation. By the way, I have read Clayton's books and I enjoyed them very much.

Consider how disruptive innovation might impact your company. Especially if your company is the 'disruptee' and not the 'disruptor'. I am sure Blockbuster and Sears would agree that disruptors such as Netflix and Amazon had a devastating impact on their business models. If you knew anyone working for either of those formerly profitable companies, chances are they are working somewhere else now – I hope.

Here are more examples of companies that have disrupted entire industries. Some are already household names, but some of the upcoming companies and the industries they are disrupting may surprise you. Is your industry on the list?

- Salesforce (R) – sales
- Airbnb (R) – travel accommodations. They own no hotels or real estate but are valued more than many major hotel chains
- Coursera (R) – education
- Klarna (R) – electronic payments
- Snapchat (R) and Instagram (R) – photos
- Oscar (R) – health insurance, health care
- Mapques (R)t – maps (remember paper maps)
- Apple (R) – many industries including portable music players – remember the Sony (R) Walkman – I do!
- devRant.io (R) – tools for niche specific social networking
- Tesla (R) – car industry, battery industry, space exploration industry, travel (Hyperloop). We need more visionaries like Elon Musk's in the world!
- Waze (R) – driving directions, walking directions. I give credit to Garmin and Tom-Tom as both pivoted to health trackers
- LinkedIn (R) – recruiting – They disrupted recruiters, who now make up a significant portion of LinkedIn's revenue stream
- Uber (R), Lyft (R) – moving people from place to place. They not only disrupting the taxi and limo industries (without the cost of ownership) but an Uber (R) owned company successfully made the first commercial deliveries of beer in the U.S. Their subsidiary autonomous tractor-trailer delivered 40,000+ cans of Budweiser (R). It was autonomous (self-driven) on the highway and then a driver, who was in the sleeping bay, drove the last-miles in the city. But soon a truck will do end-to-end routes and in the future, there will be no drivers needed
- iTunes (R), Spotify (R) – rewrote the music industry
- 23andme (R) – affordable genetic testing, ancestry
- Craigslist (R) – newspapers – those little classified ads were a big revenue stream for newspapers back-in-the-day, but not anymore

A few things you should start thinking about so you do not get a nasty surprise:

- Do you have a way of identifying disruptors in your industry?
- Does your company innovate?
- Could you possibly get blindsided today, next week, next month or next year by a couple of visionaries working in a garage? It does not take a big staff or a lot of advertising to become a

185

disruptor. Keep in mind, a company like Uber did not even own taxis and was able to disrupt an entire industry. It only requires an idea and a creative plan to execute the idea. Disruptors can use low-cost Internet guerrilla marketing techniques to own an industry

Technology has been a great enabler of new platforms. Innovative startups can roll out product quickly and grab market share. The disruptive nature of technology will continue to become more powerful and available in the coming decades as the cost for the three most critical technology components: chip power, data storage and bandwidth their assault on approaching nearly 'free' or too small to measure. For a great book on this phenomenon I recommend you read, *'Free: The Future of a Radical Price'*, by Chris Anderson.

It is important for your company to have a pulse into what is occurring in your industry. Fortunately, there are tools that can help you. Google alerts is a good free tool. Twitter also has a search capability. The trick is to turn this avalanche of raw data available to us into insights. In the technology section of the book I discuss how we can leverage situational awareness tools in more depth.

Market research tools can also provide great insight in a rapidly changing environment. These tools intrigue me as my favorites use cutting edge technology to gather, analyze and publish rich information in a timely manner. Brilliant technologists are leveraging sophisticated machine learning techniques and predictive analytics to identify meaningful insights buried in terabytes of data. Rather than simply passing the raw data through, they add value that matches a business's needs. They monitor thousands of news sources plus social media. Many of the sources are commercial grade subscription services that they have partnered with.

Importantly, some use machine learning and predictive analytics algorithms to provide insight into what may happen next, before it happens! I am not saying it is a crystal ball but it does give you sort of a peak into the future and potentially a competitive advantage.
I was impressed so I passed on some of the insights to friends in the business plus a few supply-chain professionals. They told me it generally took them at least half a day to discover what I had produced in minutes and in some cases they would never have stumbled across the information that was automatically generated by the system while I was sleeping.

Mapping the results from these tools to your BIA and RA can help you create the ultimate near real-time business continuity threat, risk and opportunity tool. This dynamic information can give you an edge in the marketplace.

I do not recommend tools in the book as the landscape changes and new tools come on the market. If you are interested in my current favorite tools please contact me – marty@ultimatebusinesscontinuity.com.

The bottom line is you must keep disruptive innovation on your radar. Always be the disruptor not the disruptee!

59

HEALTH IMPACTS - ACHOO!!! HOW THE 100 MPH - 20 FT SNEEZE CAN BECOME A SERIOUS CONTINUITY CONCERN

People are our most important asset. I cannot tell you how to run your business but I will suggest when people are sick they be encouraged to work from home or take a sick day. Germs and disease can trigger a crisis.

Many of us work in close quarters in our offices. There is great danger in spreading disease throughout the office if someone is contagious. Consider implementing awareness and 'when not to come into the office' policies to protect employees and your business.

Public transportation is another hot-spot where disease can easily spread. I often experience firsthand people on the train sneezing and coughing into the air. The germs then hang around and spread. By some estimates sneezes can travel 100 mph and up to 20 feet! It may be a bit extreme but I recently changed my seat on the way home three times during a 45-minute train commute due to rampant sneeze blasts. On a positive note, I rarely get sick. Uh oh, I hope I did not just jinx myself.

During pandemic planning we seem to tighten the reigns on this issue. When pandemic is no longer front page news it seems, we go back to our old ways.

Flu can easily be passed from person-to-person. Our primary concern is the health of our employees. Also, consider the business continuity aspects if a high percentage of people get sick because of the unnecessary spread of germs.

If people are sick and insist on coming to work, they should be considerate when sneezing and coughing. They should sneeze or cough into their arm. They should use care when touching objects that others may use, such as door knobs.

Tip – Keep safety masks in your office if someone wants to wear one.

Tip – Keep disinfectant dispensers at high traffic points throughout your office.

Six tips from the Center for Disease Control (CDC):
(Click here for additional CDC good practices to help prevent the spread of germs)

1. Avoid close contact with people who are sick. When you are sick, keep your distance from others to protect them from getting sick too.

2. If possible, stay home from work, school and errands when you are sick. This will help prevent spreading your illness to others.

3. Cover your mouth and nose with a tissue when coughing or sneezing. It may prevent those around you from getting sick.

4. Clean your hands. Washing your hands often will help protect you from getting germs. If soap and water are not available, use an alcohol-based hand rub.

5. Avoid touching your eyes, nose or mouth. Germs are often spread when a person touches something that is contaminated with germs and then touches his or her eyes, nose, or mouth.

6. Practice other good health habits:

- Clean and disinfect frequently touched surfaces, especially when someone is ill. Get plenty of sleep, be physically active, manage your stress, drink plenty of fluids, and eat nutritious food
- Cover your mouth and nose with a tissue when you cough or sneeze - https://www.cdc.gov/flu/protect/covercough.htm
- Put your used tissue in a waste basket
- If you don't have a tissue, cough or sneeze into your upper sleeve, not your hands
- Remember to wash your hands with soap and water after coughing or sneezing
- Keeping your hands clean through improved hand hygiene is important to avoid getting sick and spreading germs to others. Many diseases and conditions are spread by not washing hands with soap and clean running water
- If clean running water is not accessible, as is common in many parts of the world, use soap and available water. If soap and water are unavailable, use an alcohol-based hand sanitizer that contains at least 60% alcohol to clean hands

Cough etiquette is especially important for infection control measures in healthcare settings, such as emergency departments, doctor's offices, and clinics. More information on respiratory hygiene and cough etiquette in healthcare settings may be found on CDC's seasonal flu pages.

Stay well!

189

CYBER SECURITY - C'S IN THE HOT SEAT

I compiled this ready to use list in case your management is not paying attention or does not understand the criticality when you alert them to cyber threats, vulnerabilities and infrastructure risks. You can cherry pick some examples from this list that just might get their attention.

Unfortunately, this list expands at an alarming rate, often on a weekly basis. When a cyber security breach occurs, it is often the 'C' (Chief executive) that is held accountable, and loses his/her job. The well-coiffed public story may that he or she resigned to spend more time with family or he or she retired... In reality, it is most likely they were either fired or pressured to resign. The impact is, the person who was in the seat before the cyber issue is no longer employed by the organization.

Cyber security breaches, malware and hacking are big issues to C levels. When I interview C levels one of my questions is, as you have heard me say over and over, *'what keeps you up at night?'* The past few years it has ALWAYS been data breaches, ransomware, viruses and critical systems not being available. Many realize that just one cyber-attack that paralyzes the organization and they may be 'retired'!

Here are an unlucky 13 breaches from the past. I am sure, with minimal research, you can add many more:
Sony Pictures (R) – Co-Chair – OUT
Sony Playstation (R) – CEO – Resigned – OUT
Target (R) -CEO – Resigned – OUT
Target (R) – CIO – Resigned – OUT
Ashley Madison (R) – CEO – OUT
Experian (R) – CEO Resigned – OUT
Anthem (R) – investors said time to remove the CEO
AOL (R) – CTO – OUT
Utah State Department of Technology Services – Head of Technology Services – Fired
Austrian aerospace parts manufacturer FACC (R) – CEO – Fired
U.S Office of Personnel Management (OPM) – CIO – Resigned
Maricopa County Community College – CIO – Fired
Bangladesh Central Bank – Bank Chief – Resigned

CYBER SECURITY - YOUR LAPTOP HAS 'LEGS'

The fact that modern laptops are small, light and mobile means they can also be high-risk for us and low-hanging-fruit for criminals. That is a dangerous combination. Whether the criminal's intent is to resell the hardware or sensitive information stored on the laptop the impact to you and your company can be extremely high. One stolen laptop with sensitive data can lead to a devastating cyber security problem for your organization.

True story: I learned of a company that left laptops unlocked and un-encrypted on cubicle desks near exit doors. A thief shoulder-surfed behind an employee and easily gained access to the office. Supposedly it was a secure work area but unless you are using a turnstile or there is an unusually alert $10 an hour guard on duty, you know as well as I, not everyone badges-in. Few employees entering a building question the person behind them, especially in mid and large companies where you only know a small percentage of the employees. This is way too easy an opportunity for the bad guys!

The shoulder-surfing thief easily got access to the office, grabbed six laptops, threw them in a backpack and scooted right out the door. Sure, the entrance and exit doors were under video surveillance but by the time the video was reviewed the thief, laptops and more importantly the un-encrypted sensitive customer data was long gone. Probably the data was already on the dark web being sold to all takers for pennies on the dollar by the time the theft was realized.

In another true story an executive placed his laptop under his seat in an airport waiting area for 'just a couple of minutes' to go to the bathroom. The laptop might as well have had a sign on it 'Please Take Me'. Well you guessed it, when he got back from his 'business' his laptop was gone-baby-gone. The executive was shocked and panicked. I could list hundreds of similar stories and I am confident you could as well.

Here are some tips to help protect your laptops AND especially your data:
Tip – Create a laptop security policy and publish it to all employees.

Tip – Laptops should have remote tracking devices activated. Depending on your employee/union environment this may be a challenge to implement. Partner with HR and legal, if necessary.

Tip – Physically secure your laptops in the office. The story I described is but one of many of criminal's shoulder-surfing or otherwise social engineering their way into lightly secured workplaces and stealing laptops. Remember, it only takes one laptop with sensitive customer or employee data to put your company in the headlines, for all the wrong reasons.

Can your office environment be compromised? Think about it. No, better than thinking about it take a walk around your office, factory or warehouse. Shoulder-surf in behind people you do not know. Let management know that you are going to perform a 'laptop theft scenario' in advance so you do not get in trouble.

Place a test laptop in a cubicle and then come back and walk out with it. Did you meet with resistance or did the security guard that does not know you hold the door open for you? If you were stopped and questioned, great! If not, mitigate this risk asap.

If there is even a remote possibility that your laptops and data can 'walk', fix this risk today. Losing $5k-$10k of laptop hardware is bad but possibly losing sensitive data can be devastating. Fines can be in the millions of dollars and high level C heads will roll.

Tip – Desktop and laptop USB ports should not accept unauthorized USB drives! They can be disabled or programmed to only accept authorized devices. There are many horror stories caused by USB drives planting malware and viruses. One shiny new USB drive picked up in a parking lot by an unsuspecting employee and popped into a networked laptop USB port can bring down a network, after sensitive customer data has been siphoned off. Believe it or not, this happened to one of the top data security companies in the world and it impacted many of their global clients, including some of the largest companies in the world. All from one evil USB found in a parking lot by an HR employee and innocently popped into a networked laptop.

In addition to USB drives planting viruses they can be used to steal gigabytes of data. If you watch enough TV shows that deal with hi-tech crime you will know that using a USB drive is no secret.

192

Tip – Laptops should ALWAYS be kept close-at-hand and attended to when traveling. Let me stress that – ALWAYS!

Tip – Laptops should never be left in the trunk of a parked car. Cars do get stolen and criminals can follow you after seeing you deposit a laptop in your car trunk. Trunks are easy to break into in seconds. Blink, and your laptop and data is gone!

Coincidentally, I had written the above tip a couple of weeks prior to a government laptop with sensitive data being stolen from an agent's car trunk. Supposedly, the laptop drive was encrypted, although encryption can be broken. I wish I published earlier and the agent had read the book. Maybe the agent would have taken the laptop out of the trunk and the theft would not have occurred.

The bottom line is partner with IT, Cyber Security, Physical Security and Safety to beef up your mobile policies and employee awareness as soon as possible.

CYBER SECURITY - PERSONAL CLOUD DATA STORAGE RISKS ARE SERIOUS!

I broke this alert out so there is no chance of you missing it... Employees storing organizational data on personal cloud drives is a serious concern!

If employees are storing company data on services such as Dropbox or Box in their personal accounts there could be big cyber and data security issues in your future. These services are valuable for personal use but not unauthorized professional use.

I have received knowledge of companies where employees are saving sensitive organizational information to their personal cloud storage accounts. Some companies may have thousands of these types of risks floating around in the cloud. Speak to your IT or Cyber Security department if you think this is a risk at your organization. Communicate any risk to management as well.

Employees can become disgruntled and when they leave your organization do you really want them to have access to potentially sensitive organization and customer information?

- Imagine if a competitor got hold of this information!
- Imagine if the cloud vendor was hacked and sensitive data fell into the hands of cyber thieves. Your organization could be libel for not properly protecting the data. You could be subject to severe fines!

Be very careful. Create a data policy, if you do not have one in place or add this to your existing data security policy.

The bottom line is storing company data on a personal cloud storage account is bad and must be mitigated before it is too late.

CYBER SECURITY - THREATS AND VULNERABILITIES 101

Warning: Please do not read this chapter before you go to sleep.

Threats to the security of desktop, mobile devices and the data on those devices has exploded in recent years. We all know of organizations that have been compromised. There is a saying that there are only two types of companies; the ones that have been cyber compromised and admit it and the ones that have been cyber compromised and do not admit it. The vast majority of cybercrime instances are not publicized.

When I interview high level leaders in organizations and ask the very important question, '*What keeps you up at night?* ', the number one operational concern in recent years has been cyber security and systems related issues including ransomware, viruses, malware, data-breaches, latency and critical systems not being available.

I realize most people reading this book are not Cyber Security or IT experts, although I sometime straddle the line, but if sensitive data is stolen from your organization that has not been encrypted or malware originating from a desktop or mobile device infects your intranet, encrypts all your files and demands ransom or else everything will be deleted, you will have a major business continuity event on your hands.

This chapter is not intended to be a comprehensive course on cyber security. My goal is to make you aware of threats, vulnerabilities and in an upcoming chapter discuss best practices that can help you avoid a nightmare scenario. Consider these chapters a launchpad for you.
I do feel it would behoove you to learn as much as you can about cyber security, especially if it interests you. Unfortunately, it will only become more important in the coming years as cyber-attacks become more complex and occur more often. It can also open new career avenues for you. I know business continuity professionals that transitioned to red-hot cyber related positions such as Chief Information and Security Officer (CISO). You are in the perfect position to learn as much as you want to about cyber security as it will help you do a better job. It is the cousin of business continuity and resilience. In many organizations cyber security, IT, risk and business continuity report to the same

management. Knowledge of business continuity, resilience and cyber security will put you in an enviable position.

information in this chapter spans mobile and desktops threats and vulnerabilities. Most of the threats apply to both platforms. Where a threat is mobile specific I try to point it out.

The use of mobile devices including phones, tablets and Internet of Things (IOT) devices is growing exponentially. Billions of devices beyond traditionally tethered desktops now ride the internet and often have access to our internal networks. Business Resilience – Business Continuity (BRBC) Professionals should be VERY concerned that these devices have proper security controls. Many of them do not! Mobile and desktop vulnerabilities that are exploited can become high profile difficult business continuity events. Upper management should understand that heads will roll.

Malware (software intended to do evil), ransomware, phishing, viruses, worms and theft of portable devises increases every year. Vulnerabilities are out of control in many organizations. Cyber criminals use a variety of attack methods, including intercepting data as they are transmitted to and from mobile devices and inserting malicious code into software applications to gain access to users' sensitive information. These threats and attacks are facilitated by vulnerabilities in the design and configuration of mobile devices, as well as the ways people use them. Common vulnerabilities can be as simple as the failure to enable password protection and include operating systems that are not kept up to date with the latest security patches.

You can use a lot of the info in this chapter when speaking with your IT people. We do not want anyone to lose their job as a result of being complacent and thinking 'it won't happen to me' – until it does!

Examples of nasty, expensive, embarrassing disruptive events include:

- Fines against a company for distributing malware versions of an application that triggered mobile devices to send costly text messages to a premium-rate telephone number.

- Many Android devices in China were infected with malware that connected them to a botnet. The botnet's operator could remotely control the devices and incur charges on user accounts connecting users to pay-per-view video services. The number of infected devices able to generate revenue on any given day ranged from 10,000 to 30,000, enough to potentially net the botnet's operator millions of dollars annually if infection rates were sustained.

196

Believe it or not that number of botnet devices is relatively small compared to botnets numbering in the millions of devices!

- An ex-NSA contractor allegedly stole 50 terabytes of data including top secret documents. That amounts to over 50 million pages of information. To put it in context the Library of Congress print collection is 'only' approximately 15 terabytes!

- The FTC reached a settlement of an unfair practice case with a company after alleging that its mobile application was likely to cause consumers to unwittingly disclose personal files, such as pictures and videos, stored on their smartphones and tablets. The company had configured the application's default settings so that upon installation and set-up it would publicly share users' photos, videos, documents, and other files stored on those devices.

- I discuss the alleged cyber-attack by North Korea on SONY (R) Corporation later in the chapter. It was reported that that virus was sitting in their network for months before the attack

- The Las Vegas Sands(R) Corporation, owner of major casinos, had a major cyber-attack in 2014 that was not revealed until 2016. Malware crippled thousands of servers and workstations on their network.

- The WannaCry Ransomware attack hit on Friday, 12 May 2017. Within 24 hours it was reported to have infected more than 235,000 computers in over 150 countries. I can confidently assure you it was more damaging than the publicized numbers. Speaking with cyber security friends, I know of many companies impacted by the event. In my opinion had the malware been released earlier in the week it would have caused a much bigger financial impact. Many companies had the weekend to 'hopefully' clean up the mess. I say 'hopefully' in the hope that it did not leave 'sleeper agent software' on networks. The kicker is the virus was completely avoidable if systems had simply been patched. We will discuss patching and other best practices in the upcoming 'Cyber Security – Best Practice Tips' chapter.

- Please also read the 'Cyber Security – C's On The Hot Seat' chapter a bit later in this part of the book for a buffet of other cyber causalities.

Sources of Threats and Attack Methods Vary

The increasing prevalence of attacks against desktop, mobile and IOT devices makes it important to assess and understand the nature of the threats they face and the vulnerabilities these attacks exploit. We do not need these threats to manifest into serious business continuity events.

Threats can be unintentional or intentional. Unintentional threats can be caused by software upgrades or defective equipment that inadvertently disrupt systems. Intentional threats include both targeted and random attacks from a variety of sources, including botnet operators, cyber criminals, hackers, foreign nations engaged in espionage, disgruntled employees, students and terrorists. These threat sources vary in terms of the capabilities of the organizations, their willingness to act and their motives. These include monetary gain, political advantage or anger at a specific organization. For example, cyber criminals are using various attack methods to access sensitive information that is stored on and transmitted by connected devices. There is a lot of profit in selling sensitive data or encrypting it and demanding ransomware to 'set it free'.

Here is a short list of people that can compromise your network and take you down:
*Some of the information below originates from the GAO report: 'Information Security – Better Implementation of Controls for Mobile Devices Should Be Encouraged', with my additions and annotations.

Threat – Botnet operators:
Botnet operators use malware distributed to large numbers of desktop and mobile devices to coordinate remotely controlled attacks on websites and to distribute ransomware, phishing schemes, spam, and further malware attacks on individual mobile devices. When you read front page news about Distributed Denial of Service (DDoS) attacks making popular websites inaccessible, they are often initiated by large botnets. Botnets can be in the tens of millions of computers directing traffic at a targeted site. DDoS is very difficult to stop and can bring a business that is not prepared to a standstill. Botnets and the underlying bots are getting exponentially more sophisticated.

Threat – Cyber criminals:
Cyber criminals generally attack devices for monetary gain. Ransomware is becoming a weapon of choice. Cyber criminals may use viruses, worms, spam, phishing, and spyware/malware to gain access to the information stored on a device, which they then use to commit identity theft, online fraud, and computer extortion. They may encrypt files and demand ransom in the form of electronic currency to decrypt the files. In addition, international criminal organizations pose a threat to corporations, schools, government agencies and other institutions by attacking mobile devices to conduct industrial espionage and large-scale monetary and intellectual property theft.

198

Threat – Foreign governments

Nation-state attacks are launched by foreign countries. Some are extremely sophisticated. It has been suggested that North Korea attacked SONY and Russia hacked the Democratic National Convention. Both front page news. It is often difficult to track the origination to a particular country. There have also been suggestions various nation states have gained unauthorized access to sensitive governmental systems. In fact, it has been widely reported that Russia initiated 6,500+ cyber-attacks against the Ukraine within a 60 day period.

Tip – A great book on cyber warfare is, *'iWar: War and Peace in the Information Age'* by Bill Gertz.

Tip – I have a lot more to communicate about the coming Cyber Wars in chilling articles in the Ultimate Business Continuity Tips, Techniques and Tools Newsletter. I will also be describing nation-state system probes and damaging attacks that have already occurred against critical infrastructure.

Not a Threat – Ethical Hackers – the good guys

Before I describe unethical hacking I just want to mention that in the software development profession the term 'hacking a system' and 'ethical hacking' can mean coming up with something creative or testing a system to discover vulnerabilities and close them before an unethical attack.

Threat – Unethical Hackers – the bad guys

I enjoyed the movie War Games with Matthew Broderick, back in the day. It still holds up in a quaint sort of way. Unfortunately, unethical hackers can cause havoc on mobile devices. Hackers may attack mobile devices to demonstrate their skill or gain prestige in the hacker community. While hacking once required a fair amount of skill or computer knowledge, hackers can now download attack scripts and protocols from the Internet and easily launch them against desktop, mobile and millions of IOT devices. It does not take a lot of technical talent. The Dark Web is packed with scripts and stolen sensitive data including credit card and social security numbers for sale to all takers. I strongly suggest that you do not venture onto the Dark Web.

Terrorists

Terrorists may seek to destroy, incapacitate, or exploit critical infrastructures such as computer networks to threaten national security or damage public morale and confidence. Terrorists may also use phishing schemes or spyware/malware to generate funds or gather sensitive information from mobile, desktop or IOT devices.

Common Attack Techniques Used by the Groups Described Above:

Browser exploits:

These exploits are designed to take advantage of vulnerabilities in software used to access websites. Visiting certain web pages and/or clicking on certain hyperlinks can trigger browser exploits that install malware or perform other adverse actions on a mobile device. Older versions of Internet Explorer had many browser exploits, as it was targeted due to its popularity. Additional details on a few types of common browser exploits are listed below.

Data interception:

Thieves can easily pick up open Wi-Fi and read (sniff) unencrypted data. If you send un-encrypted data on the Internet it can pass through many servers in clear (readable) text. Only send un-encrypted data if you do not mind anyone reading and using it. Data on the Internet travels in funny ways. Using IP (Internet Protocol), messages sent to your friend who lives on your street can traverse the globe and go through many servers. The message can be intercepted and read at any point. It is quite easy to intercept (sniff) messages.

Keystroke logging:

This is a type of malware that records keystrokes on desktop or mobile devices in order to capture sensitive information, such as credit card numbers. Generally, keystroke loggers transmit the information they capture to a cyber criminal's website or e-mail address. This is very dangerous and very prevalent. At a dinner-party a while back a friend asked me if his spouse could intercept what he was inputting on his desktop or mobile device. My answer was, *'yes, it is easy with a keystroke logger.'* His face turned red – uh, oh!

Malware:

Unfortunately, too many people have been a victim of malware. Malware targets desktops, mobile devices and IOT devices. Malware is often disguised as a game, patch, utility, or other useful third-party software application. Malware can include spyware (software that is secretly installed to gather information on individuals or organizations without their knowledge), viruses (a program that can copy itself and infect the mobile system without permission or knowledge of the user), and Trojans (a type of malware that disguises itself as or hides itself within a legitimate file).

Once installed, malware can initiate a wide range of attacks and spread itself onto other devices. The malicious application can perform a variety of functions, including accessing location information and other sensitive information, gaining read/write access to the user's browsing history, as well as initiating telephone calls, activating the device's microphone or camera to surreptitiously record information, and downloading other malicious applications. Repackaging—the process of modifying a legitimate application to insert malicious code.

Malware can also install **sleeper agent software**. It is insidious code that lies in a waiting for a particular trigger, such as a future date, to launch itself and attack your systems. It can also open ports, back doors and/or steal your data.

One malware attack on your organization can bring your network and business to a standstill. Be careful, malware is a very serious concern. I will have more to say on malware prevention and mitigation in the cyber best practices chapter.

Old Operating Systems:

Operating systems that are out of date or being phased out can pose great risks. For example, systems running on XP are probably not being patched and can be easy targets for hackers to gain entry to your network. I know of critical systems that were still being run on XP log after it was actively supported and perhaps are still a risk. I have a feeling if I had a dollar for every computer running XP I would be a rich man.

Unauthorized location tracking:

Do you want the bad guys to know where you are OR are not? It is like saying, 'I am not home, come break into my house and rob me!' Location tracking allows the whereabouts of registered mobile devices to be known and monitored. While it can be done openly for legitimate purposes, it may also take place surreptitiously. Location data may be obtained through legitimate software applications as well as malware loaded on a user's mobile device. Also, use care when posting pictures on social media. The pictures can contain location metadata that can be used by criminals.

Phishing:

Phishing is a one of the most popular scams. A phishing attack frequently uses e-mail or pop-up messages to deceive people into disclosing sensitive information. Internet scammers use e-mail bait to "phish" for passwords and financial information from mobile users and other Internet users. I have done ethical phishing tests for organizations where 70% of users clicked on a link that, had it not been a test, would have infected a network. Phishing emails are hard to detect from the real thing. I have suggestions on dealing with phishing in the next chapter. I also have a recommendation on a phishing prevention company that I respect.

SCADA software and hardware:
Supervisory control and data acquisition (**SCADA**) is a system of **software** and hardware elements that allows industrial organizations to control industrial processes locally or at remote locations. It also can monitor, gather, and process real-time data. The risk can be great and physically dangerous. Often SCADA systems are not patched in a timely manner or at all if the vendor no longer exists or does not publish a patch. An attack on a SCADA system can melt down critical infrastructure components or spin a nuclear centrifuge out of control. Both have happened. I go into more detail on SCADA risks and breaches in the Ultimate Business Continuity Tips, Techniques and Tools Newsletter.

Spamming:
Spam is unsolicited commercial e-mail advertising for products, services and websites. Spam can also be used as a delivery mechanism for malicious software. Spam can appear in text messages as well as email. Besides the inconvenience of deleting spam, users may face charges for unwanted text messages. Spam can also be used for phishing attempts. Spamming goes back to the dawn of email decades ago. If you think it does not work you would not be correct. Unfortunately, spam can be very profitable as the cost to send spam is so inexpensive. Some spammers can make a fortune with click thru's of only one in a million.

Spoofing:
Attackers may create fraudulent websites to mimic or "spoof" legitimate sites and in some cases, may use the fraudulent sites to distribute malware to mobile or desktop devices. Email spoofing occurs when the sender address and other parts of an e-mail header are altered to appear as though the e-mail originated from a different source. Spoofing hides the origin of an e-mail message. Spoofed emails may contain malware. Security firewalls and software sometimes will mistakenly think an address is being spoofed when you actually want to have a large number of emails come into your intranet. An example of this would be the use of an outsourced mass notification tool. In that case your IT department

202

can white-list the vendor IP address sending the emails to your employees. Otherwise the messages will be blocked.

Zero-day exploits:
This is a difficult one to deal with. A zero-day exploit takes advantage of a security vulnerability before an update for the vulnerability is available. By writing an exploit for an unknown vulnerability, the attacker creates a potential threat because mobile devices generally will not have software patches to prevent the exploit from succeeding.

Now let us discuss a range of vulnerabilities below which can become serious business continuity events. Some of these are mobile specific and many apply to mobile and desktops. In the chapter after the next we will talk about compensating controls for many of these vulnerabilities. You can even use some of that information as awareness tips in your newsletter, tabletops or website.

Mobile, desktop and IOT devices are subject to numerous security vulnerabilities that can facilitate attacks, including password protection not being enabled, the inability to intercept malware, and operating systems that are not kept up to date with the latest security patches. While this is not a comprehensive list of all possible vulnerabilities, the following 11 vulnerabilities can be devastating. Fortunately, many are easy to correct.

- **Devices often do not have passwords enabled.** Mobile devices often lack passwords to authenticate users and control access to data stored on the devices. Many devices have the technical capability to support passwords, personal identification numbers (PINs), or pattern screen locks for authentication. Mobile devices running IOS and Android also include a biometric reader to scan a fingerprint for authentication. However, many employees do not use this feature. As racewalker and runner I have found when my fingers sweat the biometric reader does not work – grrrr. Additionally, if users do use a password or PINs they often choose passwords or PINs that can be easily determined or bypassed, such as 1234 or 0000 or their spouses first name... Without passwords or PINs to lock the device, there is increased risk that information from stolen or lost phones could be accessed by unauthorized users who could view sensitive information and misuse mobile devices.

- **Two-factor authentication is not always used when conducting sensitive transactions on mobile devices.** According to studies, people generally use static passwords instead of two-factor authentication when conducting online sensitive transactions while using mobile devices. Using static passwords for authentication has security drawbacks: passwords can be guessed, forgotten, written down and stolen, or eavesdropped. Two-factor authentication generally provides a higher level of security than traditional passwords and PINs, and this higher level may be important for sensitive transactions. Two-factor refers to an authentication system in which users are required to authenticate using at least two different "factors"—something you know, something you have, or something you are—before being granted access. Mobile devices themselves can be used as a second factor in some two-factor authentication schemes. The mobile device can generate pass codes, or the codes can be sent via a text message to the phone. Without two-factor authentication, increased risk exists that unauthorized users could gain access to sensitive information and misuse mobile devices.

- **Wireless transmissions are not always encrypted.** Information such as emails sent by a mobile device is usually not encrypted while in transit. In addition, many applications do not encrypt the data they transmit and receive over the network, making it easy for the data to be intercepted. For example, if an application is transmitting data over an unencrypted WiFi network using hypertext transfer protocol, http rather than secure https, the data can be easily intercepted. When a wireless transmission is not encrypted, data can be easily intercepted by eavesdroppers, who may gain unauthorized access to sensitive information. Chat systems often do not use encryption, so be careful.

- **Mobile devices may contain malware.** Employees download malware unknowingly because it can be disguised as a game, security patch, utility, or other useful application. It is difficult for users to tell the difference between a legitimate application and one containing malware. One piece of malware can wreak havoc on your network.

- **Mobile devices often do not use security software.** Many mobile devices do not come installed with security software to protect against malicious applications, spyware, and malware attacks. While such software may slow operations, and affect battery life on some mobile devices, without it, the risk may be increased that an attacker could successfully distribute malware such as viruses, Trojans, spyware, and spam, to lure users into revealing passwords or other confidential information.

- **Operating systems may be out-of-date.** Security patches or fixes for mobile devices' operating systems are not always installed on mobile devices in a timely manner. It can take weeks to months before security updates are provided to devices. Depending on the nature of the vulnerability, the patching process may be complex and involve many parties. For example, Google develops updates to fix security vulnerabilities in the Android OS, but it is up to device manufacturers to produce a device-specific update incorporating the vulnerability fix, which can take time if there are proprietary modifications to the device's software. Once a manufacturer produces an update, it is up to each carrier to test it and transmit the updates to the consumer's devices. However, carriers can be delayed in providing the updates because they need time to test whether they interfere with other aspects of the device or the software installed on it. I know it is a hassle getting so many mobile – new updates. I do not like it either but it is important we apply the updates asap.

- **Mobile devices that are older than 2 years** may not receive security updates because manufacturers may no longer support these devices. Many manufacturers stop supporting smartphones as soon as 12 to 18 months after their release. Such devices may face increased risk if manufacturers do not develop patches for newly discovered vulnerabilities.

- **Software on mobile and desktop devices may be out-of-date.** Security patches for third-party applications are not always developed and released in a timely manner. In addition, mobile third-party applications, including web browsers, do not always notify us when updates are available. Unlike traditional web browsers, mobile browsers rarely get updates. Using outdated software increases the risk that an attacker may exploit vulnerabilities associated with these devices.

- **Mobile devices often do not limit Internet connections.** Many mobile devices do not have firewalls to limit connections. When the device is connected to a wide area network it uses communications ports to connect with other devices and the Internet. These ports are similar to doorways to the device. A hacker could access the mobile device through a port that is not secured. A firewall secures these ports and allows the user to choose what connections he or she wants to allow into the mobile device. The firewall intercepts both incoming and outgoing connection attempts and blocks or permits them based on a list of rules. Without a firewall, the mobile device may be open to intrusion through an unsecured communications port, and an intruder may be able to obtain sensitive information on the device and misuse it. Speak with your IT and cyber security experts to see if this is a vulnerability in your organization.

- **Mobile devices may have unauthorized modifications.** The process of modifying a mobile device to remove its limitations to add additional features (known as "jailbreaking" or "rooting") changes how security for the device is managed and could increase security risks. Jailbreaking allows users to gain access to the operating system of a device so as to permit the installation of unauthorized software functions and applications and/or to not be tied to a particular wireless carrier. While some users may jailbreak or root their mobile devices specifically to install security enhancements such as firewalls, others may simply be looking for a less expensive or easier way to install desirable applications. In the latter case, users face increased security risks, because they are bypassing the application vetting process established by the manufacturer and thus have less protection against inadvertently installing malware. Further, jailbroken devices may not receive notifications of security updates from the manufacturer and may require extra effort from the user to maintain up-to-date software. I suggest you never jailbreak and take precautions so that your employees cannot do it.
- **Communication channels may be poorly secured.** Having communication channels, such as Bluetooth communications, "open" or in "discovery" mode (which allows the device to be seen by other Bluetooth-enabled devices so that connections can be made) could allow an attacker to install malware through that connection, or surreptitiously activate a microphone or camera to eavesdrop on the user. In addition, using unsecured public wireless Internet networks or WiFi spots could allow an attacker to connect to the device and view sensitive information.

Ok, whew! We made it through the bad stuff. Now let us go onward and upward to discuss some possible controls to prevent or mitigate these threats. But before we do let's put a smile on our faces and say hi to little Flakes my Yorkie in the next chapter.

64

HOW MY CERTIFIED DOGGIE RESILIENCE PROFESSIONAL (MCDRP) CONTRIBUTES TO MY PROGRAM

Wow, the previous chapter was pretty scary. There are some serious cyber threats that can make our lives MISERABLE. Before we dive into the next chapter which discusses some ways we can help mitigate cyber threats, I thought I would try to de-stress you and me. The previous chapter took a lot out of me. We both need a laugh. I will also let you in on a technique that worked well for me in the software development profession that I  successfully carried over to my career in business continuity and resilience.

This is my dog Flakes. He is a chatty Yorkshire Terrier (Yorkie). I think most Yorkie's are chatty. My wife rescued him when he was 3 years old.

Flakes actually helps me write some of my business resilience plans. Seriously. As stated in the title of this chapter he earned his MCDRP certification helping me on many occasions. No, he is not unique in his ability to help. Whether an animal is real, plush or a toy they can help us solve complex problems.

If you are a software developer, you may have heard of Andy Hunt. Andy is a famous software developer who wrote a best-selling book called The Pragmatic Programmer. Many thousands of software developers including me learned from it and enjoyed it. The book discusses the popular Agile development framework, which Andy was instrumental in creating. His book also discusses the concept called 'Rubber Duck Debugging'.

Believe it or not, rubber duck debugging might actually be more popular than Andy's book and the Agile framework. Rubber duck debugging is legendary. A simple search on Google for Rubber Duck Debugging produces 23,200+ results. There are other terms for it which produces many additional results.

Rubber duck debugging encourages programmers to interact with their (usually) toy duck and solve seemingly insurmountable problems. I have seen all kinds of toy and real animals, stick figures and stress balls with faces on them substituted for a duck. Business resilience professionals have many challenges including developing effective risk reduction and recovery strategies, writing plans and creating exercises. Flakes is helpful in all those facets.

Flakes was also a significant contributor to this book! He is my 'doggie' sounding board. I asked him questions, read him paragraphs and he stared at me knowingly with his head tilting from side-to-side. He listened and bounced my ideas back to me with an interesting slant. Hmmm, maybe change a sentence in the BIA chapter or re-word a paragraph on 'The 3 Pillars of Resilience Technology' and viola – he did it!

Perhaps this phenomenon has to do with verbalizing ideas and thinking out loud. I do not mean Flakes verbalizing, I am not that far gone yet. Yes, Flakes is MCDRP, My Certified Doggie Resilience Developer.

In any event, if you get stuck or need some cheering up perhaps consider getting your own little rubber duck or real dog or cat or bird or whatever to lighten up the moment and get your creative juices flowing. You will be surprised how effective it can be!

Ok, I now we are refreshed and ready to dig into the next cyber chapter – *Let's Go!*

65

CYBER SECURITY FOR BUSINESS CONTINUITY - BEST PRACTICES FOR BUSINESS SURVIVAL

In the 'Cyber Security Threats and Vulnerabilities 101' Chapter we discussed cyber security risks that can potentially impact your employees and the continuity of your operations. Although your Cyber Security and Information Technology departments must secure mobile and desktop devices and the data on them, the survival of your business can be put at risk if your organization is attacked. Successful cyber breaches and attacks can instantly become business continuity issues.

Unfortunately, I have witnessed organizations tighten up their desktop security but leave mobile and more recently, IOT device security wide open to the bad guys. People intent on doing harm, even with low or no-level technical skills, can easily get access to programs that can severely impact your organization.

In addition to desktop and mobile devices (phones, tablets...) the popularity of Internet of Things (IOT) devices takes risks to another level. There will be **billions** of IOT devices riding the Internet in the next few years. All kinds of sensors, cameras, motors... are being connected to the Internet. These devices can very much help our programs and I discuss amazing opportunities in the technology section of the book. I have connected sensors and alarms from trusted vendors to the Internet. These devices benefit employees and our ability to understand our environment in real-time. Unfortunately, IOT security is not the first concern for some vendors selling IOT devices. The last thing we want is rogue sensors and robots adding risk to our infrastructure. These devices can change the way we do business for the better, but we must implement the proper security controls.

Perhaps, your organization has all your device security and IOT controls in place. I hope you have robust cyber security policies. If you pick out even one or two tips from this chapter, it will be well worth the short read. Venturing beyond your immediate Business Resilience duties and making helpful security suggestions to IT and management will help you in many ways.

The security controls and practices described **below are a starting point – not a comprehensive list.** I tried to map them to the threats

209

and vulnerabilities we discussed in the threats and vulnerabilities chapter. They are consistent with studies and guidance from NIST, FTC, FCC and DHS along with my experiences. Some of the information below originates and is used with permission of the GAO from their report – Report to Congressional Committees – Information Security, 'Better Implementation of Controls for Mobile Devices Should Be Encouraged'.

General Security Best Practices – Mobile Phones, Laptops, Tablets and Desktops:
(This is not a comprehensive list. You should partner with your Cyber Security and Information Technology Experts to Implement a Holistic Information Security Program)

Tip – Partner with your IT and Cyber Security experts and analyze the vulnerabilities that can compromise your organization.

Tip – Advise employees of mobile and desktop best practices. You can use information in this chapter and the preceding 'Cyber Threats and Vulnerabilities' chapter in your in-house newsletter or in your in-house blog if you wish to.

Tip – Your Cyber Security and/or Information Technology experts must implement the latest security safeguards, anti-virus software, patches and timeouts. They must do it in a timely manner. No excuse for delaying this is acceptable!

Tip – A corporate policy, with teeth, must be in place making it a violation to save critical / sensitive / unencrypted data on laptop local drives or mobile devices.

Tip – As we discussed in the previous chapter on cyber vulnerabilities phishing is a rapidly growing problem. Create awareness with all employees that they should never click on links unless the know the source of the message.

Discuss doing a series of ethical phishing tests with your IT and cyber security experts. Most likely a large percentage of employees will click on an unknown link.

You can then follow-up with them and explain that clicking on such a link can enable a virus, worm or ransomware attack. It can also lead to criminals stealing the employee's personal information. I believe as your series of ethical phishing tests take place the number of employees that click on links from an unknown source will significantly decrease.

Tip – USB thumb drives must be encrypted! They are able to store gigabytes of data and are too easy to lose. We have all read horror stories of sensitive data being stolen or lost and seriously impacting the survival of an organization. Do not let this happen to you.

Tip – Data must be encrypted at rest AND in-flight. Even with a policy in place, people will still copy data to their local drive, if it is available. Laptops have a way of getting stolen or lost (read the chapter 'Your Laptop Has Legs…'). It is the loss of sensitive data that is the bigger risk than the loss of the hardware. Laptop hardware is relatively cheap and can easily be replaced. Losing sensitive data can cost your company many millions of dollars and the loss of executive jobs at the highest level of the organization.

Tip – Make sure any vendors that have access to your data are encrypting it both at rest AND in-flight.

Tip – Office laptops should be physically secured when left on desks. In many organizations, it is too easy for someone intent on doing harm to surf in behind an employee and swipe unattended laptops. Even if you have security cameras, good luck in catching the thieves before they are long gone. It happens all too often.

Tip – **Do not** let your laptop, tablet or phone out of your sight at airports or any other public places. They should be with you always or they will 'walk'. If you do store data on the device make sure the data is encrypted, just in case the device disappears.

Tip –**Do not** text or chat sensitive information unless it is encrypted at rest and in-flight. Often these types of communications are sent in clear text. Only send in clear text if you do not mind everyone reading it.

Tip – **Do not** write your log-in credentials on a sticky note and stick it to you keyboard or desk. Oh, you haven't seen this type of thing at least once?

Tip – **Do not** keep your steaming-hot filled coffee cup next to your devices – we've all done it or seen it so you're not alone. Come on, admit it. I will be the first to admit it, it happened to me twice in one morning, yikes.

Tip – **Do not** provide login information to callers. Social engineering is rampant and an easy and effective way to infiltrate a network. You are giving them the keys to the network. No technical skills are required. Warn your employees.

Tip –**Do** put policies and procedures in place to address all areas of risk including the ones I listed above.

Tip – **Do** provide mobile device security training.

Tip – **Do** include mobile devices and IOT in your risk assessments.

Enable user authentication:
Tip – Configure mobile devices to always require passwords or PINs to gain access just as you do with your desktop devices. In addition, the password field should be masked to prevent shoulder surfing, and all

devices should have active idle-time screen locking to prevent unauthorized access.

Tip – Your organization needs a policy on desktop and mobile passwords – length, alpha-number-character, special characters, forced changes after a certain period of time.

Tip – Speak with your IT department about active directory and single-sign-on to control and reduce password maintenance complexity and risks.

Enable two-factor authentication:

Tip – Two-factor authentication is important when conducting sensitive transactions on mobile devices. Two-factor authentication enables a higher level of security than traditional passwords. Two-factor is an authentication system in which recipients must authenticate using at least two different "factors" (pieces of information) before being granted access. You are probably already familiar with two-factor authentication, as most of the popular websites use it.

Tip – Mobile devices themselves can be used as a second factor in some two-factor authentication schemes used for remote access. The mobile device can generate pass codes, or the codes can be sent via a text message to the phone. Two-factor authentication is especially important when sensitive transactions occur, such as mobile banking.

Always verify the authenticity of any downloaded applications:

Tip – Understand where the application came from. Check digital signatures. When in doubt, block, quarantine or filter the download.

Install anti-malware capability:

Tip – This one is a 'no-brainer'. Malware is rampant on the internet. You definitely do not want it in your network. It encompasses ransomware, viruses, worms, botnets and spam. It will make your life miserable and can seriously impact your organization.

Install a personal firewall:

Tip – A personal firewall can protect against unauthorized connections by intercepting both incoming and outgoing connection attempts and blocking or permitting them based on a list of organization rules.

Disable lost or stolen devices remotely:

Tip – Remote disabling is an important feature for stolen or lost devices that either locks the device or completely purges its contents remotely. Locked devices can be unlocked subsequently by the user if they are recovered.

Use automated device scanning software:
Tip – Software tools can be used to scan devices for compromising events (e.g., an unexpected change in the file structure) and then report the results of the scans, including a risk rating and recommended mitigation strategy.

Implement a virtual private network (VPN):
Tip – A secure VPN is very important if employees need to securely access your intranet from remote locations. If you are designing work-from-home recovery strategies, you need VPN access.

- **Sub-tip** – Stress-test your VPN to insure everyone can connect during high demand. I have witnessed VPN connection and latency issues during major events such as snow storms and hurricanes when thousands of employees try to connect. VPN's by design may have only one or two entry points into an organization. You must validate that there is sufficient bandwidth for all employees to connect. You do not want to discover latency or the inability to access your network during a widespread disruptive event.

Tip – Regularly do penetration (PEN) tests on your network and systems. Ethical tiger teams can test their ability to penetrate your systems and provide you with results. Your IT and cyber security teams can then focus on closing all vulnerabilities. If you need a recommendation on a particularly good company that specializes in phishing tests and can even help you with implementing cyber related policies please contact me.

Adopt centralized security management:
Tip – Centralized security management enables organization-wide control of devices including remotely disabling devices. It also includes management practices, such as setting policy for individual users or a class of users on specific devices. This is very important for scalability, patch management, hardware and software audits. In fact, I broke this out in the book as a small one page chapter so no one misses it.

Turn off or set Bluetooth connection capabilities to non-discoverable:
Tip – When in discoverable mode, Bluetooth-enabled devices are "visible" to other nearby devices, which may alert an attacker to target them. When Bluetooth is turned off or in nondiscoverable mode, the Bluetooth-enabled devices are invisible to other unauthenticated devices.

Limit use of public WiFi networks when conducting sensitive transactions:

Tip – Attackers may patrol public WiFi networks for unsecured devices or even create malicious WiFi spots designed to attack mobile phones and penetrate your network.

Public WiFi spots represent an easy channel for hackers to exploit. Users can limit their use of public WiFi networks by not conducting sensitive transactions when connected to them or if connecting to them, they should use secure, encrypted connections. This can help reduce the risk of attackers obtaining sensitive information such as passwords, bank account numbers and credit card numbers.

Minimize installation of unnecessary applications:
Tip – Users can reduce risk by limiting unnecessary applications. Once installed, applications may be able to access user content and device programming interfaces, and they may also contain vulnerabilities. Your cyber security department should control this.

Do not click on links sent in suspicious email or text messages:
Tip – Be very careful – often these links look like legitimate sites, but they can lead to malicious sites and ransomware attacks.

Limit exposure of mobile phone numbers:
Tip – By not posting mobile phone numbers to public websites, users may be able to limit the extent to which attackers can obtain known mobile numbers to attack. Do some Internet searching to see if you have exposures. It is scary how many companies have private spreadsheets and documents on the public Internet. I do mean scary!

Maintain physical control of your devices:
Tip – Always know the whereabouts of your devices. Do not leave them in any public areas where they can and will 'walk'! Please read the chapter, *'Your Laptop Has Legs'*. It applies to mobile as well.

Delete all information stored on a device prior to discarding it:
Tip – The device should be returned to your company and all data should be purged and wiped clean at a low level before discarding it. Simply deleting a file often just marks it for deletion but it can still be un-deleted. Be careful. You should also can remotely disable the device and delete data in case it is lost.

Do not modify mobile devices (jailbreak):

Tip – 'Jailbreaking' devices will expose them to security vulnerabilities and can prevent them from receiving security updates. It can also impact the warranty. Never jailbreak.

CYBER SECURITY - AUTOMATED VIRUS PATCHING AND INVENTORY AUDITING IS CRITICAL!

My interviews with C level executives convey again and again that being the victim of a cyber-attack is their worst nightmare. Imagine walking into the office one morning, turning on your laptop and up pops a ransomware demand to access your files. If you do not meet the demand in a few hours they threaten to delete all your files. That is a nightmare scenario.

You must know your network!
I highly recommend that your Information Technology (IT) department implement an automated network inventory and patching process. A process is needed to scan all servers and clients so you know in real-time every piece of software on the network including versions and patches. When updated patches are required the system must be at least partially automated for a mid or enterprise organization. Information

Technology must scan for malware, viruses and anything that can compromise your network. Remember, even one major cyber incident can seriously imperil your organization.

An automated inventory tool will also let you know if you are out of compliance with licensing or if anyone has installed pirated software on their local machine that can potentially cost your organization millions of dollars in legal fees!

Do not let these issues slip through the cracks. All it could take is one incident and that could be the end!

OUR SOFT TARGETS MUST BE HARDENED NOW!

Soft targets have deeply concerned me for many years. One way or another all our lives are touched when a soft target is attacked whether it is by an irate student, a person filled with hatred for others, nation states or terrorist organizations. As experts, we have the opportunity to identify threats, vulnerabilities, risks and prevent or control them using a number of tools.

Many of us work in organizations that could be considered soft targets – schools, hospitals, corporations, movie theaters, retail stores… We take mass transportation such as planes, buses, trains… We must weigh-in on this issue and make suggestions to harden these potential targets. First, and foremost, for the protection and safety of people and secondarily for operational continuity. **This must be a global concern. It is not limited to any one nation.**

Having a trained eye like we do in our profession, it is hard for me to accept some of the horrific soft target events that have occurred in recent years. These events must be a dire warning that we need to tighten our security now and begin using technology levers to help us beyond 'see something, say something'. My point of view is there is so much more we can do to promote safety and help our security officials. We need actionable data, predictive analytics, social sentiment indicators, machine learning for the ability to understand threats and risks in real-time or prior to their impact.

On July 23, 2012, my editorial submission 'Now is the Time to Harden our 'Soft' Targets!' was published in Newsday, which is one of New York's most widely read daily newspapers. I wrote it because I was upset and frustrated by the embarrassing lack of progress made to harden soft targets and connect-the-dots. Needless tragedies, in my opinion, are occurring on a more frequent basis and surely the worst is yet to come – possibly on a much larger scale. In fact, some of my thoughts in the article were unfortunately a chilling precursor to events that subsequently transpired.

Below is the original article I wrote (Newsday published a portion of it). I also include updates I posted to my blog in ensuing years.

I am interested in your thoughts on protecting soft targets.

Original July 23, 2012 article I wrote. A portion published in Newsday letters to the editor:

Now is the Time to Harden our 'Soft' Targets!
By Marty Fox, New York

The recent tragedy in Aurora, Colorado must serve as a wake-up call to harden our defense of 'soft' targets. The intent of this article is not to place blame or point fingers, rather it is to raise awareness of a frightening gap in our nations' security and hopefully identify some possible solutions.

The police department of Aurora acted with great courage, and without their skill and bravery, possibly more lives would have been lost. Unfortunately, this event occurred and we cannot turn back the clock and the bloodshed dealt by a madman. However, practitioners of crisis management understand that every event, whether it is man-made or an act of nature is a learning opportunity. We must seize this moment and make a commitment that we will do everything possible to harden targets which are currently the path of least resistance – 'soft' targets such as schools, hospitals, shopping centers, movie theaters, restaurants, trains...

This act was carried out by a deranged student, but imagine if it was a well-funded nation-state or terrorist organization that determined they could inflict great harm on our nation by simultaneously attacking multiple soft targets. Do we have the confidence that with our current level of security we would stop all the attacks, half, or even a few? Even one successful penetration could be catastrophic. Remember, a terrorist group would not limit their tools to bullets. They could use explosive devices or biological weapons. I know it sounds like an episode of a 24 but it is all too real and there will be no Jack Bauer riding to the rescue in the nick of time.

I believe the next phase of securing this new world in which we live must be to protect these 'soft' targets at all costs. Just as job seekers have come to realize that millions of outsourced jobs will not be coming back anytime soon, if ever, we all must realize the world has changed. The hour is at hand to implement improvements to insure the continuity of our way of life so we are not imperiled by a future event, possibly of greater magnitude in terms of casualties.

I became educated in the difficulty of protecting 'soft' targets at a Homeland Security seminar in 2006 in Washington, D.C. A high ranking Israeli security expert described the challenges and risk mitigation processes Israel implemented in theaters, schools and other

218

public places to successfully deter and detect those that would want to cause harm. He described the challenges Israel faced in protecting their citizens and detailed why the United States would face the same challenges in the coming decades. His talk made a lasting impression on me. The United States, United Kingdom, France and many other countries are larger than Israel, but there is much to be learned from their experience and knowledge.

One example is they utilize security screening in their theaters, as a small percentage of theaters in the United States do as well. Of course, this costs theater owners money and it is a bit of a hassle to theater-goers. On the other hand, if an event were to occur that could have been prevented, the cost would be incalculable to theaters in many ways. The value of a life cannot be measured in dollars. As someone who loves to go to the movies I would certainly accept the minor inconvenience of going through a security checkpoint as I do at a ball game, to be safer in a dark theater. Without this type of security, the risk/reward of watching at home on a digital TV swings towards watching from the safety and comfort of my couch.

As a career technologist, I believe there is much that can be done to empower our security officials by implementing new technologies that aid them and allow them to reduce the time to react. During a crisis, seconds can be the difference between life and death. Certainly, facial recognition is useful to match against a database of known terrorists. Pattern recognition is useful to filter out unusual behavior that could be the forewarning of a malicious act. If an exit door in a theater is opened during a screening and left ajar, an alert should be triggered and sent in real-time to security personnel. Tiny RFID tags embedded in weapons can alert us when one of these deadly objects enters a secure area – we already tag books, medicines and jewelry. These types of laser focused signals cut through the noise of data around us to pinpoint unusual events that require immediate attention.

Vigilance and 'if you see something say something' is critically important in leveraging the eyes of a nation and we must stay the course in that regard. I try to be aware but there are times I doze on the train or read a book and I know I would not realize if a package was left unattended two seats away from me or if the person just went to the bathroom. Cameras in train cars that scan for unusual behavior or abandoned packages can be of huge value. If they could alert an on-board security agent it could save many lives. Again, I do not care if someone is monitoring a train for suspicious activity if it can prevent a catastrophic event.

Finally, we must regularly test our security processes and technologies. An untested plan is a worthless plan! We must flesh out the gaps before an actual event. Tiger teams can test the validity of plans and procedures with penetration tests. Providing security personnel with comprehensive tools and training will help keep everyone safe. We must be proactive! We cannot be reactionary and wait to raise our guard after each event takes place and the damage has been done. Every great athlete knows that failing to plan is planning to fail. Unfortunately, in crisis management there often is not a second chance for the victims. The time to act is now.

Marty Fox is a technologist, crisis management and business continuity professional with a lifelong passion for applying technology to solve big problems

.

June 12, 2016 (four years later) I added this information to my blog:
Tragically, another massacre of innocent people has occurred on U.S. soil. The horrific shootings during the early morning hours of Sunday June 11 at an Orlando, FL nightclub impacts us all. My heart goes out to the families directly impacted by this event.

It is early in the investigation but all indications point to another soft target that was too easily compromised. The pattern of failing to connect the dots again once reared its ugly head. As usual the police acted heroically. They always do!

In my opinion our soft targets are more vulnerable today than they were four years ago when Newsday published portions of my 'Now is the Time to Harden Our Soft Targets' article. Four years is a long time for monsters focused on doing evil to discover new vulnerabilities in our physical structures and computer systems. Terrorists, whether they intend to do physical or cyber harm are very patient and smart. Complacency on our part is our downfall.
As a lifelong systems, process and business continuity officer with the largest corporations, I can clearly see the current federal computer systems and processes in place to 'connect-the-dots' are not adequate – even though the budget for Homeland Security has increased exponentially the past 15 years.

The warning signs once again were clearly there. This was not a Black Swan (Nicholas Taleb). Had the systems and processes worked as they should have, the Orlando event might not have occurred.

Prediction – unless we do a far better job hardening our soft targets **AND** immediately improving our systems this will happen again. It might be a theater, maybe a bus or a train or possibly a mall, but it will happen. We will once again look at missed opportunities due to the 'dots not being connected' or security not where it should be or non-existent. Statistics prove that often we do not learn from 'lessons learned'.

'See something, say something' will only take us so far. Most events happen so quickly we must be alerted in seconds, Nano-seconds and preferably before an event occurs. The technology is there to do it. We are not even using it in a primitive way. I am sure if some of the dynamic tech minds were at the helm of our federal security analytics programs, they would be more effective. Unfortunately, many of the most creative minds are in the private sector. Maybe an advisory think-tank consisting of the Elon Musk's, Jack Dorsey's and other creative thinkers/Technorati's would begin moving us in the right direction.

If Musk can get people to Mars by 2025, which he probably will, he can certainly help in some way to have systems speak to each other and close gaping gaps, such as a Florida security guard that had been questioned by the FBI being able to buy automatic weapons. That is shameful and unfortunately proved deadly to scores of innocent people. No do-overs or lessons learned can bring back those lives.

V

PART 5 - RECOVERY STRATEGIES AND BEYOND

All the detailed work you have done to this point will now enable you to develop appropriate and resilient recovery strategies, including:

- Internal recovery seats
- Work-from-home
- 3rd party vendor work-area seats
- 3rd party vendor mobile trailer work-area seats
- Additional, less formal recovery options are listed in the chapter entitled, *'Creative Recovery Sites That Saved Me'*. In fact, during one of the days I was writing the recovery strategies part of this book, I had a power outage at home and had to recover from my condominium clubhouse – seriously! I was even able to get a workout on the treadmill. Yes, I had previously tested from there as part of my recovery plan.
- I suggest you implement multiple tiers of recovery. In case the primary or secondary is not available, you can use your tertiary option. This strategy has paid off for me.

In my experience, if you build a culture of resilience and motivate employees to be creative they will find a way to work even during most challenging circumstances.

During my career, I have had the fortunate experience to implement all the recovery strategies discussed in this part of the book.

68

RECOVERY STRATEGY OPTIONS, TIPS, TECHNIQUES AND IDEAS

In this chapter, we will discuss a variety of business recovery options. It does not have to be all-or-nothing. You can mix-and-match strategies to bake maximum resilience into your overall response capabilities.

Internal Recovery – 'Sister-Sites' Option:

I always try to leverage internal recovery sites and seats into my strategies, whenever practical. Internal seats have many advantages and can be quite valuable and cost effective compared to 3rd party vendor seats. There are several case studies in the book where I effectively recovered time-sensitive processes internally.

In-house recovery advantages:

- You control the recovery environment. I have used training rooms, meeting rooms, conference rooms, lunch rooms, 'quiet rooms' (these are neat little rooms) and 'bouncing' (in nice ways of course) employees with less time-sensitive process requirements to accommodate employees with more time-sensitive recovery needs. Walk around your locations. Is it practical to recover in-house? Remember, be creative and think 'outside the box!

- Cost savings – In most cases you can still use the designated in-house recovery areas for production meetings with the understanding that you will commandeer them during a crisis. Get this agreed upon in writing with management, facilities, IT and other critical partners. Make sure they understand the in-house rooms will be used to recover processes during a disruptive event. Otherwise, at time of a crisis some big head SVP may make a fuss on giving up his/her daily BS coffee-klatch meeting. Trust me, it could happen.

- Testing – You can test internal recovery as often as you want to. With a 3rd party vendor you will have limited hours specified in your contract during which you can test.

- If you are using shared space with a vendor you will be subject to 'first come-first serve' and may not get the seats you need in the most convenient location.

- You can train 'shadow staff' in the internal recovery location to 'stand up' the process within minutes. That can enable you to meet even the most aggressive RTO's. I have done this successfully with Customer Serve and Trading and describe it in this book.

Internal recovery seat challenges:

- You will need equipment. Employees may have their laptops available during a disruptive event, but in a scenario such as a fire during the work day (evacuation) they would need recovery equipment. If you are using a training room and it already has computers and phones, then it is not as much an issue. Otherwise, think it through. Also, read the chapter, 'Reduce Expenses and Improve Resilience with The Laptop Re-use Project' in the book on leveraging retired laptops for recovery purposes.
- You must keep the equipment and software up-to-date. You must apply patches. That is very important. You should consider an automated tool that pushes the patches and updates to the laptops and desktops to make this manageable.
- The recovery location must be a safe distance from the production site. This is a concern for multiple reasons. You will want to be out of harm's way. You will want to be on another electrical grid, although a campus environment can work if only one building is impacted and the sister building is functional. I have used campus recovery effectively when the scenario dictated it. In addition, there could be regulatory rules stating a recovery site must be at least 50 miles or 100 miles from the production site.

Tip – When planning internal recovery seats at sister sites plan closely with the recovery location Incident Commander and facilities person. Communicate your needs. Learn what space they have available and how many seats you can use. Remember, they may have already promised seats to someone else. You may also have to partner on building out conference or meeting rooms to meet the expectations of the recovering employees. Communicate with the sister site regularly to determine if anything has changed in the way of available space.

Tip – Store special equipment and supplies at the recovery location or a central location.

Work-from-Home Recovery Option:
If you have been building recovery strategies for a while you have probably noticed a trend for processes to work-from-home as their primary recovery strategy rather than going to a vendor site or even a sister site.

I believe work-from-home can be a great recovery strategy in many scenarios, especially when travel is difficult or impossible, schools are closed or employees have responsibilities to care for their parents. In a real crisis, sometimes people that said during planning they would recover 50 miles away in actuality cannot or will not do it. Sometimes I cannot blame them.

There are many office processes where people can effectively recover at home, although not so for those in the factory, warehouse, retail, health or delivery processes, to name a few. In fact, when practical, telecommuting on a regular basis has a lot of advantages for employees and organizations.

I worked primarily from home for six years as a business continuity senior analyst. Working-from-home actually improved my productivity. I had less distractions than being in the office and a 6 second commute from by bedroom to my home office. I also received a stipend for supplies and equipment. Not too shabby, right? My employer was a Fortune 100 Company. They saved a lot of money on rent and utilities. Multiply that by thousands of employees and the bottom line popped, in a positive way! Plus, the most talented people wanted to work for that company as work-from-home is a great perk.

Tip – Stress test your VPN. Otherwise you may find out the hard way that you cannot support enough work-from-home employees simultaneously during a widespread disruption. I have experienced it whereby employees incur latency issues and the inability to log onto VPN. If you think you will need to support a maximum of 12,000 simultaneous users leave room for growth and plan to support 24,000+.

Tip – If employees are using hard-tokens to get onto VPN make sure they have re-certified their VPN chip according to your security policies. You do not want to find out during a crisis that employees have old chips and cannot access the network. Work with IT to make sure you have 'all your ducks in a row'.

Establish a work-from-home policy:
If you have employees that are primarily work-from-home, as I was, your company should have a well-documented work-from-home policy in place that every work-from-home employee must agree to and sign-off on. This can address security issues and having a separate room or area dedicated to work. HR will have information on this.
If your company has work-from-home, a smart thing to do is to establish 'hoteling' areas in your major locations.

These are work areas where work-from-home employees can book a seat when they need to be in the office for meetings. These areas also make excellent workstation recovery strategies in the event of a disaster. They are very useful when people do not have power at home, are impacted by flood, fire… you get it. For business continuity, these hoteling areas make us more resilient. Hoteling is a win-win scenario in my opinion!

Compliance:
Depending on your industry you should check about any compliance issues with employees working from home. For example, securities trading is highly regulated but during a crisis when people cannot safely travel, regulatory rules may be adjusted. Determine that in advance with the regulatory agencies and document it in your plans.

Security:
Another big consideration is if you will allow people to use their home computers (not corporate issued) to access your network. If this is the plan you should be thinking about security, security and oh yeah, security. You must work closely with your Information Technology and Cyber Security experts to implement this properly.
- Who has access to the home computer?
- What are the base requirements for the hardware and OS?
- How will you provide technical support when the inevitable questions arise?

One idea is to control the environment by creating virtual machines. Employees can use their home computer but they will be limited to a 'sandbox' terminal environment. I have done this and it works well. Think about it.

Tip – Work-from-home employees must be in-scope for recovery exercises:
Even if in-office processes indicate they can work-from-home, they should still send representatives to the workstation area recovery exercises at the 3rd party locations, sister sites or mobile trailers.

In the event there is a power outage in their home, they will need a place to work. In an evacuation scenario during which they leave their laptop in their office, they will need a place to work. It is critical they validate they can work from an alternate recovery location. You do not want to identify gaps at time of disaster. We never want that!

I suggest you have a small percentage of people test from home on a regular basis. Rotate people during normal business periods so that during the course of a year everyone who is expected to work-from-home in a crisis validates they have no issues. Having people test from home is one of the easiest requests you will make in business continuity. I have never had a complaint about testing from home.

Survey work-from-home employees after they test. Ask questions and ask for comments. Below is a starter set of questions. Please add your own:

- Was the test a success? Why and why not?
- Could you access our network from home through VPN?
- Were you able to reach all your critical applications?
- Did you have any ergonomic issues?
- Did you have any phone issues?
- Did you have any supply issues?
- Did you have any equipment issues?
- Did you have any compliance/oversight issues?
- What could be improved?

3rd Party Vendor Work-Area-Recovery Seat Option
Using a 3rd party vendor for recovery seats can be a viable recovery solution especially if you do not have internal sites you can leverage. The advantage of a 3rd party vendor is you do not have to dedicate space or maintain up-to-date computers and software.

The downside is limited test time and if you are using shared seats, you will most likely be competing for seats with other companies on a first to declare basis. If you are using dedicated seats in a vendor hot site it can get expensive but you have great control over the environment and test time.

I have had great success using 3rd party vendors for testing and recovery during real events. I discuss details on using a 3rd party vendor in the Interchangeable Work-Area-Recovery Exercise (IWARE) chapter in the Testing part of the book. Below are some tips:

Tip – Build relationships with hotels near the vendor recovery site. This may be critical for recovery employees so they do not have to shuttle great distances every day. Consider shift work – 3 days on and 3 days

227

off. At time of crisis many companies may be vying for limited hotel space. If you have high impact highly time sensitive processes, it may make sense to have an agreement in place with hotels to insure you can accommodate your recovery employees.

Tip – If you are recovering multiple processes in one large vendor workstation area recovery room consider any "Chinese Wall" separation of processes regulations. In the financial securities industry, it can a be concern that trading is not commingled with certain other processes. Research this in advance.

Tip – During the BIA it should be determined if processes can work during regular, mid and night shifts. Shift work may be difficult with customer facing processes but there are other processes that may be able to do it, thereby enabling you to share recovery seats. For example, one person during the day, another during the second shift and possibly a third during the third shift. Using only one seat for all the shifts (3 people) can save significant money
and produce more work in a 24-hour cycle.

Tip – Build relationships with transportation companies. You may want to use buses or vans to transport groups of employees to the recovery site. That will make it easier for them. Group transport is also valuable during winter storms or transit strikes. Sometimes it is preferable to have a professional driving.

3rd Party Vendor Mobile Trailer Recovery Option
Using 3rd party vendor trailers can be a good strategy for certain scenarios. I have implemented this solution for management, customer service and many operations teams. Depending on the vendor you use, each trailer seats approximately 20 and 40 employees. You can daisy-chain multiple trailers for larger staff recovery requirements. I have done setups for 100+ employees.

The nice thing about trailers is people do not have to travel long distances to a physical recovery location. As you know, during certain scenarios, people will not want to be away from their family for an extended period.

Modern vendor recovery trailers are very impressive. Their features include:
* Comfortable seating (but watch the overhead credenzas – I used to hit my head, but fortunately the credenzas were padded)
* Bathrooms

228

- Kitchen space
- Televisions
- Computers
- Most important (well the bathrooms are equally as important) they have satellite connectivity for telecommunications. Therefore, critical customer facing teams can answer incoming and make outgoing calls.

Challenges:
- You probably cannot meet aggressive less-than 24-hour RTO requirements as the trailers must travel and be set up
- You need space to park them
- You might need permits due to their size
- There is not as much seating space and 'elbow room' as in an office
- Possible latency issues may be encountered when bouncing the calls off the satellites. You should test to get used to it.
- Although testing may be pricey, I suggest you do at least a couple of rounds of tests from the trailers. It is also important you have your IT and telecom folks closely involved and in the trailer as they will need to image the computers and work on any telecommunication issues that arise.

As I mentioned I have implemented all the solutions described above with great success and so can you. Have fun and contact me with any questions!

229

69

TIME SENSITIVE CALL RE-ROUTING CAN KEEP CUSTOMERS HAPPY AND ADD NEW CUSTOMERS + REVENUE

Super resilience through the re-routing of customer facing toll free telephone numbers is critical in keeping customers happy and keeping them as customers during and after a disruptive event. You can even turn this super resilience into additional revenue by adding new customers after a disruptive event. Sales can make it part of their pitch that your company was taking orders when the competition was serving up a stale voicemail for hours or days!

Re-routing toll free numbers must be thought through carefully and documented in your plans and telecom routing tables. Attention to detail and team coordination will enable your organization to recover these critical communication numbers in any disaster in a time-frame meeting or exceeding business requirements.

I have successfully re-routed customer facing toll free telephone numbers for customer service and various securities processes during my career. These types of processes typically have an RTO of <4 hours. In each disruptive event I have encountered, we were able to recover within 1 hour and often in just a few minutes. Yes, you can exceed expectations!

I have re-routed calls internally to recovery staff at sister-sites (warm and hot-sites), vendor recovery sites, vendor mobile recovery trailers and work-from- home locations. Each can be a viable strategy, depending on your needs and resources.

Here are Tips for Your Consideration:
Tip – Toll-free numbers can often be redirected in the cloud utilizing a telecom routing table. You should team with your telecommunications experts to implement this strategy. The telecommunications team can often build out the underlying infrastructure with the flexibility to re-route calls to any site or desktop.

When speaking with process owners always ask if they have any customer facing toll-free numbers. Ask it during initial interviews, BIA, plan maintenance and tabletops. Remind them that if new toll free numbers are activated to add them to their business continuity plan and let you know so you can build a recovery strategy. Often new customer facing numbers are added and unless there is a process in place and awareness they may not be captured and SURPRISE – they will not be available at the time of crisis. Customer calls that terminate with a canned voice-mail 'we are experiencing a disruption...' or drop into a black hole are **BAD** for your company image and for your career! You could lose customers and revenue.

- **Sub-Tip** – if you are using a sophisticated BCM system you can set a trigger to alert you whenever a new toll free number is added to a plan.

Tip – After you have identified the customer facing toll free numbers, work with the process owners and the telecommunications team to fine tune your strategy. This may include setting up sub-prompts off the main toll free numbers so customers can get to proper skilled professionals who can best answer their specific questions or take their orders.

Tip – Level-set expectations with the process owner. Like we always preach, it might not be business as usual (BAU) during a crisis, unless they want to pay for it and even then, depending on the availability of employees they may have to compromise to a certain degree. Most likely the process will have a smaller than usual number of recovery staff taking calls, especially during the first 4 to 24 hours. They may want to plan to consolidate some of the sub prompts into one extension.

Tip – Recovery staff should be cross-trained before-hand to at least can speak intelligently and answer basic questions that customers may have. Complex questions could then be escalated to a supervisor. Call-forwarding should be tested beforehand.

Tip – A valuable related project goal can be to discover all the critical customer facing toll free phone numbers in your organization. Depending on the size of your organization and the data available to you this can be a large, but worthwhile, project. As a special treat, please read the chapter, 'Spinning Data into Gold', in Part 1 of the book. It may give you an idea to unleash additional value from this project.

Working with a Third-Party Work-Area-Recovery Vendor as the End-Point for the Customer Calls:
Tip – When you re-route calls to a third-party recovery vendor site you and your telecommunications team will partner with the vendor's telecommunications team to channel the re-routed calls through their phone system to the proper end-point skill-set employee(s). Your

recovery staff must have the flexibility to log-in from any desk and begin accepting calls for a particular queue.

Depending on the vendor's phone system this may take some getting used to by employees. Encourage employees to attend every work-area-recovery exercise to practice using the phone system. If additional testing is required, you can speak with the vendor about bringing a few employees over for an 'unofficial' test. Vendors usually try to accommodate their clients, if possible.

Tip – Your job is to manage the project. I promise, you do not have to be a telecommunications geek to successfully re-route toll free phone numbers.
1. You must understand the business requirements and risks
2. You must bring your telecommunications team together with the third-party recovery vendor telecommunications team. They speak the same language and they will then handle the technical implementation. You will be the key person to ensure that the proper business requirements are achieved
3. You must clearly document everything!
4. You must test!

Testing the Toll-Free Phone Numbers at the Recovery Site is Critical – Critical – Critical!
After the back-end work is completed and documented do an initial test with a few 'dummy' calls:
1. Your telecommunications expert can probably tag your desk or cell phone in the routing table so that when you call in from that number to a certain customer facing toll free number in scope it is then re-routed to the recovery site. A vendor rep at the recovery site can answer the call. This enables you to test without impacting any production calls. The production calls will not be re-routed. This is good as you might need to do some fine tuning to the re-routing process.
2. Next, bring a small percentage of recovery personnel to the recovery site. Test re-routing a small percentage of production calls. You and your telecommunications team may have to play with the percentage of calls on-the-fly. If you only get 20 calls a day on a toll-free number, re-routing 1 percent of the calls for that number to the recovery site might have people sitting around for hours waiting for a call. The percentage of re-routes depends on the number of calls and number of recovery people you have at the site. The process owner can provide a good approximation of the percentage of calls to re-route for this part of the test.

232

Generally, changing the percentage up or down takes a minute or so for the telecom team.

3. **IMPORTANT** – After a test or a real crisis remember to re-route the calls back to the production site. I repeat, after a test or a real crisis remember to re-route the calls back to the production site. If you forget to do this, it can understandably get ugly. Trust me, with all the excitement, it can be overlooked.

The bottom line is re-routing toll free customer facing telephone numbers sounds complicated, but it is not. When it works, it is a beautiful thing and of course your organization will be able to 'sleep nights' knowing this has been planned and tested! Good luck and let me know how it works for you.

If you have any questions on this subject or need further suggestions, please contact me – Marty@UltimateBusinessContinuity.com.

70

REDUCE EXPENSES AND IMPROVE RESILIENCE WITH THE LAPTOP RE-USE PROJECT

I am guessing your company refreshes laptops every 3-5 years or replaces them at 'end-of-life'. I doubt too many of you are still using Osborne 1's or Compaq 35 pound 'luggables' at this stage (been there, done that.) Possibly your organization is migrating sales people from laptops to tablets and there are hundreds or thousands of laptops being returned (also been there, done that).

Why not try using these as recovery laptops during a disruptive event. Ok, some may not be usable, some you may have to 'bump up the RAM'- but the value of these machines in cost savings and RTO benefits will be significant over buying new machines that hopefully will never be used.

Feeding the ability to use slightly older laptops for recovery purposes is the mass migration in recent years of enterprise systems running from the cloud rather than from local machines. This provides many advantages for business resilience. For laptop recover it means they often do not require top of the line configurations to keep the business going in a disaster. Perhaps, they can be used a stopgap until an alternate recovery site is available. This can mean the difference between a <1 hour RTO realization and a 24 or 48 hour RTO realization.

In a fire scenario, your employees will hopefully evacuate quickly and according to protocol, as the safety team and you have trained them to do. They must never waste any time trying to get their laptops on the way out. Having backup laptops can be critical to your meeting your business recovery requirements.

Imagine, the fire department is on the scene in your parking lot and advises that the building has sustained significant damage and is uninhabitable. It is unsafe for anyone to go back in to retrieve anything. Everyone is standing at the rally point. Your Senior Vice President's next question is directed point blank to you – 'hey <<your name goes here>> what is the recovery plan?'

Now, remember, all the laptops are in the building and have already melted. Many users have work-from-home as their primary recovery strategy – but no machines. Hmmm, interesting!

Well, hopefully you have a 3rd party recovery site or a sister site in which you can recover. Unless you have a nearby hot site, employees may not be able to get to the 3rd party site until the next day or the second day following declaration. It depends on many factors such as distance, care for children or parents and your service level agreement (SLA) with the vendor. A critical question arises, do you have enough spare laptops at your disposal to support work-from-home or to work at a sister-site to keep the business going?

Perhaps after reading this book you wisely look into utilizing all those returned, fairly new laptops.
1. You have IT image them
2. You test them
3. You have employees test them
4. You store them in a secure location

Congratulations, today those laptops are going to make you a hero! No don't thank me – thank you.
I have successfully implemented this strategy several times at enterprise, mid-size and small companies. In one case, for an enterprise sized company, we used hundreds of returned laptops. The estimated savings was $411,000+ the first year, with similar recurring savings every 4 years. We stored the laptops in strategic locations. The laptops were available for multiple sites in case of a disruptive event, getting us even more 'bang for the buck'.

Maybe, to get started, poke around a bit (or better yet a byte), talk to management, talk to IT, talk to purchasing and see if there are some laptops you can leverage for business continuity purposes. You very well may find there are lots of laptops sitting in closets collecting dust. You may also be pleasantly surprised by managements' enthusiastic reaction to you creatively protecting the business AND saving them significant money!

Tip – If you cannot find in-house recovery laptops you may want to consider using Chromebooks. I have had great success with these off-the-shelf extremely inexpensive laptops. They do not have much power but for your purposes you may not need a beast of a machine. Speak with your information technology department about testing Chromebooks to see if they can do the job.

If you give this a try or are using this strategy already, please let me know. Good luck!

71

SPECIALIZED EQUIPMENT OFFSITE STORAGE TIPS, TECHNIQUES AND IDEAS

When you performed your BIA dependency analysis interviews with process owners, I know you asked them about any specialized equipment they will require during a disruptive event. In fact, we discussed probing for specialized equipment in the Chapter 'Recipe for a Successful BIA'.

It is important to store these offsite, either at the recovery location or a central site that can send the equipment to multiple sites.

Remember, the disruptive event could be regional and equipment could be difficult to attain when other companies are competing with you for limited resources. It is critical to plan for this.

Examples of specialized equipment:
- MICR printers (check printing)
- Checks (blank)
- Custom forms
- High-speed scanners
- Rubber stamps
- Headphones
- Mice
- Extra batteries…

Tip – Do an inventory audit of the specialized equipment and supplies stored offsite. Do it on a regular basis. Requirements can change and certain supplies such as batteries will need to be replaced over time.

Tip – Sometimes processes require costly equipment be available, such as high-speed scanners. One strategy I use is to use recently retired high-speed scanners and store them at a 3rd third party recovery vendor. The equipment can then be leveraged for multiple sites in the event of a disruption.

If the specialized equipment requires a computer with special drivers it may make sense to store both the fully configured computer and the specialized equipment together and ready to be shipped at time of a disruption. I have 'been there, done that' with high speed scanners and fully configured computers, it works well.

If you will not be storing a computer, make sure you have a copy of the scanner drivers available or you can download and install them at the recovery site at time of disruption.

If you are storing equipment with a third-party vendor here are a few tips:

Tip – Test the request and delivery process to the recovery site(s) prior to a real disruption. A perfect time to do it is during a work area relocation exercise.

Tip – You may find issues the first few times you test recalling equipment from a vendor. Work on the issues and test delivery again until it is perfect.

Tip – Make sure you have the proper phone number to call to retrieve the equipment. Is it in your business continuity plan?

Tip – Make sure you are on the authorized list to recall equipment and that you have backup team members that understand the procedure to recall the equipment if you are not available.

Tip – Make sure you have your customer number and your password if it is required to initiate a request to have the equipment sent from storage to the recovery site.

72

ESTABLISH EMPLOYEE WORK-FROM-HOME AND LAPTOP TAKE-HOME POLICIES AND PROCEDURES

Laptops and tablets have replaced desktops as the primary work tool for many employees. This can be a plus in building resilience. With a laptop or tablet and a good virtual private network (VPN), a large percentage of your organization can work securely from anywhere they can get an Internet connection and in some instances connectivity may not even be required.

Working from home can be a valuable part of a robust recovery strategy and in certain disasters is a must. We know people will be reluctant to leave their family during many types of events. There could even be the circumstance where your business is open but schools are closed and employees have no one to take care of their children.

Scenario 1 – your building is open but schools are closed policy:
A friend described this interesting scenario which occurred early in her career as a consultant. There was an early season ice storm in Connecticut. Schools were closed BUT the company's facilities team did such a great job opening one of their major sites by flipping on the generator and clearing the parking lots. So, the building was officially open BUT they did not have a policy for allowing children to accompany their parents to work. Employees certainly could not leave their children home and HR could not give the local Connecticut management team a definitive answer as to whether employees could bring children to work. There was then the question if employees stayed home would they be charged for personal days?

Ultimately local management allowed employees to bring their children to the office and set up all kinds of entertainment and food for them. The employees were so grateful and indebted to the company for doing this.

The point is you should prepare for these types of situations by discussing them with your HR and Legal experts. I have experienced these types of questions arising during tabletops. Develop policies and procedures in advance. Create awareness with management and employees so they can properly prepare. This will eliminate confusion during a disaster.

Scenario 2 – organization issued laptop take home policy:

You may experience people leaving their laptops in the office rather than taking it home. They may leave it in a desk drawer or on the desktop. As we know, a disruptive event often happens outside of regular business hours. In that case people would not be able to work from home without their laptop.

I was advising a company a few years ago that faced this problem. Digging into the data we found the issue of not taking laptops home was more prevalent in urban environments, where they had to be 'schlepped' on mass transit as opposed to rural environments where they could be transported in the trunk of an employee's car. In any event the organization had a continuity problem. Here are a few tips that can help. It is important to get the backing of management to make this work:

Tip – Develop a policy to the effect that when employees receive a corporate laptop and their primary recovery strategy is work-from-home, they must take their laptop home every night, unless they have a second corporate issued computer at home.

Tip – On occasion test employees by stationing your business continuity team at guard posts in the lobby to check if employees are bringing in their laptops in the morning or if they had left them in the office overnight.

Tip – Walk the office floors at night to see which employees left their laptops on their desks.

Tip – Instruct employees who have a legitimate reason they cannot transport their laptop home on a daily basis to speak with their manager. In some valid cases perhaps they can secure a second machine for home use or your company can create a sandbox virtual machine environment on their home computer so they could securely access corporate systems. If the person has a critical recovery role, purchasing a second machine for them may make sense.

Tip – During unannounced recovery exercises do not allow employees to go to into the office to retrieve their laptops. When word gets around about this, people will hopefully have more incentive to take their laptops home. Otherwise let them know they will be reported to management. People do not like being reported to management. Use 'you will be reported to management' whenever you really need something done when building your program.

In my experience these tips can help. Be consistent with your message and eventually a large majority of your organization's company's employees will take their laptops home every night. For the company I was advising, it paid off. They had to enact their recovery plans on several occasions and each time a great majority of the employees could work from home on their laptops.

73

BUILD A VALUE LADEN IN-HOUSE RECOVERY HOT-SITE

I know you can do it, because I have done it multiple times, for many clients! Every scenario is different; however, I have saved $150k+ (and much higher) annually in some instances. Enormous savings are achieved due to the high expense of a using a third-party vendor for dedicated seats (as opposed to shared seats) and the compressing of RTO to minutes rather than hours or days – depending on a vendor's service level agreement.

In one instance building an in-house hot-site recovery trading floor was a big win for me in my business continuity career. I patterned much of my future thinking and many of my subsequent successful projects on this type of innovative low cost/high return on investment solution. You can extend this thinking to any type of very time-sensitive process you need quickly recovered.

Here are some suggestions based on my success in building in-house recovery solutions:
Processes, such as customer service and securities trading, require extremely aggressive RTO's and RPO's. If you are down even a couple of hours it can mean missing very large financial opportunities, reputation impacts and regulatory implications. The goal is to build recovery capability with a less-than-1-hour RTO. That would mean critical systems must be available and butts need to be in recovery seats ready to trade in less than one hour. So, let's push the envelope. By the way, I have achieved this scenario and ultimately surpassed our goal and delivered customer service and trading rooms that had a <15-minute recovery time!

Your alternative is to have a hot site with a third-party vendor. I have used this solution as well and it can be very good. You will incur a significant expense, but it may make sense if the impact of the process not being available is significant. I have also used a combination of an in-house hot-site recovery solution and a vendor solution to attain maximum resilience.

Here are some tips that may help you if you are considering building an in-house hot site recovery solution:

241

Tip – Bring together a formal project team to map out the details. You will need the backing of your senior leadership, as it is a big project. You will also need the business process you are building the recovery solutions for, IT, facilities and other professionals working as an integrated team. In my experience, it takes a great team and a couple of intense months to build the solution. I come from a project management background integrating data centers and building enterprise software solutions so it was easy for me to build a comprehensive very detailed plan. You may want to include someone from you project management office for this project, otherwise if they do not have a resource you can do it.

Tip – Consider using a conference room or similar work-space. I have utilized conference rooms and training rooms at sites located an appropriate distance (not too far or close) from the production site.

Tip – Use cloud computing solutions where appropriate. I use a mixture of cloud and internal infrastructure where it makes sense from a capability and security perspective. The cloud solution simplifies recovery from any location.

Tip – Spend as much time as necessary to get the telecommunications part right. If you are re-routing customer facing toll free numbers make sure you have captured them all and built routing tables. You will then be in a resilient position to re-route your toll-free numbers anywhere in minutes. I go into more detail in the chapter, 'How Time Sensitive Call Re-Routing Can Keep Customers Happy AND Add New Customers/ Revenue' in this part of the book.

Tip – Partner with IT and regularly image and patch the desktops and laptops. This should be an automated process, if possible. Test aggressively. Having the solution in-house reduces travel time and any hassles using the vendor's infrastructure – so there are no excuses not to tested.

Tip- Read the chapter 'Reduce Expenses and Improve Resilience with The Laptop Re-use Project', about utilizing retired laptops as recovery machines. I have found 'not so old' retired laptops or inexpensive Chromebooks can be great recovery machines. With more and more systems going to the cloud you can often use laptops with 'lighter' configurations as opposed to systems that require heavy powerful 'client machine' configurations. The best way to determine if all systems are working is to partner with IT and test – test – test. You will discover if there is any latency or system conflicts. Perhaps, you are not expecting

242

business as usual during a crisis so a small amount of latency might be acceptable to keep the business continuing.

Tip – The secret to getting from <1 hour to <15 minutes is in the people! If you can, train shadow staff at the hot-site recovery location to assume recovering the process until the primary recovery staff can arrive at the location. I have done this on numerous occasions for customer service and trading. The business process managers have to take ownership of the cross training; however, it will be worth the effort to compress any potentially very expensive down-time impacts.

Tip – Success is in the details. Do tabletops and workstation recovery exercises based on having to activate your in-house hot-site. Think about forms, special equipment, headsets, batteries, stamps… the devil is truly in the detail.

Tip – In my experience, management just loves and values this type of win-win solution.

74

HOW I SAVED MY BUTT USING CREATIVE RECOVERY SITES AND YOU CAN TOO!

There may be times that your primary work location is impacted by a disruptive event and you cannot conveniently work-from-home, a sister site, a third-party-vendor or a mobile recovery trailer. In those scenarios, you must be resilient and think outside-the-box.

I have been in those types of situations during my career. In fact, I think disruptive events know where I am and try to get the best of me! On those occasions, we must reach deep-down and embrace the challenge! Here are a few tips gleaned from creative alternate recovery sites that saved my 'butt'. I am sure you have your own innovative strategies ready just in case:

Tip – Starbucks (of course) – Saved me numerous times. On one occasion, I worked from there during a power outage resulting from a hurricane. It was comfortable and no one hassled me. I love their coffee and I even have a gold card! Starbucks rules! P.S. a healthy portion of the book you are reading was written in Starbucks.

Tip – McDonald's – I was snowed-in during a major winter storm a few years ago. The snow drifts were 24+ inches in height. My power at home was out BUT there was a McDonald's approximately half a mile from my house that got power back before anyone else in the neighborhood. So, in snow up to my knees, and higher in spots, I trudged my way to McDonald's and worked from the comfort of the world's largest hamburger chain. Thank you, McDonald's!

Tip – Public library – I used it when I had no connectivity at home. I needed to send a mass notification alert at 7 pm. The second floor of my local library became my temporary command center. Wireless access, printers... thanks Syosset library!

Tip –Dunkin' Donuts – Somehow the Long Island Railroad got me to Dunkin'. I got off the Long Island Railroad and was stranded then there for three hours during a raging blizzard. I also had to manage a crisis and do multiple mass notification alerts. Dunkin' made my evening! Great dinner consisting of coffee, 'old-fashioned' AND chocolate cream donuts and more coffee and more coffee! Hey,I am not complaining. If you are going to get stranded, I recommend Dunkin' Donuts!

Tip – My friend's den – On another occasion my condo had lost power. A friend a few blocks away saved the day.

Tip – A small sales office of my large company. They graciously set me up in a tiny room the size of a big closet but it was nirvana to me! Everything I needed to continue working. I fortunately had this recovery option documented as part of my planning strategy.

Tip – Hotel business office center (I was not even a registered guest) – The hotel management allowed me to use a desktop and printer. I VPN'ed into my corporate infrastructure and worked like I was in the office AND the hotel staff treated me to coffee and fruit!

Tip – My condo clubhouse – I wrote a couple of chapters of this book during a brief power outage. I had done prior testing for this recovery solution – and it paid off! I also found time for a workout on the treadmill!

Think resilience and get it done! Think about interesting places you can use as a recovery location. With a laptop, tablet, smart phone, cellular or wireless connectivity, VPN access… you probably can work from almost anywhere. Throw in a satellite phone and I would venture you could work anywhere on the planet!

Where is the most creative place you have worked from?

VI

PART 6 - BUSINESS CONTINUITY PLANS

This part of the book will focus on documenting and re-thinking the possible options for your business continuity plans.

Often people, not knowledgeable in BRBC (Business Resilience / Business Continuity), think documenting plans is our only value. Although documented and tested plans are critical, this book demonstrates it is only the tip of the iceberg in the value we provide.
As usual, I will offer some creative ideas. Imagine offering business continuity plans in eReader format or a tiny format! 'Easy peasy', as you will 'see-zy' (ouch – I could not resist that one).

I will share plan data elements and formats that have worked well for me. All organizations are different, so the plan data and formats I present may work for you or perhaps they will not. Hopefully, you will take away a few idea nuggets that you can expand on for your own benefit.

We will also discuss the value of a business continuity management (BCM) system rather than word processing documents or spreadsheets as scalable solutions for your plans and beyond!

75

CREATE LASER FOCUSED BUSINESS CONTINUITY PLANS FOR DEPARTMENTS

The department (process) level business continuity plan is the 'cookbook' to recovering a department and sub-departments (sub-processes). There is no one 'right way' to document a plan. If you do some research you will find well over 100 styles of business continuity plans. Decide on a style that meets the needs of your management and your process owners. I hope some of the ideas I present below will be beneficial to you.

I have created thousands of business continuity plans in my career (yes thousands – not hundreds) and the information in this chapter has worked well for me. More importantly, this information and simple straight-forward plans have worked for my department owners during disruptive events including hurricanes, tornadoes, earthquakes, blizzards, power outages, pandemics and more. Remember, it is all about 'them' – the people that must use the plans.

Please do not feel you must use this information exactly as presented. In fact, I would be quite surprised if this information is exactly mapped to the needs of your organization. I suggest you extract what makes sense for your organization, and disregard the rest.

Listed below are examples of departments and teams I have created plans for in various organizations. Please customize for your organization:
1. Accounting
2. Auditing
3. Brokerage
4. Business Continuity (somehow this process is often forgotten)
5. Compliance
6. Customer Service
7. Delivery
8. Executive management
9. Facilities
10. Factory Operations
11. Human Resources
12. Information Technology
13. Legal
14. Marketing

15. Purchasing
16. Research and Development
17. Risk Management
18. Safety
19. Sales
20. Security
21. Securities Trading
22. Upper Management
23. Warehouse Operations

Each department can have one or more sub-departments. For example, Human Resources may be comprised of:

- Benefits
- Employee on-boarding
- Recruitment
- Training

The department and sub departments would have been identified during the Business Impact Analysis (BIA). The data captured during the BIA should automatically flow into your business continuity plans, provided you are using a good BCM tool. If not, you can do it manually.

Tip – Keep the department level plans as simple and clean as possible. During the stress of a disruptive event a 150 page 'kitchen sink' plan, beyond the goal of recovering the process, will be counterproductive and often useless.

If you are using a BCM tool it should provide simple ready-to-use templates for department (process) level plans. If the system is designed properly it will easily roll department information up to wider scope location, division and even to the enterprise level plans. There should be zero manually effort in doing this. We discuss wider scope plans in the next chapter.

In addition, you should be able to view functional plans across your organization, such as a plan for all of customer service encompassing multiple sites. The ability to automatically 'cut the data' various ways will provide management with a holistic view of your organization. More on that when we dig deeper into BCM tools and 'how a database works 101' in the technology part of the book.

Tip – Succession planning is sometimes overlooked. Plan the orderly succession for ALL key executives and managers. The primary person

248

may not be available at time of crisis. People also leave, retire, etc. Do a holistic review of your succession related risk.

Tip – Where it adds value I suggest you break out dependency requirements at the sub-department (component) level, rather than at the department level. You do not have to do this for every dependency as some dependencies will not easily map to sub-process granularity. Do it where it adds value.

You can then configure your BCM tool to automatically summarize the sub-departments at the department level (and above). Dependencies can be described over a series of time recovery time buckets. I typically break these buckets down to <4 hours, 24 hours (Day 1), 48 hours (Day 2), 72 hours (Day 3), 168 hours (1 Week) and finally 'Defer'. You should decide on time buckets that make sense for your organization's recovery goals.

This type of time-line implementation can be very useful in many ways. For example, to fuel a dynamic employee recovery seat requirement report in which you can map recovery employees to the capability of each of your recovery locations to understand if any locations have been oversubscribed to. For example, recovery site A has 40 seats but processes using that as their primary recovery location require 100 seats in total. Your system can automatically analyze this each time a piece of data changes and it can email you if there is a gap. I describe this dynamic, automatic, real-time process in detail in the assessment part of the book.

You can still do this analysis manually in word processing documents or spreadsheets, etc. but it is much more difficult, error prone, time consuming and will provide far less value in the short and long term. Most importantly, instead of being real-time it will often be outdated and wrong.

Tip – In addition to dynamic data in the plans, department business continuity plans should include maps, directions and any static instructions that will help recover the department. I once had a very dedicated Vice President map out detailed public transportation routes to the recovery site – by walking part of the route and then riding a bus to the site!

However, you are not getting paid by the word. It is more difficult to make the plans simpler, but you should strive to make them as brief, clean and simple as possible without losing functionality. There will be a lot of stress at crisis time and people only want and need information that helps them recover.

Tip – Use checklists wherever possible. I am a great proponent of checklists. If you think checklists will not cut it, you may be interested to learn that airline pilots use simple checklists before every flight to insure they do not miss any safety steps prior to takeoff. Medical professionals use simple checklists before every operation. In each case, they provide great value or they would not still be used.

If you need more proof that checklists are beneficial, I recommend you read, *'The Checklist Manifesto: How to Get Things Right' by Atul Gawande*. It describes various types of checklists and the impact they have on many professions. Also please read the chapter in this book – *'How Checklists Can Change Your Life and Supercharge Your Program'*

Tip – Plans are 'living documents' and MUST be kept current. All plans must be maintained on a regular basis during an official maintenance period – I would recommend quarterly. In addition, plans should be updated whenever there is a change to the department. Reinforce the importance of keeping plans accurate during tabletops and recovery exercises. Also, create awareness using all the tools we will discuss in the awareness part of the book.

Tip – Plans must be assessed whenever changes are made to them to determine the probability of recovering the department and to ascertain new risks that might be raised by the changes. Assessment after the regular maintenance period is a step in the right direction but we want to do much better. In the plan assessment chapter I will describe where we want to go in achieving real-time world-class assessment!

Tip – It is critical to test the department level plan on a regular basis. We talk about that in detail in the next part of the book – Testing.

Tip – Awareness of plans and the roles people are responsible for during a
disruptive event must be part of your corporate culture. The details cannot be buried in the plan and not understood until time of crisis. That won't work!

Tip – Keep in mind all crisis events have their own defining wrinkles. The business continuity plan probably will not be perfect. The plan **must** provide for resilience through adaptability. Build out a resilient culture and you will have a great chance to survive and thrive.

250

Below is a list of entities I have included in department plans. You should add, delete and modify to match your needs:

- Crisis team contact information
- Crisis communications policy and public agency contact information (police, fire, hospitals…)
- A brief description of the department
- Assumptions
- Department manager and alternate manager contact names and contact information.
- Department RTO's and RPO's
- Department inputs (upstream)
- Department outputs (downstream)
- Alternate recovery strategies. For example – on day two – three employees will work from home. On day three – five employees will work from ABC site… I maintain this in a narrative field and as structured data elements to produce gap analysis reports against recovery space, etc.
- Recovery employee contact info. You may also be able to map the employees to your mass notification tool thru an API (application programming interface) that can enable you to access their contact information and to initiate notifications. This type of data integration aligns to our mantra of maintaining the same data in as few places as possible which has many advantages. I discuss this throughout the book as it relates to data quality, integrity and normalization.
- Telecom section. DID's (local exchange phone numbers) and critical customer facing toll free phone numbers. To properly recover toll free numbers routing procedures must be implemented in telecom routing tables and tested prior to a disruption. When new toll free's are added to plans in the telecom section, it should trigger an email to your team so you can research if the toll free has been accounted for in the telecom routing table and properly tested. I discuss this in-depth in the Recovery Strategies part of the book. You do not want to learn at time of crisis that a critical customer facing toll free telephone number has to be re-routed and it is not properly set up
- Software application section – all critical applications must be listed with RTO and RPO. You can develop application impact analysis (AIA) reports to identify business recovery requirements versus the actual recovery capability of the systems defined by the information technology department

- Equipment section – all critical equipment must be listed in the plan. You should store critical equipment such as MICR printers, scanners, rubber stamps, forms… at the recovery site or in a central location to be delivered at time of crisis to one of many recovery locations. I store equipment in various locations depending on my company's location assets. We discuss specialized equipment storage ideas in the Recovery Strategies part of the book.
- Vendors section – all critical vendors AND backup vendors should be listed with full contact information included down to the rep level
- Customers section – if you have a small number of customers consider documenting them in the body of the plan with contact information. If a department has thousands of customers perhaps you can give them the option of attaching a customer list to the plan. You also might want to add your customers to your mass notification tool for proactive notification during a crisis. Customers appreciate status notifications
- Vital records section – Is there anything in the production site (e.g. case folders, tracking spreadsheets, etc.) that would be critical to recovery?
- Team Leader, Alternate Team Leaders and Team Members – These roles and the people appointed to them will have responsibility for performing tasks to recover the department. Always plan for the possibility that department owner and Team Leader may not be available during an event. Tasks must be understood by the backups. Everyone on the team that is assigned a task should understand exactly what they must do.
- Tasks – step-by-step list of action items that will guide the department owner and recovery team through the crisis response and recovery phases. Task development will most likely be an iterative process. I suggest using team roles rather than individual names when attaching responsibilities to each of the tasks. Try to include manual workarounds, where possible, in the event software systems are not available. Have someone other than the person that built the task list read through the tasks to see if they can follow the progression and if anything has been left out of the plan. Keep it as simple as possible
- Location of your process ready-box(s). Options include: at a sister-site, 3rd party recovery vendor, Iron Mountain…The box(s) can contain forms, rubber stamps and anything else that will be required to recover the process. If these are only available at the

production site and it is gone, you have a single point of failure. You need redundancy

- Location address and detailed directions to the alternate recovery site(s). Include public transportation if it exists
- Attachments. Very important. Get process owners thinking about attaching supporting documents to their plan. Word processing, spreadsheets, etc. that will be critical to recover their process. If you are using a BCM system, it should provide an option to simply and securely store the attachments in the cloud and to optionally have them printed as part of the plan
- Confidentiality Statement – use care when distributing the plan. It contains employee contact information and other sensitive process information. It should only be distributed to people with responsibility to carry out the plan. Individual section contributors will only need specific information to do their job. Information should be published on a need-only basis

Plan Availability:
1. Plans should be kept at home and in the office
2. Plans should be kept in the command center
3. Information from the individual plans should be rolled-up in higher level regional and enterprise plans

Tip – The plans must be easily accessible always. Both digital and paper versions are ideal. Later in this part of the book I describe some new ideas to make plans more accessible than simply available in the traditional 8 1/2 x 11 format.

76

CREATE WIDE SCOPE 'ROLL-UP PLANS' - INFO AT YOUR FINGERTIPS

On a higher and wider scope level than the individual department business continuity plans, which we discussed in the previous chapter, you can attain additional value by creating larger, more comprehensive plans. These plans can consolidate business information at varying levels in anticipation of disruptive events that may impact a wider scope of your organization.

These types of plans, depending on your organizational hierarchy, can provide value at the enterprise, global, regional, divisional and/or location level. These hybrid plans are in addition to your focused Crisis Management, Crisis Communications, Emergency Response and Disaster Recovery Plans.

I will caution you that it is important to make sure these larger information roll-up plans are designed with usability in mind. It is critical to organize the information as simply and elegantly as possible. During the design phase obtain input from the people who will be using the roll-up plan. Understand what will be important to them at time of crisis. If you have a communications or publishing department in your organization, also speak with them regarding good design.

These larger 'one-stop-shop' plans can also incorporate crisis management, response, scenario specific static and dynamic response steps, as well as the business process roll-ups to the hierarchy level you desire. In my experience, it is advantageous to use checklists where possible. These wider scope plans would be overkill and too confusing for individual 'boots on the ground' process owners who are laser focused on recovering their department.

If you are like me, you and your crisis team will find value having everything at your fingertips. You will not have to go searching around during a pressurized situation for important information. Imagine having to consolidate business requirement dependencies sifting through individual plans. Imagine scavenging around for a phone number or address of the 3rd party recovery site and your customer identification number? That would not be the best use of your time.

The cool thing is, if you are using a flexible business continuity management (BCM) tool powered by a relational database that has properly separated the presentation and data layers (more on that in upcoming chapters), you should be able to automatically populate the 'roll-up' dynamic data in the higher-level plans.

For example, you could roll-up all the business processes and underlying systems impacted at a single location, region or even globally. You will also be able to create reports, checklists and metric dashboards in any amount of detail or summary that you and management require.

Your BCM tool should have the ability to slice, dice and present the information any way you want and need it – with minimal effort. You should also have the ability to create 'ad-hoc' on the fly reports with minimal effort. In the technology part of the book I describe these benefits and many more that I require from a BCM tool.

Think of plans in a BCM tool as template containers. They can access information stored in the underlying database in fields, records and tables AND integrate those with static information. Static information does not change and can be 'hard-coded' into the plan templates. For example, descriptions of recovery role responsibilities or the emergency hotline telephone number might be consistent throughout your organization. You could hard-code these into the template.

We are in a data business. To make you more comfortable with these data concepts we will dig a bit deeper into the workings and power of a relational database in the technology part of the book. I promise it will not turn into an advanced database tutorial. I just want to demonstrate how a database can help you and help to level the playing field when you are speaking with vendors trying to sell you solutions along with your internal IT partners.

I am available for follow-up technical questions. I try to answer every question, if possible.

HMMM, DO YOU HAVE A BUSINESS CONTINUITY PLAN FOR YOUR BC DEPARTMENT?

Ok, be very honest – did you remember to build a plan for your Business Continuity/Resilience Department?

Did you include the Business Continuity/Resilience Department in your BIA?
Did you include the Business Continuity Department in the Executive Report you created?
Do you have a documented plan for the Business Continuity/Resilience Department at the enterprise and local levels?

Do you have your Business Continuity/Resilience team backup assigned and trained? Are tasks listed in the Business Continuity / Resilience business continuity plan?

It seems like a 'no-brainer'. Business Continuity / Resilience is so important to the survival of our organization. It is somewhat embarrassing but I have reviewed programs where building a plan for our department is overlooked. There is no documented plan and we are the people that develop the plans!

Fortunately, this is an easy one to fix. Simply include Business Continuity/Resilience throughout your documented resilience program.

WHY DIGITAL AND PAPER PLANS ARE BOTH CRITICAL

Although I love technology I am going a bit old-school with this one so we leave nothing to chance.

Create awareness among process owners that they should always have access to a paper 'hard' copy of their plan. Also, tech it out by making plans available to them in a secure location of your intranet. An internal website is a great place to store plans. Just make sure employees only have access to the plans they own. In addition, consider providing access to plans in a secure app. Good BCM systems include robust apps.

Paper is important as under certain circumstances the digital copy may not be available and the paper copy can be a business-saver.

You can use this as a template for your awareness message or customize as you see fit:

Dear <<process owner name>,
Disruptive events have a strange way of happening at the most inconvenient times. Your business continuity plan is your 'cookbook' for responding and recovering to any disruptive event so it is important to:

- Keep a printed copy at home (I keep it in my bedroom)
- Keep a printed copy at work
- Keep a mini-plan with you always

You can also access your plan on <<name of accessible site – if you have VPN>>. But remember, we are a resilient organization. We frown on single points of failure. You must have access to a paper copy of your plan in case you do not have power OR your network infrastructure is the disruptive event and you cannot get to the digital copy of your plan.
Please contact me if you have any questions.
Thank you,
<<Your name and contact info goes here>>

END-OF-EMAIL

HOW TO CREATE TINY PLANS

I often asked myself, '*Why do all business process plans have to be 8 1/2" x 11"?*' I could not come up with a good answer so I began experimenting. In this chapter, we look at another approach, 'How tiny can be beautiful!'

There is definitely a place for large, detailed, wide-scope, well-written corporate crisis management plans 75+ pages at 8 1/2" x 11". They can be critical when managing a crisis at a high level, such as the enterprise, regional or divisional level. Although, in my experience, at the process and sub-process level more can be less and less can be more!

If a disaster conveniently occurs when you are at home or in the office and you have easy access to the large plan that is great. Unfortunately, disasters time themselves when we are travelling, at the movies or running 5k's – been there, done that! It is uncanny how they occur at such inconvenient times. You may be able to access the digital version of your plan but in certain types of disruptions, such as a power outages, it could be difficult or impossible to get access to it.

For years, I sat among the business process owners. The only time I heard an urgency on their part to review their over-sized plans was 30 minutes before a tabletop exercise when they would yell to team members, 'where the heck is that huge plan we had to create last year?' Well, often it was in the corner collecting dust or being used to prop a door open. I decided early in my career to deliver a simpler more streamlined type of plan and it has worked well for process owners though many disruptive events. The paper version of the plan was still 8 1/2" x 11" but it worked well.

Here is my 'take the 8 1/2" x 11" streamlined plan to the next level' idea:
For each business process create the larger, traditional size plan. In addition, create a 'mini-plan' which is a tiny, compact, portable plan that people can carry in their pocket or pocket book. These 'mini-plans' must include all of the critical information required to respond to and recover a business process and its' sub- processes. It should be customized with important contact info to reach public agencies, the employee hotline, safety, security, the business continuity team and management.

My' mini-plan' is a compact 4" x 5" booklet containing checklists, dependencies, recovery info and process tasks... all the essential information its' bigger cousin has, but it is a heck of a lot more portable and a heck of a lot cuter!

The little guy should be data driven. Focus on people, location, equipment, systems and importantly tasks! Strip out unnecessary static info. Keep only actionable information.

The 'mini-plan' should easily fit in a pocket book or pocket and can even be folded over if necessary to 4" x 2.5" and carried in your wallet! I even ran a 5k last year with a tiny plan in my shorts pocket and won my age group! I will bet I am the first person that won a 5k with a business continuity plan in his pocket.

While developing the 'mini-plan' I experimented with many other sizes, both smaller and larger, portrait and landscape. The 4"x 5" size seemed ideal so I went with it and I am happy I did. At the time of this writing, I am also having success developing and testing a 'teeny-tiny-plan' 1/2 the dimension of the 'mini-plan'. I will be writing about this in an upcoming issue of the Free Ultimate Business Continuity Tips, Techniques and Tools Newsletter.
Best of all the 'mini-plan' prints as a booklet on standard and relatively inexpensive A6 laser paper. Many standard printers can use that size paper.
I give process owners the big cousin for home, office and audit purposes and the little cousin for everywhere else.

I hope the 'mini-plan' provides you with an idea you can further develop for your own use.

80

HOW TO MAKE LONG-LASTING EREADER READY PLANS

I always keep my antennas up for new ways I can improve
business resilience / continuity. Sometimes I come up with
ideas that utilize manual improvements but often, my ideas
involve technological solutions. The idea we will discuss in this
chapter came to me in a round-about way. Here is what
happened:

A short while back I was researching some new racewalking and running
techniques to hopefully improve my 5k and 10k racing times and to
lessen the likelihood of getting a running related injury. I decided to see
if there were any books that might be of use to me.

I found a book on Amazon that looked interesting and most of the
reviews were decent, but not great. Then POP BANG HOLY
BATMAN! the next review I read mentioned a book that the reviewer
thought was fantastic! He said the author was a former world-champion
runner and that the book was packed with easy to implement
information to improve times and lessen the likelihood of sustaining a
running related injury by teaching proper technique. The book had
helped the reviewer significantly improve his racing times and avoid
injury. It seemed on-target for my needs.

Although I had never heard of the book I was intrigued and wanted to
know more. Easy enough, I would find it on Amazon, read the inside
sample chapters, buy it, read it, lower my racing times and not have to
worry about getting injured! Hey, I had a plan! We always need a plan,
right?

Well, as you know, sometimes things do not work out according to our
plan and we must be resilient. Remarkably, the book was not on
Amazon. What! How could that be? So, on to plan B; we always have a
plan B.
Perhaps I had the wrong name of the book or the author. I started
Googling and lo-and-behold the book appeared in the search results. It
seems the book was decades old and not available on Amazon. It was
available on several running websites but only in pdf format.

Next, I downloaded the pdf. The content was just what I was looking for but it was over 100 pages and I did not want to read it on my desktop or a tablet. I do not enjoy reading books or very long documents on my tablet. The screen seems to tire my eyes. I much prefer reading on my Kindle back-lit DX.

Unfortunately, there is a big problem reading lengthy pdfs on a Kindle BUT fortunately there are some really cool solutions. The solutions might even provide nice value to your business resilience program, otherwise this chapter would not have made it to the book.

The PDF to eBook Process:
So, how do we get a pdf on a Kindle? I had downloaded and read hundreds of .MOBI Kindle formatted eBooks and documents from Amazon but I did not even know how to get a pdf on the Kindle. A little digging demonstrated it is easy. You simply email the pdf to your Kindle email address. You can find your address in the Amazon Digital Content Settings. It will be something like <<your user name>>@kindle.com.

I tried emailing the pdf and it worked on the Kindle! I was so happy and I was about to write the solution up for the article you are reading. Imagine simply saving your plans as pdf's and having them available on an inexpensive/long battery life e-reader.

We all know how critical it is that we are able to access and use our business continuity plans during any disruptive event. We cannot count on having power or even back up batteries when traveling. Even with battery-backups, a tablet may only have enough power for a couple of days. My Kindle easily holds its' charge for 2+ weeks. It is also back-lit, even though it is a dinosaur compared to some of the newer Kindle and Nook devices, which are still really cheap.

When I opened the pdf on my Kindle I instantly had the wind knocked out of my, '*hey Marty you think you are so smart*' sails. The font size was really small. I mean teensy-weensy small. I mean magnifying glass required small.

I figured I could adjust the font as I do with .MOBI formatted eBooks on the Kindle. Unfortunately, that is not the case in pdf format. If I enlarged the font size the words scrolled off the screen, which made it almost impossible to use. There was no way I could read that 100 page running document unless I held a magnifying glass in front of my eyes.

I started Googling again. Every post I read indicated the solution is to not read pdf's on a Kindle. Just use your tablet. Not exactly the solution I was seeking. Then at 2 am after digging through hundreds of posts (I never give up) I came upon one that mentioned PDF4Kindle. Hmmm. PDF4Kindle is an online pdf converter whereby you upload your pdf and it converts it to a .MOBI file. That is the format used by the Kindle to do all the neat formatting and page turning. When I visited the site I was met with a notice in big letters saying they were 'taking a break' and not available at this time.

I searched some more and stumbled upon a different cloud conversion solution. I ran the running pdf through it and it did a fairly good job. A few formatting errors here and there and the table of contents was not perfect but definitely a solution that would enable me to read a long document or book and it would save my eyes. But I was not satisfied! I wanted great formatting and I had no intention of using a third party cloud solution for security reasons.

I continued my research and came upon what I think are two great pdf to eBook conversion solutions. Both seem to be secrets to many people. I want to share them with you:

Solution 1)
Very easy. Email the pdf file to your Kindle and simply put **'convert'** in the subject line. That will convert the pdf to .MOBI and queue it up for the next time you synch your Kindle. The final product is readable and has all the .MOBI options available to you **including resizing fonts to fit the Kindle screen**. It is a good solution but for my needs it did not stack up to Solution 2, which I found much more powerful with only a little more work to convert the pdf.

Solution 2)
Very Powerful. This solution takes approximately a minute to convert a pdf to .MOBI but for the negligible additional time investment it provides incredible benefits allowing you to fine tune the final .MOBI book. You can even brand your final product with your company information and create custom search tags. In addition, it can be used for many other input and output files including ePub which is used by many other e-reader devices including The Nook.

The product I use is called Calibre - - https://calibre-ebook.com/. It offers many conversion and formatting options. It took me a minute to download the conversion program from calibre-ebook.com. I installed it and was amazed by how easy it was to import various types of documents and output to formats such as .MOBI, ePub, DocX, RTF,

Zip and many more. It is a very powerful program. As of this writing of this chapter Calibre is free because a large community of software developers devote time and energy to the Calibre solution. Hopefully, when you read this chapter it will still be free.

I converted the running book pdf using **Calibre**. I tweaked the settings a few times testing various output options. I then emailed the .MOBI file to my Kindle email address. Lastly, I synched the Kindle and it found the new file and installed it on my device within 15 seconds. So cool!

I was so impressed by the job Calibre did!! The formatting was comparable to any eBook you would purchase on Amazon. Calibre has so many features. It even has a built-in heuristic option that allows Calibre to figure out how to improve the formatting of the raw pdf. By default, heuristic it is not enabled and you may not need it. Try it both ways.

Ok here is the Business Continuity payoff: I experimented using Calibre to convert a few business continuity plan pdf's to .MOBI. It did a great job every time. The newly converted plans were very usable on the Kindle. I did have to scroll a few of the wider tables in the plans to view them on the limited Kindle screen but I was able to minimize that by re-sizing the fonts on the Kindle. I was able to do that as the plan was now in a true .MOBI format.

I also adjusted the source output that produced the plan from my BCM system so the pdf that Calibre uses to convert to the .MOBI file would be more conducive to the limited Kindle screen. Fortunately when using a BCM system the data is stored in a database. This separates the data from the presentation layer. I was therefore able to easily export a more narrowly formatted e-reader specific version from my system in addition to maintaining the wider paper version and a desktop version.

Finally, to make sure I was not the only person on the planet that did not know how this can be accomplished, I ran it by a few very tech savvy friends. They were impressed and now use the solution for their pdf conversion-to-eBook needs.

Tip – If you will be storing plans on your Kindle or Nook I strongly suggest you enable a password on your eReader. On the Kindle DX it is located from: Home, Menu, Settings – Device Options.

All-in-all I am very happy with the two solutions I described. You should give each a try and see which works best for you and your users. In my case Calibre was the better choice but the first solution may be useful to you, especially if you are not at a desktop that has <u>Calibre</u> installed on it.

I hope you get use out of this idea, whether it is for your business continuity plans or for use in your personal life. Imagine, now any pdf, and many other types of documents, can be enjoyably consumed on a light, cheap e-reader.

Have Fun!

VII

PART 7 - TESTING YOUR WAY TO RESILIENCE

This part of the book drives home the importance of exercising all components of your resilience program. An untested plan is a plan that is doomed to fail. Test, Test, Test.

Although I favor the term 'exercise' when communicating with employees to lower stress and increase learning, I am going to use the terms 'test' and 'exercise' interchangeably in the book.

TESTING YOUR WAY TO RESILIENCE - OVERVIEW, SCOPE AND EXPERIENCES

All Plans, Critical Systems, Recovery Strategies, Cyber and Call Trees / Mass Notification Call Lists must be tested and reviewed on a schedule that aligns to your policies and requirements.

Testing must validate your plans and systems and improve the resilience of your organization. In sports, smart athletes 'practice with a purpose' to improve their weaknesses. We must test with a purpose. Each of the testing types listed below is described in much more detail throughout this book.

I recommend you develop a comprehensive test schedule and publish it during the October or November time-frame of the year prior to the scheduled tests. That will provide you with ample time to communicate the schedule to stakeholders and to adjust where the business has valid date/time concerns.

Although you must maintain and assess the results of the tests, you do not necessarily have to personally host and conduct all of them. From my experience, if you and your team try to do it all by yourselves, your program will suffer. It will not scale as well and it will not be as resilient as taking a more decentralized approach.

If you have established business continuity liaisons at the local sites they could be responsible for the actual conducting of some types of tests that do not require your direct involvement. Perhaps they could conduct mass notification call list tests. An Interchangeable Work Area Recovery Exercise (IWARE) would be beyond their expertise and would require your team to be heavily involved, as it is a relatively complex exercise.

Mass notification is an excellent example of resilience through decentralization. At one point in my career a partner and I were doing all the tests for a Fortune 50 company. It was a lot of work but if it made the organization more resilient I would not have minded conducting the tests. In fact, it worked against us.

The business continuity liaisons were not getting enough practice in doing notifications so when it came time for them to do one during a crisis situation they did not have the level of confidence they required.

When we modified the process so that the business continuity liaisons started doing the mass notification tests, they quickly gained a level of comfort that vastly improved their ability to create and launch notifications during real crisis events, such as tornadoes and hurricanes. Everyone benefited from their direct involvement.

High Level Test Tips (additional detailed information is included in the individual test type chapters throughout the book):
Tip – A comprehensive annual test schedule must be created and adhered to.

Tip – The test schedule must be communicated to management late in the year prior to the upcoming year that the tests are required. For example begin communicating the 2020 schedule late in 2019.

Tip – Upper management must be made aware of results and risks in dashboard reports and as part of your Steering Committee Meetings.

Tip – All tests must have documented goals and measurable success factors. It is important to understand what you want to achieve from each test you conduct. After each test, measure the results to the desired success factors. Then determine the areas you must improve on – and test again.

Tip -Test results must be analyzed and retained. I favor maintaining the results in a business continuity management (BCM) system, rather than silo'ed spreadsheets or word processing documents. The results will be centralized, enabling you to perform interesting gap and trend analysis.

Tip – If you schedule a work area recovery exercise for March and March happens to be one of the busiest month for the accounting department to prepare taxes, you will definitely get push-back from management. You will most likely have to adjust the test dates to get maximum buy-in from the business. Even then, some people will agree to a date and try to beg-off at the last minute. Upper management must have-your-back on the importance of testing. They should publicly declare that all critical processes must participate in all required tests. No exceptions!

Tip – Your responsibility is to design and conduct robust tests without negatively impacting business production. Clearly communicate to process owners that tests will not impact production. Doing so will work in your favor. For example, when doing a work area recovery exercise, set a threshold that each process must send a minimum of 10% or 20% of recovery staff to validate their recovery strategies. You will accomplish the goal of validating the ability to recover the process without raising risk that recovery staff cannot do production work if you find gaps at the recovery site. Another way to say it is, 'Don't put all your eggs in one basket'.

Always encourage the process owners to send a higher percentage of recovery staff if they so desire. The more the merrier! I have done Interchangeable Work Area Recovery Exercises (IWARE) with 150 employees in attendance. It is a really valuable experience for all involved.

Tip – You may find people will push back going to the recovery location but once they arrive and realize how effectively they can recover their department and continue to work during a disruptive event, they will thank you! In fact, I have had many people tell me that they would prefer to work from the recovery location than their production site! The kicker is, some of these people were the ones that balked the most about participating in an exercise. Sometimes the recovery site bandwidth and system response time is better than the usual production site and sometimes the recovery location can be a better commute for them compared to their regular production site journey.

Tip – After the tests are conducted thank attendees and management for their participation in making the tests successful.

Tip – Testing brings people together and strengthens relationships. People talk and sometimes magic happens. These relationships can be critical at time of crisis.

Tests in scope for your program should include but are not limited to:

Site evacuation drills. These may be the responsibility of the Safety Department. In fact, I believe it should be. Clearly document who has responsibility. I suggest creating a RACI chart and getting sign-off so there is no miscommunication down the road.

Manual call tree or automated call list exercises. Call trees with branches typically indicate manually calling versus call list exercises (no branching) using a mass notification system. Automated mass notification systems scale much better than manual call trees. In my experience using manual call trees for mid to large organizations often

268

do not work. They can easily break down when you need them the most. I strongly encourage you to utilize a mass notification system, if possible. I discuss this throughout the book.

1. Tip – Do both location and process based call-list exercises. Your tool should be able to slice and dice contact info to satisfy all conditions

2. Tip – I generally schedule exercises on a semi-annual basis or as often as the business requires them to get to a satisfactory level of successfully reaching employees. If you are requiring two a year, make sure you spread the dates so there are not two exercises one day apart, such as June 30 and July 1

3. Tip – Do not overdo the quantity of notification tests such as on a weekly basis, as employees will become desensitized to the messages and will not pick up the phone. You want them to be conditioned so that when a call, email or text is received from the branded emergency phone number or name you are using they realize it is important, and they must listen to it or read it

Plan walk-throughs, workshops or orientation seminars. These are designed to familiarize team members with emergency response, business continuity and crisis communications plans and to validate their roles and responsibilities as defined in the plans. Walkthoughs allow for validation of plans in a low stress setting. They are good starter exercises after plans are created to uncover obvious gaps and opportunities for improvement.

Tabletop exercises. These are scenario based exercises. I do these for an entire site, a process or multiple processes. You can walk through one or multiple scenarios in a conference or training room. Include crisis management, emergency response and continuity of operations in your tabletop exercises. Tabletops are very effective if done right.

Interchangeable Work Area Recovery Exercise (IWARE) – fully announced. The process owners and employees know the date of the exercise. Recovery staff physically recovers in accordance with the recovery strategies documented in their business continuity plan. The goal is to validate they can work from a recovery location(s) and to uncover/mitigate all gaps.

Interchangeable Work Area Recovery Exercise (IWARE) – partially unannounced. I position this between fully announced and fully unannounced in terms of maturity level and participant stress.

Interchangeable Work Area Recovery Exercise (IWARE) – fully unannounced. The is the most aggressive type of exercise. Carefully work up to this type of exercise. Never begin here. It is as close to being in a real crisis as possible. You can recover one site or, if you have the 'chops' and maturity level, multiple dependent sites! If you are currently doing completely unannounced exercises for multiple sites simultaneously let me know so I can personally congratulate you!

Critical Systems disaster recovery – All critical systems must be tested on a basis that adheres to your corporate policies. Users must be involved to validate the testing.

- Partner with IT and the business on these
- There should be comprehensive user scripts and sign-off by the business authority
- I recommend that the results be stored in your BCM tool, if possible. You will get the most 'bang for the buck' in analyzing the results mapped to business processes and roll-ups to higher regional or line-of-business levels. This will empower you to include insightful information as part of the real-time dashboard metrics that management will have at their fingertips

SELL THEM ON THIS - 'AN UNTESTED PLAN IS A USELESS PLAN'

'Hi-Ho-Hi-Ho a Gap Hunting We Will Go!'
ALL plans must be tested on a regular basis!

Tip – Process owners should bring their plans to tabletops and workstation area recovery exercises. They should use them as-is during the exercise.

Tip – Plans and strategies must be validated. Our goal is to identify gaps preventing the plan from working – before a real disaster occurs.

Tip – During testing, process owners will often discover gaps and updates they must make to their plans including:
• Incorrect RTO
• Incorrect recovery seats required during various time-frames
• Critical systems not listed in their plan
• Employees that are no longer part of their process that remain in their plan
• New employees that must be added to their plan
• Recovery team members no longer in their department
• Equipment
• Vendors
• Customers
• Customer facing critical toll free phone numbers not listed in their plan
• Tasks that must be added, deleted or modified to recover their department

To fully validate plans and identify gaps, use multiple types of tests including those listed in this part of the book. The last thing you want to discover are gaps during a crisis. My advice is to start testing and hunting today.

TABLETOP HOSTING TIPS AND TECHNIQUES

Hosting tabletop exercises is one of my favorite activities. I suppose that is a good thing, as I have hosted 200+ tabletops during my career. Tabletops have so many valuable aspects. They are a low stress way to test your current plans, identify gaps and improve your ability to respond. The more we test, the better we will be prepared at time of crisis.

There are many ways to perform tabletop exercises. If you look at 20 tabletops on the Internet, you will see each has a different style. You can pick and choose the ones that fit your organizational culture and customize the content.

Below are some tips I would like to share with you. They have all been learned through experience. After the list of tips, we will walk through a typical tabletop exercise. I will add suggestions where I think it might help:

Tip – You should always have goals and objectives defined for your tabletops. Know what you want to accomplish, communicate and learn from the attendees. Then work backwards to incorporate the content that will help you achieve your goals. I mentioned a couple of times in the book that when I used to develop complex software systems I would always ask the users (clients) what they wanted to accomplish with the system. What type of output and reports would they need? What metrics would make them happy? What would be the most pleasing layout for input forms (user experience)? I would then design each module in the system to achieve all the user's desires (requirements). I found it a recipe for success every time. In the software / project management profession this is typically called a requirements document. On occasion, I called it a desires document!

Tip – Make the exercise interactive! The more the attendees get absorbed in the scenario, the better. When interactivity takes over I smile! It can be a magical experience!

Tip – Make it fun! I suggest you use slides with pictures and audio to liven up the exercise. Putting a few humorous slides and/or anecdotes in scope will do wonders building rapport with the attendees. The squirrel slide works every time!

Tip – Be careful not to use too many slides. Sometimes, less is more!

Tip – Make it low stress! Not – no stress so they fall asleep – but low stress, so they are not sweating bullets and wondering if they will be 'called on', like in school. This is especially true the first few exercises for a location or process. You are there to improve and partner with them, not to embarrass them. Before hosting tabletops as a business continuity professional, I was an attendee as an IT Senior Technical Officer. It is easy for me to empathize with attendees of exercises I now host.

Tip – Add value. Add value. Add value…You have a great deal of expertise and you must share it. Share and you will receive.

Tip – If you do it right you will often hit on a topic that turns into an amazing discussion. That is great! You also must keep control or one hot topic could use up the allotted time. If you need to, schedule separate more focused discussion solely on that topic.

Recently there was a slide I was debating whether I should include in my next tabletop. I was not sure if it would be on target for the group of attendees. I finally said, 'what the heck' and added it. Well, it hit a big-time security nerve and I was really happy I had included it. In fact, people did not want to leave that slide. Everyone was chiming in. Finally, I did have to take control and move on, with the promise that we would break that topic out into a follow-up discussion – and we did.

Tip – Please do not – I repeat – do not make it a lecture. If you make it a lecture and load up 100 slides with a bunch of densely packed textual information you will lose them fast. You may even hear some snoring in the room. Keep it interactive, fun and lively!

Tip – Nervousness – Trust me, the first few exercises you host you may be nervous. I certainly got nervous the first 4-5 times I hosted tabletops. It is fine to get nervous. Some of the most popular actors and actresses get nervous before a live performance. If you are a little nervous it means you care. Remember, most people are afraid to speak in front of a group of people. You are brave by getting up and speaking.

You are providing a critical service each time you host a tabletop. People will thank you. Even if they pick up one useful take-away it can be lifesaving or business saving. Just getting the key players in the same room to talk about emergency response and continuity of operations is

273

a huge win for your organization. So, before you say the first word you have already won! Now have fun.

For the first few, remember to loosen your shoulders, emphasize certain words, use your hands to emphasize points and speak slowly (especially finishing sentences). Do a little check-down before starting. I always do my little check-down whether hosting a tabletop or racewalking a 5k. It always works to my advantage and it will for you.

After your first few tabletops you will be very confident and loose. You will no longer be nervous and you will look forward to hosting tabletops. It is really fun! The attendees will learn a lot and you will learn as well. You can add what you learn to future tabletops. It is a virtuous cycle – it gets better-and-better with every tabletop you host. I promise you!

Planning and Running Tabletop Tips:
Planning:
Tip – Tabletops must be included in the comprehensive business continuity exercise schedule you create and share with management.

Tip – Plan for the month of the tabletop, not an exact date. If you suggest an exact date, give the Incident Commander some flexibility to adjust. They may have valid production reasons to modify the date. They will appreciate your partnership in finding the best date and time for the exercise. It is hard finding a date that accommodates the schedules of most of the attendees.

Tip – My tabletops generally run between 2.5 and 4 hours. I plan for 3 hours and always finish on schedule to respect the time of busy individuals. I always offer to stay longer to discuss all issues. Sometimes, when I begin the tabletop I joke, 'we should be finished in 6 hours' and everyone gets this really concerned look on their face and then I mention 'I was only kidding' … 'approximately 3 hours' and they laugh and appreciate the shorter time-frame. In sales that is called 'framing' (say a big number and psychologically the smaller number appears even smaller than it is)

Tip – The presentation should be customized to address threats that could realistically impact a location. For example, in the mid-west I discuss tornadoes, in the east hurricanes and in the west earthquakes… Prior to deciding on which tabletop scenario to present for a specific location you should do some situational research. Hopefully, you have a knowledge-base of location based incidents and geographical hazard maps (State Emergency Management Offices will have hazard maps and stats).

Is the location in tornado alley or on the San Andrea fault? ... Speak with the Incident Commander to determine if a specific threat has a high probability of impacting his/her location. Then you can customize and present that scenario. If there is not a specific threat, I usually begin with a tabletop like the fire scenario that follows in this chapter. Fire can occur anywhere as a primary event or as a cascading event from an earthquake or tornado.

Tip – Coordinate with management on the location well in advance of the tabletop. Confirm the date and the requirements. Stress that all processes must be represented, as well as the Crisis Management Team, Emergency Response Team, and the Emergency Operations Team. It is also advantageous to have public officials such as police, fire and EMS make a brief appearance to share knowledge.

Tip – I have hosted tabletops ranging from 10 to 70 attendees. Through experience I have found if there are more than 40 attendees it is best to divide the tabletop into two sessions – morning and afternoon. The Incident Commander should be at one and the Alternate Incident Commander should be at the other session. It can be valuable training if the Alternate Incident Commander must step-in for the Incident Commander during a real crisis.

Tip – Either you or the Incident Commander should reserve the conference room and invite the attendees. I have found it is more effective if the Incident Commander sends the invites. The attendees know her/him. Another benefit is, if you are hosting many tabletops having the Incident Commander do the invites will save you a lot of time.

Tip – Horseshoe seating is my favorite where I am at the front. If that is not possible classroom or square is fine. I have done them all and you can too. Use the seating arrangement you are most comfortable with.

Tip – If the Incident Commander is new to the role you should do a brief meeting with her prior to the tabletop. In fact, even if she is experienced speak with her before the tabletop. This will instill knowledge in her, make her more confident and make the exercise more enjoyable.

Tip – The Incident Commander must stress in the email invite to attendees that people must attend. There will be occasions process owners or their alternates will be traveling. In those cases, a conference

275

line can be provided a day or two prior to the exercise. You really do want as many people to attend in person as possible.

Tip – You should provide the email invite template to the Incident Commander.

Tip – The Incident Commander should order appropriate light refreshments.

Tip – Send the Incident Commander the presentation at least 10 days prior to the date of the tabletop. He can have copies printed for the attendees or they can distribute an electronic copy after the tabletop. It makes a nice take-away. Bye the way, I see nothing wrong with distributing the presentation in advance. The goal is for people to learn and be prepared. If they want to prepare in advance that is great!

Tip – The Incident Commander should assign someone to take notes and document follow-up **Tip** – Process owners should bring a copy of their plan to the exercise.

Day of the tabletop – finally!
Tip – Arrive early.
Tip – Visit the Incident Commander and say hello. Put him/her at ease. Confirm that he/she will do a short intro kickoff to begin the exercise.
Tip – Test the audio and video early.
Tip – Insure the refreshments are ready.
Tip – Have the sign-in sheet ready near the doorway when attendees arrive. Ask them to please sign-in.
Tip – Greet people as they arrive and introduce yourself.
Tip – Start the exercise on-time!

During the tabletop – our goal is to have fun and learn – let the attendees know that:
Tip – The Incident Commander should say a few words thanking everyone for taking the time to attend and letting them know the importance of this exercise. She can say a few words about emergency response and business continuity at the location. Perhaps reference a recent disruptive event that will strike a chord with the attendees. Then she should introduce you. If possible, be there in person. There have been times I have had to host by phone due to travel delays and cancellations. Remote hosting can work.

Tip – Smile and say hello. Thank the attendees for participating in this important exercise. Let them know how happy you are to be there. Put

276

them at ease. Say something amusing – seriously – I mean say something seriously amusing. Attendees are often uptight, especially high level managers. They think they must score 100%. They might feel they will be embarrassed if they do not know everything. As you and I know, nothing can be further from the truth.

Tip – Let them know there is no pass/fail, if that is your methodology. Just by attending and actively participating we all win. The goal is to identify gaps in plans prior to a crisis event and close them.

Tip – Ask that they go around the table with all the participants introducing themselves. Have them include their process name and their role in the plan. People and roles change. New people join organizations and others leave. You might be surprised how siloed an organization can be. In my experience, people you think might know each other often do not.

Tip – Have fun. Every tabletop I have given I have enjoyed. I have learned really interesting things as participants relax and open up.
I learned about Google Voice and ICE (in case of emergency), both of which I speak about in the book, from participants while hosting tabletops. These are just a couple of the many things I have learned during tabletops over the years. If you strive to make your tabletops interactive and fun everyone will clearly see that the tabletop is not so much a test them, rather it is a review of the plans as they are currently written. The attendees do not have to score 100% during the exercise. As I mentioned before, let them know that the goal of the exercise is to uncover gaps and close them prior to a real crisis.

Tip – If you are using a PowerPoint do not make it wordy. Use 6 bullets or less in a large font on each slide. Using a lot of pictures keeps it interesting. You do not want to put people to sleep or have them squinting to read an 8-point font from 30 feet away.

Tip – The person taking notes (scribe) should capture areas that need more research. The notes are really important so that nothing falls through the cracks. Remember to have the scribe assigned by the Incident Commander prior to the tabletop. The takeaways must be worked on after the tabletop. You can also list the takeaways on large easel pads. Review these at the end of the presentation and ask if we forgot to include anything.

Tip – At the end of the presentation thank the participants for their active participation. Ask them if they have any other questions or concerns. Let them know you are available to them 24x7x365 and mean it!

Tip – Provide them with a feedback survey, either printed or online. It is important they complete it the day of the exercise while things are fresh in their mind. Feedback helps you improve.

Tip – Be prepared for 'thank you comments' from attendees and emails letting you know how much they enjoyed and valued the tabletop.

Special Online Bonus!
Online tabletop example outline – Fire Scenario
As a special bonus, I have included an outline of one type of tabletop I have found works well for the attendees and I really have a lot of fun hosting. You can locate the tabletop at:

http://www.ultimatebusinesscontinuity.com/index.php/testing-tabletop/

I put the tabletop online for a few reasons:

1. To improve it over time. I tweak it often. That keeps it up-to-date and fresh.
2. In the not too distant future I intend to add augmented reality and perhaps virtual reality to the exercises I host. I have already started reviewing a few possibilities. That amazing level of realism will add significant value and attendees will love it! I will keep you informed of progress through the Ultimate Business Continuity Tips, Techniques and Tools Newsletter.
3. The sample exercise will be more accessible to you when you are designing and hosting your own tabletops.

You will also find links to additional scenario based tabletops in the Hazards Central chapter in the Testing part of the book. My suggestion is for you to take the best of each tabletop and build your own customized version.

Some of the slides in the presentation can be re-usable for other scenarios – especially the crisis management and emergency response slides before the specific fire, earthquake scenario section. Use what works best for you. Update as you develop improvements. Customize for your organization.

Fire can occur in any locale, whereas a hurricane, winter storm or tornado is more regional in nature. This tabletop covers a lot of ground. The injects at different points in the tabletop keep it interesting and get people thinking. You should add additional injects.

278

Remember, prior to deciding on which tabletop scenario to present for a location do some situational research. Are they in tornado alley or on the San Andrea fault? Stay away from a volcano for a New York location. Speak with the Incident Commander to determine if a particular threat has a high probability of impacting a location. If there is a need then customize and present that tabletop.

Remember, do not make your tabletops lectures. The best tabletops, in my experience, are the most interactive ones. Use multimedia when possible. I have used audio and video to liven up the scenario. It can get amazing as people are drawn in and really get into the scenario.

84

TABLETOP MEETING INVITATION TEMPLATE - TWEAKED TO PERFECTION

If you have not yet created an invitation, this one may give you some ideas. You can use it as-is or customize it to meet your needs.

I vary tabletop invitations to fit the situation. Below is one of the invitations I find useful and well accepted by participants.

You or the Incident Commander can send the invitation. I recommend it be sent from the Incident Commander.

The main goal of the invitation is to communicate that the tabletop is very important and will be fun and low stress. We are testing the plans – not the people. We want to find gaps prior to the real event… that is the goal of the exercise!

When I was a Senior Technical Officer I was on the other side of the fence. I was a tabletop attendee, rather than the host. Prior to a tabletop:

- All the attendees, including myself, had stress
- We thought we had to know all the answers
- We thought we had to score 100%
- We thought we might be reported to upper management if we did not have all the answers
- We thought we would be embarrassed if we did not know everything to a 'T'. Of course, nothing could be further from the truth!

The more you can get people to relax and eager to participate, share and learn, the more successful your tabletop will be. Tabletops can be one of the most fun and valuable services we provide. I have enjoyed every one of the hundreds of tabletops I have had the pleasure to host, and so will you.

Sample invitation below. Please customize for your organization: (items in brackets <<…>>> are variables. You should pop in your specific information.

Hello Team,

I am happy to announce we will be having our annual Business Continuity tabletop exercise on <<Day>> <<Month>> <<Date>> beginning at <<Start Time>> to <<End Time>> in <<Building location>> Conference Room <<Conference room identifier>>. Please arrive a few minutes early to sign the attendance sheet and we will be able to start promptly at <<Start Time>>. Light refreshments will be served.

This is not a test. The goal of the tabletop is to share information and insure we can respond to and recover from any disruptive event we encounter. We will review our plans and if we discover gaps we will close them prior to a real event. The expectation is not that you have all the answers.

During the tabletop, we will work our way through a disaster scenario. It will be a facilitated discussion and an open dialogue forum. All viewpoints will be respected.
We will be respectful of your time. The exercise will last no more than the allotted time – possibly a little less.

If you are not able to attend, please designate a person in your department that can represent you. All departments **must be represented** at the tabletop. If you can attend you are welcome to bring an additional attendee.
Please let me know in advance.

Please review and bring a copy of your business continuity plan to the exercise.

If you have any questions or concerns, please let me know. I promise the exercise will be informative, fun and low stress.

Sincerely,

<<Incident Commander or You>>

85

TABLETOP READINESS CHECKLIST TAKE-AWAY

Whenever I host a tabletop exercise I provide a handy-dandy checklist to all participants. It is a valuable take-away. It helps guide them when reviewing their plan for completeness and finding gaps. It is also a starting point for readiness discussions with their team members.

I hope you enjoy the list. Consider it a starting point. Please customize for your organization.

When I give this away I get a lot of *'thank-you Marty'* comments from attendees and I think you will too.

Yes / No	Do your recovery employees know how to get to the designated alternate recovery site?
Yes / No	Have employees that are designated to work-from-home during a crisis tested their ability to reach all their critical systems?
Yes / No	Is the employee section of your plan, including contact information, complete and up-to-date?
Yes / No	Have you exercised your call tree(s) within the last quarter? If not, how do you know the phone numbers are correct?
Yes / No	Is the telecom section complete?
Yes / No	Do you have critical customer facing toll free numbers that must be re-routed?
Yes / No	Have you tested re-routing toll frees to your recovery site?
Yes / No	Have all your processes and sub-processes been documented in your plan?
Yes / No	Are the RTO's and RPO's appropriate for each process and sub-process?
Yes / No	Is the critical software application section complete?
Yes / No	Is the equipment section complete?
Yes / No	Is the vendors section complete?
Yes / No	Is the customers section complete?
Yes / No	Is the vital records section complete?

Yes / No	Is there anything in your office (e.g. case folders, tracking spreadsheets, etc.) that you would deem critical and would cause you significant problems if you relocated to your designated recovery site and did not have access to them?
Yes / No	Is the task section of your plan complete and up-to-date?
Yes / No	Have you developed a manual work-around procedure to support your business if critical systems are not available?
Yes / No	Was your plan missing information and do you need to modify and / or add recovery tasks to accommodate your findings?
Yes / No	Do you have a ready box stored off-site with important supplies, forms and equipment?

86

TABLETOP EXERCISE SIGN-IN SHEET: WHY DO THE WORK IF I ALREADY DID IT FOR YOU?

All departments must have representation at tabletop exercises. The process owner / alternate process owner or both must attend.

Position the sign-in sheet near the doorway so people see it as they arrive and you greet them. Before the exercise begins ask if everyone has signed-in so they will get credit for participating.

You can do a telephone follow-up exercise for no-shows **but** if people simply blow off the meeting for no good reason consider 'dinging' them with management. Otherwise, it will set a precedent and you might wind up with an empty conference room down-the-road. I am a very nice guy, but *'you gotta do what you gotta do.'*

If a process owner is travelling the day of the tabletop I permit him/her to call in. Just do not publish an optional call in to everyone two weeks prior to the tabletop or again you might wind up as the only person in the room.

Tabletop: Name>>	<<Location Meeting Date: June 9, 2018	
Facilitator: Name>>	<<Your Place/Room: <<Conf Room.>>	<<Location>> /
Name (Print and Sign)	Department and Role	

87

INTERCHANGEABLE WORK AREA RECOVERY EXERCISE (IWARE)

Interchangeable (Mix-and-Match) Work Area Recovery Exercise!
VALUE * VALUE * VALUE

If you have never done a work area recovery exercise, you are in for a treat. If you have had the good fortune of doing them, you already realize why I am so excited about this chapter.

Let's examine some of the incredible value you will receive from the IWARE:

- Testing your ability to reach the Incident Commander OR their Alternate with or without letting them know the exact time you will be calling them.
- Testing the validity of the Incident Commander to contact Incident Command, Emergency Operations team members and all the process owners either through an automated call list or a manual call tree.
- Testing the ability of the Incident Command team to meet at a physical or virtual command center to make decisions
- Testing recovery staff knowledge of traveling to the alternate work area recovery location(s), working from home or working from a mobile trailer
- Testing the ability of recovery employees to work productively from the alternate work area recovery location(s)
- Identifying and closing all gaps **prior to a disruptive event**
- Testing the transfer of customer facing toll free phone numbers to the alternate recovery location(s) (a very cool part of the exercise)
- Insuring you have critical special equipment available at the recovery site. For example, high speed scanners, MICR printers, rubber stamps, form letters...
- Testing the ability to transfer equipment from a third-party storage facility/vendor to the alternate recovery site
- Validating all plans are accurate
- Validating call tree procedures are accurate
- Validating work-from-home recovery employees can log in during the exercise and reach all their critical systems

285

- Verifying image configurations and the ability to access production systems from the alternate recovery location(s)
- Building relationships – getting to meet new people, putting a face to a name, making friendships
- Working closely with IT (you may not like it but I 'grew up' there, so please be nice…)
- Having a great lunch! That is critical! Don't cheap out. More below…
- Generating new ideas for improvements from attendees
- Doing a post event meeting (I stopped calling it a post-mortem, as it seemed like a depressing term). Listing each item that needs fixing, assigning responsibilities and deliverable dates and tracking until closure!
- Getting high praise from the people that attended AND your management!!!

Ok, that is a lot of really cool stuff. I 'affectionately' call it the exercise that just keeps giving!! To pull this exceptional exercise off coordination, dedication and management support is required. If I was able to do it, you certainly can. You will ace this exercise!

A bit of history:
I have happily completed more than 100 IWARE's thru the decades for various companies. Just thinking about them brings back such great memories. Some had 150-200 attendees and others had 10 attendees. All of them were great, valuable, educational and fun!

More importantly, the value clearly demonstrates you can enact your plans and recover to a vendor work area, sister-site, mobile trailer(s) or work-from-home. The IWARE is a key component in preparing and mapping to the actual response AND recovery processes you currently have documented. Yes, there will be minor tweaks at crunch time, but that is where the resilient culture you are building will shine.

Possibly your team is virtual, such as my current team is now and all my former teams were. The IWARE brought us together during exercises throughout the United States and overseas! There were late dinners (after setting up the network and workstations of course) and time to have fun and rant about many things. I treasure the moments working with such great teammates through the years and how much we achieved.

Value-wise I really like the IWARE because it tests so many different components of your program while never impacting business production. The business will love it as well. You will hear the inevitable excuses not to participate, but once the exercise starts the value will be realized and you will see quite a few smiles.

On one occasion, I did an exercise for 150 people in Massachusetts as the sole representative from our business continuity team. My DR partner was ill and understandably could not attend. It was a real challenge but fortunately, like you, I embrace and enjoy challenges. I had to handle both the DR and Business Continuity facets of the exercise. It was a huge success and a great memory! Although I live in NY, I always eagerly volunteered for the Massachusetts recovery exercises when we created the testing schedule. Boston is my favorite city. I loved going up there and to smaller cities including Lowell, MA.

I have so many memories. I am a devoted basketball fan and once I timed an exercise to coordinate when the New York Knicks were playing the Boston Celtics in the old Boston Garden. I started out from Long Island and about 30 minutes into my trip I was called back to attend to a local disruption.

I was so disappointed, but duty called. I never did get to the old Boston Garden. Ok, not such a great memory. Hey, they can't all be good. But I suppose my subsequent 'bucket-list' trip to iconic Fenway Park to see the Red Sox vs. the Yankees made up for it. Seeing the Green Monster in person was surreal!

Ok, down to business:
The IWARE can be conducted in three ways as a fully announced, partially unannounced or fully unannounced exercise. It can be held over two or more days. You should align the exercise to the BC maturity level of your company:
- Fully announced IWARE: during the preparation phase the process owner and all employees are aware of the start date of the exercise. There are no surprises. If the business has done tabletops to this point and this is their first work area recovery exercise, I suggest conducting the IWARE as a fully announced exercise
- Partially unannounced IWARE: during the preparation phase the process owner and all employees are aware that the start date of the exercise will be during a certain month or quarter. This positions the exercise as more stressful and realistic than the fully unannounced. If the business has done tabletops and one or two

fully announced IWARE's then the partially unannounced is a nice step up in realism

- Fully unannounced IWARE: Surprise! – the preparation phase is done within your team. The exercise is a complete surprise to the process owner and all employees. This positions the exercise as the most stressful and realistic scenario, short of a real event. I have matured programs to such a high degree that upper management and process owners actually requested we do fully unannounced exercises. It is great preparation, but you must be at a high maturity level

The off-site recovery phase of the exercise is conducted the same whether the exercise is fully announced, partially unannounced or fully unannounced.

Tip – You will meet success if you have patience and map out a step-by-step project plan so nothing falls through the cracks:

Here is a sample timeline I like to use and the coordination of steps leading up to and thru the exercise. The exercise provides many opportunities to tweak and customize the timeline and scope to precisely fit your needs. Have fun with it:

Prior to the exercise:
- Schedule the exercise the year prior to the actual event. So, if the exercise will be during June 2020, distribute the proposed date when your yearly exercise schedule is published, probably during November or December 2019 (the prior year). This leaves room for the Incident Commander to communicate conflicts. It provides flexibility in case you must adjust the month
- Begin the actual coordination of the exercise approximately two – three months prior to the date of the exercise
- Schedule a webinar overview with the Incident Commander and the Alternate Incident Commander
- Schedule a webinar overview with the process owners. If there are multiple locations in scope you may need multiple meetings, as there will be questions during the webinar and it can get out of hand with too many people. I try to limit these meetings to a max of 40 process owners and their backups, otherwise it can lose the personal touch
- Perform the webinar overview with the Incident Commander and the Alternate Incident Commander. Leave time to answer all questions and concerns

- Perform the webinar overview with the process owners to review the exercise. Leave time to answer all questions and concerns. The Incident Commander and/or Alternate Incident Commander should attend these calls.
- Determine whether the exercise is a 'go or not'. There may be excuses by local management but upper management should back you up in that all processes must participate
- Determine if there are customer facing toll free phone numbers in scope for re-routing to the alternate recovery location(s). Gather call re-routing requirements. Coordinate with the vendor and your telephony people. (I detail call re-routing in a separate chapter)
- Coordinate which recovery rooms and seats you will use with the third-party recovery vendor and/or coordinate with the facility director if the exercise will be held at your sister-site(s)
- Coordinate with IT and DR teams to insure systems can be accessed from the recovery site. This will entail a series of meetings up-to and including the day of exercise

Exercise execution:
I am going to describe the exercise as a three-day exercise below. You may get to the maturity level where you can compress it into two days. Day 1 being the notification and day 2 having recovery employees report to the recovery locations as documented in their plans:

Day 1 – Tuesday evening approximately 7:30 pm:
- Place a phone call to the Incident Commander. If you cannot reach him or her call the Alternate Incident Commander. You can also follow-up with an email. Depending on the type of exercise, he or she may or may not be surprised to hear from you
- **TIP –** I say this in a loving way – Some Incident Commander's will do anything and everything possible to find out the exact date in advance. They may bribe you, they will check your calendar, they will speak to your friends. They can be verrrry clever. So, use care
- When you call the Incident Commander you will let him or her know the exercise is beginning. They are usually very positive about the exercise. Describe a scenario – fire, flood (something appropriate for the location). Let them know the first step is for them to activate their process owner and crisis teams call lists. They should instruct the process owners to meet at 9:00 am the next morning (Day 2) to discuss the exercise in a conference room

289

– that you already secretly reserved. Again, be careful when you reserve the conference room. The cunning ones will be looking for that reservation with your name indicated when trying to figure out the 'surprise' start date of the exercise. So, have an admin schedule it for a fake meeting. As you see, there is a lot of interesting espionage in this exercise

- After you finish your call with the Incident Commander or multiple Commanders if multiple locations are in scope for the exercise, you should send a progress update to management and everyone else who should be in the loop. In fact, progress updates throughout the exercise are critical. Always send them

That is all for Day 1! Easy Peasy!

Day 2 -Wednesday (three-day exercise)
*** if you are running an aggressive 2 day IWARE then Day 3 Recovery would be performed on Day 2. Some of the steps below would then be performed on Day 1 after the phone call to the Incident Commander:

- The emergency operations team meets in the reserved (secret) conference room at the production location and a conference line is opened up for those that have to call in due to travel. It is good to have both
- You or another member of your team should either attend in person or be on the call. You may have to travel to the recovery site on Day 2, so the conference line is important. Also, if multiple sites are in scope for the exercise, you can either stagger the start time of the Day 2 meetings or assign a different BC Team member to attend a different site meeting
- The Incident Commander should open the meeting and briefly discuss the exercise and its goals. The Incident Commander should also discuss the success or gaps in the previous night's outreach to contact the team. For instance, they may have tried to contact someone and reached a bar. That actually happened to me many years ago during a disruptive event. Fortunately, we had backup contact numbers for that person! If there were problems reaching people the prior night, these are wonderful opportunities to close gaps before a real disruptive event occurs. I have used that valuable line thousands of times in my career – have you?
- The final take-away from the meeting is each of the process owners must indicate who will be participating (recovering) on Day 3 (the next day for the 3-day version of the IWARE). The recovery testing should align with what they have stated in their

business continuity plan. So, if they stated the primary recovery location is a 3rd party vendor site, then people should test from there. One caveat though, if their primary recovery location is work-from-home, you should encourage them and perhaps make it mandatory that a small percentage of their recovery team test from the 3rd party vendor recovery location in addition to testing from home. This is valuable in case work-from-home is not a viable option at time of disaster.

- Determine the minimum number of staff that must recover during the IWARE. It should be a number that validates true recovery but not high enough to impact production work if there is a problem at the recovery site. I generally require 10%-15% of the normal recovery staff to participate but I always encouraged process owners to send as many people as they would like. The more the merrier! If their strategy is 20 people would recover during an actual event, a minimum of 2-3 people is required to attend the exercise. You should set a percentage that makes sense for your organization. All processes should be in scope, even if their primary strategy is work from home.
- Remember to send those progress report(s) to management and all stakeholders
- During a 3 day exercise, you and your team will be setting up the recovery environment, turning on the network repeaters, imaging workstations, insuring the attendee list is in place... if it is a 2 day exercise you would have covertly done it on day one or prior to the exercise.
- Make sure if a 'Chinese Wall' is required to separate departments for regulatory reasons that you account for it when designing the seating plan.
- Print and place attendee's names in front of the workstation they will be assigned to
- Depending on the number of participants you might finish setup at 7pm or 1am
- Grab dinner during setup if it will be a late night or dine at a nice restaurant if you, hopefully, finish setup early
- Get a good night's sleep. The final day will be busy but so much fun!

Day 3 – Thursday – Recovery:
***If the IWARE is performed as a 2 day (rather than 3 day) more aggressive exercise, recovery would be on day 2.

This part of the exercise remains consistent for fully announced, partially unannounced, fully unannounced, 2 day and 3 day exercises.

- Set 3 wake-up alarms so there is zero chance that you will oversleep. Especially if you and your BC buddies were out late the night before
- Allow plenty of time to get to the recovery location. Have a backup plan if your car does not start
- Buy breakfast for the attendees
- Set up shop at the recovery location with your team. I like to begin final day prep at 6:45 am for an 8 am official attendee start time
- Even if you had set the exercise time for 8 am some people will get there early. Some people may arrive as early as 7:20 am, which is fine. Other people will have trouble finding the vendor site – but that is ok as it prepares them in the event they need to relocate during a real crisis
- Greet participants as they arrive. Escort them to their seats. Thank them for attending and introduce members of the BC team and any IT support people
- Let managers know that they can use private meeting rooms if they need privacy and show them where they are
- Address the recovery associates as a team early when most people have arrived. Thank them for attending and explain where the bathrooms are located, where emergency exits are located, when lunch will be served, etc. Let them know that by raising their hand you or IT will help them with any issues. Ask that they complete a survey before they leave. Make them aware of where they can get the coffee, bagels and donuts you bought earlier in the morning – probably a break-out room
- Recovery associates should work from the provided desktop to validate each of their critical systems and to report any issues and gaps. They should also report any ergonomic concerns. You must compile all the feedback
- After they have validated their systems some people are more comfortable working from their laptops (if they brought them). I allow them to work from the laptop at that point
- Test and review the inventory of supplies, headsets, high-speed scanners, MICR printers. Replace batteries where necessary. Make sure there are backup batteries and check the expiration dates. Ok I will admit it, I got bit by bad batteries one time.
- If equipment is required from a 3rd party storage vendor, request it be sent over. Keep track of how long it takes to arrive. I have

discovered and closed gaps doing this. You will need that equipment during a real event

- Take lunch orders – remember do not 'cheap out' on the lunch – it is critical to success
- Serve lunch in a break-out room
- If management permits it employees may be finishing up at 2 pm or 3 pm. It is important for you to circulate a survey mid-day and instruct people that they must complete the survey before they leave while everything is fresh in their minds. The survey can be on paper but I prefer using Survey Monkey or another online tool. Be sure to include the work-from-home people and management in the surveys
- As people leave thank them for participating in this important event. You will probably get lots of thanks you's from them
- If you tested in a shared recovery space, make sure to clear your desktop computer image off the vendor machines and shred any paper artifacts left behind!
- Send equipment back to the proper storage facility or place in on-site lockers
- Perform a hot-wash meeting with the business management team at the end of the day. It is valuable to speak with them the same day, if possible, while everything is fresh in their minds. Discuss what worked, what did not work and what you can do to improve going forward
- Send a report with high level final results. Make sure upper management is included on the report. Again, thank everyone for participating and 'making this important exercise a success'. Always give credit – where credit is due
- Finally, say goodbye to your teammates in BC, DR and IT until next time

Post exercise meetings

The week following the exercise meet with your BRBC team and DR. Review issues and opportunities for improvement captured

- Determine a plan to close all open issues
- Formalize an executive summary and publish it to management and process owners. Remember to thank everyone for their participation in this valuable exercise
- You may want to also do a follow-up meeting with management to review all the issues in the executive summary
- Remember to indicate in the exercise schedule database that the exercise was completed for each location and process in scope

VIII

PART 8 - ASSESSMENTS AND GETTING TO REAL-TIME

In this part of the book we will discuss maintaining and assessing your plans.

I present ideas on the value of automating plan maintenance and assessments. In my experience, automation provides tremendous value to organization's

Automation will also make your life less stressful and more profitable.

REAL TIME ASSESSMENTS = EXTRAORDINARY VALUE AND THE ROAD TO NIRVANA!

Developing a real-time understanding of every facet of
a resilience program is a passion of mine! In this chapter I will
share some ideas on the value it has provided in empowering me
to do real-time assessment analysis with minimal manual effort.
A major goal of this chapter is to get you thinking about how you
can get to real-time and why it is so valuable to you and your
organization.

I would just like to mention that my door is always open to you. After
reading this chapter if you get excited but are not sure about next steps
on automating your program, please contact me. I would be happy to
'talk shop' with you.

The criticality of assessing your plans:

Plans are 'living documents'. They MUST be kept current. Plan owners
or coordinators must maintain (update) plans on a regular basis during
officially scheduled plan maintenance periods. Many organizations
schedule plan maintenance and assessments once or twice a year. In my
opinion, this is not adequate.

In addition to the scheduled maintenance periods, plan owners and
coordinators must update their plans whenever there is a change to their
process requirements. The plan MUST reflect the current state of the
process. This is the only way to ensure that we can analyze the process
to the capabilities to recover. If plans are outdated, we are 'flying blind'
and there will be unpleasant surprises at time of disruption. I have seen
it get ugly.

I suggest you reinforce the importance of keeping plans accurate during
tabletops and recovery exercises. Also, create awareness using all the
tools we will discuss in the awareness part of the book.

To properly assess a plan, you must:

- Review critical fields in the plan and underlying BIA
- Compare dependency requirements against capabilities
- Score the 'recoverability' of the plan against a set of rules and
  thresh-holds you create with your business partners. Some fields
  will carry more 'weight' than others when defining criticality. You
  will program this into the assessment formula.

There are many moving parts in your organization and the underlying plans. Risks and requirements can change on a daily or weekly basis. Here are just a few critical elements that must be analyzed as part of a process plan assessment:

- RTO and RPO
- Recovery seats and location requirements
- Staffing requirements
- Upstream and downstream systems requirements
- Telecom requirements
- Equipment requirements
- Skillset requirements
- Supplier requirements
- Vendor requirements

In addition to the above, you should add additional dependencies that are important to your organization

But wait, there is more to the assessment process... Prior to the 'official' assessment analysis you must email process owners to remind them to review and update their plans. Ideally, this should include a series of reminder communications as the official start date gets closer. The email and process updates are often separated out into the maintenance phase, but for the purpose of this chapter we will group it into automating the assessment process.

After the assessment analysis, you will want to provide the process owners with a scoring of their plans as far as the ability to recover the process. You will customize the scoring rules for your organization. Critical gaps, such as the omission of phone contact numbers or the indication of only a primary recovery location instead of the required primary and alternate recovery location, may require the process owners to make updates to their plan. In that case, there would be additional emails to be sent back and forth.

The problems with assessing plans manually:
As you can see from the paragraphs above, it can be very time consuming to get process owners to update their plans. It also takes a great deal of time for you to do the analysis against many fields in the plans and to subsequently contact the process owners to report the probability of recovering their plans. In many cases, depending on the scoring, the cycle will continue. The process owners must do additional updates to their plans to make them 'recoverable' or they may have to get a waiver to accept the risk of a delayed recovery. Then you must re-assess the plan and send additional emails. It can be two or three

iterations to get to a 'Green' recovery probability. Honestly, this process gets me tired just thinking about it.

Tip – Whether you do assessments manually or through automation, when the process attains a 'Green' or 'Recoverable' status send the process owners a nicely formatted digital 'Certificate of Success'. They worked hard. They deserve it and they will appreciate it. I have passed many offices where process owners framed and proudly displayed the certificate you sent them.

When you factor in the need for you to report progress and gaps to management and other stakeholders the reality is if you are a mid to enterprise size organization there is **no cost-effective and real-time way** for you to properly manually assess all the information in your program. As they say at the race track, *'you are leaving serious money on the table'*.

I have consulted with organizations that have devoted hundreds of hours to manually assessing their plans on a semi-annual or annual basis. It is a tedious and error prone process. BRBC teams are lean-and-mean. Can you really afford to dedicate highly skilled professionals to this task when there is an alternative that makes this pain go away?

It is troubling that at any time during the six month or annual assessment window that your plans may become 'unrecoverable' due to changing dependencies. Unfortunately, you would not even realize the risk until the next round of assessments, which might be too late. It would keep me up at night.

Fortunately, we can make all this pain and inefficiency go away. In doing so we will also save our organization money. Finally, management will be very happy.

Automating your program can make all the difference in quality and getting your life back:
A well designed assessment system can assess, score and report metrics on hundreds or thousands of BIA's and plans in less than 5 minutes. The BCM system, or your mass notification system, can send notifications leading up to the assessment and post analysis. Your new end-to-end automation will provide tremendous return on investment.

Tip – If you set up your pre-assessment and post assessment email notifications in your BCM or mass notification system, it makes life very easy for you and provides value to the recipients.

297

Your automated system should have the capability to extend upstream and downstream to identify hidden gaps that can impact your organization. This will enable you to map and analyze in real-time internal and external threats. For example, your customer service process may have an RTO of <4 hours but may be dependent on a process upstream that has identified their RTO as 48 hours. This type of gap is easy to flesh-out in real-time with an automated system. Some off the shelf systems provide this capability as part of their base offering. You can build it in other systems using rules and workflows. You can also develop it in-house if you have the programming resources and time. Trying to do this type of analysis manually would be impossible.

Your automated assessment system will happily work 24×7 and it will never need a coffee break. In my opinion, it does not get any better.

Automation will allow you to identify changes that impact your organization from end-to-end. You can build simple or complex rules (algorithms) and workflows to trigger events and alert the right people at the right time. Generally building these algorithms does not require programming.

Tip – Include the supply chain in your end-to-end analysis. Critical gaps often lurk in tiers 1, 2 and 3.

The impact/risk insight you will derive from the system allows you to automatically report details to process owners and to provide a summary to middle and upper management in a dynamic colorful high level dashboard. You will be serving each audience with exactly what they need to do their job.

Imagine a cool real-time dynamic graph that changes color to alert the right people of risks and opportunities – green, yellow and red. It will provide them with a holistic real-time vision of the organization. You can also develop critical reports that are automatically emailed to the proper people.

The key is having all your information in a central repository along with your business continuity requirements which will empower you to do some very nice analysis.

Do I sound excited? Well, darn it I am excited!!!

Tips on building your new automated system:

The best way to begin building your system is slowly. As BRBC professionals, we preach the value of preparation. When designing a software system, preparation is key to building a tool that will meet your business requirements. The biggest mistake and the primary reason most new systems fail in organizations, is lack of preparation. New programmers sit down and start coding without understanding and documenting the business requirements. It is critical that the business drives the system requirements, not IT.

Earlier in the book, in the BIA and plan creation sections, I stressed that you should insure you are capturing the proper information that will enable you to do the analysis and produce reports and metrics that you require. I realize you will need ad-hoc reports as you mature but for now try to determine your near-term needs. What sort of metrics and reports do you want the system to produce? What are your program and plan requirements? What makes a plan recoverable or not recoverable? Mock up what you will need from your new system and you will have a clear understanding of what needs to be captured. Think world-class for output and insight. Don't hold back. Think about reports, alerts...then work backwards.

Examine, in detail, how you are currently doing your manual assessments. List each step. You may be able to automate the steps you are currently using and/or you may find opportunities for improvements to extract additional value from the process. If another teammate is doing the manual assessments, sit with that person and document the steps. I am sure he or she will be thrilled that you are trying to automate this tedious job. There are more interesting things they can be doing.

Depending on the size of your organization you may want to engage a project manager to help you build the assessment process automation requirements analysis. If you are a small company, you can build a requirements document on your own. The requirements document will clearly spell out what you need out of the system.
You set the rules – the system does the work!

Here are a few examples of the types of criteria that may be important to you when assessing the viability of your plans. Each of these, and most every other field in your system, is an opportunity for automation, predictive analytics, real-time metrics

and custom notifications. These are just examples that you must set to your own criteria:

- All team members must have two or more contact numbers
- All processes must have a primary and secondary recovery location listed
- All process plan recovery locations must be 10, 25, 50... miles from the production location
- All underlying IT systems must have the capability to deliver the appropriate RTO and RPO required by the process
- All IT systems and processes upstream and downstream must have RTO's and RPO's to meet business requirements
- I like to add additional interesting and fun analysis that I can follow-up on such as:
- Comparing normal staffing to recover staffing requirements. For example, if the sales process has 100 employees and requires 100 third party recovery seats, I would want to question that. I speak more on recovery seat analysis automation below as an opportunity for automation. I build a threshold rule once for each process and the system does the work

Tip – If a process has zero updates to any data during the past couple of maintenance cycles in the past year or two years, it may indicate that the process owner is not thoroughly reviewing the plan and just checking off the 'review complete' checkbox while watching TV. The system can track this and it can email you an exception report so you can further analyze to insure the process is being properly reviewed.

Build or Buy?

You have two choices to make your new automated system a reality. You can build it in-house or purchase a third-party Business Continuity Management System. The system requirements you and your IT team document will help you make a decision to either build or buy. Although I am an experienced professional programmer, I have found 'buy before build' often makes sense. Of course, even when I buy I am very demanding that my team has the ability to dig into the system and customize to our hearts content. You will see that come through in the following chapters on selecting BCM and mass notification systems. The interesting thing is that good vendors love my questions and know I am 'pushing them' to help make their products better.

Tip – If you have an organization with scarce database programming skills or a full slate of projects in the pipeline it might make sense to buy.

300

Tip – If you have an organization with good in-house database programmers that are not fully dedicated to current projects, then building a system in-house might make sense. You will also want to factor in future upgrades and system maintenance in your decision to build or buy.

Whether you build your system in-house or buy a solution, it is critical that it has the capabilities to not only act as a repository for data and to build simple reports, but it also has capabilities for you to easily design rules, triggers and workflows, enabling you to analyze thousands of inter-dependencies in minutes.

Before we finish this chapter please allow me to share one example of how automating a previously time consuming, error prone analysis can provide great benefits for many years to come. While reading this use-case please use your imagination and think of all the complex analysis you would like to do that is currently impractical or impossible using manual means.

Through automation anything is possible! When someone tells me, a process cannot be automated that is when I get super excited and I prove them super wrong. You will be able to analyze all your data in real-time if you think it out and execute the development of your new system properly.

In this example, we will work through a Recovery Seat Gap Analysis I created. Over the years, I have matured the analysis from a laborious, error prone manual endeavor to an automated real-time gap and metrics powerhouse.

In this example, the term 'recovery seats' bundles recovery people, desks, desk-phones and computers. I describe the process from end-to-end. The general approach described can apply to other types of analysis.

You will see that once you build the logic you can often re use it and extend it. In the tech world that is called using extensible objects. There is no need to go there in this chapter though.
We will follow the basic implementation process of preparing and keeping it simple which I described above and in other parts of the book.

Decide on the output you want the system to deliver (working backwards as described above):

The output of the recovery seat analysis is universally useful, whether you are using internal recovery, external recovery or a combination of the two. Understanding your recovery seat requirements can mean money in your pocket. You do not want to overbuy, where you would have too many seats and waste money. You do not want to underbuy, and not have the necessary number of seats. On many occasions, I have significantly reduced expenditures using these real-time metrics and trend-analysis reports.

I like to produce detailed reports listing each recovery site and the number of seats subscribed. If it is oversubscribed, the system will automatically highlight the gap red and trigger the appropriate notifications.

I also like to do summary dashboard metrics for management that changes in real-time (including the colors if the location is oversubscribed). When I do a demo of the system for management I show-off the real-time changes as they watch in awe. Often, they comment it reminds them of a real-time stock chart. Again, this is not hard to do.

Capture the right data (described above and in the BIA and plan development chapters):
Tip – During plan building make sure you discuss recovery requirements with process owners. Consider implementing primary, secondary and tertiary recovery contingencies. This provides you with great resilience to activate depending on the scope of the disruptive event you are encountering.

Process owners will describe their seat requirements and all other dependencies. You will capture and document the information they provide. During subsequent maintenance cycles, they will update their recovery seat requirements in the BCM system without your involvement. Analytics will automatically be triggered and communicated when they complete their updates.

Automate it!
As information is captured you must rationalize if you have adequate seats at each recovery location to support the business. For example, if Production site ABC has 13 processes with 200 recovery staff and they want to recover at local internal site DEF which has 35 available seats or a 3rd party vendor site which has 75 shared seats, then you and the process owner must understand the gaps. The only way you will know this is to analyze the data. You can then buy more seats or

recover at another location. It will depend on your assets, resources and the impact of the process not recovering in the required time frame as documented in the BIA.

You will want to map the employee recovery requirements against the available internal and external recovery locations. Break it down by primary, secondary and tertiary requirements and by time frame buckets. I typically use <4 hours, <24 hours, < 72 hours, <96 hours, <168 hours (1 week) and > 168 hours. I recommend using the hourly buckets so you can 'apples-to-apples' easily analyze trends and requirements. These results will give you instant insight into your gaps and risks. Depending on the results of the analysis your system will perform specific actions including scoring the ability to recover the process and sending the appropriate emails to the process owner and management.

Your powerful 3rd party or in-house developed BCM relational database solution should allow you to build rules and workflows to compare the seat requirements of the process versus the capabilities of each recovery location. The matching process is pretty simple. The building of the algorithms (rules) should also be easy with the right system. A key feature of a system which I value, and I discuss in the chapter on BCM tool selection criteria, is the ability to build rules using simple Boolean logic (and, or, between) and conditional branching (if, while…). Boolean logic + conditional branching = Success!

Manually this type of analysis would be a hassle at the very least and impossible to do every time a seat requirement change was made by a process owner in their plan. I know first-hand, as I used to do it manually and it was awful, inefficient and error prone! There was serious 'lag-time'. Unfortunately, disruptive events could not wait for me to manually review hundreds of plans and recovery locations to identify gaps. Fortunately, my automated system takes milliseconds to complete the analysis for as many plans as required, with no manual effort.

The new data recovery seat requirement is automatically matched against the recovery location capability table record and analyzed with a relatively simple algorithm I cobbled together. The right people are immediately alerted if there is a gap. For example, imagine the sister recovery site has a total of 30 available seats. The process in question had originally indicated 25 seats. The process has grown through success and the new recovery requirement is 40 seats. Obviously, we do not currently have enough seats so there is a gap that must be addressed. An email is automatically generated and sent to the authorized people and yourself of course. Decisions can then be made on perhaps increasing the recovery seats at the sister site or using another site, mobile trailer, etc. **The last thing you want is critical recovery staff fighting over too few recovery seats at time of disruption.**

This is a simplistic example of easily creating value through automation. The point is, no matter how complex the issue is, it is possible for your system to analyze everything in real-time, provided it has the data and the capabilities. True real-time automation is a beautiful thing and so much fun to build!

I hope this chapter whet your appetite. Improving your program from manual to automated is like going from a horse-and-buggy to a Ferrari! Have fun and let me know if you need any suggestions.

IX

PART 9 - AWARENESS + FUN + ENGAGEMENT = BIG RESULTS

In the Awareness part of the book we will discuss ways to communicate important emergency response and business continuity information to your employees.

I consider awareness an important, fun, 'think-outside-the-box', 'get creative' phase of a business resilience program. There are so many ways to get the word out to the masses.

Hopefully, some of the suggestions I provide in the coming pages will plant seeds you can harvest.

Have fun!

NEW EMPLOYEES NEED AWARENESS OF CRITICAL EMERGENCY RESPONSE AND BC PROCEDURES

Emergency Response and Business Continuity must be part of your new employee orientation process.

If this is not the case in your organization it would be a very big win for you to partner with HR, Safety, Security and Learning & Development to help all new employees be better prepared.

Tip – Each employee must be made aware of evacuation procedures and rally points. Awareness of proper evacuation procedures and the whereabouts of rally points can be the difference between life and death, for both the employee and possibly a fireman that needlessly goes into harm's way to save an employee when he actually jumped in his car and went for a bite instead of going directly to the rally point to be accounted for. Unfortunately, no one ever communicated to him the correct procedure to follow.

Tip – Process owners (department managers) must discuss their business continuity plan with new hires and let them know their role(s) in the plan.

Tip – An online video or introductory course is a great way to provide consistent information to all new employees. If you have a Learning & Development team they can help develop this.

Tip – During every tabletop that I host I ask process owners if they provide new employees with emergency response and business continuity information. Try it. When you do your next tabletop ask attendees, *'by a show of hands do you include emergency response and business continuity during your new employee orientation process?"*

If 100% of your employees currently receive this critical information as part of their new employee orientation process you are very fortunate. So many things happen when a new employee joins an organization that emergency response and business continuity can be overlooked.

TASTY LUNCH-AND-LEARNS: FULFILLING, FUN AND OH SO VALUABLE

I highly recommend 'lunch and learns'! They are great opportunities to communicate important info in a fun and stress free environment to a wide number of people.

Here come the tips (you guys know me by now):
Tip – Provide ample pizza, pasta, sandwiches, salad, snacks, coffee, tea, soft drinks... They will love you for it. Been there, done that!

Tip – Invite speakers from the Police, Fire, Emergency Management and Red Cross.

Tip – In addition to business related information include interesting sessions and visual displays that will help employees develop personal response plans. For example, 'Why You Need a Plan for Your Pets', 'Why You Need an Emergency Kit at Home'.
People will appreciate it. It is the right thing to do and remember, if your employees have issues at home during a disruptive event they may not be able to come to work.

Tip – Distribute brochures and value-laden pamphlets they can take with them.

Tip – Distribute simple to use action-item checklists.

Tip – Distribute your business cards and newsletters.

Tip – Run a raffle or contest. Give out some cool prizes. If your budget is tight give out t-shirts, hats or Amazon eGift cards.

Tip – Distribute a circular magnet or coffee cup coaster divided in eight interlocking colorful slices. Print each slice with a piece of awareness you want to communicate.

CREATE A BC NEWSLETTER - 'EXTRA, EXTRA READ ALL ABOUT IT'

'Extra, Extra Read All About It' **– You need a business continuity newsletter! It is a great way to promote awareness. In my experience newsletters are fun to read and just as much fun to write.**

Your newsletter is a perfect complement to your business resilience blog and portal.

Below are a few tips to help you get started:

Tip – Come up with a catchy name – 'gamify it', as discussed in the gamification chapter. Hold a contest to name your new newsletter. A quick win is that you will begin spreading awareness through the contest. Give out a nice prize to make people happy. It does not have to be expensive. Free lunch or an Amazon Gift Card are perfect. Hey, I would gladly enter your contest!

Tip – Write your own articles and augment with carefully curated FEMA type government info where appropriate.

Tip – Your newsletter should be customized and branded to make it interesting and valuable for your employees – do not only use curated information.

Tip – Consider special 'Get Prepared' editions for Hurricane Season, Tornadoes, Earthquakes and Snow Storms. These geographic specific scenarios can be distributed to locations that have a high probability of being impacted by the threats.

Tip – Publicize business resilience and continuity successes (maturity milestones) in your newsletter. It is ok to 'brag' a little. You are doing great and important work and people will appreciate reading about it.

Tip – Discuss successful emergency response initiatives by your company and your team.

Tip – Encourage employees to submit articles, tips and questions. You can ask for themed articles for the next edition – their favorite tips, apps…

Tip – Invite Upper Management, Safety and Security to submit 'guest' articles. If they do not have their own newsletter it would be especially valuable for them to 'speak to the people' through yours. They may even want to publish a regular series of articles in each of your newsletters. Even if they say they do not have the time, they will appreciate that you extended the invitation to partner.

Tip – Remind people they are part of the emergency response and business continuity process. If they are unsure of their role, ask them to speak with their manager or your team. Provide your phone and email information so employees can easily contact you.

Tip – Remind people that their plans are 'living documents' and it is important to always keep them up-to-date.

Tip – Include fun contests, surveys and/or quizzes – see the gamification chapter for more ideas.

Tip – Include articles that readers can apply to their personal recovery strategy beyond the business environment. For example, how to create a plan for their pets or what go-bag items they should consider keeping at home.

Tip – Ask for feedback and suggestions – it is important to be interactive.

Tip – When you write, remember 'it is all about 'them'. Write from the heart. Write for the audience.

Have fun developing your newsletter!

92

'GO-VIRAL' RESILIENCE PROGRAM

How many emails do you send out every hour and every day? If you are involved with business resilience / continuity / safety / security / compliance or own a company, I will bet you send out a great deal of emails! Well, you can add significant value to each email with no extra effort by fully leveraging your email signature (sig).

A sig is the signature at the end of your email. A sig typically includes a name, title, email address and phone contact numbers. You are most likely including that information already. Smart marketers (including business resilience marketers) go a step further and wring additional value from their sig. They turn it into a value-laden billboard!

There are many stories throughout the history of the Internet of companies that used their sig to make their message go 'viral'. For example, Hotmail back-in-the-day had a sig that was instrumental in building their company into one of the hottest products on the Internet which eventually led to them being acquired by Microsoft for $500 million dollars.

In the business resilience world, you can help employees by providing valuable information in your sig'.
Tip – Include a deep-link in your sig that directly links to cool articles on your business resilience internal blog and website. It is important that you deep-link to the content rather than linking to your home page. You will get a much higher click thru rate over a long period of time.

Tip – When describing the deep-link in your sig think like a marketer. Make it interesting and powerful. Use action words rather than passive words.

Tip – Track the click-thru's. You may need an assist from IT on that but it is really easy in most cases. You can then analyze the click thru metrics and understand which descriptions and articles 'pull' the most. Build on that information.

Tip – The data can be used as lagging and leading indicators of trends and areas for focus. For example, if you send a link regarding evacuation exits and 90% of the people you email click the link, there is significant interest. You may have an opportunity to improve awareness in that critical area, which you already started doing with the deep-link to the article. You can also let your safety director know that some training may be needed. Again, you have provided value beyond core business continuity.

Tip – Mix in some deep-links to your personal emergency plan, such as how to develop a plan for your pets, In Case of Emergency (ICE), etc. Employees really appreciate that type of information and it improves resilience for your organization.

Tip – Include a little survey with each destination article. Ideally you will receive feedback from the reader which can lead to valuable insight. Congrats! You have now entered the exciting world of content marketing! Tons of fun and sooooo valuable.

I like to apply 'going beyond' technology to a process, when it makes sense.

Here is what I did: I developed a program that automatically inserts a short business resilience related quote or a deep-link leading to valuable custom content through a link in my sig. I coded this solution over a long weekend. If you do not want to code the solution yourself I have identified a couple of good custom signature tools that will enable you to achieve what I built. Contact me if you need specific product capabilities and names.

Each day a new quote or deep-link is pulled dynamically from a database I built which contains the master list of content. Rotating through the content helps keep it fresh and brands our resilience team. Even beyond business resilience, these quotes motivate people in their business and personal lives and makes them more productive. Management loves it.

Finally, I improved the program over time from a simple rotation through the quotes and deep-links to specifying custom sub-groups to rotate through. For example, I have winter weather preparation messages, tornado tips, evacuation best practices... I simply added a group field to the database and make that active through a web form I can access on my mobile device or laptop.

The next benefit I am adding is the ability to customize the messages to align with user's geographic regions. For example, if I am emailing someone in California my message might have an earthquake preparation tip and if my next email is to someone in New York, it might

311

include a hurricane preparation tip. I just have to finish this book, and I will dive into that fun new benefit. I am going to make it my own little Marty Hackathon Challenge at Starbucks. I think I can code most of it in a weekend.

Here are a few of the resilience related quotes I use in my email sig, newsletters and during tabletops:

- "By failing to prepare, you are preparing to fail."
  — Benjamin Franklin
- "I will prepare and someday my chance will come."
  — Abraham Lincoln
- "Give me six hours to chop down a tree and I will spend the first four sharpening the axe."
  — Abraham Lincoln
- "The best preparation for tomorrow is doing your best today."
  — H. Jackson Brown Jr.
- "An ounce of prevention is worth a pound of cure."
  — Benjamin Franklin
- "He who is best prepared can best serve his moment of inspiration."
  — Samuel Taylor Coleridge
- "Spectacular achievement is always preceded by unspectacular preparation."
  — Robert H. Schuller
- "I believe luck is preparation meeting opportunity. If you hadn't been prepared when the opportunity came along, you wouldn't have been lucky."
  — Oprah Winfrey
- "The key is not the will to win. Everybody has that. It is the will to prepare to win that is important."
  — Bobby Knight
- "Success depends upon previous preparation."
  — Confucius

93

TRY MY 'WALK DOWN THE HALL' AWARENESS ASSESSMENT

I have used my fun 'walk down the hall awareness assessment' to gauge the level of awareness in my organization and to meet people. It may not be the most scientific exercise, but you can instantly get both qualitative and quantitative feedback. In addition, you will be branding yourself with every person you speak with.

*If you do not know the person you are speaking with, you should introduce yourself with a 10 second elevator pitch. Otherwise, I promise you will get some 'who the heck are you' stares.

1. Walk down the hall and ask 3 or more people what they would do in an active shooter situation (they get 3 seconds to answer this one)
2. Walk down the hall and ask 3 or more people where the nearest evacuation exit is located (they get 3 seconds to answer this one)
3. Walk down the hall and ask 3 or more people where the rally points are located (they get 3 seconds to answer this one)
4. Walk down the hall and ask 3 or more people if they know what business continuity or business resilience is
5. Walk down the hall and ask 3 or more people where their business continuity plan is located
6. Walk down the hall and ask 3 or more people what their role is during a disruptive event
7. Please add your own question
8. Please add your own question
9. Please add your own question
10. Please add your own question

I enjoy gamifying this exercise. When someone answers all the questions (or 9 out of 10) correctly… BINGO they win a prize! When word gets around that you are roaming the halls and they can win lunch or an Amazon gift card, people will prep and they will hope you stop them in the hall. They might even start following you to be a contestant!

The more people that play, the more word will get around. Most importantly, awareness will improve and that is the goal. This is definitely a positive feedback loop!

I would suggest doing this exercise at least once a week if you have the resources. Over time you can gauge if your training and awareness initiatives are effective or if they need adjustments. Analyze the results to determine where you must focus going forward. For instance, if no one can identify where the exits or rally points are located, you know you have life threatening emergency response issues that need to be worked on immediately.

I suggest you hand people a little cheat sheet and your business card after they answer the questions to increase their awareness.

As your program matures change the questions to continually raise the maturity level of your program and to keep it interesting.

Have fun!

94

GAMIFY YOUR RESILIENCE PROGRAM FOR BIG WINS

If you make your program fun and exciting, you will be pleasantly surprised with the great results you achieve. Interest will skyrocket. People will be talking at the water cooler and they will stop you in the hall. Fun rules!

Gamification works well in business resilience.

If you have never heard of gamification here is Wikipedia's definition: *The application of typical elements of game playing (e.g., point scoring, competition with others, rules of play) to other areas of activity, typically as an online marketing technique to encourage engagement with a product or service. Gamification is exciting because it promises to make the hard stuff in life fun.*

I will vouch for the definition. It works!

Here are some tips on ways to gamify your program. I am sure you will come up with a great many more fun ways to learn ideas:
Tip – Whatever type of game you use make it a fun **learning experience**. Keep the contest, puzzle, etc. on topic. Map it to a phase of resilience you want to emphasize.

Tip – Ready, Set, Go! – First employee to correctly answer a short list of business resilience / continuity related survey questions gets sports tickets, movie tickets, pizza lunch, a coffee mug, etc. You can get fancier and allow points to accumulate over multiple contests toward more rewarding prizes earned over time. People love climbing up the leader board. It can be more rewarding than the actual prize! Check out IOS and Android apps and see how some creatively use points and leader boards. Some make a fortune doing it. Your fortune will be in creating a highly resilient organization and the rewards that go with it.

Tip – Trying to solve a problem? Name a newsletter? Improve processes? What about a take-off on the X-Prize? Employees submit ideas to solve the problem. Sort of resilience crowd-sourcing. If the prize (incentive) is attractive enough you will receive a great deal of participation. In fact, it may go 'viral' in your company. Employees love these types of contests. If you publicize the winning entries, it will create a positive feedback loop for future contests.

Tip – Use your newsletter, website, email body, email signature and text messages to deliver and create awareness for your BC games and contests.

Tip – I often include a quick trivia contest or quiz with prizes as part of my tabletop and relocation exercises.

Tip – During national strategy meetings with leaders and BC liaisons incorporate themed games such as Business Continuity Jeopardy and Business Continuity Employee Departments Feud (Accounting versus HR...).

Let your imagination run wild. Have fun!

X

PART 10 - AUTOMATION, TECHNOLOGY AND BEYOND - THE SECRET SAUCE

If you have read the book sequentially, you are well aware that my sweet-spot, passion, excitement, 'love'… is where technology and business continuity/resilience intersect and produce superior value to organizations.

To recap: a few types of technology solutions we have discussed earlier in the book include:

- In the crisis management part of the book we discussed near real-time automated situational awareness alert systems
- In the crisis communications part of the book we discussed emergency hotlines
- In the crisis communications part of the book we discussed mass notification systems
- In the awareness part of the book we discussed an automated email signature (sig) awareness database system
- In the BIA, Plan, Maintenance and Assessment sections we discussed the value of a comprehensive Business Continuity Management (BCM) system

In this part of the book we will dig a little deeper and get more comfortable with technology solutions. I will share the tools and technologies that have enabled me to build powerful value-laden automated technology driven programs.

We will discuss:

- The 3 Pillars of Resilience technology. The key components of a world-class resilience program
- Automating threat identification and crisis communications
- Data quality issues and solutions. Low-hanging fruit that can score big wins for you and your organization
- When to use a spreadsheet or database and why you should use one versus the other
- Questions to ask technology salespeople that are trying to sell you the latest and greatest system – how to 'keep them honest'
- The importance of piloting systems BEFORE making buying decisions – skip this chapter at your own risk

317

- Ideas on using cutting edge and over-the-horizon technology to go where no resilience program has gone before. This chapter includes some of my favorite new tools, toys and ideas that may benefit your organization now or in the future.

Disclaimer:
Although I am a passionate technologist I also value the beauty of simplicity and sometimes that means 'going old school'. Earlier in the book we discussed the benefits of simple paper checklists, tiny printed BC plans and land-line phones powered from a central office. Each offers value.

THE 3 TECH PILLARS THAT CAN SUPERCHARGE YOUR PROGRAM!

By now you know that I believe the right technology, implemented the right way, is the X factor that can move a business resilience program from good to 'world-class'.

Throughout the book, I have clearly professed my belief that technology provides value that is not attainable from siloed word processing and spreadsheet entities. Word processing documents and spreadsheets have their value, but not as the cornerstones of a mid to enterprise size resilience program, in my opinion.

Let us begin our discussion at a high level defining my three technology pillars. Later in this part of the book I will serve up tips on automating phases of your program and offer a scrumptious buffet of current and future technologies that can ignite your program for years to come. I also provide you with the questions I always ask when researching and vetting prospective technology vendor solutions. These powerful tools can also help us produce opportunities 'far beyond BC' value, which management loves and makes us indispensable.

In my opinion listed below are three major technology components you should consider incorporating into your program:

1. A robust situational awareness tool-set. This can be from one vendor or a mixture of commercial and free tools. You must understand your surroundings and what can impact your business and employees. This information is critical to employee safety and potentially the sustainability of your business! Great situational awareness tools go beyond just serving up alerts after they happen. Some use predictive analytics and machine learning to help us 'see the future'.

2. A powerful and easy-to-use business continuity management (BCM) system to centralize all entities that comprise your program. In scope for centralization are BIA's, RA's, Plans, Testing, Maintenance and Assessments. The system can also be leveraged by other teams such as Safety, Security and most definitely IT, Cyber Security and Compliance/Audit. This corpus of data will provide insight far beyond the individual parts. You will be able to derive unique insights in the workings of your

company. You might be able to spread the cost of a great system over many departments rather than solely from your budget. Importantly, this central repository is a great 'data silo' breaker!!!

3. A powerful intelligent mass-notification tool that empowers your organization to send hundreds, thousands or tens of thousands of consistent interactive notifications to employees or customers. The ability for the recipients to respond is critical for you and management to understand in real-time where employees need assistance.

If you implement these three pillar components they can be epic in elevating your program to 'near' world-class'. You will be able to serve your corporation in a highly efficient way.

Yes, I said 'near world-class'. In order to get to Marty's 'top-of-the-mountain world-class' status it is not easy, but well worth it. Here is what I currently demand of my programs:

- Each of the three pillars must be benefit laden for your company. Forget the worthless bells and whistles.
- Each pillar must give the end-user a great experience. Each must provide a user experience that is simple, elegant, clean and rewarding. If the tools are complicated, convoluted and 'kludgy' people will not use them – including your team.
- **The three pillars must complement each other. They must make each other better. The sum of the trifecta must be greater than the individual parts.**

The three components must behave like a championship sports team. Every professional team has great athletes but to be a championship team, the players must make each other better. This would include talking on defense and passing the ball to people where they can do the most with it. I coached youth basketball for many years and my best teams were easily the ones where the players made each other better. The ones that had a selfish 'superstar' and minimal teamwork fell by the wayside. Your technology tools must play as a championship team!

Tip – When you speak with vendors about their solutions ask them how they integrate with other systems. Have them provide examples, case-studies and white-papers. We will discuss system integration further in the upcoming chapter, *Let's Get Visionary*.

Please keep in mind there are many other important technologies we discuss in the book but let's make sure we have the three pillars in place as a foundation or at least consider their value. We can then add all sorts of beneficial technologies including some amazing Internet of Things tentacles. As we move through this exciting part of the book much will become clear.

96

DO A PILOT BEFORE BUYING CRITICAL SOFTWARE

If you are in the market to purchase a new critical software tool, such as a mass notification system, situational alert system, BCM plan repository... and have determined the finalists please do an in-house pilot!

You MUST 'kick the tires' and play with all facets of the system BEFORE signing on the dotted line!
A pilot is a free trial of the software you intend to roll out to your organization. If the vendor insists on a small fee to do a 'proof of concept' it may be acceptable.

I have purchased many enterprise systems and I have written and sold enterprise software solutions to some of the largest companies, educational institutions and governments in the world. I have a perspective from both sides of the fence:

Tip – Even if you have done a thorough product/vendor feature, benefit, cost analysis and you have attended the 'dog-and-pony' demo by sales and pre-sales engineers and seemingly received the answers you were looking for in your request for proposal (RFP) – it is simply not enough. That is the starting point. Now is the time to do the pilot!

Tip – You must also stress-test the system. Trust me, poorly designed systems can behave VERY differently with 200 records than with 20,000 or 200,000 records. The last thing you need is a system that was snappy and peppy when the vendor demo'ed it but in production it turned into a slooooow dog. Users will not tolerate latency; *'this ain't the 1990's World Wide Wait'*. You do not need that aggravation.

Tip – A pilot is the ONLY way you can truly be sure the system is right for you! I really want you to do this for your own sake and that of your company.

Tip – During a pilot you will see the imperfections that the salespeople conveniently forgot to mention during the dog-and-pony demo. Be especially careful when it is near the end of the quarter and the sales person puts on the hard-sell to make his/her quota or bonus. Think before biting on their pitch.

Tip – Ask your IT team to attend any of the technical meetings with the vendor. They will see and hear red flags that you might not. Get their blessing on the technical aspects of the system before signing the contract.

Tip – I suggest you have a few users on different levels of technical comfort/discomfort try out the new system. Don't only have power users. Have 'newbies' as well. They will give you great feedback, both good and bad. Speak with them and survey them:

- Do they like the user experience (UX) and – interface (UI)?
- Do they like the canned reports?
- Is the system overly complex?
- Is it slow?

Then buy them lunch or give them a cool t-shirt for testing the system.

Any quality vendor will be happy to help you do a pilot or free trial. They want to insure you are getting what you expect. Otherwise, it will bad for you and bad them down the road. It will not end well if you are both not on the same page. Please accept my advice on this one.

Tip for Vendors – As a buyer I feel good when a vendor strongly advises I do a pilot. It shows me your product will speak for itself. Words are cheap – 'the proof is in the pudding.'

The Bottom Line – Do a pilot EVERY TIME you are considering a new system. You will save yourself time, money and lots of frustration. Yes, I would be happy if you send me a thank you if this saves you from aggravation in the future.

97

SITUATIONAL AWARENESS - A LIFE SAVER AND REVENUE GENERATOR

Why situational awareness is critical:

During a crisis or during business as usual we MUST understand what is happening that can impact us. Situational awareness enables us to understand the probability of threats. Accurate information is critical and it must be available in a timely manner.

During a crisis making fast accurate decisions can be the difference between life and death. Situational awareness alert systems and Internet of Things tools such as sensors, cameras, robots and traffic cams provide extraordinary value.

During business-as-usual situational awareness can provide bottom line value. For example, understanding where to build or not build a new facility. What is the history of the region? Is the proposed new location on an earthquake fault-line or in a flood zone? Are there new business disruptors entering our sector? That is import information and we can get it if we know where to look in a sea of data. Does the upcoming seasonal weather forecast pose revenue opportunities or threats. I have first-hand knowledge of spinning informational advantages into bottle line revenue.

Situational awareness tools:

Think about it, wouldn't even a few additional seconds or minutes be critical if you could warn your employees of an approaching tornado so they could gather in the core of your building and away from windows or prevent them from going to lunch and driving toward extreme danger? What about a near real-time alert of an earthquake? What about being forewarned of a rapidly approaching tsunami? During a recent tsunami ocean sensors coupled with notification systems saved many lives. I certainly would value that extra time to get my employees to higher-ground and safety. It can be life-saving priceless information.

Notice I stressed the information must be accurate. Inaccurate information can be worse than no information. I have seen some very bad alerts. Some can be dangerous and some just down-right embarrassing. I got burned once... before I knew better I acted on an inaccurate piece of info I received from a vendor and communicated it to management. It was embarrassing. I had to sheepishly retract it. Hey, fool me once, shame on you, fool me twice it's shame on me. It will not happen again to me and I hope it never happens to you.

Analyzing situational alert vendors and their capabilities:
One way for you to begin learning about the types and quality of alerts that are available is to visit some of the top situational alert vendor sites. Read everything you can. Get familiar with the strengths of each vendor. The type of data they specialize in, case studies, their technical infrastructure, source and breadth of the data they use and provide...
Then contact the vendors to get a demo of their service. Pilot the ones that seem like they may provide the type of alerts important to you and your employees.

Depending on what you are looking for, one vendor may fit your company better than others. For example, if you are seeking risk information for executives that travel to foreign countries one solution is very strong. They have a great deal of information on foreign infrastructure and risks. They even have a service that can assist you in extracting executives in peril.

Some vendors are very strong with weather alerts. They even have in-house meteorologists to advise you. Other vendors are great with beyond weather situational alerts. Some are very good with providing threat awareness mapped to logistic delivery routes. You can use their information as-is or customize as necessary. If you need some recommendations for my favorite situational alert vendors, please contact me. I will be happy to send you a special report suggesting my favorite tools, depending on your needs.

Some vendors use rooms full of analysts to cultivate their alerts and others use computer algorithms

Most vendors have informative dashboards and push alerts. Formatting of the alerts is often structured in a consistent manner meaning if you are creative you can grab the alerts, parse them and do something actionable with the results.

Some have an API integration with mass notification systems. This gives you the ability to forward information to the appropriate people so they can act on them in a timely manner. It can save you valuable seconds and minutes.

Some systems include historical information of previous alerts that you can use to do a risk analysis on geographic threats. This can be useful in site selection and for predictive analytics of possible future events.

How to roll your own situational alert solution:
If commercial vendors cannot provide the type of alerts you are looking for or you do not have a budget or you want to supplement the alerts you get from vendors, you can create your own streams of situational alerts. The Internet is rich with data. You might be familiar with the term 'big data'. The Internet is 'really big' data. It includes very large sets of structured and unstructured data.

Structured data is often stored in relational databases or spreadsheets. It is neatly formatted data. Structured data fits nicely in the rows (records) and columns (fields). Product orders, customers, vendors…
Unstructured data includes all social media. Twitter, Facebook, blogs and websites. Harnessing this type of big data for situational alerts and predictive analytics can be worth its weight in gold. There are gigabytes, terabytes, petabytes, exabytes, zettabytes and yottabytes (1,024 zettabytes) of data to analyze so it is no easy task to determine patterns and make predictions. But it is doable and incredibly valuable to be able to 'connect the dots!'

Off topic tip but really interesting – This very cool site describes in real world terms the size of gigabytes, terabytes, petabytes - https://www.computerhope.com/issues/chspace.htm…

I will whole-hardheartedly admit I am a data freak. I scour the internet seeking interesting data sources and connections. I have started a few businesses based on mashing up data to 'connect the dot' value. Some were even back-in-the-day before the Internet. The exciting thing is that the available data-sets get better every day and opportunities are all around us to benefit. The more up to date the data the more useful. There is even a website
that tracks API's for popular and often free data-sets.

Tip – On a basic but very effective level you can begin seeking free sources of public information you trust and sign up for their alerts. For example, I find great value in Notify NYC for local New York alerts. I have received many actionable alerts from them in a very timely manner.

Tip – Search local sources of alerts including your Office of Emergency Management, Police and Fire departments. More and more are sending alerts. I subscribe to many of them.

Tip – I also make use of API's, JSON, XML and RSS feeds to access public government from NOAA, USGS and many other sources as the information is updated to their sites. The feeds are automatically available in my homegrown reader system. There are many free reader apps available. Let me know if you need guidance in finding good ones.

Tip – An example of a great feed is that of openweathermap.org. They have a free version as well as reasonable priced subscriptions, if you are making many calls to their database.

Tip – A great source of API feed listings is www.programmableweb.com. Do a search on that site for 'weather ' and I think you will agree.

Tip – A great source for RSS feeds is Google News: https://support.google.com/news/answer/59255?hl=en

Tip – For one example of just how good this data bonanza can get go to –
http://w1.weather.gov/xml/current_obs/seek.php?state=ny&Find=Find

Tip – I also use Google Alerts daily. It has provided me with timely situational awareness information plus lots of other powerful information.

Tip – Try Hootsuite to data-mine Twitter information.
The bottom line is I think you will find the data you need is out there, whether it is a commercial solution or one you craft on your own. Start investigating and testing data sources or contact me for further suggestions on situational awareness solutions.

In the upcoming 'Let's Get Visionary' chapter I discuss interesting technologies that can help you with situational awareness and beyond.

98

HOW TO SELECT YOUR BUSINESS CONTINUITY MANAGEMENT (BCM) SYSTEM

I strongly believe a great Business Continuity Management (BCM) system is a critical pillar of any mid to enterprise size world class business resilience program. In many ways, it is the centerpiece of your technology stack. With a great BCM system you may be able to put much of your program on auto-pilot as I have multiple times!

If you do not own a great BCM system you are probably not getting the full insight into inter-dependencies, risks and opportunities. In my experience plans, dependencies, upstream and downstream gap analysis maintained in word processing documents and spreadsheets can get ugly real fast. Perhaps, you realize those solutions do not scale well. They will inhibit you from spinning finely sliced and diced data into the actionable and insightful metrics and reports you, management and your employees deserve.

BCM Systems Selection Criteria, Suggestions, Tips and Vendor Questions:
If you decide to research the value of a BCM system, I have some suggestions in this chapter that might help make your life a little easier, and your system evaluation more comprehensive.

- I will describe features and benefits I seek in a great BCM system.
- I will provide you with questions that you must ask vendors to separate the 'wheat from the chaff'
- I will reinforce the advice we discussed in the 'You Must Pilot before Buying' chapter. Remember, never skip this step!

I have successfully researched and implemented multiple BCM systems for mid and large enterprises, so I speak from experience. It took a few bumps and bruises until I perfected my research and implementation process. These systems were instrumental in bringing each program I worked on to a world-class level. In addition to my suggestions, you must perform thorough due-diligence during your evaluation process.

Tip – Your first step is to conduct a thorough needs analysis within your organization. Decide on what you want to get out of the system.

328

That will drive your system selection. When I was a software developer and built enterprise database systems I started at the end and worked backwards. I would discuss what reports and data input fields were valuable to the client. I would then build user friendly forms so it was simple for users to enter and maintain their information. It pays to be detailed and thorough in documenting what you will want and need from your new BCM system.

Tip – Do research. There is no one-size-fits-all. There are great, good and not so good systems on the market. You might overpay for features that are of no value to you or you may get a low-ball price and buy a system that does not have the benefits you require. You do not want to go there. Contact me if you need assistance. As I said at the beginning of the book, I am here for you.

Tip – Read case studies and review the vendor's website. If they have on-line videos watch them. Look at their reports and input screens. If you like what you see, speak with a salesperson and have him/her conduct a high-level webinar for you and your team. You can use some of the tips and questions in this chapter but don't ask them all on the first webinar. The first webinar will have info about the company, which is important, and then they will go through a high-level demo of their product. We call it a dog-and-pony webinar.
If you like what you see and hear, you can do another more in-depth webinar and get all your more detailed questions answered. Do not hold back. Make sure the salesperson has a pre-sales engineer on the call that can answer some of the tech questions in this chapter.

Tip – Be sure to ask for current and past references from the vendor and speak with each reference. Read between the lines as they provide information. Drill down on their responses when it makes sense.
However, these references are the people the vendors are giving you, so they probably will be positive – ya think? Definitely go beyond these cherry-picked references. Do your Internet research and see if there are any horror stories out on the web. Then pick up the phone or send an email and try to get the scoop. They might give you critical info. If they got burned they may want to prevent the same thing from happening to you. Hey, the worst that can happen is you make a new contact and maybe they say 'no comment'. It is worth the effort. I can also give you advice on good and not so good products.

But there is more you have to do! You must pilot the finalists. You must kick the tires and really learn the capabilities of each system!!!

Doing a pilot is essential. If you skip the pilot it very well might come back to bite you. You will get bit and you will sigh, *'I should have listened to Marty, he really knew what he was talking about.'* I have seen it play out too many times. A pilot will provide clarity. It takes the guess factor out of the equation. During or after the pilot you will know if the system is right for you.

A pilot should be easy for the vendor to set up. Ask for 30-60 days to test. Modern BCM tools often live in the cloud so it is simply a matter of 'instantiating (spinning up) an instance' (tech talk for setting up a test site) for you and getting you access. 24-48 hours is all it should take for you to begin testing. It sidesteps the yester-year complicated and time consuming requirement of installing on your infrastructure. If you want to show off your tech chops and impress everyone on the call ask the rep if she can, 'instantiating an instance'.

Tip – During the pilot make certain to stress-test the system with dummy (masked) data – nothing sensitive. If you expect to have 10,000 records in the system, then put 20,000 or more dummy records and see how it performs. If there is latency during testing it should be a red flag for you.

If you are a vendor reading this: as a buyer, I feel good when a vendor strongly advises I do a pilot. It shows me you are confident that your product will speak for itself. Words are cheap – 'the proof is in the pudding.' Impress us.

Below are features in a BCM system that are important to me because they provide benefits and value to my company. If a feature is included in a system but it does not provide any benefits for my company, I do not need valueless bells-and-whistles.

A word of advice: In my opinion your great new BCM system should be a 'product' rather than solely a 'framework'. By 'product' I suggest it should include a high percentage of what you will need from your new system on the day you buy it – 'out of the box' - without any customization! That includes reports, dashboards, input screens and a normalized database structure.

If you are buying a 'framework' understand that getting to production likely will take additional time, effort and perhaps consulting fees.

Your new system should be built on a robust relational database. It must be powerful to scale yet easy to use. Even if you have 1 million records it should be fast.

Your new system should quickly and easily produce consistent detailed reports and dashboards for management. It should include a BIA, RA DR, inter-dependency mapping, IT gaps, RTO inconsistencies and more – on Day 1 – when you buy it.

The 'product' should also be customizable. You should be able to build on the 85%+ solution the vendor has supplied. It should be easy to add additional input forms, reports, dashboards, triggers and workflows. Finally, it must also be easy to migrate your existing plans and data into your new system.

Questions for the vendor- As part of your evaluation, webinars and request for proposal ask about the following. The *benefits* of each are in *italics*.
Mr. / Ms. vendor please tell me:

- Dashboards – are they dynamic? Do they include real-time data? Show me. Please change data in a form/table and show me how the dashboard changes. Do I have to refresh the page for updated results? = *Management will use these – so blow them away with* **great real-time dynamic dashboards***!*

- Do you have a flexible form builder so I can easily build user friendly intuitive forms? How much control do I have over the look-and-feel of the form? Can I use field color properties and background images? Please demonstrate = *Users will be spending time in front of the User Interface (UI) so no 1990's dated interface. If it is too hard for them to input data into the system and they have to first input into spreadsheets or word processing documents and then you enter it in the system you will have big trouble.*

- What properties do fields have? Colors, size, phone masks (111)-222-3333, conditional on the data in previous fields? = *The more properties fields have the more control you will have in customizing the user experience*

- How are sub-forms (child) linked to master forms (parent) on an input form? = *You will want to do this to take advantage of the relational qualities of the system. It should be easy to do with minimal clicks*

- How do users input sub-form data into a master form? For example, in a business continuity plan how do we add software systems or vital records dependencies to the Customer service business continuity parent form. = *Think one-to-many items which can*

331

be tedious unless the system makes it easy. Do you have to click to another form or is there a 'data-grid' type object on the master form? Those extra clicks add-up very quickly and become very time consuming and very confusing to users. You will get complaints if it is not fast and easy

- Please show me how do I do real-time dependency mapping and gap analysis both upstream and downstream for processes and systems? = *The ability to understand upstream and downstream dependencies and critical gaps is important. The BCM tool should make it easy to create analysis reports between any fields in the system. Doing this type of analysis manually can be next to impossible*

- Is the presentation layer separated from the data layer? = *If it is then the underlying data can then be easily displayed in a form or report in multiple ways for different users. If the data is bound to the form it is not as flexible. I have seen it both ways. Unbound is better, in my opinion*

- Tell me about your core BIA / BC Plan(s) mobile app. Is it included in the base price? Is it responsive built with HTML 5 or native IOS / Android? = *Plans must be available on mobile platforms. When you ask these types of questions they know you are steeped in tech knowledge. If you are really nice, you will say you read about this in my book:)*

- Tell me about your incident management capabilities? Do you have a dedicated incident management mobile app. Is it responsive HTML 5 or native IOS / Android apps = *The ability to manage an incident from anywhere. Mobile is a must*

- Please show me your customizable BIA template(s) = *You want something to get you started quickly that you can easily customize for your needs*

- Please show me your customizable Risk Assessment template(s) = *You want something to get you started quickly that you can easily customize for your needs*

- Please show me your customizable BCP template(s) = *You want something to get you started quickly that you can easily customize for your needs*

- Please show me your customizable report templates. = *You will need a lot of reports so they must get you started quickly with a buffet of reports that you can easily customize for your precise needs. There should be no need to build everything from the ground up*

- Please show me your full-featured report writer to create powerful new reports. Please build a report for me while I watch. Please join a few tables in the report you build = *You will need to easily create new reports over time as your system grows. Asking them to join tables makes sure they do not just show you an 'easy-peasy' report*

- Please describe the user access security configurations. How do we set up individual and groups of users? Do you support role based access? How do we limit (filter) the data that users can access? =

User access is very important, especially if you are maintaining employee data with personal contact information. Role based access is an important concept.

- Do you have a rules engine? Please describe the capabilities. Can we set rules and triggers or do you have to do it? = *This allows you to build logic into your forms without the need for coding. You can customize behaviors and automate processes.*

- Do you have a workflow engine? Please explain how it works? Can we customize it or do you have to do it? = *This allows you to get sign-offs, send emails, create tasks...*

- Do you have both an on-line and written user guide? Can I please read it? = *pdf is fine – skimpy short often outdated videos are not fine, in my opinion*

- Do you have both an on-line and written admin guide? Can I please read it? = *pdf is fine- but it must be thorough. Skimpy short often outdated videos are not fine in my opinion*

- Do you have an Application Programming Interface (API)? Can you please send me some documentation for my technical team to review? = *A good API will enable you to integrate (connect) with other programs such as situational awareness systems and mass notification systems. Ask which types of systems they currently integrate with. Your IT team can review the API with you*

- Please describe and demonstrate your methods for data imports = *You will most likely want to do nightly feeds of automated SFTP uploads and/or manual imports using spreadsheets, especially if you are migrating from another system or maintaining word docs and/or spreadsheets. Also, you may want to import existing BIA's and Plans into your new system. Make sure it can be done. If you do a pilot, ask them to import a plan or two and show you the results*

- Do you have the capability to localize to various languages? Which ones? = *Important if you are a global enterprise. I have used systems with scores of languages.*

- Who hosts your platform? What is their up-time? Can you send me a third-party audit of their data center(s)? = *Very important! You must be up-and-running!*

- Will our data be in a separate database instance or in a shared database with other company's data? = *If shared – Red Alert!*

- Will our database instance be located on a shared server or a dedicated server?

- How often is our database instance backed up? What sort of backup is used? Who on your team and the hosting team has access to our data? = *Your legal, auditors, HR and IT security teams will need to know this, as you are storing sensitive data in the cloud.*

You can also use some of the questions in this chapter as part of your request for proposal document (RFP). You can then compare and rate various systems in a structured manner.

Track each of the responses in a vendor evaluation spreadsheet. When you get to the finalists you must do a pilot of each system!

Business Continuity Management Systems are constantly changing. The system you select must align to the needs of your organization. To name my favorite mass notification systems in this book would not have been fair to you. I do review and recommend solutions in my newsletter.

If you urgently need suggestions, please contact me and I will get back to you with my recommendations and supporting information.

99

HOW TO SELECT YOUR MASS NOTIFICATION SYSTEM

I have emphasized throughout the book the value of a robust mass notification system. If you have a mid to enterprise size organization I believe it is essentially to have an automated system.

Manual call trees break down fast. Every second can count when notifying people. Think tornado, tsunami, earthquake... I have successfully implemented multiple Mass Notification System solutions so I speak from experience. Mass notification is one of my favorite subjects and I consider it one of my top specialties.

In this chapter I list the questions I ask of vendors. As a technologist, my questions cut to the core capabilities of their products. You might find some questions in the list that you can add to your list. Perhaps, this will make your evaluation more comprehensive. Of course, you must do thorough due-diligence in your evaluation process.

* If you read the How to Select a Situational Awareness Tool chapter that precedes this one you can skip the next few introductory paragraphs as they contain similar important information or you can browse them as a refresher.

Features in a Mass Notification system are important to me if they provide benefit to my employees. If a feature is included in a system but it does not provide any benefits, I do not care about those empty bells-and-whistles.

Your first step is to do a thorough needs analysis within your organization prior to embarking on a tool selection project. The tool you ultimately select will depend on your specific needs. Decide on the value you need. Be thorough in what you expect from the system.
Do your research and/or contact me for my short list of systems that might meet your needs. Read case studies. Go through vendor's websites. If you like what you see speak with a salesperson and have them do a high-level webinar for you. You can use some of the tips in this chapter during the webinar but don't ask them all on the first webinar. The first webinar will have info about the company and then they will go through the product.

If you like what you see and hear you can do another more in-depth webinar with them and get more in-depth questions answered.

Along the way be sure to get current and past references from the vendor and speak with them. But remember, these are the people the vendors are giving you so they probably will be positive – ya think? Definitely go beyond those cherry-picked references. Do your research and see if there are any horror stories out there. Then pick up the phone or send an email and try to get the scoop. They might give you critical info. The worst that can happen is you make a contact and maybe they say" no comment'. It is worth the effort.

But there is more you have to do. **You must do a 'pilot' for each of the finalist's products!!!** Kick the tires and really learn the capability of each system. It will be well worth the effort. If you skip the pilot it very well might come back to bite you and you will have no one to blame but yourself. I have seen it play out too many times not to warn you. A pilot will provide a lot of clarity.

If you are a vendor reading this: as a buyer, I feel good when a vendor strongly advises I do a pilot. It shows me your product will speak for itself. Words are cheap – 'the proof is in the pudding.' Impress us.

Intelligent Mass Notification Tools are constantly changing so to name my favorite mass notification systems in the book would not have been fair to you. Please contact me if you are interested in my current recommendations.

Below are benefits I seek when evaluating mass notification systems. The value of each benefit is in italics. You can mix these in with your own questions on vendor calls and in your RFP (request for proposal):

- Ease of use to learn the basics. If the system is not easy users will hesitate to use it. *This becomes critical during a crisis event when every second may count*
- Intuitive user interface. *You are seeking a simple, clean and robust interface in their app and desktop*
- Robust documentation that empowers admins to 'deep dive' and 'stretch' the product. *Sometimes vendors lag in providing robust documentation. I will temper this in saying that, from vendor feedback, I dig deeper than most any admin which I attribute to my technical background. In the long run, they appreciate my 'stretching' their product and making suggestions – in a nice way*

336

- User security. *If security is lacking, you will likely be in for big issues*
- Strong in-house (not outsourced) 24×7 tech support. *There will be times you or a user will need to reach the vendor for support. It may not be frequently but when you need to reach them – you need to reach them*
- Mobile- do they provide native apps or responsive HTML5 – Android and/or IOS. *In my opinion, native is not a requirement if they have a good HTML 5 or cross-platform app*
- Localized language sets for multilingual messages – be careful of the translations. *Test thoroughly to insure the proper message is being conveyed in the translation or there could be trouble*
- Inbound bulletin board to check-in, get messages and post crisis pictures
- Application Programming Interface (API). Is it free or is there an extra fee? What other tools, security hardware, sensors do they currently integrate with through the API? Ask for a couple of client case studies that align with your goals
- Employee contact feeds – SFTP, JSON, other methods. What type of upload file do they accept – CSV, Excel…?
- Employee contact hot syncs with SAP and BCM tools. Can they instantly update contact info based on triggers?
- The ability to create custom fields. *I find it important to have that option to add customized fields to the contact record*
- Strong non-proprietary relational back-end database with the ability to easily query the data
- Who do they host with? Do they utilize hot-hot failover with zero down-time?
- Which BCM systems do they currently integrate with? Is it two way or one way integration?
- Does their system identify duplicate contacts during an activation? *Important! If an employee belongs to multiple groups in scope for an activation you do not want them to receive multiple calls. Do that with a 'Finicky VP' and you are toast!*
- Strong secure network infrastructure, redundancy and security. *They will be hosting sensitive data*
- Strong / flexible internal user entitlements to access employee records, activations and reports. *It should be easy to filter what users can and cannot see and do. It should include the ability to assign users to groups with common rights. Role based access is a good methodology*
- Multiple replicated data centers – geographically dispersed national and International
- Triple DES Encrypted Data or similar high encryption if hosted in a 3rd party data center

- Corporate vision – is the vendor innovative? Do they stay on the cutting-edge? Do they have plans for social media communication modes including Twitter, Facebook, LinkedIn and other modes of communication LED signage, push notifications and desktop alerts?

Activation requirements:

- Easy to activate under pressure. *If the demo is confusing multiply that by 1000% during a stressful real activation*
- Multi-modal methods of communication – voice, email, SMS (text messaging), push notifications, desktop alerts, IP phone displays, signage…
- Two-way interactivity. *The recipient must be able to provide feedback by toll free number, email link, SMS*
- Boolean language (AND, OR, EQUAL TO…) support to build and mash-up dynamic groups on-the-fly. *One of my favorite benefits! The ability to filter data and build on-the-fly ad-hoc granular lists in seconds can be critical.*
- The ability to create user definable custom groups – both static and dynamic – using departments, cost centers, company codes and any other fields you desire…
- Polling / Survey capabilities – Yes/No, Multiple choice. How many questions can you ask in a notification? *Getting feedback from recipients can be critical*
- Follow-up notifications linked to the response received from an initial notification. *For example, if you ask 'Do you need assistance' and recipient responds 'Yes' – a follow-up customized notification is automatically sent by the system without human intervention*
- Variables in outgoing messages – in the body of a message the ability to embed variables pulled from backend database related records. Hierarchical/relational logic if possible (*very hard to find but at least one solution has it*)
- Multiple activation options:
- o Blast – all devices at once to everyone in the activation
- o Escalation – for all people in activation escalate through their devices – stop contacting that person when one of the devices is answered
- o Person-to-person (P2P) – sent sequentially to one person at a time. Do not use for a mass crisis alert. A use-case for P2P would be a system error that needs one technician to fix it. If the first person responds the activation stops
- PIN Support for sensitive messaging. *Do not use for time sensitive mass crisis alerts*

- Call-in message creation (usually limited functionality but valuable in a pinch). *Activator can call a phone number and trigger an activation with a code*
- Text-to-speech message creation – and the ability to easily have it played to you before sending the notification
- Real-time activation delivery tracking is important. *You need this information during an activation – as it happens*
- Support for phone extensions – *and ask how they do it. For example, what do you have to provide in the contact record to indicate an extension umber*
- Support for VOIP
- Support for GIS
- Multi time-zone sensitivity. *The ability to consider multiple time-zones in activations*
- GEO Fencing – *the system must understand when an employee is travelling or badges-in at another location*
- The ability to send a notification by web, app or dial-in to toll free number
- Drop-in conference call bridging – *make sure the vendor provides sufficient conference call numbers by default or if you can add your own. Also, if they provide the lines, ask how many attendees each conference line supports. You do not people to call and hear, 'the line is full' during a crisis meeting!*
- Customizable caller ID so you can brand outgoing calls. *This will greatly increase recipient responses. Otherwise, many people will think it is a telemarketer calling, and they will not answer the call.*
- SMS Short Codes *supplied for free to brand text messages. Vanity codes will cost extra.*
- Call can be delivered without recipient having to say 'hello' or another verbalization? *Test this. The capability varies from vendor to vendor. Even if they tell you we use 'whisper technology' – test it.*
- The ability to schedule future activations. *I have been responsible for global programs – so this allowed me to sleep rather than having to be at the keyboard to send a test at 3 a.m.*
- SLA for activations. *The vendor must provide robust message through-put even at high utilization periods during a widespread crisis event*
- 24/7/365 system and support availability – if you need the system it MUST be available

Reporting:
- Activation status report must be real-time! *You cannot wait until everyone has been contacted to create a status report*
- Canned reports must be included with the default system. *You must have the ability to clone these to create your own custom reports*

339

- You must have the ability to create new reports using a flexible report writer

Other thoughts and considerations:
- If competing products are equal in functionality consider tools that integrate well with your BCM and/or situational awareness tool(s)
- Does the product include situational alerts? Some systems now have them although usually limited for free but can integrate with commercial situational alert vendors through an API
- If possible, standardize the tool across your enterprise. This will provide the ability to leverage and cross-train associates as well as possible contractual advantages
- You want a flat rate for sending unlimited messages, including call list tests, rather than metered domestically
- How are international voice messages sent: international data center, VOIP / phone company… is there a charge?
- Panic button – at least one vendor has a great implementation. Simply tap an app button and an alert is sent out AND they have a very visionary feature/benefit where you do not even have to act to send an alert. Imagine you are travelling and feel you might be in danger in route to your hotel. Simply set the panic button on a predefined time – say 5-minute countdown. Every time the app counts down to zero it must receive an acknowledgement from you – or it triggers an activation. An elegant solution if you are not able to pull out your phone and click the button

Remember, when you get to the finalists you must do a pilot for each system! Also, you must send a thorough request for proposal. The pilot and RFP will greatly enhance your ability to decide on the best tool for your needs.

Intelligent Mass Notification Tools are constantly changing so to name my favorite mass notification systems in the book would not have made sense. Contact me –
Marty@UltimateBusinessContinuity.com if you are interested in my current favorite systems that meet your needs. I have a couple of solutions that are best of category in my experience.

100

YOU ARE ONLY AS GOOD AS YOUR DATA - SO LET'S MAKE IT BETTER

'You are only as good as your contact data.'
(Suggestions in this chapter focus mainly on employee contact data but are helpful with vendor and customer data as well).

In the previous chapter, we discussed how to select a good mass notification system. In this chapter, we will discuss contact data quality and integrity. They go together. The greatest system in the world with poor employee, vendor, customer contact data will not succeed. You need a great system and great data for world-class success.

Combining a great system with great data has enabled me to:
- During Hurricane Sandy I performed numerous notifications to 38,000+ employees. We quickly accounted for everyone.
- During the Boston Marathon I did notifications to employees located in towns that were on lock-down. The ability to create custom dynamic notification lists on-the-fly was a great benefit to recipients and enabled us to account for employees and produce comprehensive reports for management.
- During tornadoes, I often did notifications to cities in Oklahoma, Texas, Iowa and Ohio. I released multi-modal messages to employees in a timely manner. We practiced and practiced and each time we shaved precious seconds off ensuing notifications

It might surprise you to know each time I implemented a mass notification system the biggest challenge was improving the quality of employee contact data. The technical implementation of the mass notification system was relatively easy. I have heard similar accounts from many organizations throughout the world.

Tip – When you plan your mass notification system implementation and estimate a production date make sure you leave ample time to:
- Get your initial employee data upload approved by your Legal and HR departments. This can take time especially if the data will be stored in a vendor's data center in the cloud
- Insure the quality of the data is at the level you require. If the data is of poor quality, contacting people will be difficult or impossible,

which defeats the purpose of the system. Improving the quality of data is something I have been through many times and I will share some tips that have worked for me

Tip – Whether you use manual call trees to communicate with employees during a crisis or an automated mass notification system each is only as good as the quality of the underlying HR contact data.

Tip – Data quality and integrity is often a challenge, especially in mid-size and enterprise companies. In my case I have worked with employee databases between 23,000 and 82,000.

Tip – In some cases you might even be breaking new ground in your organization to improve the quality of employee data across the enterprise. I have encountered this in many organizations and I promise you that the effort you put into improving the data will benefit your employees and your company in many ways beyond crisis management and business continuity.

For example, while implementing an automated mass notification system for a fairly large company I reviewed the employee contact data in SAP (a popular HR system) and for many people their contact data had never been updated. I did some random testing by trying to manually contact employees. It was no surprise to me that many phone numbers were incorrect. I encountered many disconnected numbers, numbers no longer in service, pizza places (we have a lot of pizza places in NY), a stationary store and even a bar (perhaps the employee spent a lot of time there).

The Road to Better Data
Even before you evaluate and purchase an automated mass notification system it is important to speak with HR and legal about what type of employee data you can and cannot use to contact employees. Depending on your policies and procedures you may or may not get permission to add personal contact information to the system without specific 'opt-in' from employees. In most of my implementations we had to implement an opt-in or opt-out process for personal data. Work data can usually be used by default without opt-in, but verify that with HR and legal just to be certain.
Implementing an opt-in process can be time consuming. You must consider how you will communicate the program to employees and how you will capture the opt-in permission from them.

342

I suggest when you go out to the employees for their permission to include their contact information you offer them the opportunity to also review and update their current contact data. When people move and/or change landline and mobile phone numbers the last thing they think about is updating their employee contact information with HR. Do not be surprised if a large percentage of your data needs updates. Getting this important data up-to-date and accurate is a big win for you and your organization.

There are many options you can offer employees to review and update their contact data. You may already have a self-service portal for employees. Another option is to send them an email with a secure link. When they click the link, they can sign-into a form which will display their current contact information. They can then review the data, add or update contact methods and click the opt-in checkbox.

It is important to sell the opt-in as a win-win for employees. Let employees know that the opt-in contact information will only be used in emergencies as part of the crisis management program. You can give a few examples of scenarios during which it is critical and advantageous that you can reach them. For example, if there is an ice storm in their area and their work location will have a delayed opening you can contact them to try to prevent them from needlessly driving to work.

In my experience, you still might have a low opt-in percentage. The opt-ins will likely improve when you have the system implemented and you begin doing call-list exercises.

During these exercises, typically people that had not opted-in hear that their friends received cool notifications the night before and they did not receive any. At that point you must first check if they are in the system. It is possible they had opted-in and the system did not contact them or it did contact them and perhaps someone in their family listened to the call and did not mention it to the employee.

You can check the notification reports for details of what occurred. Most likely the employee had not opted-in. You should have an easy process for them to opt-in at that point. Perhaps, an email could be sent with a form to review their contact information and an, 'Opt-Me-In' checkbox. Otherwise, if your opt-in process is not automated you can use paper opt-in forms.

Unfortunately, in my experience some people still will not opt-in. When a crisis happens and they do not get a call they will probably then want

343

to opt-in but of course it is too late for that event. Well, you did your best.

IMPORTANT TIP – If you are a global company and have international employees located in various countries pay close attention to laws regarding where employee data is permitted to be stored. Can it be maintained in a server based in the United States? I encountered this type of issue when running a global program spanning 30+ countries. Work closely with the international countries, HR and legal to get it right.

But wait, there is more!

If you are working with a vendor, where will the employee data reside? In your local network or in the cloud? Most likely it will be stored in the cloud in their data center or probably in an outside data center such as AWS (Amazon Web Services). If that is the case here are some tips:

Tip – Ask the vendor which data center they use. Do some analysis on their infrastructure. Make sure they are solid and well secured. I know of major data centers compromised by hackers that were down for days! Research their history. Do some Googling. Do your homework.

Tip – Vendor resilience – Review the vendor's disaster recovery and business continuity plans. Ask if they run hot-hot for system recovery. Can they instantly flip from one data center to another? Ask about single points of failure. Have your network, cyber security and IT teams join in the conversation so they can ask hard questions to make sure all is great and you won't lose sleep over their up-time down the road.

Tip – Vendor security -Imagine if the vendor is hacked and your employee data is stolen. Make sure you do an audit of their infrastructure or have them send you recent independent audit findings. Ask if your data will be encrypted 'at rest' and 'in-flight'.

Tip – Vendor disaster recovery testing and results – Ask how often they test their backups. Ask for the results of the three most recent disaster recovery exercises they conducted. Ask about their uptime SLA.

Ok, let us assume all is great and you did a comprehensive pilot of the system and finally you have a signed contract for the system. You will meet with the vendor to map fields from your HR system to their mass notification tool. The data will be stored in a database table in the vendor's data center. The data may be stored in a flat file as part of a relational database. Some mass notification vendors do not normalize their data model. This can be ok in this use case. Had this been a BCM system, red flags would go up if the system were not normalized.

You will work with IT and the vendor to map your internal fields to their database. It is relatively easy. The good vendors provide you with a lot of flexibility for core contact fields plus additional custom fields you can define. Custom fields plus Boolean logic will enable you to slice and dice the data in a great many ways. For example, you may want to initiate a notification to one or more cost centers or zip codes. Some systems make that impractical and others make it 'easy peasy'.

What you do not want to do is to manually maintain the employee contact information directly on the vendor system or manually upload spreadsheets every night. I strongly urge you to set up an automated secure ftp (SFTP) process from your internal network to the vendors site. When the nightly file arrives, it should trigger a job on their end that automatically imports the contact information – adding, updating and deleting records without any manual intervention.

Ask the vendor how long the process of importing the data takes on their end. You would be surprised. Even a small upload of 10,000-15,000 employees could take an inefficient system hours to import. It really should only take a matter of seconds. Anything over 10 minutes, I would question. Stress test this BEFORE you buy the system. You should use masked data for the test.

Important Mass Notification System Tip – Deleting Employee Records
I separated this one out as I have heard horror stories of people no longer with an organization getting contacted. It is critical that a foolproof process is in place to delete employees from the system who are no longer with your organization. You must do everything in your power to insure the system does not send notifications to these people.
You do not want to call the family of an employee who is no longer with your company. Possibly the employee could have passed away.

I have also heard of occasions where people fired by an organization were subsequently contacted during a call list exercise. You do not need the aggravation.

There is also the important issue that you may have personal data sitting in a third-party database when the individuals are no longer part of your organization. This is a liability. Imagine if the vendor was hacked and you had to notify the people to explain why their contact data was still in the cloud!

It is important that the vendor deletes the employee records and does not simply tag them as deleted and leaves them in the database.
Make sure you pay close attention to the delete process. Test it thoroughly. It is critical.

Improving your data over time
With all the above you will still most likely have data challenges. However, you are making progress. Often you are doing something that has never been attempted in your organization. It can be a big project. It takes time. You will get there if you do not give up.
You must continually test and improve the quality of your contact data. Analyze your data and improve it until you reach a threshold you feel is acceptable.

Your mass notification system must be able to provide you with detailed reports indicating wrong numbers, busy signals, hang-ups, etc. This will allow you to finely focus on where you must continue to improve the data. Create a feedback loop with employees so they can update their record with the correct information and test again.
Each test you perform will improve your contact connection results. Employees will contact you to opt-in after you launch the first few call list exercises. Word-of-mouth will encourage employees, who may have been wary of opting in to do so, as they will want to be included in future alerts.

I do have to warn you if you test to a couple thousand employees you will get questions from some employees as to why they did not receive a call or email. Be prepared to comb through the call list results. It is all part of the effort to build data integrity, prior to a disaster. Been there, done that many times.

Tip – The more contact methods you have for an employee the greater the probability you will be able to reach them in an emergency. Strive to have employees list as many work and personal contact points as possible including voice text and email.

Tip – Report the results of the call list tests to management. Let people know the results go to management and they will be eager to participate.

In summary…
In my experience improving contact data quality can be a challenge. Do not minimize the time and effort this endeavor may require, especially if you are a large organization.

Tip – HR should own the employee contact data. Purchasing can own vendor contact data. Sales can own customer contact data. You should provide support and guidance, but they own it. If you own it, it will sap your time. If they say you own it, you might want to 'push back!'

Tip – Expect to find a lot of disconnected or wrong home phone numbers, cities and states. People move and do not always update their information with HR.

Tip – You may discover disconnected work cell phone numbers that you may still be paying for. Check out the chapter in the book entitled 'How to Spin Data Into Gold'. It can be a big opportunity for you beyond business continuity.

Tip – You will find incorrect personal email addresses. There will be a lot of bounce-backs. Be ready.

Tip – Instruct people to white-list the email address you are using to send email to their personal email account. Otherwise, it can be rejected or go into spam,

Tip – Have HR request, on a regular basis, that users update their HR information. Make it easy for the users to do so.

Tip – Gamify your automated call list exercises. Get management involved. Make it a friendly competition for the divisions. See who can get the highest connection percentage and send praise their way. Send 'gentle reminders' to the lowest scoring divisions to help them improve.

FINAL IMPORTANT TIP – Opt-in versus Opt-out
Each organization is different and the decision to have an opt-in or opt-out policy to load contact data is an important decision in terms of the percentage of data that gets loaded into the mass notification system.
If the decision is that each user must opt-in to have their data included in the system, you will likely start with a low percentage of contact information. However, if you are permitted to use an opt-out process to load the initial data into the system your initial user contact information will SKYROCKET! This may be a decision for HR and legal.

DATABASE OR SPREADSHEET? YOUR CRITICAL DECISION

You may wonder why I have written a chapter on 'Database or Spreadsheet?' for a book focused on Business Resilience / Business Continuity (BRBC). There are many good reasons which I will discuss in this chapter.

I have known a lot of great BRBC people and unless they came from IT they can sometimes be at a disadvantage:
1. Understanding which is a better solution for different use cases – a database or a spreadsheet
2. Understanding the true power of a well-designed database solution and how to implement it properly

Using the wrong tool or implementing the wrong vendor solution can result in a nightmare for you and your organization. It can become:

- Life threatening to your employees
- Expensive for your organization
- A frustrating drain on your limited resources and very difficult to reverse for you and your team

In this chapter, we are going to stay away from complex tech jargon. We do not need to go there. We will keep it at a high level. Our goal is to get you comfortable with the basic concepts. When you consider building a solution in-house you will have a good idea which tool to use. When you get on a call or webinar with a vendor you will have a head start. Database concepts will not be completely foreign to you. Many people are not comfortable with database concepts and I can completely understand it.

Hopefully, this short chapter will start you in the right direction and you can further research on your own with a simple database book or video. There are some very good ones available. If you prefer you can contact me for some suggestions. As you know my door is open to you.

In my experience people throughout corporations, education and the government, not just BRBC, often use the tool they are most familiar with rather than the one best suited for the job. The result can be like using a screw driver to hammer in a nail. This has become a pet peeve of mine. I think organizations are doing themselves and their customers a disservice when they think spreadsheet first and only. I am not a spreadsheet hater. I use spreadsheets. Spreadsheets can have great value. Sometimes a spreadsheet is the appropriate tool and sometimes it is not.

In Business Resilience, we work with oceans of data and it is increasing every day. Often we have to analyze how data 'elements' relate to each other. For example, creating a dashboard of the important metrics derived from hundreds or thousands of plans and determining the relationship of processes upstream and downstream. This type of data-analysis plays to the strength of databases. You need to be able to spin these large data-sets into insight, knowledge and decisions using the best possible tool. Picking the wrong solution will undermine this and it will waste your time.

Making the Decision – Database or Spreadsheet:
To be 100% transparent, I have written eight books on database development that have been used by professional programmers globally. Don't worry, this chapter is not meant to be a database programming course and I am pretty sure most of you would not want it to be. I promise I am not going to get too techie here, as it would be counter-productive. I will pose some ideas and suggestions that will help you decide if a database or spreadsheet is the proper tool to use.

There are occasions where developing a simple database can be faster and much more valuable than building complex macros in a spreadsheet to make it 'almost' like a database. I will also point out use-cases where a spreadsheet is preferable to a database.

I will then conclude the chapter with some common database concepts and terms that will help level the playing field for you when speaking with your IT folks or vendors trying to sell you their expensive software solutions. When you ask them questions about fields, records, properties, data normalization, data models and API's, they will see you on a different level. You will be in the top 1% of business users in terms of understanding the power of a database. The questions will help you select the best solution for your needs. It is critical to ask the right questions before you buy.

If fact, ask 10 of your non-IT business friends what data normalization is or what a data model is and I will bet close to zero will not have any clue what you are talking about. They may roll their eyes.

Most importantly, the information you will learn will allow you to get a feel for how robust a vendor's solution really is, not strictly what they are telling/selling you. I mean, we trust them to a certain degree but they may be slightly biased in favor of their product, ya think? Poor database design can indicate a poor product and trouble ahead. Great database design can provide incredible value and can be a foundation to your program.

When you use one of the concepts such as an API or normalization in a question to a technology salesperson and he or she says, *'hmmm I was never asked that before. Great question, I will speak with our tech people'...*, let me know. You will make my day. I hear it from salespeople often and I hope you do too!

Spreadsheets in BRBC:
I am guessing you are pretty good with a spreadsheet. The clear majority of people I have met are more familiar with using spreadsheets than developing database solutions.

You probably know a spreadsheet is a paper based or software program that captures data in rows and columns. The data can be in one worksheet or in multiple worksheets in a workbook container. Excel and Google Sheets are examples of spreadsheets. I started with Lotus 1-2-3, back in the day. I have seen spreadsheets used for almost every application from word processing to a home spun FTP (file transfer protocol) program using VBA (Visual BASIC for Applications). In fact, I have built some very complex spreadsheets using VBA. In my opinion it is a fun and easy to learn language.

In a spreadsheet, individual data elements such as first name, last name, city, state and zip code are captured in cells that intersect rows and columns in the worksheet. A1, B12, D5... sounds like a bingo card, right?

I commonly use spreadsheets for simple contact lists, vendor features/benefits analysis and sometimes for reports from my business continuity management tool or mass notification tool in which I need to apply a further level of numeric analysis beyond what I can do in the core vendor tool. I also use spreadsheets for checklists and simple project plans. I find each of these use cases shine in a spreadsheet.

Spreadsheets can get us into trouble when many people need to contribute or access information.
You have probably seen spreadsheets emailed to 10, 20 or 50+ people for input. You have multiple people updating a BIA or updating their contact information. Each person enters information and returns it to the sender. It then becomes cumbersome and error prone to integrate

and present the results. Keeping the spreadsheet up to date can be a time sapping nightmare.

At that point, if you are good with spreadsheets, you may start designing complex macros, programming in VBA or developing cross-worksheet formulas and pivot tables to produce the metrics and summary results you and management need to do your jobs. Then, when you finally complete that effort, the need to produce additional metrics triggers another larger than necessary effort. This type of use case is 'easy peasy' using a more flexible database solution.

Spreadsheets also have the propensity to breed faster than rabbits. Siloed departments often have their own 'secret' version of 'the truth' or the 'not so gold copy' stored in spreadsheets out on their share drive, either on an official corporate drive or perhaps on their personal drive in the cloud, which is a huge security risk. This can get ugly real quickly when there are many versions of 'the truth'. Which one do you believe? I have witnessed very expensive organization-wide data cleanup projects dedicated to trying to consolidate and 'normalize' this data, after the fact.

Overview of Databases in BRBC:
A database is a central repository that can manage vast amounts of data. If the database is designed properly gigabytes, terabytes, exabytes and even zettabytes of data can be sliced and diced any way you need it in fractions of a second. For example, a database with 1,000,000 employee records, 100,000 vendors and thousands of systems and organizational locations is trivial. A database comprised of 2,000 business continuity plans is 'easy peasy' for modern database systems.

A database is an excellent tool when you need input from many people AND when you want to present the data in different ways to a variety of users with varying permissions. You can easily control what they can input and view. You can easily hide data they do not have permission to see.

The information in a database is most often stored in tables (relational database) or in nodes (graph database). As of this writing relational databases are much more popular than graph databases, primarily because they have been around far longer. Most, if not all, HR systems, business continuity management systems and mass notification systems use relational databases.

351

Although graph database systems make up only a small portion of the database universe as of 2017 that will change drastically in the future, as there are many interesting uses for graph databases. Graph databases allow us flexible and easy analysis of millions or billions of data nodes. Advanced situational awareness and real-time gap analysis are two of many uses. Employee skill and certification information can be a graph database solution as well. Facebook manages their billions of users in a graph database. Graph databases can help us discover critical well-hidden inter-relationships between entities in our organizations or any other facet of life. For example, graph databases are key to mapping DNA and discovering the causes of disease.

Perhaps in a future edition of this book we will dig deeper into how we can leverage graph databases. In the meanwhile I will keep you up to date on graph database solutions in the free Ultimate Business Continuity Tips, Techniques and Tools Newsletter.

Basics of a relational database:
A relational database stores information (data) in **one or more tables**. Each table stores a common set of data in rows and columns. Employees, equipment, vendors, customers and applications should be stored in their own dedicated table, rather than one huge table.

A well-designed database solution separates the presentation layer (what the user sees) and the data layer (the back-end data tables). This allows you extraordinary flexibility and control in presenting and accessing data to users. Make sure the layers are separated.

Tables are made up of the following:
Each table will be made up of 'records' and 'fields'. Each field will store a particular data element which is a single piece of information. For example, in the employee table 'first name', 'last name' and 'employee ID' would be stored in individual fields. Employee ID, if unique, can be a special field called a primary key. Each table requires a primary key that defines the uniqueness of each record in that table. In some instances, a primary key can be the concatenation (combination) of more than one field.

Primary keys and uniqueness may be a discussion point during your vendor calls and definitely when importing data to a BCM or mass notification system. I speak a little more about primary keys below, as it is an important concept for you to be comfortable with.

Records: are comprised of groups of fields. That would include the three fields I just mentioned and more – city, state… in total for one person which would constitute one record. For a Vendor record, fields might include: Vendor ID, Vendor Company Name and Vendor Representative.

A simple analogy with a spreadsheet is that database fields are columns, and records are rows.

Tables: are comprised of multiple records. As I mentioned you will have an Employees Table, Vendor Table, Applications Table...

The amazing thing is, if the database is properly designed, data about a person, a process or any other asset might be spread across multiple tables but it will be easy to bring everything together in reports and display information at a detail or summary level.

Proper database design is an important concept. If the relational database is treated as a 'flat file', sort of like building one big spreadsheet in the database, it will cause trouble down the road. It can easily become an expensive re-design and it will cause you lots of nights thinking about how to fix the mess. Your database MUST use the power of proper powerful relational design.

Here are a few database terms you might hear on vendor calls or in meetings with your IT liaison. You do not have to memorize them. Just get a feel for them. You can also further research any that especially interest you:

Primary Key – is a special relational database table field (or combination of fields) designated to uniquely identify all records in each table. A **primary key's** main features are: It must contain a unique value for each row (record) of data and the primary key cannot contain null values. An example of a primary key might be employee ID's. Even if 10 people have the same first and last name they can be uniquely identified by the primary key.

Primary key definition will be an important part of any BCM and mass notification tool discussion and implementation. When you update the records in the database you will most likely cut a file from your HR system and upload it to the BCM or mass notification tool to delete, update or add records. The match will be accomplished using the primary key.

Foreign Key – is a field (or collection of fields) in one table that uniquely identifies a row of another table or the same table. In other words, the **foreign key** is used in a second 'related' table, but it refers to the primary **key** in the first table. This is how the link between the

353

tables is established. Often it is used in a one-to-many relationship, which we discuss below.

For example, your Accounting 'process' may use many types of software which need to be linked in their Business Continuity Plan. In that case 'process' would be the master table and software would be the child table. A 'join' would be created between the tables using each tables key field. The system will use these linked fields to produce reports in a variety of formats. Joins are really important.

Normalization – is the process of organizing the columns and tables to reduce data redundancy and improve data integrity. Normalization occurs by breaking out repeating data into related tables. In my experience, there are instances in database design where partial normalization makes more sense from a response perspective.

The three levels of normalization are:

First Normal Form
- Eliminate repeating groups in individual tables
- Create a separate table for each set of related data
- Identify each set of related data with a primary key

Second Normal Form
- Create separate tables for sets of values that apply to multiple records
- Relate these tables with a foreign key

Third Normal Form
- Eliminate fields that do not depend on the key

Don't worry if the three levels of normalization do not make sense. The practical use of normalization is more important. Here it is… if you are implementing a BCM tool you should be **very concerned with normalization and quality of data.** You will most likely set up master tables for employees, equipment, applications and other dependencies.

If the data is not normalized, what can happen is the same application can be called by multiple names – Microsoft Office, Office, Office 365… When it comes time to produce reports on a particular piece of software, you will have a mess on your hands.

The reporting demands will quickly turn into 'kludgy' (tech term for messy) solutions in an attempt to produce quality output. Worst case is, you can wind up with a very expensive cleanup and database re-design on your hands. Trust me, you DO NOT want to go there. The best solution is for the database to be designed properly upfront and the data should be automatically imported or manually entered into the system abiding by strict rules for consistency. Users can select dependencies to link to their plans, but your team controls the dependency data in the master tables.

Repeating data in tables can also turn into a maintenance nightmare if you need to change a piece of data throughout your system. You will have to find and change every occurrence if it throughout the database.

By having it in one master table and linked to other forms when you need to use it, you will only have to change the information in one place and the change will automatically be reflected (ripple) wherever that piece of data is used in relationships. Change it once and the change is reflected everywhere in the system.

If you are fortunate enough to have corporate central 'gold sources' of data within your company with unique identifiers (primary keys) you may want to upload that data to your BCM systems master tables. You can even set up automated SFTP uploads to add, modify or delete data as often as required. The unique identifiers (primary keys) must not change, as that is what the BCM tool will use to match the records!

One-to-many relationship – this is the most common type of relationship you will encounter in whichever database system you use. A parent record in a table can refer to zero to many child records in another table. The child record can only have one parent record. For example, a department can link to many dependent applications, vendors or any other dependency or asset.

Data Model – this is a diagram of how the tables and the underlying data is connected and stored in a database system. To the trained database professional analyzing a data model can be **very valuable** in determining the normalization degree of a database and in the ability to create complex reports. In my experience, some vendors are hesitant to release their data model. Having it can save you time. If you do not have it you can figure it out, if you know databases.

Structured Query Language (SQL) – a programming language designed for managing data stored in a relational database. I know many languages and I rate SQL very easy to use for basic updates and reports. It can get pretty complex depending on the type of table joins and actions you need to perform. You will most often be using inner joins. There are also outer, left, right, cross and self joins that can prove useful.

HTML, JavaScript, ASPX... – these are powerful and fun front-end scripting languages that allow you to quickly build web-based and mobile app forms that connect (interact) with the back-end database. Always start with 'Hello World' as your first script. I do and it gets me off to a fast start and brings me luck. Ask vendors if they support any of these industry standard languages. If you are building your own simple database system you should be able to learn to build forms and manipulate data with one of these languages and online/book resources.

* In the 'Golden Opportunities to Generate Beyond BC Value Streams' Chapter in Part I of this book toward the end of the Chapter I discuss 'Data Referential Integrity'. This is an important consideration when designing databases. It is also low hanging fruit when analyzing data problems in organizations. As data moves horizontally from department to department bad data can become very costly. You can provide extraordinary value identifying data issues and bringing them to the attention of management and IT. Please be sure to read the Golden Opportunities Chapter.

The bottom line is databases might sound complicated but they are not. Just take it slow and build your skills at your own pace. It really is fun and it is a very valuable skill to know. As a BRBC professional no one expects you to develop complex databases. Knowing when to use a database as opposed to using a spreadsheet or another tool is very important to your success. Contact me with any questions, concerns or ideas you may have.

102

DISASTER RECOVERY SYSTEM TESTING MUST BE DONE BEFORE GOING TO PRODUCTION

Your organization needs a robust disaster recovery program in place. The days of going back to manual workarounds in the absence of core critical systems is forever fading for many time sensitive processes. In fact, often the people that used to do the work manually are retired or have moved on to other positions. If critical systems are down for an unacceptable period of time it can severely imperil your company.

- Information Technology (IT) should have direct responsibility for disaster recovery. You should work with them to map the current availability of systems (RTO and RPO) to the business requirements
- All systems must have a run-book
- All systems must be tested per your company's policies (more on testing below)

System information, run-books and disaster recovery test results should all be maintained in your automated BCM tool, rather than in spreadsheets. Maintaining this type of data in spreadsheets has many drawbacks. A few include:

- Spreadsheets are difficult to keep up-to-date
- Spreadsheets have a limited audit trail
- Spreadsheets tend to become siloed
- Spreadsheets make it more difficult and time consuming to analyze application data against upstream and downstream applications and business processes

Using a BCM tool makes all those negatives go away. You can maintain data in structured fields and use attachments if additional information in spreadsheets or word processing documents are required, such as network diagrams.

Having all this information in a BCM central repository along with your business continuity requirements will empower you to do some very nice automated analysis including real-time gap pulse reports. For instance, if changes are made to any system in your enterprise it can be analyzed in real-time and a risk profile can be updated. A robust BCM tool can use rules and workflow to deliver alerts to the right **people** at the right time!

I get excited just thinking about it. I have set up these types of rules, triggers and workflows on many occasions and it is great!

It is important you are capturing the information that will enable you to do the analysis and produce the reports and metrics. As a long-time successful software developer, I learned to start at the end. I realize you will need ad-hoc reports as you mature but for now try to determine your near-term needs. Mock up some reports. Think about reports, alerts...then work backwards to understand what information you need to capture to make your dreams a reality.

Do I sound excited? Well darn it, I am excited!!!

Some of the information you might want to capture in your system will include the following. Be sure to add more to meet your needs:
- Application name
- Description
- Application owner and contact info
- Purpose of application
- Processes that use the application
- Vendor name
- Vendor representative (name/email)
- Critical (Yes/No)
- IT System RTO (hours)
- IT System RPO (hours)
- Run-book completed? (Yes/No)
- Disaster recovery plan completed? (Yes/No)
- Was last DR test successful? (Yes/No)
- List of issues from the last DR test
- Production data center
- Backup data center
- If vendor hosted, was a SAS-70 or data center walk through completed? (Yes/No)
- If hosted locally – must it be local?
- Number of users
- Number of servers
- Type of server (dedicated, virtual, operating system....)

- Contract / license expiration date
- Owner of equipment
- Fail-over tested (Yes/No)
- Is the application being recovered in the primary data center? (you would be surprised)
- Full back-up frequency
- Incremental backup frequency
- Type of backup (digital tape, vaulting...)
- If backup is tape, where is it stored?
- If backup is tape, who transports it?
- Systems dependencies – input
- Systems dependencies – output
- Comments, concerns, results

I know it is a lot and IT may not have it now but it is important to get the ball rolling. Engage them and find out where they are. This is critical stuff.

You MUST do your disaster recovery tests 'before the baby is born'!

Your policy should be that **prior to any new system going into production** a disaster recovery test be completed with the business **actively participating**. The results must be signed off by the business owner. I will repeat one more time – there must be a written, tested and approved disaster recovery plan in place – **PRIOR to going live**.

If your organization has a Project Management Office (PMO) they should make disaster recovery testing and sign-off a 'toll-gate' part of every new system implementation. If the user has not signed off on the Disaster Recovery User Acceptance Test (UAT), the system cannot go into production, until it is completed.

In my experience, as both an IT and BC professional, once a critical system has gone into production the urgency and incentive to complete a disaster recovery test is greatly reduced to 'someday' or 'when we have time'... which often never comes. The DR testing will be pushed back indefinitely or likely forgotten as teams move on to the next critical project.

Unfortunately, your butt will be on the line when the untested system goes down or a virus hits and there is no backup, incompatible tape backup, RTO/RPO does not meet the business requirements or maybe all of the above!

So, I strongly advise you not to wait until 'after the baby is born'. When the production system goes down is NOT the time to test or to think – woulda, coulda, shoulda.

Next step tips regarding disaster recovery testing:

Tip – Ask IT when the last disaster recovery testing was done and where the results are stored. Review them for critical systems information results, gaps and issues. Were they corrected and tested again? Did the business sign off on the corrections?

Tip – Ask IT if disaster recovery testing is on the new system development roadmap. If it is not, it must be added asap.

Tip – Make all requests in writing and keep a copy of the email trail and the final decision. Otherwise, your butt will be on the line when issues arise.

Tip – Partner with IT and management to develop the enterprise 'before the baby is born' disaster recovery testing policy and get it signed off on.

Tip – If a policy is subsequently put in place it is a significant accomplishment to be highlighted on your next annual job review.

Tip – If a policy does not get put in place, the email trail just might save your job when a critical system is not available during a disruption and the inevitable finger pointing begins. I have seen this play out, so please be forewarned.

103

HOW TO BUILD YOUR BUSINESS RESILIENCE WEB SITE AND MOBILE APP

A Business Resilience / Business Continuity (BRBC) website or mobile app are great ways for employees to easily access important information. These are also wonderful branding opportunities for your program.

Your website can include:

- Breaking news
- Critical emergency phone numbers
- Best practices
- BC team member's bio's
- BC team members contact info
- Links to important websites such as NOAA, FEMA, Weather.com
- Local alert services reporting nearby incidents – use geo-location if you have multiple sites geographically dispersed
- Simple secure metric reports tied to a back-end database. You get extra credit for building this feature/benefit!
- New Business Continuity Plan request form. So, process owners can populate and send you basic information on their process

Consider a section focusing on the well-being and safety of your employees outside of work. For example, a personal plan template and information, a pet plan template and information, an In Case of Emergency (ICE) wallet card template and a home emergency supply kit template. Remember, if people do not have a personal plan and supplies, it probably will impact their ability to come to work during a disruptive event.

You can also include the ability for users to view their business continuity plans on the site, but that will raise the bar on security and role based access. I believe this is better served in a BCM tool, which can be linked to your web portal or mobile app.

Building your website:
If you have basic html skills, you can easily design a simple website. It does not have to be fancy. Start simple and grow. If your company uses SharePoint, you can build a simple SharePoint repository and blog. You can even buy an inexpensive web template on a site like 99designs.com

that will look professional and can be customized by your team. I have created hundreds of custom websites and several SharePoint portals.

Another excellent alternative is WordPress. I am quite impressed how far it has come. You can quickly easily build a full featured blog, which is great for interacting with employees or you can use WordPress to build a full feature web site. If you host WordPress on your own server, you can choose from thousands of themes. Each theme's look and feel can be customized through an easy to use interface.

If you have basic HTML, CSS and PHP skills you can even dive into the underlying files that make up a WordPress theme and customize every detail of your site.
WordPress also has thousands of plug-ins that can be installed in minutes and provide some very nice benefits.

To learn more about WordPress visit WordPress.org. If you decide you do not want to host your WordPress site, you can have it hosted on WordPress.com. If you host the site, you will have more customizing options.

By the way, 95%+ of my programming skills are self-taught. Little-by-little I improved my skills and ultimately, I built enterprise database solutions for some of the largest companies in the world.

My advice is to start on small projects first and learn. Every programming language I learned I started with a tiny 'Hello World' program. It provides a simple win and it has become a good luck tradition for me. There are many great books and websites devoted to building websites.
If you need advice contact me -
Marty@UltimateBusinessContinuity.com

Building an App:
If you love to code like I do or you just want to learn and have fun, you can try your hand at building an app for your employees. It is not hard. There are three ways you can build apps. I list each below from the simplest to the most difficult:

HTML5 app development:
If you used HTML5 to build your website it will work on mobile devices as well. HTML5 is 'responsive' which means it will adapt to desktop screens, tablets and mobile phones. HTML5 is easy to learn and fun to use. The downside is, it does not have as many features as native or

cross-platform tools but you most likely will not need those 'bells and whistles'.

Tip – If you use HTML5 be sure to test on various mobile devices. You may have to tweak the code for your site to look good on different device.

Cross-platform app development – a powerful development solution:
Believe it or not, it really is not that hard to create a cool looking app that runs on multiple platforms.

Rather than programming your app in the latest native language specific to IOS or Android, which will entail developing and maintaining a couple versions of the code, you can use one of the powerful cross platform developer tools built specifically to 'write-once' and run on multiple platforms. These tools use a higher-level language such as JavaScript to develop apps. Higher level scripting languages are powerful and much easier to master than lower level languages such as Java, Swift or C# (C sharp).

I have built native apps as well as cross platform apps. For business resilience related apps, I think it makes more sense to go the cross platform route.

Tip – Cross platform app development tools have greatly matured in the past few years. They are more reliable and feature laden then 3-4 years ago. Many successful companies are thriving using cross platform developed apps.

You will most likely have to do some minor tweaking to have your app run on both IOS and Android, but compared to developing at a lower level for each platform, it is a minuscule effort. Also, updating the apps is much easier than maintaining multiple code bases.

Native app development:
Beside wowing your management, a native app allows you to take full advantage of a mobile devices hardware and software features. You can interact with contacts, phone, notifications, cameras, accelerometers, etc..

Tip – I will warn you that developing native apps can be time consuming and complex. Unless you are a programmer, this might not be the best choice for you.

Whichever method you choose I commend you for taking on the challenge.

Happy Coding!

104

LET'S GET VISIONARY - WHAT'S HERE NOW AND COMING NEXT!

Technology has been key to many of my career successes. Researching, testing and sharing technology gems is what I would do even if I did not get paid for it. It is my passion and it is my hobby. Leveraging technology solutions can provide resilience and hyper return on investment.

In this fun and visionary chapter I will first recap some of the technologies we have discussed earlier in the book and then suggest some ideas for you to consider to take your program to the next level now and in the future.

Throughout the book, we have discussed how we can leverage technology to achieve world-class programs and make our lives easier by:

- Implementing the three-critical business resilience 'pillar' systems:
  - Situational Awareness – to clearly understand our surroundings, risks and opportunities
  - Business Continuity Management – to scale our programs and derive real-time insight with minimal effort. Insight that would be impossible to uncover through manual means
  - Intelligent Mass Notification – to provide critical two-way multi-modal communication to the right people when they need it
- Implementing an incoming emergency hotline
- Building a business continuity website to share critical information
- Building our own custom apps to share critical information
- Creating fully functional portable eBooks, from any of our plans
- Creating highly portable 'mini-plans'
- Knowing when to use a spreadsheet versus a database – the right tool for the right job
- Understanding the fundamentals of how a database works
- Using Internet Protocol (IP), satellite phones and push to talk for critical communications, when other channels may not be available
- Identifying potentially disastrous laptop vulnerabilities and mitigation strategies

- Identifying potentially disastrous mobile vulnerabilities and mitigation strategies
- Identifying potentially disastrous network vulnerabilities and mitigation strategies

All the above is critical to building a solid foundation for your resilience program.

Now, let's have some fun and travel to the next level...

Visionary software and hardware vendors are already embracing opportunities to provide added value to their products. Systems are gaining the ability to learn, predict, make fast/intelligent decisions and communicate the results to the right people – without human intervention! Interesting and often inexpensive new hardware components are improving our work and personal lives.

Tip – When you speak with vendors about their solutions, always ask about their roadmap to the future. Ask how they currently integrate with other systems and hardware components. Request use-cases of how their current clients are creatively using their products.

Ask about their application programming interface (API). An API is a bridge to other systems and Internet of Things hardware. It is similar to playing with building blocks. You can snap software and hardware components together.

There are limitless combinations of value that can be created by mixing, matching and mashing software, hardware and data. I can think of many multi-million dollar companies that were built on that notion. The only limits – are our imaginations.

Situational awareness, BCM and mass notification tools are aggressively moving toward tighter integration. Some mass notification tools are offering compelling situational awareness solutions and situational awareness tools offer certain mass notification capabilities as part of their product offerings. These two critical pillars can also speak with your BCM tool.

In addition, your incident command app should be able to leverage information from your 3 pillar systems. Maintaining plans and tasks in your BCM system and using it elsewhere will prevent multiple versions of the same data and the significant issues that it creates.

366

Consider mashing in situational data using API or XML feed to build your own situational awareness tool. One of my favorite situational awareness tools is strong on transportation and supply chain threats. It can dynamically overlay threat ratings on your transportation routes, geo-fencing your commercial vehicles in real-time to alert them to threats.

Listed below are a potpourri of ideas you can use to leverage off-the-shelf technology:

Traffic cameras (cams) – can be your eyes on the ground during a dangerous natural or man-made event. They often provide near real-time situational awareness information on a website that can be valuable to your team's decision making. I have used local traffic cams on many occasions to view local travel conditions near my locations in many states during blizzards, tornadoes and hurricanes. I even had the occasion to monitor roads in Hawaii as a volcano emitted lava near one of my locations. There are many directories on the Internet that list traffic cams.

Robots – can augment your security and safety teams. These guys take mobilizing the concept of using a camera to identify threats and impacts to a whole new level. Robots can provide cost-effective mobile surveillance and situational awareness during a disruptive event. They can easily be fitted with additional inexpensive off the shelf sensors. In some cases they can be sent to locations too dangerous for people. They have provided great value during and after earthquakes, sniffing out bombs, etc.

Robots can be valuable during non-crisis times as well. Imagine doubling or tripling your ability to view threats. Robots can be programmed to patrol hallways, offices, warehouses and factories. They will work 24x7x365 and never complain. I am familiar with robots that can climb over objects and go around them. Industrial and military grade robots are tough. They can take a pounding and happily do their jobs. Prices for industrial robots have decreased dramatically recently.

Drones – I used a drone to film a video for a resilience program kickoff meeting. It wowed 40 attendees as it flew over our locations recording some amazing videos. Drones are being used for security and safety. I recently met with a company that automates the flight path of security drones. The drones can be programmed through a friendly interface to fly specific pre-programmed routes. They can survey multiple locations simultaneously and send video streams that are consolidated in a central command center console.

367

Drones are also delivering medicine and other critical supplies to areas impacted by natural events, such as earthquakes.

Internet of Things (IoT) sensors are proliferating. Temperature, motion and geo-positioning are a few examples of low cost, off-the-shelf, sensors often costing less than $10. Sensors can be placed in desolate and dangerous areas. They can be coupled with a Raspberry Pi / Arduino low cost microprocessor and a tiny solar panel so there would be no need for an electrical outlet. Coupling sensors, software and communications channels will provide you with critical information anywhere in the world. Use your imagination where you can put these devices.

A great simple use-case would be to monitor humidity in a food or beverage warehouse. These inexpensive sensors can integrate with notification tools to notify the right people when humidity is above a threshold level. This can avoid costly spoilage.

Another interesting sensor application is monitoring conveyor lines for threats, such as anthrax or mechanical breakdowns. Certain sensors can identify packages on a conveyor that emit a dangerous odor or visual anomaly. My favorite mass notification tools can communicate with many IoT devices and automatically send notifications based on custom triggers we create.

The best news is, what I described above does not take complex programming to implement. It is not difficult and it gets easier every day. It is almost like snapping building blocks together.

Physical (hard) panic buttons – I also mention these in questions to ask a mass notification vendor. These are tiny physical devices that you can hold in the palm of your hand and, in the event you are in danger, you can press a button to send an alert. The right panic device coupled with a mass notification tool can be of life-saving value. The location of the device can be shared with public authorities or family.

Satellite technology – I use satellites for communications and tracking assets.
Satellite phones – can be a lifeline when cell towers are not available (which is often the case during a widespread event). You can make and receive voice calls from practically anywhere on earth.

On the lower end of satellite communications there are some really cool 'ping' tracking transceivers such as the Iridium RockBlock and

368

Globalstar's Spot Trace. These are very inexpensive devices that transmit latitude – longitude coordinates off low-orbit satellites. Software programs can then plot the coordinates on a map. I am currently using a Spot Trace to track a 21st Century Message in a Bottle project as it, hopefully, crosses the Atlantic Ocean.

Spot Trace is a 2" x 3" device, smaller than a deck of playing cards, which integrates GPS, satellite transceiver and power in a compact casing. It is a one-way communication from the device. In my testing the pings can go through wood, plastic and glass. It has difficulty penetrating metal. It is a great solution to monitor the movement of devices. It can be hidden under a truck, car, boat, etc. so they can be tracked in case they are stolen. It stays in sleep mode to conserve battery life and activates when it senses movement. Three AAA batteries can last months. I discuss Spot Trace as it applies to resilience and the bottle project in much more detail in the *Ultimate Business Continuity Tips, Techniques and Tools Newsletter.*

Iridium Rockblock has the ability to provide two-way communication. It can transmit latitude – longitude and additional information such as temperature or salinity readings from the middle of the ocean or outer space. You can also send it instructions from anywhere on earth. It can be coupled with many types of IoT sensors and motors using an Arduino or Rasberry Pi microprocessor for added intelligence. Rockblock is more difficult to set-up than Spot Trace, but in certain use-cases it is the preferred solution. I will be using it in 2018 on an exciting project – not the ocean, but you can probably guess the direction.

Miniature microprocessors – Arduino, Rasberry Pi, etc. – These super fun to 'play with' tiny and very inexpensive ($5 – $40) computers can be coupled with sensors, transceivers, motors... almost anything you can imagine. They can be programmed and have great potential for resilience, security and safety applications. I provide some very cool use-cases in more detail in the *Ultimate Business Continuity Tips, Techniques and Tools Newsletter.*

3D Printing – 3D printers are an incredible step forward. Some of the current use-cases boggle the mind. One example is printing body parts. A prosthetic hand can cost thousands of dollars. Children can quickly outgrow a prosthetic hand as they get older. e-NABLE network, - http://enablingthefuture.org/ - which is a volunteer network, now makes it possible for so many children to have a new prosthetic hand for a fraction of the cost by printing them with 3D printers. If you visit their website and watch a couple of videos I think you will shed some tears of joy.

Many other types of body parts are being 3D printed and have proven critical in emergencies.

If airplane and cars parts can now be 3D printed, why not specialized parts required during a disaster? For the right company or possibly disaster struck city, that could be valuable and perhaps lifesaving. If a company uses a wide variety of parts it could get very expensive to insure there are adequate supplies of all parts on-hand. If emergency parts could be 3D printed and perhaps customized to unique scenarios, imagine how helpful and economical that could be. I am sure some forward-thinking organizations will be using 3D printers for continuity of operations purposes in the near future.

<u>Finder – NASA JPL</u> (I discovered this potentially lifesaving device on an episode of Chuck Pell's, Xploration Earth 2050 – one of my favorite technology shows):
In the wreckage of a collapsed textile factory and another building in the Nepalese village of Chautara, four men were rescued, thanks to a NASA technology that was able to find their heartbeats. A small, suitcase-sized device called FINDER helped uncover these survivors — two from each destroyed building — in one of the hardest-hit areas of the 7.8-magnitude earthquake that rattled Nepal.
The technology detected the men's presence even though they were buried under about 10 feet of brick, mud, wood and other debris.

FINDER, which stands for Finding Individuals for Disaster and Emergency Response, is a collaboration between NASA's Jet Propulsion Laboratory in Pasadena, California and the Department of Homeland Security's Science and Technology Directorate in Washington.

Virtual meeting Room Tools:
Virtual meeting room environments take conference calls and webinars to a whole different level. They provide many benefits, such as reducing travel expenses, while fostering collaboration. Two interesting products are SoCoCo and Second Life. I have tested and used both.
SoCoCo is a business tool that lays out a realistic office environment with private offices and conference rooms in an online environment. You can have public and private meetings. You can even shut your door to speak with someone privately.

Second Life is a world unto itself. You are represented as an avatar which you can customize. You can meet with your team in custom offices in buildings you own. You can even create the buildings from the ground up! Large companies have purchased choice real estate on Second Life for offices and store-fronts. It even has its own currency – Linden dollars that are traded in the physical world. For some companies, it did not live up to commercial expectations, while others have realized its value. Some individuals claim to earn $100,000+ annually on Second Life.

Virtual and augmented reality training:

Virtual and augmented reality training solutions are on the verge of becoming popular methods to train employees

For example, Forklift Simulator (http://www.forklift-simulator.com) and 3D Forklift Trainer (http://www.tactustech.com/3dforklift) are immersive environments that can be used to train warehouse workers to operate forklifts in a safe virtual reality environment. Drivers can make mistakes and learn without worrying about getting injured.

Before we leave this chapter I want to share one more example of creative thinking that excites me. Great ideas mashed up with great technology can make a positive impact on people's lives, when they need it most.

Here is just such an idea applied to disaster recovery:
LuminAID (https://luminaid.com/) is an inspiring small company that had a great idea:
Two graduate students created an innovative way to provide light to people impacted by disasters, including Hurricane Sandy, Typhoon Haiyan and the earthquakes in Nepal.
Great ideas can spread virally and that happened to LuminAid. Word spread globally and their lights are now being used in over 70 countries. In third world countries, where power can be unreliable or non-existent, children can now study by safe clean LuminAid lights rather than dangerous smelly oil based contraptions. The solution is also used by hikers in Yosemite, backpackers in Whistler, and emergency workers in Nepal. Even the reality investment show ABC's Shark Tank saw the LuminAID vision irresistible, and invited the two founders on the show for a chance to premiere their product on prime-time.

If you found this chapter interesting, you will love the newsletter. I would be happy to share other interesting tech products and tips with you with a free subscription to the free *Ultimate Business Continuity Tips, Techniques and Tools Newsletter.*

XI

PART 11 - BUSINESS RESILIENCE / CONTINUITY AS A CAREER

The Business Resilience / Business Continuity (BRBC) Profession is rapidly growing in importance. Our skills are needed by every business to insure their survival when confronting disruptive events.

We can also identify revenue creation and expense reduction opportunities because of our unique cross-functional and end-to-end view into organizations.

We are steadily getting a seat in upper management.
For the right person, Business Resilience / Business Continuity can be a great career choice.

In the next few chapters I offer my experiences and views on:
✓ What it takes to be a great Business Resilience / Business Continuity Professional
✓ Switching from IT to the Business Resilience / Business Continuity Profession.
✓ Managing Stress

105

HOW TO BECOME A GREAT BRBC PROFESSIONAL - ATTRIBUTES, APTITUDE AND ATTITUDE OF THE SUPERSTARS

I have found that great Business Resilience / Business Continuity (BRBC) professionals come from many different walks of life. Often, we begin our careers in a different, but somewhat related discipline. You probably do not know too many people that came right out of school and entered our profession.

My background is in Information Technology (IT) and Operations. Many other successful BRBC professionals I have worked with came from finance, risk, logistics, security and the government.

When I was a little kid I did not say, '*Mommy, when I grow up I really wanna be a BRBC Pro!*' Although, I do attribute her reading, 'The Three Little Pigs' story to me as planting a lifelong seed in my brain on the importance of preparation, planning, situational awareness, threat identification and risk mitigation...

When I came out of college there was not even a BC profession! I am confident in the future as word spreads about what a great profession BRBC is that will change!

Hopefully, this book will spread the word on how valuable we are for achieving organizational resilience AND producing 'beyond BC Value $treams'.

Qualities, Mindset and Some Tips:
- The desire to help people
- A passion to learn
- Energy
- Confidence
- Focus and fortitude to finish what they start
- Attention to detail
- Good communication skills
- Creativity and an innovative mindset
- The ability to envision what the future-state can become – beyond what the current state is

Below I have listed a real-world potpourri of qualities, skills and tips I believe contribute to the success of a BRBC professional. These can be built over time and on the job. If you have some or all these qualities, you may enjoy a BRBC career.

- **Enjoy working with people** – Unless you are strictly doing IT system disaster recovery (DR) work you will be working with many people at different levels of the organization. If you simply want to 'hang in your cubicle' all day – BRBC is not the right career for you. You will not be happy and being happy in your work is so important. Life is too short to be doing something you do not enjoy for 60+ hours a week (my editor suggested a work week is 35 hours – haha – not in our world)

- **Be a good listener** – Active listening skills are critical in all facets of life. 'They' should be talking and you should be listening. You probably heard of the saying, 'that is why we have two ears and one mouth.' 'They' should be talking more than you talk. You only learn when 'they' are talking. While 'they' are talking, you should not be thinking of the next thing you will say. You should build on what 'they' say. It is all about 'them'

- **Ask insightful 'open-ended' questions** – Rather than asking a question where the person can simply answer 'yes' or 'no', (unless you need a yes or no response) ask probing questions, where the person must elaborate. You can then build on their answers with follow-up questions. The "5 Why's" works! Ask a question and when they respond just ask 'Why?' to their response if you need more information. Keep doing that. By the 5th 'why' you will get to the root of the cause. Salespeople use this technique with great success

- **Have technology / IT knowledge and skills** – This scares some people! I treat this one separately in the following chapter '*Are you thinking of a career move from IT to BC?*' We have discussed a lot about technology throughout the book so hopefully that has helped you. I grew up in IT and for me it is a passion. It is not critical to be immersed in IT though, so do not stress about it. Just get comfortable and pick up technical knowledge as you progress in your career.

- **Expect to be on call at odd hours and weekends** – That said, you should also have a backup so you are not on call 7 x 24 x 365. Trust me, disasters have a way of happening Monday morning at 3 am when you are probably sleeping or perhaps on a beautiful Saturday afternoon when you are soaking up the rays and enjoying the surf at the beach. It's like they know when it will be least convenient for you. During events, such as hurricanes Sandy and

Katrina I was on conference calls throughout the night and it paid off. So, be ready to dive right in because 'it goes with the territory'. When disaster strikes all the planning you did comes to the forefront. I always think of it in terms of 'where the rubber meets the road'. If you thoroughly planned and tested correctly it is likely you will be an unsung (or not so unsung) hero. Don't hide or stay in the background. Give it 100%. Everything will work out, you'll see. I am writing this on a Sunday during some turbulent winter weather. I fully expect to be working tonight, possibly doing mass notifications to keep our employees well informed and doing whatever else helps our team

- **Always make it all 'about them'** – They will love you for it. Be confident, friendly and professional. Be sure to check your ego at the door

- **Have the ability to multi-task** – I have never seen a BRBC department that is overstaffed. More likely, your department is understaffed but you must 'find a way' to get the work done, which often means long days and nights. This is especially true if you are supporting domestic and international locations. Hey, if I am wrong on this one please let me know. I lived it, having supported domestic AND global programs for many years

- **Stay calm and focused when those all around you are losing it – and some folks will be losing it** – Embrace pressure, or at least accept it because it will come. During a crisis event, everything moves at 1,000 miles an hour. Even the best documented plans will most likely need to be adjusted during an event. A culture of resilience will pull your team through any disruption. When preparing plans, we can't plan for every type of disaster scenario. Bringing the right people together and the ability to think on our feet is critical. Believe me, teaming with the right people and focusing on the moment and what must be done will enable you to respond and recover

- **Be honest and straightforward with management and process owners** – When RTO's are misaligned and disaster strikes the s*!t will hit the fan and your butt will rightfully be on the line. I have seen this happen and it is not pretty. So be honest and make sure the process owners are honest on the true RTO requirements even if it will cost more to deliver a shorter recovery time-frame. Let management make the final decisions.

- **Have good written communication skills** – Hopefully, you are comfortable writing. You don't have to be Stephen King or J.K. Rowling. If you need to improve your basic writing skills, you can read a book or take a class or two. I promise you, you will be

375

writing a lot of emails, newsletter articles, exercises, presentations…so, sharpen your skills. If you already enjoy writing and are good at it you are way ahead of the game. Here are some writing tips:

o Know your audience
o Write simply and straight-forward
o Let your personality shine through
o Write from the heart
o Don't use big words to impress – you won't impress, you will only confuse
o If you want some great advice on writing I suggest you read Stephen King's book – '*On Writing*'. It tells you everything you need to know in 'down to earth' terms. Check out the hundreds of positive reviews on Amazon. The book is approximately $10 and tells it all. Hey, maybe you even have a book in you! I have had 10 in me, with more to come. I may not be the most talented writer but I love to write and I do my best to deliver valuable information to my readers.

• **Have good verbal communication skills** – At various times in your career you will be working one-on-one and presenting to small and large groups. Don't worry, we all get nervous in front of groups of people in the beginning (public speaking is rated scarier than death to many people in some polls) but your jitters will quickly fade away as you get a few presentations under your belt. Relax, you will have fun. A little nervousness is actually good; it means you care. Even successful actors and politicians are nervous before a performance or speech but they do not show it. Never let them see you sweat

By the way, there will come a time when you are giving a presentation and you encounter some sort of technical 'glitch'. Think of it as a rite of passage. It happens to everyone. Stay cool and keep moving forward. Again, never let them see you sweat.

True story; Early in my career, I did a series of software demos with a co-worker who was also a good friend. Of course, the fateful day came when we encountered an audio/video issue in a room with 100+ attendees. Naturally it did not happen when there were two or three attendees. While I was resolving the issue Mike, my co-presenter, started cracking a few jokes and then to everyone's amusement he hoisted himself onto the presentation table and started tap-dancing like a mad-man. Arms all over the place, going in circles, so bizarre and funny! The attendees loved it! I continued working on the 'glitch' and eventually fixed it. By then everyone was in a great mood. We had a great presentation. I think half the people were disappointed when I fixed it and Mike stopped dancing.

Funny, this happened quite a while ago when I was a young technologist on Wall Street. Every time I think about Mike 'the dancing machine' doing his thing up on that desk with a big smile on his face, I laugh. *Way to go Mike.*

106

THINKING OF A CAREER MOVE FROM IT TO BC LIKE I
DID? READ THIS...

**Quite a few of us in the Business Resilience / Business Continuity
(BRBC) profession began our careers in Information Technology
(IT). I am one of those people. If you are in IT and thinking of a
career change or you know someone that is considering it, this
chapter may be helpful.**

I loved being an IT professional and I worked my way up to a Senior
Technology Officer in a Fortune 50 company, but I have never regretted
switching from technology to BRBC. A technology powered BRBC
program is incredibly valuable to organizations. Having the opportunity
to work with both technology and BRBC is the best of both worlds.
Going to work every day is fun for me because I love what I do!

In my case, the IT to BRBC career transition came about while I was
working with a global company. My specialty at the time was in database
system design and development as well as managing large data center
migrations and consolidations. Over the course of my technology career
I developed more than 100 B2B database systems. Many were for large
corporations and others were for my entrepreneurial ventures. All were
fun!

I was not too familiar with BC at the time. Not too many people were.
Our company already had a business continuity specialist. He and I
became friends and I learned what BC was all about. It offered a lot that
interested me including working with systems, a great deal of data
analysis, planning, working with people and the chance to positively
impact my company in innovative ways!

Timing is important in life and the BC director decided to leave for a
different opportunity. I quickly applied for the position and I got it! For
the next two weeks, he was supposed to train me in what he was doing
but that never happened.

It was not that big a deal. I dove right in and soaked up every article and
class I could find although the BC industry was just getting into gear
and it was hard to get good information. I wish I had the book you are
reading when I started. In fact, that was a key factor in my writing this
book so I could help the people that follow me in our wonderful

profession. It would have made the process easier and provided more value for my company in a shorter period of time. I was learning as I was doing. I made mistakes – but never the same one twice.

Fast forward 17 years and BC has provided me with a long and interesting second half of my career. If you have a background in technology it can be a huge asset to any organization. When you transition to BRBC, that knowledge will provide a unique view into business resilience, business continuity and disaster recovery.

The disaster recovery (DR) portion is obvious. Understanding system recovery and infrastructure strategies gives you a big advantage. You will be speaking with the IT folks on their level. They will respect that. Without the systems background, it can be challenging to get up-to-speed on disaster recovery technologies. That said, even without an IT background aspiring business continuity professionals can learn the DR portion well enough to do a good job if they apply themselves.

I also firmly believe any mid-size to enterprise-size organization needs to have a high degree of end-to-end automation powering their resilience program. The business deserves it! Having read this book, you most likely realize my personal and professional over-riding goal is laser focused on building technology-driven, world-class business resilience programs.

Coming from a technology background you will also understand integrating tools, such as situational awareness systems, business continuity management (BCM) systems, intelligent mass notification systems, etc. You will be able to integrate the tools so they can 'talk to each other' thru API's, JSON, XML, SFTP... You will also be able to integrate 'Internet of Things' sensors, alarms, cameras, satellite location devices... This integration is extremely valuable. It may come naturally to you but can be a challenge to people not steeped in technology. I have seen people struggle at that level but I also know if they apply themselves they eventually get there. I am proud of my teammates over the years who were not initially tech savvy but they became so. Perhaps, I had a little influence on them. I hope so.

As a former technology professional, you will be able to easily research and leverage technology. Also, you will understand technology better than the sales reps trying to sell you their solutions. Your business resilience teammates will want and appreciate you being on every call, especially when you are analyzing new enterprise systems.

You will ask the techie questions and you will keep the vendors 'honest'. You will not get 'sold'. Without bragging, I think I am often that guy. There is so much I learn from my teammates every day. A great team consists of people with different strengths and the willingness to openly share all information for the success of the team.

A few final thoughts:
If you are contemplating moving to BRBC from IT be sure you read the previous chapter so you know what you are getting into. For example, make sure you enjoy working with people – every day. I know that sounds strange but many of my IT friends strictly want to work with technology as I did for a portion of my career. In many ways, it is simpler and less complicated to work with machines. If you do not want to mix with 'users' every day do not move to BRBC unless you are strictly doing DR and even then, you will be working with users at times.

To be honest, my career transition to BRBC was easy. I was ready. It presented many new and interesting challenges. I enjoy helping people. I enjoy developing and implementing resilience technology. I like being the 'go-to-guy' when it comes to the intersection of BRBC and technology. That can happen to you as well. Now is the best time to be in BRBC.

I would be interested in hearing from other people on your experience moving from IT to BRBC. If you have specific questions or concerns on making the transition, please contact me Marty@UtimateBusinessContinuity.com).

HOW INSTANT MESSAGING + HOSTING A WEBINAR = CAREER DISASTER

During your career, you will do a lot of instant messaging and you will host a lot of webinars. But please be forewarned, mixing the two can be toxic to your career if you are not careful. Please read on...

I have witnessed the following scenario play out many times during my career. Sometimes it sits in waiting for a few years but then BOOM there it is again and again. In each case the person that fell into the insidious trap was smart and savvy but somehow it just happened.

The outcomes were really embarrassing and in some cases career damaging. Other times, it was sort of humorous. I could see this happening to me and I never want it to happen to you. So, if you use an instant messenger product like Slack or Skype for Business you might want to invest a couple of minutes scanning this tale. Names have definitely been changed to protect the embarrassed.

Our tale begins innocently enough, like any of the zillions of webinar meetings I have hosted or attended throughout my career. Having had responsibility for business resilience / continuity programs that spanned thousands of domestic and international locations on every continent except Antarctica, I have done a lot of webinar meetings at all hours of the day and night.

I really enjoy webinars. Through webinars I get to cover a lot more ground and save a lot of money rather than globe-hopping. I also get to be with my family and sleep in my bed, which is a nice comfort.

Once upon a time in a land not so far away there was a Kickoff Meeting for an offsite work area recovery exercise being planned for our Oklahoma locations. Eleven Oklahoma high ranking senior executives were on this webinar plus three Enterprise IT Directors (Ellen, Jim and Bob) who would support the business from the systems side throughout the exercise.

The plan was for Sam Otto, our Midwest Director of Business Continuity to host this webinar. Sam had hands-on experience recovering to our third-party recovery site vendor and he always did a

381

great job. He motivated people to attend the exercise with the coolest breakfasts and lunches you could imagine. Donuts, bagels, pizza, wings, scrumptious salads, sandwiches, beverages and desserts. He was great with people and made it a lot of fun.

At the last minute, Charles 'Don't Call Me Charlie' Ego-Smith, the Global Business Continuity Senior Vice President, decided to grand-stand Sam. He demanded the reins to the webinar. Pulled a last-minute power-play and made himself the host and presenter. You have probably seen the move at some point in your career. I guess the old saying, *'be careful what you wish for'*, has some truth to it – read on and let me know if you agree…

So, Charlie, I mean Charles, begins hosting the session and greets all the attendees. Hey, good so far! He starts showing some slides in the PowerPoint presentation and he fields a few questions, comments and requests from the Oklahoma executives. The usual easy to handle requests such as, 'what if we are too busy to do the exercise', 'what if we recover all our processes from home', 'what if we have high profile visitors that month?' Hey you can't blame them for trying. You are probably thinking to yourself, 'been there – heard that!' But luckily our experienced team had anticipated the push-back. Fortunately, Senior Management 'had our backs' and committed that all processes must participate – so these were just softball requests, 'easy-peasy' to handle. But wait, we are just getting started!

Now the fireworks begin. Bob, one if the Enterprise IT directors started asking a bunch of questions. Well, Charles had somewhat of a history with Bob from previous exercises and did not take kindly to Bob's string of questions. Charles started getting defensive and while Bob was speaking Charles started IM'ing. He's firing off one instant message after another to me and our teammate Sam. This book is PG rated so I am not going to use the gutter words he used when referring to Bob, but here is the PG version;
This idiot Bob is the biggest pain in the ass that I ever worked with'; 'he doesn't know shit', 'he never shuts up', 'I want to go over to his office and kick his ass…!'

Unfortunately, Charles had control of the webinar and was sharing his screen so every message he sent was seen by all the attendees! Yeah, everyone including Bob and the Senior Oklahoma executives! We could not instant message him to stop as everyone would have seen our warnings, so we tried to call Charles' cell phone and text him but he did not pick up. He just kept firing ridiculously embarrassing IM messages and I guess we were all so stunned we just sat there bewildered. We finally bit the bullet and IM'd him to STOP ALREADY!!! Whoa, talk about an embarrassing silence!

I really felt sorry for Bob. He is a good guy. Deservedly, Charlie 'Yes I am going to call you CHARLIE' got in big time hot water after the webinar with upper management. For one reason or another he only lasted another year or so at our company. Maybe this event played a part in his demise.

So, the morale is, if you use IM – turn it off during a webinar if you are the host. If you must use it, be very careful what you say, who you say it to and pray nothing embarrassing or personal is sent to you for everyone to see.

Quick Update – During the writing of this book I participated on many webinars with enterprise software vendors trying to sell me expensive solutions. Most of the vendors had their IM going while doing webinars and training. Some very embarrassing things came flying across our screens. You learn a lot reading those messages when they pop-up on the presenters' screen, both personal and business related.

My advice to employees and vendors is to sign-out of IM before hosting a webinar. Otherwise, it just might destroy your credibility and possibly your career.

MANAGING STRESS - BE GOOD TO YOURSELF

I will leave you with this final chapter. Some people may consider it off topic. I believe it is important.

Business Continuity, Safety, Security, Operations... sometimes it gets stressful. Especially during a real disruption. We handle serious situations. Our employees and management count on us to get it right. This can lead to stress.

Below are some ideas that have helped me manage stress. I am sharing them but I am not a doctor. If you are experiencing extreme stress it is best to get guidance from a medical professional.

I admit it, early in my career I was bad at handling stress. I let little things get to me. The danger in this situation was that I did not realize how bad it was getting.

The Internet Revolution was just getting started and, as usual, I found opportunity. I was working my full-time day job in technology and coding websites for clients every night and weekends. In those days, there were not too many hosting solutions and I wound up hosting my client's sites with this cowboy in the Midwest. He really was a cowboy, which was kind of cool. His name was Bill and he asked that I call him Buffalo Bill, which was also cool.

A lot of the Internet technology, hardware, software, network infrastructure, was new and not fully understood. Unfortunately, Buffalo Bill's server went down regularly. I came to believe that his data center was in the barn. Possibly the server was being trampled by his buffalo or horse. Regardless, I was getting complaints practically every night from clients all over the world. I would keep my laptop next to my bed hitting the refresh key over-and-over at 3 am to make sure client sites were working. Looking back, the extended hours were good training for my future BC/DR career, but at the time I was not handling it very well.

- I was losing a lot of sleep but I did not think much of it
- I stopped exercising
- I had a bad diet
- I was putting on too much weight

- My blood pressure was rising into the danger zone

Still, I marched on stressing about keeping the sites online and meeting unrealistic deadlines. I was trying to make everyone happy.

One day it all came to a head. I was strolling in a shopping mall on a Saturday morning with my young son. We were on our way to see a new Pokémon movie. It should have been the most relaxing of times. I remember holding his hand and out of the blue he says, '*dad why is your arm shaking?*' I did not know. I did not even realize it was shaking. But it was definitely shaking. I consciously tried to stop it. My arm momentarily stopped shaking and then a minute later it started again and again and again. My body was in a high state of anxiety, even on a Saturday morning when I should have been enjoying precious time with my son. I knew it was time for some drastic change…and change I did!

I went for a medical examination and found my blood pressure was very high. I also purchased a book that a friend had recommended, '*Don't Sweat the Small Stuff, It's All Small Stuff: Simple Ways To Keep The Little Things From Taking Over Your Life*', by Richard Carlson.

The book made so much sense to me. I made the decision to stop 'sweating the small stuff'. My resilience kicked in. 'I had bent but I had not broken'. I realized nothing I was doing was as important as staying healthy to be there for the people that loved and needed me. I stopped trying to make everyone happy. I ate better. I took my newly prescribed blood pressure medication and eventually my pressure went back to normal. I played basketball regularly for decades after that. I lost weight. I became much better at my job as I was more relaxed and I began enjoying life again. I came back stronger than I was before… and yes, thankfully my arm stopped shaking!

Fast forward 20 years and I still work a lot. Day, night and weekends on many occasions. However, I love it. I understand I am still something of a perfectionist but I have a much better mindset. I am still an A type personality, but it works for me. Life is good and I would not change a thing!

How walking helped me:
I believe Steve Jobs had it right. When he wanted to have a conversation with someone he would often get up and say, '*walk with me*'.

The Business Continuity component of resilience will always have a stressful component. We are on call 24x7x365. We are often dealing with disruptive events, both large and small. I have responded to disruptions from a Dunkin' Donuts in the middle of a raging snowstorm, at the movies during a rare 'date night out' with my wife and in Atlantic City on an even rarer mini-vacation.

Often, we are required to sit for long periods of time doing BIA's, Risk Assessment's and writing plans. We also have a great deal of meetings during developing and maintaining our programs. Sometimes too many meetings, right? It goes with the territory. It is what we do and I embrace it all!

Walking helps me clear my mind, relax and re-charge. It helps keep me healthy and happy. It makes me a better Business Continuity Professional. I brainstorm many of my most creative business continuity and personal project ideas during short walks and my 6-12-mile trail walks. Many of the ideas in this book originated in the midst of those walks. Some of the chapters I 'wrote in my mind' while practicing racewalking and running.
According to my trusty Fitbit, as of this writing I have logged 17,146,473 steps (8,409 miles) during the past couple of years. I know, it is a bit over the top, but you know me by now and I enjoyed every step.

Many studies have indicated that sitting too long is bad for us. I find walking helps relieve stress. The secret is to do it regularly. Carve out time on a regular basis to get up from your desk and walk. I have integrated walking into my regular routine at work and at home. It has become a big part of my life. I have even incorporated walking into my daily commute, racewalking 1.5 miles each way to and from work.

If you do decide to walk, be careful about multi-tasking. I have eliminated texting and emailing while walking after a few serious close calls – one bordering on fatal. For example, a few years ago in Baltimore while I was walking and texting, I came within a few feet of falling into Baltimore Harbor. But that did not stop me.

Last year I was walking and texting and I took a bad fall. I went flying and luckily broke my fall with my right palm on jagged concrete. I tore up my hand (pretty nasty picture) but I could have easily hit my head, which would have been disastrous. But that did not stop me either. More recently, I was walking and texting and I almost walked off a three-story structure to a concrete floor 30 feet below. That one stopped me! Yes, it did the trick! No more walking and texting. It made me real careful going forward. I still get chills every time I pass the spot of that near tragedy.

If you are interested, here is a feature article from the widely circulated Newsday in NY - UltimateBusinessContinuity.com/newsday/racewalk that describes how my lifelong belief in perseverance and resilience enabled me to quickly bounce back from a serious basketball. For me it was my 'When One Door Closes, Another Opens' moment!

Singing:

I read that singing out loud for 10 minutes every day is a good stress reliever. Unfortunately, I am such a horrendous singer that if I did it my wife's stress level would go way up. So, that will not work for me, although I do admit to singing quietly in the shower on occasion.

Having an outlet for stress change your life as it did mine. It can be fun, help you solve problems and positively impact your health. Caution – always check with your doctor before starting any type of strenuous physical activity.

XII

PART 12 - FREE BONUS GIFTS

I have included two Free Bonus Gifts to continue building our relationship. I hope you enjoy them.
Marty

THE ULTIMATE BUSINESS CONTINUITY ONLINE ROADMAP

The perfect complement to The Ultimate Business Continuity Success Guide!

The Online Roadmap:
(http://www.ultimatebusinesscontinuity.com/roadmap) is a special sequential step-by-step roadmap that will guide you toward the reward of resilience. There are approximately 200 steps that have proven valuable to me when building resilience programs.
It is important to use the roadmap in conjunction with The Ultimate Business Continuity Success Guide. Many of the steps in the roadmap correlate to in-depth chapters featured in the book. Where possible, I tried to cross reference Column A of the roadmap with the chapter(s) that provide more detailed information and instructions.

My hope is that the Online Roadmap becomes a collaborative effort. I will continue to add to it plus I want to open it up to you to help nurture and grow it. If you have ideas, tips, innovations and techniques that have helped you build your program, I would love to hear about them. Simply email them to me and maybe we can include your ideas in the Online Roadmap.

THE ULTIMATE BUSINESS CONTINUITY TIPS, TECHNIQUES AND TOOLS NEWSLETTER

Great news!

Happily, this is not the end, it is only the beginning. I would like to continue building our relationship by offering you a free subscription to the Ultimate Business Continuity Tips, Techniques and Tools Newsletter.
Every issue is packed with my latest resilience tips, techniques, tools and technologies to help you improve your program.

To begin your free subscription please click here -> Ultimate Business Continuity Tips, Techniques and Tools Newsletter -

http://http/www.ultimatebusinesscontinuity.com/index.php/newslett er

.

Sincerely,
Marty Fox
Marty@UltimateBusinessContinuty.com

RECOMMENDED READING

Listed below are some of my favorite books:

The Resiliency Dividend: Being Strong in a World Where Things Go
Wrong
by Judith Rodin

Five Days at Memorial: Life and Death in a Storm Ravaged Hospital
by Sheri Fink

The Unthinkable: Who Survives When Disaster Strikes
by Amanda Ripley

iWar: War and Peace in the Information Age - by Bill Gertz

The Checklist Manifesto - by Atul Gawande

The Go-Giver: A Little Story About a Powerful Business Idea
by Bob Burg

X-Events: The Collapse of Everything - by John Casti

The Butterfly Defect - by Ian Goldin and Mike Mariathasan

The Black Swan: The Impact of the Highly Improbable
by Nassim Nicholas Taleb

Bursts: The Hidden Pattern Behind Everything We Do
by Albert-Laszlo Barabasi

The Risk Driven Business Model: Four Questions That Will Define
Your Company - by Karan Girotra and Serguei Netessine

Future Babble: Why Expert Predictions are Next To Worthless and
You Can Do Better - by Dan Gardner

Free: The Future of a Radical Price - by Chrsi Anderson

ABOUT THE AUTHOR

Marty Fox has achieved success as a Business Resilience-Continuity Director, Senior Technology Officer, Software Developer, Technology Rainmaker and Entrepreneur. He has authored ten popular technology books, developed B2B database software systems sold world-wide and created unique content based web properties enjoyed by thousands of people. He has been featured on television, radio and in major newspapers, blogs and national conferences.

Marty enjoys building successful business resilience programs for organizations of all sizes. He and his teammates have successfully led major organizations through disruptive events including hurricanes, tornadoes, earthquakes, blizzards, pandemics, power outages and terror related events.

Marty's passion is leveraging technology to improve business resilience, intelligence and streamline processes. He believes there are vast opportunities to build world-class resilience, increase revenue and reduce costs through the creative use of new tools, technologies and techniques.

Recently Marty used his professional resilience techniques in his personal life to rebound from a life-threatening basketball injury. To fill the void of no longer being able to play' bball' Marty learned to racewalk. Within 6 months he became a state champion and within 10 months he became a national champion. His inspirational story has been chronicled online and in major newspapers. He has inspired people to believe-and-achieve. Marty will be sharing his 3P's success formula in an upcoming book, with the goal of helping people embrace challenges and attain business and personal fulfillment.

Marty is available for advice and speaking engagements.

Made in the
USA
Monee, IL